MW01115678

THE RED SARI

When life is the price of power

Javier Moro

You and this book were born together,
and I dedicate it to you,
Olivia

INDEX

OPENING

Lead me from darkness into light, from death toimmortality.

Vedic prayer

1

New Delhi, May 24th, 1991.

Sonia Gandhi simply cannot believe that the man she loves is dead, and she will no longer feel his caresses or the warmth of his kisses. She will never again see that sweet smile that one day swept her off her feet. It has all been so quick, so brutal and so unexpected that she still cannot take it in. Her husband was killed in a terrorist attack two days ago. His name was Rajiv Gandhi; he has been Prime Minister, and he was about to be Prime Minister again, according to the polls, if his electoral campaign had not been cut short in such a tragic way. He was 46 years old.

Today the capital of India is preparing to say farewell to the remains of this illustrious son of the nation. The coffin containing the body is lying in the great hall of Teen Murti House, the palace residence where he spent his childhood when his grandfather, Jawaharlal Nehru, was Prime Minister of India. It is a small colonial palace, surrounded by a park with large tamarinds and flame trees, their red flowers standing out against a lawn that is yellow from the heat. Originally designed to be the home of the Commander-in-Chief of the British forces, after independence it became the residence of the leader of the new nation, India. Nehru moved in, with his daughter Indira and his grandchildren. The gardeners, cooks and other members of staff, who, together with thousands of fellow Indians, have come today to pay tribute to their assassinated leader, find it hard to believe that the body lying in state here is that of the little boy who used to play hide and seek in those rooms as big as caves, with ceilings six metres high. It seems to them that they can still hear the echoes of his laughter when he chased down those long corridors after his brother, while his grandfather and mother received some head of state in one of the rooms.

A large photo of Rajiv with a white garland round it stands on the coffin which is covered in a yellow, white and green flag, the nation's colours. His bright smile is the last thing the thousands of people filing through Teen Murti House, in spite of the temperature of 43°, take away with them. It is the image that the members of his family will also take away, because the body of this man that women found so handsome has been so badly disfigured that, in spite of their attempts at reconstruction, the doctors have not managed to put the amorphous mass of flesh left by the bomb back into shape. They say that one of them fainted during the attempts to embalm him. So they have simply used cotton wool and bandages, and plenty of ice so he will last until the day of the cremation.

"Be careful, please. Don't hurt him," says his widow with a grief-stricken look to the men who come periodically to put in fresh ice, because the heat is increasing inexorably, and the temperature will go on rising until the beginning of July, until the monsoon rains come. Her only consolation – that she could well have ended up the same if she had gone with him, as she so often did – does not help her because right now she would like to die too. She would like to be with him, always with him, here and in eternity. She loved him more than she loves herself.

Her children are by her side. The younger one, Priyanka, 19 years old, is a tall, dark haired girl who is strong both in character and physically. She has taken charge of the funeral preparations and is very attentive to her mother. She insists that she eat something, but just thinking about food makes Sonia feel sick. She has got through the last two days on water, coffee and lime juice. Her old companion, asthma, which has been with her since she was very small, has reappeared. Two nights ago, when they informed her that her husband had been the victim of a terrorist attack, she had such a violent attack that she almost lost consciousness. Her daughter found her anti-histamines and gave them to her, although she could not comfort her. She is worried that the heat and grief may bring on another attack.

Rahul, the elder, is 21 and has just arrived from Harvard where he is studying. In her son she sees her husband: the same gentle features, the same smile, the same expression of goodness. She looks at him with infinite tenderness. How young he seems to light his father's funeral pyre, which is the role of the son according to Hindu tradition.

At one o'clock in the afternoon, the arrival of three generals, the representatives of their respective armed forces, signals the official start of the State funeral. Just before the soldiers lift the coffin with the help of Rahul and other family friends, Priyanka approaches to caress him, as though she wanted to say goodbye to her father in this way before he starts out on his final journey. Her mother, who has been busy greeting so many personalities, keeps herself a certain distance away, watching the scene with tears in her eyes. She is dressed in a pure white sari, as is customary for widows in India. She has spent more than half her life living here, so she feels Indian. Last February she celebrated her 23rd wedding anniversary with Rajiv having dinner in a restaurant in Teheran, where she was accompanying him on an official visit. She is still very attractive, just as she was at 18, when she met him. Her black hair, streaked with incipient grey, is carefully combed back, tied in a bun and covered by one end of her sari. If they were not swollen with grief, her eyes would be big. They are dark brown in colour, with long, carefully plucked eyebrows. She has a straight nose, plump lips, very white skin and a strong jaw. Today she looks like one of those tragic heroines from an Indian blockbuster movie, although her profile and proud stance evoke a goddess of the Roman panthcon, pcrhaps because the sari she wears so naturally is similar to the tunic women wore in ancient times. Or perhaps because of her physique. She was born and brought up in Italy. Her maiden name is Sonia Maino, although she is known as Sonia Gandhi, now Rajiv's widow.

More than half a million people defy the heat to see the funeralcortège go by on its way to where the cremation will take place, some ten kilometres away, behind the walls that the Mogul emperors erected to protect old Delhi, in splendid gardens on the banks of the River Jamuna. Escorted by five detachments of 33 soldiers, the wheeled platform bearing the coffin decorated with marigolds is pulled along by a military truck, also covered in flowers. On the seats inside it are the heads of the General Staff. After it come the cars carrying the family. Some of the onlookers manage to see Sonia remove her enormous sunglasses in order to wipe her face with a handkerchief and, with a trembling hand, dry her tears. The cortège heads down Rajpath Avenue, bordered with well-tended gardens where generations of city dwellers have strolled in the shade of its huge trees, mostly *jambuls* over a hundred years old, with black fruit like figs. Most of the trees were planted against the heat, when the English decided to make Delhi into the new capital of the Empire, to the detriment of Calcutta. They built a pleasant garden city with wide avenues and grandiose views, as was appropriate to a capital of the Empire. The vista down the centre of Rajpath, overflowing with a crowd carrying orange flowers, the holy colour for Hindus, brings memories to Sonia of a past of happiness, so close in time and yet so far away now... On this same avenue, opposite India Gate, the local version of the Arc de Triomphe in Paris, she stood on January 26th, the national holiday, watching the military parade with Rajiv... How many times has she watched it? Almost as many as the years she has been in India. A whole lifetime. A lifetime coming to an end.

To add a touch of mockery to the tragedy, her car stops and the driver cannot get it going again. The engines suffer with this heat and at this pace. Sonia and her children leave the vehicle and the crowd immediately hurls itself at them, forcing the Black Cats, the special black-garbed security commandos, to deploy quickly and make a human chain around them to protect them while they move to another car. Then the cortège gets going again, to the measured rhythm of the guards of honour. Later, in the narrow streets near Connaught Place, the crowd becomes a human tide ready to invade everything, as though wanting to swallow up the cortège, and the security system can barely manage to keep it at bay. The faces in that crowd show exhaustion, dripping beads of sweat, and their dark eyes focus on four military trucks full of journalists from all over the world. Men and women, children and old people throw flower petals at the coffin with expressions of grief on their faces and tears in their eyes.

The cortège reaches the place where the cremation is to take place at half past four in the afternoon, an hour later than expected. There are so many people that today the flowerbeds cannot be seen, only the huge trees, like eternity's sentries casting their benevolent shade over those present, many of whom are dressed in black, such as John Major or the Prince of Wales, others in military uniform, such as Yasser Arafat, and all of them pouring with sweat. The funeral pyre, made up of half a ton of wood, is ready. Behind, on a platform dominating the pyre and built specially for the occasion, stand the closest members of the family. Some three hundred metres to the north are the mausoleums of Nehru and his daughter Indira, built on the exact site where their cremations took place, and which will never be able to be used again, according to the tradition. Soon Rajiv will have his too, made of stone carved in the shape of a lotus leaf. The family alltogether in death.

Some soldiers take Rajiv's body out of the coffin and place it on the funeral pyre, with his head to the north, according to the ritual. Then the generals of the three armed forces carefully fold the flag that wraps the mutilated body and cut the strings of the white shroud that holds it. The family is standing side by side. The priest, an old man with a long beard as white as snow, looking as though he has come out of an ancient tale, goes through the steps of the Vedic rites and says a short prayer: "Lead me from the unreal to the real, from darkness into light, from death to immortality..." He is an old friend: he also presided over Indira's funeral. He hands Rahul, dressed in a white *kurta*, a small jug full of holy water from the Ganges. The young man, barefoot and with his head lowered, is lost in thought behind his black framed glasses. He walks three times round the pyre as he splashes drops of water over his father, thus carrying out the rite of purification of the soul. Then he kneels beside the remains and weeps inside, without anyone being able to see. He weeps for a father who was always tolerant and compassionate and who adored his children. Dry tears well from a wound which, he feels, will never close. His mother and sister Priyanka, whose serene dignity moves those present, approach the pyre and carefully position the logs of sandalwood and rosary beads on the body, in gestures that are recorded on television all over the world.

Now it is time to say goodbye. Sonia places an offering on the body, over the heart. It is made of camphor, cardamom, cloves and sugar and it is supposed to help remove the imperfections of the soul. Then she touches the feet in a sign of veneration, as is customary in India, places her hands together at breast height, and bows to her husband for the last time before stepping back. Through the television cameras the world discovers this stoic woman who reminds everyone of Jacqueline Kennedy twenty-eight years before in Arlington. It is five twenty in the afternoon.

Five minutes later, her son Rahul walks seriously and decisively three times round the pyre before placing the flaming torch in his hands among the sandalwood logs. His hands do not tremble: it is his duty as a good son to help his father's soul to free itself from its mortal body and get to heaven. For a few seconds it is as though time has stopped. There is no smoke or flames to be seen; only the Vedic psalms can be heard among the crowd. Sonia has hidden her face behind her sunglasses again. They must not see her cry. She has to keep herself composed, as she has done until now, whatever the cost may be. As composed as Rajiv was when it was his duty to light the funeral pyre of his mother Indira Gandhi, only seven years ago, while little Rahul cried in his arms. As composed as Indira herself when she attended the cremation of her father Jawaharlal Nehru, and then that of her son Sanjay, the apple of her eye, her designated heir, killed when his plane crashed one sunny Sunday morning, eleven years ago now. A date that Soniacannot forget, because after that day nothing was ever the same as before.

She has had to find strength from the very depths of her being to be here today, because the Hindu priests refused to allow her to be present at the cremation. It is not the custom for the widow to be there, even less if she is of another religion. But here Sonia was inflexible. She reacted as her mother-in-law Indira would have done, not permitting herself to be cowed by either prejudice or archaic customs. Under no circumstances would she stay at home while the whole world went to witness her husband's second death. That is what she told the funeral organizers. She did not even have to threaten to take the matter to the highest authority in the land because they backed down before the strength of her determination. Sonia Gandhi well deserved to be an exception.

But now she has to rise to the occasion. No hesitating, no fainting, no losing heart. Go on living, even if it is difficult to do it when the only thing you want to do is die. How hard it is not to let oneself be overcome by emotion when the Vedic psalms give way to cannon salvoes, and the soldiers, standing in perfect line, present weapons to the sound of cornetsand fire at the ground as a sign of mourning. When the dignitaries who have come from all over the world, the generals in their jackets full of colour with so many medals and the representatives of the Indian government, with their cotton clothes wrinkled and soaked after having waited so long in the midday sun, stand up in unison, immobile, like stone, in a brief, final homage. When the friends, who have arrived from

Europe and America to say their last farewells, cannot hold back their tears, Sonia recognizes Christian von Stieglitz among them, the friend who introduced her to Rajiv when they were students at Cambridge. He is there with Pilar, his Spanish wife.

And then the murmur that suddenly increases, like the sea in the distance, coming from the furthest corners of the city and perhaps from the remotest parts of the immense country. It becomes a single cry, terrible and guttural, the cry from thousands of throats that seem to become aware of the irreversibility of death as the fire suddenly catches in an explosion of flames and in a few minutes envelops the shroud in a fatal embrace. Rahul steps back a few paces. Sonia sways. Her daughter puts an arm round her shoulders and holds her until she regains her strength. Through the wall of flames, the three of them witness the ancient, tremendous spectacle of seeing how the person they most love is consumed and turns into ash. It is like another slow and penetrating death, so that the living may remember that no one can escape the inevitability of destiny. Because it is a death that comes in through the five senses. The smell of burning, the bright colours of the living through the scorching air rising from the blaze lifting up swirls of ash, the taste of sweat, of dust and smoke that sticks to the lips, and then the cries of "Long live Rajiv Gandhi!" that emerge from the crowd, make up a scene that is renewed and eternal at the same time. As the flames rise, Rahul gets ready to carry out the last part of the ritual. Armed with a bamboo stick about three metres long, he strikes a symbolic blow to his father's skull, so that his soul can go up into heaven to await its next reincarnation.

For Sonia there are no words to describe what she is seeing, the enactment of the terrible sense of loss that is tearing her apart inside, as though an invincible force were ripping at her entrails. Never more than at this moment has she understood the deeper meaning of this ancestral custom. She remembers that she pulled a face in disgust when, as soon as she arrived in India, she heard about the existence of *suttee*. How horrible, how barbaric! she thought. In olden times, the people adored widows who had the courage to hurl themselves on their husband's funeral pyre in order to set out on the journey towards eternity together with their loved one. Those that gave themselves heroically to the flames were considered deities and were worshipped as such for years, some for centuries. The rite of *suttee*, which has its origin in the noble Rajput families, the warrior caste from Northern India, then became popular among the lower classes, and finally became corrupted. The English prohibited it, as did the first democratic government of India later, because of the abuses committed in itsname. But in its origin, becoming *suttee* was the supreme proof of lovewhich a woman can only understand when she sees the body of her adored husband burning. Like Sonia at this instant, seeing the fire as a kind of liberation, as the only way to put a stop to that total grief that overwhelmsher soul.

"React", she tells herself. You mustn't let yourself be dragged down by death. Life is a struggle, as she well knows. Physical contact with her children comforts her. Then, with her strength renewed, opposing feelings spring up: a desire for justice, wishes for revenge for what has been done to her husband, and a deep-seated feeling of revulsion, because what has happened is unacceptable. Could it have been avoided? she asks herself all the time. She tried as far as she was able, scrutinizing the faces of everyone who came near her husband at electoral rallies, trying to make out therevealing bulge of a weapon under a shirt, or the suspicious gesture of a potential assassin. Because she always knew that something like this could happen. She knew it from the day Rajiv gave in to what his mother, Indira Gandhi, then Primer Minister, asked of him, and got into politics. That is why, two days ago, when the phone rang at ten to eleven at night, such an odd time, Sonia turned over in bed and covered her ears as though to protect herself from the blow she knew she was about to receive. The worst news of her life was actually expected news. It was even more expected since Sonia found out that the government had taken away the degree of maximum security from Rajiv, which was his right as an ex-Prime Minister. In bureaucratic jargon, he was category Z, and that gave the right to protection from the SPG (Special Protection Group), which would have protected him from a terrorist attack. Why was that taken away from him, however much she had demanded it? Out of carelessness? Or because that so-called "lapse" was in line with the designs of his political adversaries?

A hard, sharp, indescribable sound brings her back to reality. It sounds like agunshot. Or a small explosion. Anyone that has attended a cremation knows what it is. Some people lower their heads, others look up, yet others are so captivated by the spectacle that they appear to be hypnotized and keep looking. The skull has exploded from the pressure of the heat. The soul ofthe dead man is now free. The ritual is over. The people throw flower petals into the flames, as another disturbing sight emerges. The long, fine hands that caressed his children or repaired an electronic device or signed international treaties are exposed and show blackened fingers that rise and curl in a heartbreaking parting from the other side. Goodbye, farewell.

Sonia bursts into sobs. Where is the comfort for her? With which God should she seek it? What God can allow a good man like Rajiv to be blownto pieces by the fanaticism of other men, who also have families, who also have children, who also know how to caress and love? What sense can she make out of all this tragedy? Her children, worried that the mixture of smoke, ash and intense emotion might cause another attack of asthma, stand on either side of her, while she calms down and watches, broken inside, how her dream of living many years of happiness with her husband becomes so much smoke. *Ciao, amore*, until another life. The whole of India will remember her like this, standing motionless as stone, stoical, indifferent to the cries of the screaming crowd, while fire consumes the body of her husband. She is the living image of controlled grief.

The roar of an army helicopter drowns out the singing and the cries of the crowd. The people look up into a sky that is white with heat and dust and receive a shower of rose petals that fall from the vehicle going round and round above the pyre. As the body finishes burning, the family goes down from the platform. With hesitant steps and grief-stricken faces, they receive a few words of condolence from the President of the Republic. In very typical Indian disorder, the other personalities crowd closer. They all want to say a few words to Sonia: the American Vice-President, the King of Bhutan, the Prime Ministers of Pakistan, Nepal and Bangladesh, former Prime Minister, Edward Heath, the Vice-Presidents of the Soviet Union and China, her old friend Benazir Bhutto, etc. But no one can get close to the widow because suddenly chaos breaks out. And the fact is the body does not belong only to the family, or to the foreign dignitaries. The crowd, of which the first rows are made up of militants and organizers of Rajiv's party, feels that it also belongs to them. They are only a tiny fraction of the forty million members of the party which, under the banal and rather unattractive name of Congress Party, represents the largest democratic political organization in the world. It was born in the mid-nineteenth century as an association of small political groups to demand equality of rights between Indians and English within the Empire. Mahatma Gandhi turned it into a solid party whose goal was to win independence through non-violence. Nehru was its president, then his daughter Indira, and Rajiv was the latest. In spite of the scorching, unbreathable air, now the militants want a close look at the mortal remains of their leader turning into ashes. They all want to lick the flames of death and memory, so they tear down the wire fences as though they were straw and rush towards the fire shouting: "Rajiv Gandhi is immortal!" The Black Cats, the elite commandos, are forced to intervene. They make a human barrier around the family, and decide to beat a hasty retreat, step by step, amid the hysterical cries of the now unrestrained crowd, until they reach the cars and safety.

*   *   *

In the following days, in a state of shock, Sonia takes refuge inside herself. She lives engrossed in her memories with Rajiv, breaking into sobs when she comes out of her trance and finds herself face to face with the terrible reality of his absence. She cannot stop thinking about her husband; she does not want to stop thinking about him, as though stopping were another way of killing him. She does not even want to separate herself from those two urns that contain his ashes, but it is part of the ritual that death turns again into life.

On May 28th, 1991, four days after the cremation, accompanied by her children, Sonia boards a special carriage on a train that takes them to Allahabad, the city of the Nehru family, where everything began over a hundred years ago. In the carriage, which is totally draped in white cloth scattered with

23

marigold and jasmine flowers, the urns are placed on a kind of stand next to the framed photo of a smiling Rajiv. Sonia, Priyanka and Rahultravel sitting on the floor. The train stops at a string of stations packed with people who have come to pay tribute to the memory of their leader. The outpouring of emotion exhausts Sonia, but she would do her utmost to wave at those poor people with bony faces stained with sweat and tears who, in spite of everything, smile to offer her their comfort. The smiles of the poorof India are an immaterial gift, but one which settles in the heart. Nehru, her mother-in-law and her husband all said so: the trust of the people, the warmth of the populace, veneration and, why not? the love they show you make up for all the sacrifices. That is the true nourishment of a politician born and bred, the justification for all the troubles, what gives meaning to hiswork, to his life. During the twenty-four hours that the train, baptized by the Press with the name *The Heartbreak Express*, takes to cover the 600 kilometres of the journey, Sonia is able to measure the intensity of the people's affection towards her in-laws – "the family", as Indians know them,so popular that it is not necessary to specify which family it is. A family that has governed India for more than four decades, but has been out of powerfor four years. Sonia looks at her son Rahul, who has fallen asleep between stations. With any luck the family will never come to power again. Priyanka stares ahead in a daydream; she is also exhausted. She looks very like Indira, the same bearing, the same shining, intelligent eyes. God help us.

In Allahabad, the ashes are placed in Anand Bhawan, the ancestral mansion of the Nehrus, which, when she was named Prime Minister, Indira turned into a museum open to the public. A Moorish-style patio with a fountain in the centre is a reminder of the original owner, a Moslem judge inthe Supreme Court. In 1900 he sold the mansion to Motilal Nehru, Rajiv's great-grandfather, a brilliant lawyer who earned so much money that, according to the legend, he used to send his clothes by ship to a dry cleaners in London. That heavily-built man who always had a thick moustache and dressed like a gentleman, who was outgoing, lavishly generous, *bon vivant* and witty, adored his son Jawaharlal, perhaps because he was the last son he had, having lost two sons and a daughter beforehand. That intense, reciprocal love was in the origin of the struggle for independence of a sixth of humanity. Motilal wanted his son to develop all his potential, whichmeant giving him the best possible education, even if it meant being apart from him: "I never thought I would love you so much as when I had to leave you for the first time in England, at the boarding school", he wrote to him, because he could not get over the anguish of having left him alone, so far away, and only thirteen years old. What Motilal earned in a year would have been enough to start up a business for him and set him up for life. But for thefather that was an easy, egoistic point of view: "I think without a trace of vanity that I am the founder of the fortune of the Nehru family. I see you,my dear son, as the man who will be able to build on the foundation I have created and I hope to have the satisfaction of one day seeing a noble venture arise which will reach the skies..." The noble venture ended up being the country's struggle for independence, in which father and son became involved with all the strength of their convictions.

The life of the Nehrus changed when Jawaharlal introduced his father to a lawyer who had just returned from South Africa and was organizing resistance against the colonial power of the English. He was a strange man, dressed in *dhotis*, raw cotton hand-woven pants. He had disproportionately long arms and

legs that made him look like a long-legged bird. His little black
eyes closed when, behind his metal-rimmed glasses, he gave his
typical smile, half malicious and half good-natured. Venerated
as a saint by his disciples, he was however a skilled politician
who possessed the art of simple gestures that could touch the
soul of India. Young Nehru considered him a genius.

And so Mahatma Gandhi came into contact with that family
and changed it forever. The extravagant Motilal gave up
sophistication in favour of simplicity, and exchanged his flannel
suits from Savile Row and his top hats for a *dhoti*, like Gandhi.
He gave his house and fortune to the cause of independence.
Motilal changed the huge sitting room into a meeting hall for
the Congress Party and the Nehru home gradually became the
home of the whole of India. There was always a crowd of
sympathizers at the gate hoping to see the father and the son,
hoping to have their *darshan*, the ancient tradition of religious
origin that consists of seeking visual contact with a highly
venerated person in order to receive their blessing in this way, if
unable to touch their feet or hands. Towards the end of his life,
suffering from fibrosis and cancer, Motilal shared a cell in the
Nainital jail with his son, who took care of him as best as he
could. The patriarch died without getting to see independence,
without knowing that his son, whom the world would come to
know as Nehru, would be elected the first Head of State of
the nation. He died in this house in Anand Bhawan, one day in
February 1931, with his wife beside him and his son cradling
his head on his lap.

The rooms, painted sky blue and cream, hold the same
pieces of furniture, the same books and the same photos and
knick knacks of the people who lived in them. Mahatma
Gandhi's room has a mattress on the floor, a chest of drawers
and a spinning wheel that he used for spinning cotton and

which he turned into a symbol of resistance against the English. Nehru's room has a simple wooden bed, a rug, lots of books and a little figurine of the three monkeys that symbolize the Buddhist commandments: see no evil, hear no evil, speak no evil.

Sonia remembers the first time she ever visited this place. It was Indira, her mother-in-law, who showed it to her. On that visit she did not notice the tremendous symbolic and historic effect this house has on the history of India. She was simply visiting the home of her in-laws' ancestors, the house where first Nehru and then his daughter Indira had been born. She had not been able to gauge all the meaning enclosed by the walls of this mansion, in spite of the fact that Indira showed her the secret meeting room, in a cellar, which Nehru and his companions in the incipient Congress Party used when they hid to escape the raids of the British police. Now that she has returned with her husband's ashes, she sees it all in a different way. This Victorian mansion is not the simple setting of an intense family life; its walls tell of the intrigue, dreams, hopes and setbacks of the struggle for independence. Its walls *are* modern India. The urn with Rajiv's ashes, the last object that has arrived today to be added to the others, is like the final full stop in a long sentence that Motilal Nehru began to write in the 19th century when he founded here the local section of a political organization called the Congress Party. The circle has closed.

At midday Sonia and her children leave the family home, accompanied by a small cortège, and head for the outskirts, for Sangam, one of the most sacred places in Hinduism, where the brown waters of the Jamuna join the clear waters of the Ganges, at the confluence of another, imaginary, river, the

Sarasvati. They come to an enormous esplanade of sand that leads to the river bank, dominated by an old Moslem fort whose walls are covered in ivy and which holds a one hundred-year-old Bengal fig tree. According to legend, anyone who jumps out of its branches can be freed from the cycle of reincarnations. On this esplanade the Kumbha Mela is celebrated every three years, a festival attended by millions of pilgrims from all over India. They come to wash away their sins, making this the most massive religious gathering in the world. There are many people here today too, but the place is so immense it seems deserted. On a platform over the river, *pandit* Chuni Lal, a priest who is also a friend of the family, makes an offering and intones prayers against the background noise of the tinkling of thousands of little bells and the echo of conch shells, before handing the copper urn to Rahul. The young man takes it, approaches the shore and tips it out slowly, scattering the ashes over the quiet waters which reflect the golden rays of the sun, the same waters that welcomed the ashes of Motilal, Mahatma Gandhi and also Nehru. A certain distance away, Sonia and Priyanka observe the scene, their faces tense, and then they go over to Rahul, and squatting down, caress the water with their hands. Witnesses of this scene, amongst whom is her husband's secretary, will take away with them the memory of the picture of the three of them huddled together at the water's edge. Rahul sobbing on one of his mother's shoulders, Priyanka leaning her head on the other, and Sonia, inconsolable, with her eyes full of tears which form another affluent that flows into the Ganges, the great river of life.

2

"Madam, these are the times of the flights to Milan." Sonia does not remember having asked her husband's secretary for that information. Perhaps she did, in the confusion at the beginning, when she sought protection from the enormity of the tragedy. When she suddenly thought of fleeing this country that devours its children, to seek comfort from her family, the warmth of her own people, the safety of the little town of Orbassano, just outside Turin, where she lived in her youth until the day she got married. She remembers that as soon as they got back with the remains of her husband from where the attack took place, in the south of India, she talked to her family in Italy on the phone and she was trembling. Her older sister Anushka told her they were no longer answering the phone because journalists from all over the world were calling to ask for details of what had happened and they did not know what to tell them. "We still don't know," Sonia explained to her, "it might be the Sikhs who killed Indira, or the Hindu fundamentalists who killed Gandhi, or Moslem extremists from Kashmir ... who knows. He was on the blacklist of at least a dozen terrorist organizations..." And now Sonia is sorry she did force him to demand better safety measures from the government. Rajiv did not believe in them: "If they want to kill you, they'll kill you," he said.

When she got her mother on the other end of the phone, Sonia went to pieces. Her mother was in Rome, at Nadia's house, her younger sister, who had been married to a Spanish diplomat. "Perhaps you should come back to Italy," she told her.

"I don't know ..." Sonia answered, her voice faltering from the tears.

So many questions! She thinks that leaving would be like killing a part of herself, but it is true that she came to India, adopted the customs and fell in love with the people out of love for Rajiv. Now, what sense is there in staying? Is she not tired of living surrounded by bodyguards who, when the fatal moment arrives, are incapable of avoiding the worst? She remembers when, concerned for the children's safety, Rajiv thought about sending them to study at the American School in Moscow. Sonia did not like the idea of being separated from them at all. The British tradition, later adopted by the wealthier classes in India, of sending the children to a boarding school, completely clashed with her view of herself as an Italian *mamma*. So they kept them at home, in New Delhi, and first of all tutors came to the house every morning and later they went to school with an escort to be educated in a "normal" environment, which society considered as an act of audacity, such was the weight of the threats that hung over the Prime Minister's family.

Her mother's suggestion that she return to Italy touches a sore spot. Sonia faces a conflict which she finds impossible to resolve, at least for the moment. A cruel conflict, because on one hand there is the greatest concern, the safety of her children, and it would seem logical to undertake a family move back to Italy, a total change of lifestyle, the abandonment of the whole of her husband's family tradition; and on the other hand the inertia of all the years she has spent here bearing the crushing weight of the name of Nehru- Gandhi, and to stay as they are, in the same house, as guardians of the memory, surrounded by the forever faithful friends, enveloped in the affection of so many people, knowing how hard it is to escape the web of Indian politics. In sum, to choose between safety, an anonymous life and the uprooting of a self-imposed exile or to carry on in the limelight, which couldlead to one of her children one day becoming Prime Minister and, perhaps, also being assassinated. Like Indira or Rajiv. Then she thinks, yes, it is best to change lifestyle to be safe, to forget the politics she so hates, to flee from the power she has always despised and which is destroying her.

But ... can you fight destiny? She feels very Indian, she has learned tolove the people of this country, and she feels loved by them. How can she break that link to the memory of her husband as represented by friends, colleagues and the love of the people of India? It would be a little like losing her heart. Besides, the body does not lie: her gestures, her way of walking,of shaking her head to say yes when it looks like no – so typical of Indians – her way of putting her hands together, of looking, of listening, her accent ... all her body language evokes that of a genuinely Indian person. What would she do in Italy? What kind of life would await her in Orbassano, apart from the company of her closest family? Her circle of friends is here, her world is here, 23 years of intensely happy life are here. Besides, her children are no longer small ... And will they want to go and live in a place that they have only visited on holiday? After having been brought up in the homes of two Prime Ministers of India, first that of grandmother Indira and then that of their father Rajiv, with everything that that means, could they get used to living an anonymous life in the outskirts of a provincial Italian town? It is true that they speak Italian fluently, they are half Italian, but they feel one hundred percent Indian. They have been brought up here, here they have learned from their father to love this immense, difficult and fascinating country; here they have taken in the values of their great-grandfather Nehru, the great hero of independence and founder of modern India, values that have to do with integrity, tolerance, contempt for money and the cult of service to others, especially to those most needy. Here they have been brought up, in the home of grandmother Indira, who might give them a hug while she had tea with Andrei Gromyko or Jacqueline Kennedy or help them with their homework at the kitchen table. Would her children be content with a prosperous and comfortable life at best, but far away from all they had imbibed since they were born? And for her, would it not be a defeat to go back to the town she had left behind?

"I think my life is here, Mother ..." Sonia ends up saying when she recovers her ability to speak.

"Madam, you have a visitor."

The secretary who has interrupted her remains in the doorway until Sonia makes a gesture signifying "I'll be right there", and then the man retires. She says goodbye to her mother and hangs up, wiping away her tears. As she stands up she adjusts the folds of her sari and heads for her husband's office, on the ground floor of the colonial villa where they have lived since they left the Prime Minister's residence. On seeing all his things in their place, his cameras, his books, his magazines, his papers, his radio, she thinks for a moment that he is still alive, about to arrive home from some trip or other, that what she is going through is nothing more than a bad dream, that life is going on just the same because it is stronger than death. But it is not Rajiv who comes through the door, smiling, tired and ready to hug her, but three of his party colleagues, three veterans with sad, disconsolate expressions on their faces, two of them wearing Indian shirts with high collars, the third in a kind of safari suit. Because if this terrorist attack has devastated the family, it has also left the Congress Party without its leader. And someone has to lead the Party. Who will it be next? that is thequestion these big fish who have now come to visit Sonia asked themselves only hours after finding out about the tragedy.

"Soniaji," says the spokesman of the committee, using the suffix *ji* which denotes affection and respect. "I want you to know that the Congress Working Committee, meeting under the presidency of your husband's old friend, Narashima Rao, has elected you president of the party. The election was unanimous. Congratulations."

Sonia stands staring at them impassively. Is grief not something pure and sacred? They have not even allowed her to dry her tears for the death of her husband and the politicians are already here. Life goes on, and it is cruel. Incapable of smiling, she does not have the desire or strength to pretend she is honoured by the result of the voting.

"I cannot accept. My world is not politics, as you already know. I do not wish to accept."

"Soniaji, I don't know if you realize what the committee is offering you. It is offering you absolute power over the largest party in the world. And it's doing that on a silver plate. It's offering you the chance to lead this great country. Above all it's offering you the chance to take on the inheritance of your husband so that his death is not in vain ..."

"I don't think this is the right time to talk about this ..."

"The Working Committee has deliberated for many hours before making this proposal to you. I can assure you that we have thought deeply about it. You will have a free hand and will be able to count on our full support. We ask you to continue the family tradition. It is your duty as a good daughter of India."

"You are the only one who can fill the void Rajiv has left," adds another.

"India is a very big country…" Sonia replies. "I can't be the only one out of a billion."

"But you are the only Gandhi…"

Sonia looks up, as though she was expecting that argument. "Not counting your children, of course."

"My children are still very young, and neither are they up to talking politics today."

"It is not a small thing to be called Gandhi in India …" adds another. "I know what you mean," Sonia interrupts him. "It's a name that carries an obligation, but also damns the bearer. Just look what has happened."

Actually Sonia is called that because her mother-in-law, Indira, married a Parsee called Firoz Gandhi, not because there was any relationship with the father of the nation, Mahatma Gandhi. He could have been called Kumar, or Bose, or Kapur, or any one of the common surnames in India. But chance made his name coincide with that of the most famous Indian of all, the man most loved by his people for having guided them along the path to liberty. The man who became such an intimate friend of the Nehrus that he was considered as another member of the family. Together they won independence and they did so thanks to a powerful instrument, the Congress Party, which today is fatherless. That gives the Gandhis, including Sonia, an aura in the eyes of the masses that has an incalculable value for the politicians of that party.

"Look … You are the heir of this photo."

One of them points to a photo on a side table next to the

sofa. It is in a silver frame, and shows Indira, as a child, sitting by Mahatma.

"Thank you very much, really, for thinking of me for that position. It is a great honour, but I do not deserve it. You know that I hate renown. Besides, I do not belong to the direct family, I'm just the daughter-in-law…" "You married an Indian, and you know that here a daughter-in-law becomes part of her husband's family when she gets married… You have kept all our customs religiously. You are as Indian as anyone, and not just any Indian is the wife of a Nehru-Gandhi. Look at this photo … isn't that red sari that you wore on your wedding day the one Nehru wove while he was in jail?"

"Yes, but that doesn't take away from the fact that I'm a foreigner …" "The people don't care where you were born. You wouldn't be the first woman of foreign birth to be President," interrupts the third man. "Remember that Annie Besant, one of the first leaders of the party and the first to lead it at a national level, was Irish. The idea isn't so crazy."

"Those were other times. I'm too vulnerable to take on that post. Can you imagine the attacks from the opposition? They would use the people against me, and it would be a disaster for everyone."

"Soniaji, we are making you an unconditional offer …" says the eldest man, an astute politician known for his skill in manipulation, and who seems about to pull something out of his sleeve. "Perhaps the most important thing for you is that you will once again enjoy the highest level of protection, just like when Rajiv was Prime Minister."

"I'm sorry, but you have knocked on the wrong door. I have no ambition for power, I've never liked that world, I feel uncomfortable in it and I hate being the centre of attention. Rajiv didn't like it either. If he went into politics it was because his mother asked him to. Otherwise he would still be an Indian Airlines pilot, he would still be alive today and we would probably be very happy ... So, I'm very sorry, but don't count on me."

"You are the only one who can avoid the collapse of the party. And if the party breaks up, it is very likely that the whole country will fall to pieces. What has kept India united since independence? Our party. Who guarantees the values that permit all the different communities to live together in peace? The Congress Party. Since we have been out of power, look how the old demons have gained ground: hatred between communities, between religions, the separatist aspirations of so many states ... The whole country is falling apart, and only you can help us to save it. You have prestige and the people love you. That is why we have come in person ... to appeal to your sense of responsibility."

"Responsibility? Why does it have to be this family that pays a constant tribute to the country with the blood of its members? Hasn't it been enough with Indira and Rajiv? Do you want more?"

"Think about it, Soniaji. Think about Nehru, about Indira, about Rajiv

... Your family is as closely linked to India as a vine round the trunk of a tree. You are India. Without your family, we are nothing. Without you there is no future for this great nation. This is the message we have come to bring you. We know that these are bitter hours, and we beg your forgiveness for interrupting your grief, but do not abandon us. Do not throw so much sacrifice and struggle overboard. You have the torch of the Nehru-Gandhis in your hand. Do not let it go out."

Words, words, words ... There is always a higher purpose, a

greater goal at the end of the road, a nobler cause, a better justification to dress up the final aim, which is still to take power. Politicians always find arguments and excuses to talk about the only thing that interests them: power. Because she has lived so many years in the shadow of two Prime Ministers, Sonia knows the score. She can imagine perfectly well the desolation of all the candidates who were going to stand in the elections and who today also feel fatherless. The murder of her husband has broken the dreams of many people, not only his family. She can imagine the conjecturing, the manoeuvres, the backstabbing, the trickery of all those who are fighting to succeed Rajiv in the heart of the party. A lot is at stake and that is why the big fish have come to pay their respects to her, without wasting a second. They are not thinking about her as a human being, even in these dark hours, but as an instrument for holding on to the reins of power. It is time to jockey for position within the party because power cannot stand a vacuum. In a country where resources are scarce, where there are few opportunities, political power is the key to individual prosperity.

Sonia learnt from Rajiv and Indira to keep the politicians at bay, to not allow them to use her. But they are cunning and think that Sonia will end up giving way, that she will do so, if not for herself, then for her children, to keep the family name alive, because power is a magnet from which it is impossible to escape. Do the Vedic poets not say that even the gods cannot resist flattery?

The next day Sonia sends a letter to the central office of the party: "I am deeply moved by the trust placed in me by the Working Committee. But the tragedy that has struck my children and me does not allow me to accept the presidency of this great organization." It is a jug of cold water for the faithful who cannot accept her rejection and decide to continue pressurizing her with all the means at their command. Every morning, party sympathizers demonstrate in front of her home, a colonial villa located at number 10, Janpath, an avenue in the centre of New Delhi. They carry posters and shout slogans such as "Long live Rajiv Gandhi; Soniaji for President". Sonia, annoyed, asks her husband's secretary to get rid of the demonstrators, to put an end to this spectacle that she thinks is stupid and senseless. "Let them look for another successor," she thinks. "My family has done enough already…"

Those who feel really reassured when they read the news in the newspapers are her relations in Orbassano, near Turin. "In the town we're all breathing sighs of relief," declares a neighbour. "Thank goodness she hasn't accepted her husband's job. It would have been a great risk to her and her children."

ACT I

THE GODDESS DURGA RIDES ON A TIGER

Power is there to protect.

PASCAL

3

Sonia was 18, the age at which she decided to go to England to learn English, when she fell in love with Rajiv. She was so pretty that people turned round in the street to look at her. She walked very erect, and her straight, dark brown hair framed her madonna-like face. Josto Maffeo, now a well-known journalist, at the time a classmate of hers, who shared the bus trip with her at weekends from the town of Orbassano where she lived with her family, to the centre of Turin, remembers her as "one of the prettiest women I've ever known. And besides being pretty, she was interesting, a very good friend to her friends, and quiet and well-balanced. She didn't like going to huge parties and she definitely always maintained a certain reserve towards other people."

It is not surprising then that Sonia's father, a burly man whose rugged face showed the marks of a tough past of hard work in the open air, should oppose it so vehemently when his daughter wanted to go and study English in Cambridge. This good man, Stefano Maino, with his short hair brushed back, his thick moustache that tickled his daughters when he kissed them, and his red cheeks, was very old-fashioned. To such an extent that years before, when he settled in Orbassano and found out that the village school was mixed, he refused to let his daughters go there and chose to send them to Sangano, a town ten kilometres away, to a school just for girls. As they got older, he always wanted to know where his three daughters were and who they were with. Neither was he very pleased when they went out at weekends, and that did not mean being out at night, which he would not have tolerated. They went into Turin, half an hour away by bus or train, to walk under the arcades of its beautiful avenues or, if the weather was bad, to sip a cup of hot chocolate with their friends in one of the famous *cremeries* of the city. Stefano was a man of strict principles and it was inevitable that he would clash with his adolescent daughters. The one that used to stand up to him the most was Anushka, the eldest, an argumentative girl with a strong, rebellious character. Compared to her, Sonia was an angel. The youngest, Nadia, was still too young to cause problems.

His wife, Paola, a woman with regular features, an open smile and a more refined air, made up for Stefano's severity with her flexibility. She was more open-minded, more tolerant, more understanding. Perhaps because she was a woman, she was more able to understand her daughters, although her adolescence had been very different, having been brought up in a mountain village which had fewer than six hundred inhabitants, and at a time when Italy was a poor country. Very poor. Her daughters have never had to milk cows, or work in the fields or serve coffees in the family bar. They were post-war children, daughters of the Marshall Plan, of economic expansion, of the re-emergence of Italy in Europe. They have only known poverty obliquely, when they were little, because in the post-war years it was impossible to get away from the sight of the cripples and beggars who sought the warmth of the sun and public charity leaning against the walls in the village square. And that contact marked them forever, especially Sonia. In Vicenza, the big town nearest to the village where they lived, poverty could be seen before you got to the centre, in those slum areas where the children played naked or went around in rags.

"Why do their mothers let them go out like that, stark naked?" asked little Sonia, puzzled.

"Those children are like that because they don't have any clothes. They aren't like that because they want to be but because they have no option. Because they're poor."

The child understood for the first time what a terrible thing poverty was. Furthermore, her mother added, some families went hungry. Didn't the parish priest come by the house every month to collect powdered milk, food and clothing which he then shared out among those that were the neediest? That priest knew he could always count on the Maino family who, although they too were going through hard times, were devout Catholics and practicedcharity.

"The Gospel says that the poor will be the first to enter the Kingdom of Heaven … Haven't they taught you that in Catechism?"

Sonia nodded, while she helped her mother prepare a parcel of used clothes. In the Maino household nothing was thrown away, nothing was wasted. The younger ones inherited things from the older ones. What wasnot used was given to the poor. The memory of the war was too close to forget the value of things.

Sonia's parents were originally from the Veneto region, specifically the village of Lusiana, in the Asiago mountains in the foothills of the Alps, a cattle-raising area that gives its name to one of the best-liked cheeses in Italy, known also for its marble quarries. The father's side of the family, the Mainos, were rough-mannered, honest, direct and very hardworking. A quality that did not escape Sonia's mother, Paola Predebon, the daughter of an ex-policeman who ran the grandfather's bar in the village of Comarolo di Conco, down in the valley. Stefano and Paola got married in the pretty church in Lusiana, dedicated to the Apostle James, with its tall spire pointing into Heaven resembling the minaret of a mosque, no doubt the influence of the Ottomans, who were in the region centuries ago.

Sonia was born at 9.30 pm one cold night on December 9th, 1946 in the civil hospital of Marostica, a very old, little walled city in the foothills of the Asiago mountains. "*E nata una bimbaaa!*" the good news quickly reached the village of Lusiana, and the echo bounced off the stone walls of the houses and stables, the rocky slopes and the mountains all around until it vanished in the distance, in a cascade. In tribute to the newborn baby girl and in accordance with tradition, the neighbours tied pink ribbons to the bars on the windows and doors of the village. A few days later she was christened by the Lusiana parish priest and given the name of Edvige Antonia Albina Maino, in honour of her maternal grandmother. But Stefano wanted a different name for his daughter. The eldest girl, baptized Ana, he called Anushka, and Antonia he called Sonia. In this way he kept the promise he had made to himself after getting away from the Russian front with his life. Like many Italians mired in poverty, Stefano had let himself be seduced by the Fascist ideas and propaganda of Mussolini and at the beginning of the war he had enlisted in the 116th Vicenza infantry division, a regiment that belonged to the *bersaglieri* corps, with such a high reputation in the Italian army, and in it had also served the *Duce*. The *bersaglieri*, who were known for their fast marching pace when they paraded, over 130 steps per minute, and above all for their wide-brimmed helmets with a plume of shiny black cock's feathers falling to one side, were surrounded by an aura of courage and invulnerability which the Russian campaign destroyed in one stroke. The division lost three quarters of its men in the first confrontation with the Russians. There were thousands of prisoners, among them Stefano, who managed to escape together with other survivors. They succeeded in taking shelter in a farmhouse on the Russian steppes, where they lived for weeks under the protection of a peasant family. The women healed their wounds, the men provided them with supplies, and the experience, apart from saving their lives, changed them completely. Like thousands of Italian soldiers, they returned disillusioned with Fascism and grateful to the Russians for having saved them. From then on, Stefano no longer talked politics; for him, it was all a pack of lies. As a tribute to the family that had saved his life, he decided to give his daughters Russian names. And in order not to argue with his in- laws or the priest, for whom the name Sonia was not part of the calendar of saints – Sophia was acceptable, Sonia was not – Stefano agreed to have her registered with completely Catholic names. After the christening they invited neighbours and family to a meal of cod *Vicentina*, the favourite dish of the region, with a lot of *polenta* to soak up the sauce. It was a luxury toget hold of cod, because in post-war times there was a shortage of everything, even in Vicenza, the region's capital, situated fifty kilometres away, down on the plain.

The joy of the Maino family would have been complete if it had not been for the difficulties Stefano encountered to bring up his growing family. In those years it was very difficult to escape from the clutches of poverty. They had enough to eat, to clothe themselves, but little more. The Mainos had no lands, just a few cows and a stone house that Stefano had built himself with his own hands, the last one in the Rua Maino, the street where generations of his relatives, who had come originally from Germany, had built their homes. They were spartan, but they had magnificent views over the valley. Low stone walls separated the meadows where the cows grazed, and stockbreeding was the main resource of the area because the land was poor for agriculture since there were too many stones and too many steep slopes. Sonia and her sisters grew up with the sublime spectacle of the Lusiana valley, which changed colour with the seasons. All the hues and tones of green and brown paraded in front of their eyes, from the emerald green of the trees in spring to the yellow of the fields in summer, passing through the copper of autumn and the white of winter. For the children the first snow of the year was like a celebration which they enjoyed enormously; they played at making snowmen and throwing snowballs at each other in the white streets. But the mixture of physical exercise and cold set a tiredness in Sonia's chest which soon forced her home. She liked to take refuge in the warmth of the iron stove in the kitchen, while the wind whistled through the cracks in the windows.

On Sunday mornings, the tinkling of the cowbells mixed with the ringing of the church bells, while the family in their Sunday best headed for the Mass they never once missed. They prayed that Stefano would find work, that Sonia's asthma would let up, that the general situation might improve, that the girls should have everything they needed and grow up healthy and happy. In the early 50's, Stefano finally found a job, but not in their village. It was on the other side of the mountains, in Switzerland. His experience as a builder and his seriousness merited his being given a contract several seasons. He went off for a minimum of two months and returned with his pockets full of liras that always lasted less than he had expected.

In 1956, Stefano took the decision to emigrate, as three of his brothers and so many of his countrymen were doing. The industrial centre that Turin was becoming and which had grown up around the Fiat works, was like a magnet for millions of Italians who wanted to flee the poverty of the countryside. The Mainos crossed the whole of the north of Italy by train and settled in Orbassano, an industrial town in the outskirts of Turin. They did that because Giovanni, one of Stefano's brothers whom they called "Moro" because of the sallow colour of his skin, had married a girl from a village nearby and assured them that the construction boom needed lots of strong arms. Furthermore, Stefano knew the region because in the 30's he had worked as a labourer for the army in the restoration of military forts on the border with France, in the Alps. He liked people from Piedmont, perhaps because they were mountain folk too: direct, sincere people who did not waste their time on self-indulgence.

Work, work and more work - that was Stefano's recipe to prosper quickly. He did nothing else; he was not known to have any hobbies and he was not fond of sports, although he liked to go to Pier Luigi's bar to watch Juventus in the finals on television. His daughter Sonia also visited the same bar assiduously because Pier Luigi sold the best ice creams in the area. *"Era molto vivace, molto biricchina"*, he would say about the little girl.

When he arrived in Orbassano, Stefano was by then a skilled worker and from there he came to set up his own construction company. He began with renovations, then built detached houses, small *palazzi* and later on terraced houses. "He was a very honest man," his friend Danilo Quadri, a mechanic who repaired the breakdowns of his concrete mixers and other

Javier Moro

machinery and who ended up becoming a great friend of his, said of him. They saw each other every day at coffee time in Nino's Bar, in the square opposite the Town Hall, a building with two stories and arcades, a clock on the façade and an Italian flag flying from the balcony. Next to it was the church of St John the Baptist, with its characteristic tower and its turquoise- coloured pointed little roofs where they went to Mass on Sundays with their respective families. Stefano was a man of fixed times, a lover of routine. After the daily meeting with Danilo, he would walk home along the Via Frejus, lined with graceless buildings with no style, where a block of flats could stand next to an old villa in the very characteristic post-war mixture of popular urbanism. His house was at number 14, Via Bellini, a distance of about one and a half kilometres from the village square. That three-storied villa surrounded by a little garden had been the dream of his life. When he had paid off the debts he contracted when he started up his business, he looked for a piece of land at a good price that was near the *trenino* and bus stations and bought it on the nail. Stefano built his house in record time, with the typical *taverneta* that took up the whole of the ground floor. There was not a single house worth its salt that did not have its well-cared for *taverneta*, with its bar, its counter and its fireplace, which the parents used to for meeting with their friends or celebrating anniversaries, and the children for their parties. He made the house large with the idea of dividing it up between his daughters when they were older. Apart from work, the other fundamental value in the life of Stefano Maino was the family, like any good Italian. And, naturally, religion. All values he shared with his wife Paola, and which they tried hard to instill in the girls.

Sonia was ten when she came to Orbassano. The change from a mountain village to the suburbs of a large city like Turin

48

was a shock. It was a much easier way of life, more fun and with many more possibilities. The only shadow over that new life was connected with their origins. They were *paesane*, as immigrants from the countryside were known insultingly in the north of Italy. A stigma that made them feel less than others and which gave them a complex that would last throughout their lives. In the village they had never felt different; here they did, especially at first, at school, where the other girls called them *paesane* because they dressed in an old-fashioned style in "village" clothes. Orbassano was not untouched by the class- conscious atmosphere of Turin, a conservative city where you have lunch at twelve, drink a *cappuccino* at five in big art deco patisseries and have dinner at seven. Where the ladies always have smart hairdos and the men are fashionably dressed. Where the workers want to live like their bosses and imitate them, where the bosses like the rich bourgeois of whom they would love to be part, and the bourgeois like the aristocrats they secretly admire. At that time, there was no hint of rebellion; no one wanted to hang their bosses, they all wanted to be like them. The prosperity seemed endless and allowed everyone to follow their dream of social mobility. Gradually, as their father prospered, the social status of the Maino family rose. From being the daughters of a "cowherd and bricklayer", the girls became the daughters of a builder who lived comfortably. From daughters of an immigrant peasant to daughters of a businessman. Paola, their mother, a woman sensitive to her husband's social environment, immediately picked up the tastes of the Turin bourgeoisie – their way of dressing, their manners, etc... - and passed them on to her daughters, who rapidly became conscious of their new station in life. Never to the point that they denied their origins, since they were too honest for that. But they always knew they would never attain the status of pure-blood Turinese because they had not been born there.

After finishing primary school at the girls' school in the town of Sangano, Sonia would have liked to continue her studies in the school in Orbassano, but her father was opposed to the idea. "No state schools for my daughters. For them, always the best." The best, according to the Mainos, was the Maria Auxiliadora convent school in Giaveno, a beautiful mediaeval town about twenty kilometres from home, known as a place of relaxation for many Turinese. There they would have the chance to mix with girls of "better class" than in the state school in Orbassano. Apart from the fact that they valued religious education highly, the Mainos also wanted to remove the *paesane* label. So they left the girls on Monday mornings and picked them up on Fridays. It was not a harsh boarding school, quite the opposite: it was full of kind Salesian nuns who immediately took to Sonia. "The eldest had a bad temper and was difficult, but Sonia was goodness itself," Sister Domenica Rosso, assigned as her tutor, would say of her. *"Che bel carattere, sempre gioviale,"* Sister Giovanna Negri remembers, before adding, "She only studied enough to keep out of trouble, but she was always smiling and helpful." Sonia was already showing a quality that would become of great importance in her adulthood: she was a peace-maker. "She had a special talent for stopping two classmates squabbling, or for getting a group to agree and do an activity together. She was a very calm girl, even when she was little, perhaps because of her problem, which made her mature before her time..." The problem Sister Giovanna referred to was asthma. She remembers that the fits of coughing were so intense that they had to put her in a single room. She was the only boarder that slept alone, and she didso with the windows open even in winter, in spite of the icy wind that blew down from the Alps. The boarding school, with two hundred girls, was on a hillside that looked over the town: the towers of its mediaeval churches emerged from a mosaic of old rooftops, and on the other side of the river there was a huge crag whose top was usually covered in snow. When the coughing fits passed, Sonia lay under her feather quilt, looking at that mountain, dimly lit by the reflection of the lights of the town, which reminded her of Lusiana where she was born.

Sonia learned to ski, like all the local people, for whom skiing is the king of sports. But she was never a great fan, of that or of any other sport either, because she was worried that the exercise might set off an attack of asthma. In compensation, she developed a love of reading, a passion that would last all her life. At first, as was required in Catholic schools, she read the lives of the saints. She especially liked stories about the missionarieswho gave their all to the poor in faraway countries. Being a missionary seemed to her a heroic way of life, full of meaning, because you had to give yourself for others, and exciting, because it was full of adventure. The nuns at the school regularly showed films that told the great epics and myths of Christianity – such as the life of Saint Francis of Assisi, for example – and left the girls, especially Sonia, full of emotion. But the pleasure of books lasted longer than that of films, and she could re-read them and enjoy herselfat the same time as she learned from the experiences and thoughts of the characters. Reading opened the doors of the world to Sonia. Thanks to her reading and to her innate curiosity, the adolescent Sonia developed a feeling that the nuns called *amor mundi*, love for the world, according to the exquisite description Saint Augustine had made of it.

In class she had to learn the lives of the great heroes of

modern Italian history, such as the philosopher and politician Mazzini, who contributed to Italy becoming a democratic republic; or the exploits of the peculiar Garibaldi, an idealist and fighter who struggled for the unification of the country. She learned about the *Risorgimento*, the nationalist movement in the 19th century, but the nuns taught her little about the rest of the world. For example, she never even heard about India and its struggle for independence and its emergence as a modern State. The vague figure of Gandhi rang a bell, but she could not have said who he was, like the vast majority of Italian students, and European students too. On the other hand Nehru was more familiar. She glimpsed the profile of that elegant gentleman, with his characteristic Gandhi cap on his head, on the evening news her parents were watching on television as she made her way up to bed in her nightdress.

In any case, Sonia was not particularly interested in history, or the sciences either, or anything to do with politics. She had always liked languages, for which she had a certain facility. Her father had encouraged her to learn Russian and had paid for a private teacher for her. Sonia understood Russian and spoke it, although she had difficulty reading it. She also learned French at home. In addition, languages were useful if you wanted to travel, for getting to know other people, other customs, other worlds, to discover those places that she had been able to glimpse in the lives of the missionaries.

Later, when she had left the boarding school in Giaveno and was registered at a high school in Turin to take pre-university courses, her childhood dreams gradually changed. They began to adapt to reality. The idea of becoming an Alitalia stewardess, of earning her living travelling round the world, began to seduce her. It did not require an excessive amount of work and, when she had finished her high school studies she would have almost all the requirements: she was nice-looking, well-mannered, the right height, she knew Russian and French, she had it all ... All she needed was toperfect her English.

"Daddy, I want to go to England to learn English properly ..."
"No way."

Stefano did not in the least like the idea that his daughter might make her living on planes and in hotels, and it did not seem like a proper job either. If she wanted to learn English, he would pay for her classes in a language school, she did not need to leave home. She had learned Russian with a private teacher, hadn't she? She had learned French without ever having been to France, hadn't she? Well knowing how stubborn her father was, Sonia avoided a confrontation with him, but deep down she was just as stubborn when she was convinced about what she wanted. It was in herblood ...

So she won her mother's support and while she finished her studies, she worked from time to time in Fieratorino, the organization that set up conventions and industrial fairs, such as the famous Automobile Show. Sonia took her first steps as a hostess, and even as an interpreter for Russian at a golf championship. She liked the contact with different people. Thesame curiosity she felt for languages she now felt for culture and the spirit ofthe people who spoke them. The world was definitely larger than tiny Orbassano, and those little jobs widened her horizons. Her dream of becoming an air-hostess gradually changed into becoming a foreign language teacher or, even better, an interpreter in some international organization such as the United Nations.

Like any good highlander, Stefano was authoritarian and inflexible, but not so obstinate that he did not realize that his daughters had needs. He was trapped in a dilemma common to people of his generation: on one hand he felt the need to keep them under control and educate them in a traditional manner (girls could only do certain things, but boys could do anything they liked), and on the other hand he could see that times were changing and it was no longer a matter of just waiting for them to find a husband. And even so, better that they should be economically independent so that they would not have to live under the iron rule of a man. So in view of the pressure fromhis wife who was determined that her daughters should have a profession, he gave way, and agreed to pay for Sonia's journey and studies in England. But they were not prepared for their daughter to be an *au pair* and live with just any family in any city. They chose Cambridge, the home of the most prestigious universities and colleges. At Sonia's age, it was better to place her in the best possible environment … She thanked him by hugging him and kissing him just like when she was small, getting tickled by his moustache.

On January 7th, 1965, she said goodbye to her sisters and gave Stalin, the old dog, who had been her playmate throughout her childhood, a big squeeze. Her parents went with her to Milan airport, just one *oretta* away. The morning mist lifted and gave way to a cold, sunny day. Sonia was excited about travelling alone for the first time and also afraid of the unknown. She was 18 years old and had her life in ahead of her. A life that she could not have imagined in her wildest dreams.

4

"For my girls always the best …" Stefano never stinted on his daughters. The Lennox Cook School was one of the best and most expensive language schools in Cambridge, located in a nice street a little out of the centre. It boasted of having had the famous writer E.M. Forster among its teachers of literature, although in those years he was too old and only went in from time to time to give a talk. For the cost of registration, the school also took charge of finding an English family for each student that requested it, so that they could live with them as paying guests.

Compared with Turin, the climate in Cambridge seemed depressing to Sonia: the cold froze her bones because of the damp, it drizzled constantly and got dark at four in the afternoon. Besides, it was a penetrating kind of cold because the radiators in the house were kept off most of the day to save money. To her surprise, the one in her room only worked with coins. She had thought that living with an English family would be like living with any Italian family, where they shared everything. But that was her ignorance of local customs. Taking in a paying guest was just another way of making money and, as such, everything counted. She discovered to her horror that she had to pay every time she wanted to have a bath and that it was going to cost her a lot to keep up her usual level of daily hygiene. But worst of all were the meals. She had never eaten boiled cabbage or meat with jam or potato omelette with ... potatoes. Getting up in the morning and finding herself face to face with a piece of toast with baked beans in tomato sauce put the brakes on her appetite. And the toast with soft, sticky spaghetti that they gave her one day seemed like a joke in poor taste, although when she saw that everybody else got stuck in with gusto, she realized that that was the way things were in this strange country. Added to this was the difficulty she encountered in expressing herself: she was incapable of holding a fluent conversation with her host family. In fact she knew less English than she had thought.

At first she thought she would never get used to it. Her shyness was an obstacle to her making friends with people. She avoided being with other

Italians because she was there to study and not to have fun. She spent the first days getting to know the city. The Gothic chapel at King's College and the river full of punts with tourists were two of her favourite spots. But there were many interesting places such as Trinity College chapel with its statues and plaques in honour of the great figures who had studied or researched there, like Isaac Newton, Lord Byron or Nehru himself; the "mathematical bridge", the first bridge in the world designed according to the analysis of the mathematical forces that acted on the structure ... It did not seem strange to her that Cambridge should be considered as one of the most beautiful cities in England, but that was still poor consolation for her loneliness. When she left class she used to go out walking in the streets in the city centre. From time to time she would go into one of the numerous bookshops, especially those that had foreign press, to flick through an Italian magazine or newspaper. That fleeting contact with her country was like a balm. She felt so homesick and missed her family so much that when she went back to her freezing room she was very downhearted. How the Hell did I get the idea of coming to study in a place like this? she asked herself as she took a deep breath through her inhaler.

However shy she was, it was impossible not to make friends at the age of 18 in a place like Cambridge, where one in five inhabitants was a student. There were students of every nationality and race and they did all kinds of activities during their free time, from sport to drama, as well as listening to live music or going on a picnic to the Orchard Tea Garden, public gardens in an idyllic spot that seemed out of a novel by Thomas Hardy and whose cafeteria served delicious cheesecake. They were the ones who had given the city that cosmopolitan, lively and at the same time interesting atmosphere for which Cambridge was known all over the world. And many of them were like Sonia, that is to say foreigners with no family or friends. They needed each other.

It was a German boy who spoke to her first in a restaurant where the food was decent. Christian von Stieglitz was an International Law student at Christ's College, a tall, good-looking boy with intensely blue eyes and a roguish look. Half English and half German, he spoke several languages, although he had a preference for Italian and French. And for Italian and French girls, so ... what better way to link the useful and the pleasant than by frequenting the language schools, full of pretty female students! That is how he met Sonia and convinced her to try the only place in Cambridge where you could eat decently. It was not very expensive, and neither was it far from the school. The Varsity was known for being the oldest restaurant in the city and was proud of having had Prince Faisal and the Duke of Edinburgh among its illustrious patrons, when they were students. Ten years earlier it had been bought by a Greek-Cypriot family and since then offered Mediterranean dishes to its numerous clientele, which included both dons and students. It was in an old building with a white-painted brick façade with two large square-paned windows in the upper floor. It was advertised by a discreet sign with black lettering. It was a narrow place and from the windows that looked on to the street you could see the buildings of Emmanuel College, another institution of great tradition where Mr Harvard himself had studied, and which served as an inspiration for him to found the university near Boston that bears his name.

For Sonia it was a real revelation, and some comfort for her poor stomach. It was the closest thing to home cooking she had tried since she had come to the city. And so she soon became fond of *mezze*, the apéritifs that included dipping bread in *tarama*, a paste made out of fish roe and lemon, skewers of barbecued roast meat or the house speciality, baked lamb that melted in your mouth like butter. She also liked the atmosphere there. You could go to eat on your own at the Varsity and not feel lonely. More than once she must have passed a character who limped a little at that time and was always weighed down with books. He did research into cosmology at the university and years later his name would acquire world-wide fame. This was Stephen Hawking, and he was also a regular at the Varsity.

Another character who frequented the place would leap to international renown for other reasons. Sonia had noticed him several times because, along with a group of noisy students, he occupied a long table near hers. "One of those boys stood out. He was striking in both looks and manners," Sonia would say. "He was not as boisterous as the others; he was more reserved, more gentle. He had big, black eyes and a wonderfully innocent and disarming smile."

A few days later, while Sonia was having lunch with a Swiss friend at a corner table upstairs, she saw him approach, accompanied by Christian von Stieglitz, her German friend. After the usual exchange of greetings and jokes, the German boy said to her, "Let me introduce you to my flatmate. He's from India and his name's Rajiv …"

They shook hands. "As our eyes met for the first time," Sonia would say, "I felt my heart pounding."

Rajiv had been watching her throughout lunch, captivated by her serene beauty.

"Do you like her?" Christian had asked him. "She's Italian, I know her …"

"Well introduce me to her."

The German boy was surprised because Rajiv was not a great one for the girls or a womanizer, but was rather distant and intimidated. "The first time I saw her," Rajiv would say, "I knew she was the woman for me."

That same afternoon the four of them decided to go to Ely, a town twenty kilometres from Cambridge known for its superb Romanesque cathedral built inside the walls of a Benedictine monastery. They went in Christian's old blue Volkswagen, whose roof looked as if it had chickenpox scars. The person responsible for that had been Rajiv: he had turned it over twice one day when he went out for a drive. Driving was one of his passions. As they had no money to take it to a paint and body repair shop to have it fixed, they had to get inside the vehicle and straighten out the roof by kicking it. Apart from that, the Beetle was the dream of any student because it meant having a private means of transport to escape from routine and discover the country at will.

Nothing special happened on the trip to Ely, and yet it was the most special one Rajiv and Sonia made together in all their lives. The one they would never forget. It was a rain-free afternoon, and it looked as though the rays of sunlight caressed the moss on the walls and lit up the black slate roofs that were slick from the damp. Ely was a marvellous town known for holding the greatest collection of mediaeval buildings still in use in the whole of England. A magical place, where it was easy to lose oneself among the old houses and ancient gardens, where they enjoyed spectacular views over the English countryside from the top of the towers. Christian, who knew it well, acted as guide and showed them the prettiest and most romantic corners, like a magician pulling wonders out of his hat. It was a quiet afternoon, when Rajiv and Sonia talked little, allowing themselves to be lulled by a feeling of fulfillment that seemed to overcome them. "The love between Rajiv and Sonia began right there, in the cathedral gardens, at that precise moment. It was something immediate. I never saw two people connect like that, and forever. From that moment until the day he died, they became inseparable," Christian would recall later.

Can love arise in such an instantaneous almost insolent way? When Rajiv took her hand as they were walking in the shade of the ancient walls of the cathedral, Sonia had no strength to pull it back. She thought about doing it, but she did not. That warm, soft hand transmitted a feeling of immense, profound safety and, why not say it? pleasure. As though she had been waiting all her life for that enveloping contact. She could not pull her hand away, even though her conscience told her she should.

In the days that followed, she tried to fight that feeling that set her heart pounding and caused her some anxiety because it was uncontrollable. She was determined to handle it, to not let herself be consumed by that fire that Rajiv's smile had lit within her. Women do not give way to the attempts of seduction of the first man that comes along, that is what she had been taught since her childhood. And she had given way, even if it was just letting him hold her hand, walking along as though they had been lovers all their lives. Did one not have to hold back, hide one's feelings, test one's suitors? But everything that was supposed to be done ran afoul of that smile, that look from his velvety eyes, that tender voice that cracked because Rajiv was almost as shy as she was.

"Do you want to come to the Orchard this evening?"

"No thanks, not today," she replied with a knot in her throat, unable to take her eyes away from his.

"Just for a short time, and we'll be back early ..."

She shook her head this time and smiled as though not to discourage him, because what she was really wanting to say was yes. Rajiv did not insist and stood there, not knowing what to do with his eyes or his hands, like an embarrassed child who does not know how to take a refusal. He was not the typical Italian suitor, more the opposite. He was a little clumsy around girls, but, instead of diminishing him, that increased his attractiveness. Rajiv had no guile or vulgarity; wordiness was not for him. He was a serious young man, and his smile seemed sincere. But for Sonia there was always the question ... What if he just wants to take advantage of me?

For a while she decided not to go to the Varsity any more so as not to fall into temptation and meet up with him again. Better to take extreme measures. But then her life became as

61

grey as it was before, a life without flavour ... or colour. Could the attraction to that boy be so she would not be alone? she wondered in her freezing room as she bit into an apple. How can it be real feeling, if we have hardly spoken? How can you love what you do not know? All these questions piled up in her mind as she tried to convince herself that no, it could not be, her imagination was playing tricks on her, she felt nothing for that young man. Then, in moments of lucidity, she realized that he must be very different from her in everything. He was from another country ... and what a country! Not from Europe or the United States, but a distant, exotic place about which she knew almost nothing... An Indian, no less! Of another race, with his skin quite dark and he probably had another religion, and would have been brought up with other customs, almost mediaeval. It would be crazy to fall in love with someone like that! she told herself then. Was the world not full of stories of Indians or Africans loved by European girls? Once they had them and took them back to their countries, the girls ended up as slaves. She suddenly saw herself as the passing fancy of an eastern prince, or something like that. Then, for a moment, she forgot everything and became herself again, an Italian student lost in Cambridge, wanting the holidays to come so she could go back home and put an end to the dizzying loneliness and uncertainty which, although she did not know it, was making her into an adult.

But the memory of that smile did not disappear just because she tried to wipe it out, as though it might be enough to press a button to give orders to your heart. Rajiv's smile slipped through the ins and outs of her mind and, when she was unaware of it, took a central place in her imagination again. Since it was much nicer to let herself be carried along by her daydreams than to fight the dictates of her heart, she finally gave free rein to her thoughts… What was there in that smile that seduced her like that? Was it the refinement of his way of expressing himself that touched her heart? Was it his eastern prince's composure? Rajiv spoke with the best English accent, as though he had lived in Cambridge all his life. He was polite and gallant, and a little old-fashioned, qualities that were rare among the other students. Christian, who had known him for several months now, had just found out that he was the grandson of the man that used to be Prime Minister of India, and that is impressive, or at least it whips up your curiosity almost as much as the fact that Rajiv had not mentioned it sooner. If anyone asked him, Rajiv explained that his last name had nothing to do with that of Mahatma Gandhi, but he refrained from telling about his relationship to Nehru. What he most enjoyed about England, precisely, was the peace of mind it gave him to live anonymously. All of his life in India he had been the grandson of the first head of state of independent India, an icon venerated by millions of people. Now he could be himself, he wanted to enjoy it as much as he could.

In spite of being who he was, he had no money to go out. He would have liked to invite her to one of the few night clubs where you could listen to live music. It was called Les Fleurs du Mal, but his budget did not stretch that far. Christian was surprised at the huge difference there was between the two large groups of Asian students in Cambridge, the Pakistanis and the Indians. The former usually had plenty of money and threw it away, but the Indians were always down to their last penny. The reason for this was the restriction the Indian government imposed on its citizens to limit the purchase of foreign currency. They were unable to change more than 650 pounds every time they went abroad. "The beauty of Cambridge,"

Christian would recall, "is that it was a great leveler of social and economic classes."

Nightlife was practically non-existent because they closed the collegegates at eleven o'clock. You had to go out in the daytime, and the amusements were very simple: going for a walk, punting on the River Cam, spending the evening in the digs of one friend or another... The second time that Rajiv asked her out, she accepted, and they were listening to music inthe tiny student lodgings he shared with Christian and which wasoverflowing with friends and records. Sonia ended the evening with thecertainty that Rajiv really loved her. It was a shame to see him so much inlove and yet so unable to express his feelings. Sonia perceived that he was prey to a flood of feelings that stirred him up inside as much as it did her. That day they had not taken their bicycles because it was raining, so he walked home with her, quite a distance, because she lived closer to thecentre. They were so absorbed in their conversation that they got lost in thedeserted town as he opened his heart to her. He confessed that he loved living in England because he felt free for the first time in his life. He told herthat since he was a child he had lived with an escort of security guards at home in New Delhi where his grandfather was Prime Minister. He told herhe did not like to be recognized as the son of the family to which he belonged, because it limited his movements and his freedom, because henever knew who was really a friend, as people got close to him for ulteriormotives just because of his closeness to power. He told her about thewonderful feeling he felt the first time he drove Christian's Volkswagen andthat it made him feel free, as he had never felt before. He also talked aboutthe death of his father, which had happened four years previously. About thedeath of his grandfather the year before, which hurt even more because he had loved him as though he were another father. "Yes," said Sonia shyly, "I remember that." Sonia vaguely remembered having seen pictures of Nehru's grandiose funeral, solemn and sad, on the news on television the year before.

Rajiv talked to her a little about everything, mixing things up, pouring out memories and desires, longings and hopes, yearnings and sorrows in disorder. Sonia understood that, beyond the difference in race or nationality, that young man belonged to a world to which she had never had access, about which she had never had the slightest idea. More than the fact that he was from India, what separated her most from him was the circle in which he moved, as remote from the middle-class life of an Italian girl from Orbassano as the Earth from the Moon. They were separated by everything, and yet, and perhaps because of it, the attraction they felt for each other was even stronger. For him she symbolized everything he desired: to lead a normal life. She was not Indian and she was not English; she was not identifiable on any level of the social hierarchy. She represented the anonymity of the middle class; in other words, freedom, which is what a young man of 21 who had grown up in a gilded cage most desired.

He told her about his passion for photography, for jazz musicians like Stan Getz, Zoot Sims and Jimmy Smith, although he also liked the Beatles and Beethoven. But his real passion was flying, and this had come about when he was fourteen and his grandfather Nehru took him for a ride in a glider. "The sound of the wind, the feeling of total freedom... takes you away from it all. I was hooked for life." And the beauty of flying over the plains in the north of India, with their winding rivers, their little villages surrounded by green and brown fields where the tiniest piece of land was cultivated ...

As a result of that experience he became a member of the Delhi Flying Club and every time he came back on holiday, he went out in a glider for a spin to forget the world. Now he felt he wanted to try flying a proper plane and was toying with the idea of becoming a pilot.

This young man opened the doors of an unknown world that shone like the stars in the heavens for Sonia. He was a warm-hearted boy, practical and at the same time a bit of a dreamer, but above all he inspired her with confidence. He talked very naturally and did not boast about anything because he did not need to. He was the opposite of boastful, the opposite of the typical Italian flirt that she knew so well. Walking along with him, it suddenly seemed to her that the streets were not the same as ever, that she was in another city much more beautiful than the one she had known until then. Rajiv made her dream, took her out of her shell and made her forget herself and the homesickness she had felt until then. That night, when he left her at her house, he clumsily told her he loved her, saying that she was the first girl he had really liked, and he hoped she would be the only one. He said it so honestly that it was hard not to believe him.

But even so Sonia went on struggling to get him out of her head, because she was obstinate and because her heart went from one extreme to another like a pendulum, torn between reason and desire. Subject to a storm of contradictory feelings, she felt dizzy as though she were standing on the edge of a precipice, swaying and afraid to fall. What would I do in this boy's world? What have I got to do with a spoiled child whose famous grandfather took him out in a glider? Why am I letting myself be dazzled? Sonia was proud that she had her feet firmly on the ground, and she did. But the more she became obsessed, the more distant she was with him, and that apparent coldness was for him a greater inducement to win her. The reality was that she thought about him day and night, as though he had become the very air she breathed. When she was not with him, she sought the company of girls of her own class just so she could talk about him and his overwhelming charm. The feeling that came over her served as a reason to learn English faster and better, such was her need to be good enough for him, and not to miss the nuances in conversation with Rajiv and his friends. There is nothing like love for learning a language properly! she said to herself in surprise when she noticed that she could suddenly understand a conversation, a newscast, or an article in the newspaper.

But it was exhausting to live always against herself, questioning the attraction that filled her with hope and, a moment later, with doubts and fears. Tired of those ups and downs that took her from euphoria to melancholy, one day she stopped struggling and threw herself into his arms, while the music of Gerry Mulligan was still ringing in her ears from the inside of a bar on busy Sydney Street.

5

With Rajiv, life took on another tone, another flavour. Boating down the river behind the colleges in a punt that he piloted like a real gondolier, the views from the top of St Mary's Church they so enjoyed, or sitting on the grass eating a sandwich, the smell of the parks after the rain ... The most harmless things took on unexpected aspects. One night they went to Les Fleurs du Mal to listen to live music and dance the twist, the rhythm that was all the rage at the time and which Sonia danced very well. Suddenly Cambridge was the most romantic city in the world, and she no longer wanted to be anywhere else so she could enjoy the here and now. A present that consisted of seeing each other every day, going to each other's house by bike, going on a picnic, making plans for the weekend... Rajiv was very fond of photography and soon he, his Minox camera and Sonia made an inseparable trio: he had found his perfect Muse and did not stop taking photos of her. Their romance reached such a level of intensity that the owner of the Varsity, Charles Antoni, said he had never seen "a couple so much in love ... like out of a novel."

The here and now also consisted of driving in the Volkswagen Beetle that Rajiv had ended up buying from his friend for a few pounds. They drove all over the English countryside, visited London and enjoyed a freedom that at the time seemed endless. When the windscreen broke, they continued to use the car, but wrapped themselves up in blankets.

Rajiv lived just like any other English student, working in his holidays to get some extra money. He had been an ice cream vendor, another year he had worked picking fruit, loading lorries or taking the night shift in a bakery. "Cambridge gave me a view of the world that I would never have seen if I had stayed in India," Rajiv would recall later. In Sonia he found the perfect ally. She was against any raucousness or extravagance and only aspired to what she had already known: a quiet, balanced life with no shocks or scares. If Sonia perceived the vast difference that separated her from him, she also saw all the things they had in common. They were both shy by nature and never sought to be the centre of any kind of attention. They were not attracted by either the sweetness of success or fame, but rather the opposite, those were things that it was better to flee from. "They were not interested in the outside world or life in high society ... They valued privacy above all,"

Christian would say. They both had a very similar view of family life, perhaps because in their respective cultures the family is the highest value. Rajiv lacked any kind of political ambition; he liked technical things and manual activities. He confessed to Sonia that if he had made the effort to get into Trinity College, it had only been to please his grandfather, who had studied there and who had the dream that one of his grandchildren might follow in his footsteps. But now Nehru was dead, Rajiv was seriously thinking of leaving Trinity College and following his true vocation, as a pilot. He still did not know how to tell his mother.

What he did manage to tell Indira in a letter dated March, 1965, a month and a half after they were introduced at the

Varsity, is that he had met Sonia: "... You're always asking me about the girls I meet and if there is one that attracts me specially. Well now I can tell you that I have met a very special girl. I still haven't asked her, but she's the girl I want to marry." In her reply, his mother reminded him that the first girl one meets is not necessarily the most suitable one. She wanted to moderate her son's passion. After all, he was only twenty. But in his next letter, Rajiv confessed, "I am sure I am in love with her. I know she's the first girl I've been out with, but how can you know if you're going to meet a better one?" By return post, Indira informed him that she had just accepted her first official position. She had done it a little unwillingly, but now it was done: she was Information Minister of the government of India. As such, she intended to make an official visit to London at the end of the year and she would like to take advantage of the opportunity to meet the young lady. Sonia's stomach went into knots when she heard the news. As for telling her family, she was totally unable to get her courage together. She could not even imagine what her father's reaction would be ...

But the news of Indira's arrival made her forget the present for the moment. She suddenly glimpsed dark clouds on the horizon of her happiness. Her fears came back and she asked herself if there was any future for their romance. It was too good to last. She no longer doubted her own feelings, quite the opposite, she was crazy about Rajiv, she had never known ecstasy like this, but she felt that the huge difference between their origins would end up taking its toll on the relationship, and could perhaps ruin it completely. The little she knew about India she had learned from a friend who had described it as an immense, faraway country full of snake charmers and elephants, paralyzed by poverty and backwardness. A country that lacked even the most basic comforts, a country castigated by an implacable climate; a dirty country where cows wandered at will and were more respected than the members of the lower castes, definitely a difficult and exciting country ... for an anthropologist or a yogi, but not for a girl who aimed to work for an international institution and wanted to have a trouble- free family life. Where did Rajiv fit into that picture? The Nehrus, that friend who was not exactly up to date had explained, were of aristocratic origin, from Kashmir. Somehow they dominated the society of their country and up to a point they had been controlling world politics... Beside them, what were the Mainos? thought Sonia. Just *paesani*, she told herself. What could the daughter of a small-time provincial Italian builder bring to Rajiv? She was sure that Rajiv's mother would be asking herself the same question, and that made her feel very uneasy. Sonia was aware that their families "could not be more different", according to her own words. Neither could she imagine herself telling her father that she had fallen in love with a dark-skinned man, who, furthermore, was Indian and on top of that professed, at least officially, the Hindu religion. No, that was a pill that good Stefano Maino was not going to swallow so easily, however much the grandfather had been a prime minister.

Her introverted character prevented her from sharing her fears with Rajiv. She did not want to destroy their happiness, which might be as fragile as the finest crystal. With him she was sweetness full of reserve and thelooks she gave him were full of questions. He was Indian, but in his gesturesand way of speaking, she saw an Englishman. He was distinguished and at the same time he behaved in an amazingly simple manner. Actually, Sonia experienced a strange and definitive change that led her to total, blindacceptance of what could happen to her later in life because of Rajiv, or thanks to him. She felt that in

71

the distant frontiers of her being, everything had been fixed by destiny beforehand, even before she was born.

One weekend Sonia met Sanjay, Rajiv's only brother and two years his junior. He was taking a training course at Rolls-Royce in Crewe, three hours away, and went to Cambridge from time to time to have some fun. He was very handsome, like his brother, but with a different kind of attractiveness. Sanjay had an oval face, thicker and more sensual lips and an incipient receding hairline. Just like his brother, he had impeccable manners and spoke in a soft tone of voice with a perfect British accent. Both were frugal in their habits. Sanjay did not eat much, but he talked a lot about politics and he loved parties. Rajiv did not like smoking or drinking and he was not in the least interested in politics - actually he rejected that world and preferred a quiet dinner with friends to a noisy party. Sanjay was colder than his elder brother, and did not project that feeling of quiet warmth, of a kind person who made Sonia feel so safe. And their way of looking at you was different. Rajiv did it as though he was caressing you with his almond eyes. His brother, on the other hand, had a distant, somewhat insolent look. You could tell he was very proud of being who he was, completely unlike his brother.

It was a marvellous year, perhaps the happiest of their lives, if by happiness you mean the almost total absence of worries and problems. But the academic year was coming to an end, and the summer holidays were going to interrupt the Cambridge idyll.

*   *   *

In July 1965, Rajiv and Sonia were apart for the first time. Sonia went back to Italy. She had arrived in England a few months earlier as a young girl, and now she was going home as a woman, with the firm idea of makingher life with Rajiv. She did not know how or when, but she was determined. It was a happy farewell, but also an upsetting one at the same time because although they were convinced they would see each other again, Sonia was afraid of her parents' reaction. The future was scattered with questions.

It filled her with satisfaction to realize how much her English had improved when she found jobs as an interpreter in the Turin trade fairs. What a difference, what fluency ... At least *signor* Maino had not wasted his money. It was good news for her parents. The other news, the important news, she could not find a way to put into words. However much she practiced saying it in her head, it did not come out right. "I want to tell you that I'm in love with a boy ... No, not like that, that's ridiculous!" she told herself, before trying it another way: "I have met someone very special and I want to marry him... How am I going to tell them that?" she told herself again in desperation. When the moment came to face up to it, she was petrified. "Although we were a very united family," Sonia would write later, "they were very conventional, especially my father who was an old-fashioned patriarch. In a family like that, contact between boys and girls was strictly supervised and controlled."

Rajiv did not understand Sonia's reticence when it came to talking to her parents. She tried to explain it to him: How can I suddenly tell them I have been having a passionate love affair all these months without having said a word to them? She did not know how to break the ice. "She doesn't seem able to tell them," Rajiv wrote to his mother. "I can't understand it. It must be something very peculiar. She only does what her father tells her."Of course Rajiv did not know Stefano Maino, he had never seen his reddened face or his rough highlander features and he had never heard his hoarse voice or his domineering tone when something displeased him.

"It took me a long time to get the courage together to talk to my parents about my feelings for a boy who, for them, was not only a stranger but a foreigner as well." The occasion arose after the wedding of Pier Luigi, the owner of the Via Frejus bar. Pier Luigi, who had watched her growing up, had wanted her to be the witness at his wedding. It was the great event that summer in the neighbourhood. A party with music, lots of drink in the bar, which was overflowing with people, as many as at the annual event that gathered all the neighbours like a ritual to watch the San Remo Festival on television.

"I'm in love, I love him," she told them after explaining who the boy was and how they had met.

"How old do you say he is?" "Twenty ..."

"He's too young," said her mother.

"And on top of that he's from far away!" added her father.

Just as she had imagined, they showed not the slightest enthusiasm. They reacted with total disdain, as though their daughter had been suffering from a passing attack of madness. There was nothing in that relationship to please them: the boy was barely two years older than Sonia, he was a foreigner, and he was not English or French, but from a country that only appeared in the news because of disasters; he was a *terrone*, as those from the north of Italy call immigrants from the south, with the added fact that he was not even Italian. And he had another important defect: he was not Catholic. In their opinion, Sonia had drowned her fears about feeling lonely in a foreign country for the first time by falling into the arms of the first comer.

"She'll soon get over it ..."

But she did not get over it. Even the postman joked with the family because now he was bringing three letters a day, all with the stamp from England, and all for Sonia. The "little girl" spent many long hours in her room, replying to the voluminous correspondence, or anxiously waiting for a long-distance phone call. Then there were her sisters, who understood that Sonia was really in love. The "it'll soon pass" of their parents gave way to the "what if it's really serious?" of Anushka and Nadia. The only thing that softened the mother's position was that the boy was "from a good family". At least it had done some good to send her to the most expensive school in Cambridge! That he was Nehru's grandson, that his mother Indira was in the government, left Stefano cold, but Paola did appreciate those things. And her sisters too. They already saw themselves parading on the back of an elephant in the gardens of some Indian palace. For them, the story had something of a fairy tale about it: a prince of the East had fallen in love with their sister... It was exciting.

The big argument was over her return to Cambridge. Her father did not want her to go back. According to him she already knew enough English. What he really wanted was to nip his daughter's romance in the bud. But Sonia was determined to take the exam, the Proficiency in English, and for that she needed another year. As usual, Paola's influence was decisive. She and her husband knew perfectly well that their daughter wanted to go back because she was in love, but Paola insisted on the importance of her obtaining a qualification. Sonia held firm. She told them that if they would not help her, she was prepared to do what many girls who were there studying English did: she would look for a job and would become independent. Nobody likes standing up to their parents, and Sonia less than most, because it did not go with her docile character. But love was stronger.

Her parents finally gave way, thinking that opposing their daughter's romance would only make things worse. Better for her to go back to England, they thought. At least she would come home with a qualification. They were sure that the affair, which they saw as an eccentricity, would not survive the passing of time... The only thing they could do was to advise her: be careful what you're getting into, don't rush into things.

Sonia was so respectful of family tradition, and so disliked confrontation, that she promised to keep them informed of everything. So, once back in Cambridge, and in view of the imminent arrival of Indira, who had shown a desire to meet her, she thought it best for her parents to know. Rajiv, who had been wanting to get in touch with the Mainos, took advantage of the occasion to send them a letter asking permission for the meeting between their daughter and Indira Gandhi to take place. An extremely formal and very respectful letter which left the Mainos puzzled, but what could they do? Refuse? Stefano would not have hesitated for a second, but his wife convinced him to give his permission.

6

It was winter and the road gleamed from the rain. They were arriving in the City in Rajiv's battered old Volkswagen when Sonia had a panic attack. Suddenly the prospect of attending a reception at the Indian Embassy and meeting her boyfriend's mother in surroundings she did not know terrified her and made her freeze. "What am I going to do there?" she suddenly asked herself. A flood of questions, some serious, others trivial, swirled inside her head. "How should I address her? Will I be suitably dressed? What must I say to her? What if she looks down on me? What if she's aggressive towards me?"

"Don't talk nonsense," Rajiv kept telling her.

Suddenly, Sonia's world seemed to be coming down about her ears. It seemed to her that the months spent in Rajiv's company had all been a dream that was about to fall apart. She thought she was not ready to meet his mother. Furthermore, that meeting meant becoming even more involved, and how could she do that if her own parents had been so negative about her romance?

"But they are aware of it, your father has given permission ... Are you pulling out now?"

Rajiv did not understand at all. Sonia was frightened. She thought perhaps her father was right and the moment had come to put the brakes on, to cool things and take a step back ...

"Sonia, we've arranged this, they're expecting us ..." "I'm sorry, I'm not going. I can't."

Sonia was flustered and unable to keep control of the situation. Rajiv's efforts to calm her down did not work, so he had to call his mother and invent an excuse to cancel the meeting.

They put it off for a few days later, when Sonia had calmed down. This time she promised herself she would behave properly, but it was still a difficult thing to do. Her legs shook when she went up the steps of the Indian Ambassador's residence where Indira and her best friend Pupul Jayakar, who had helped her organize the tribute to Nehru, were staying. The two of them were still worked up because the day before, after a reading of Allen Ginsberg's poetry and that of other beat generation poets, they had ended up at one in the morning in a Spanish restaurant eating *tapas* and watching the flamenco dancing. On their return, they had found the Ambassador extremely worried; he was about to call the police because he thoughtsomething had happened to them.

Indira received them in her room, smelling slightly of incense. Sonia found herself facing a fragile-looking woman dressed in an elegant silk sari. In those dark, almond-shaped eyes she saw Rajiv's. Her hair, pulled back in a bun, left a thick lock of white hair visible over her forehead, in spite of her being only 48 years old. That lock of hair, which would become a sign of her identity, conferred some considerable distinction on her. She had a charming smile, delicate manners and a prominent nose that she tried to hide with makeup under her eyes to lessen the shadows. Actually, according to what she had confessed to her friend Pupul, what she would really have liked to do was to have an operation on that nose.

"I found myself face to face with a perfectly normal human being," Sonia would say, "warm and welcoming. She did everything possible to make me feel at home. She spoke to me in French knowing I was more fluent in it than in English. She wanted to know about myself, my studies." Rajiv must have told his mother something about how nervous she was, because Indira told her that "she too had been young, terribly shy and in love, and she understood me perfectly."

Sonia, relaxed now, enjoyed that first meeting, which ended in the most familiar way possible. In fact the young couple had to attend a student party and Sonia asked if she could change into her evening dress in a room in the Embassy. But as soon as she went out, she tripped and the heel of her shoe ripped the hem of her evening gown. "Rajiv's mother," Sonia would tell, "in the calm fashion which I was to observe at close quarters later, took out a needle and black threat and proceeded matter-of-factly to stitch up the hem. Wasn't that exactly the sort of thing my own mother would have done? All the small doubts which had remained vanished, for the moment at least." A current of sympathy passed between those two women, each so different in every way from the other, except in their love for Rajiv. Indira had not told her son, but the idea of one day having a foreign daughter-in- law had disconcerted her a little. Now, after meeting her, her reservations had vanished. "Apart from being pretty," she wrote to her American friend
Dorothy Norman, "she is a healthy, straightforward girl."

Dorothy was glad to hear this news from her friend. It finally seemed that Indira was getting over the deep existential crisis she had been struggling with since the death of her husband Firoz four years earlier, and the more recent death of

Nehru, her father. First a widow, and then an orphan. Furthermore, as her sons were abroad, she had been left on her own. The day that Rajiv had gone off to Cambridge, Indira had written to Dorothy: "I feel sad. It's a heartbreaking moment for a woman when her son becomes a man. She knows he is no longer dependent on her and that from now on he is going to make his own way in life. And even though sometimes he may allow her to glimpse that life, she will always do so from the outside, from the distance of another generation. My heart is suffering."

It was very hard for Indira to get over Nehru's death, which had occurred one hot evening on May 27th, 1964. In his final days, she had not left him for a second, always attentive to his needs, giving him his medicines, supervising his diet, keeping visitors at bay. The last photo taken of them together, in which she can be seen squatting at his side, shows an expression of profound sadness and great tenderness on her face. Indira had spent the last years very close to him, organizing his agenda, coordinating the visits of foreign dignitaries such as the Shah of Iran, King Saud, Ho Chi Minh or Krushchev. She had come to act as a communication channel between him and his ministers. Nehru himself, on being named Head of State when India became independent in 1947, had asked her to take on the role of "first lady", since his wife had passed away some time previously and he needed someone he could trust who knew how to run his household for him. Indira had accepted the challenge reluctantly at first, but then with real devotion. She had done it not only because she was an obedient Indian daughter, but because her marriage was breaking up. She was tired of the unfaithfulness of her husband, Firoz. In fact, they had been practically separated for some time, so she and her children moved into Teen Murti House, the beautiful residence of the Prime Minister of India in the centre of New Delhi. The first thing Indira did was to take down the collection of portraits of heroes of the Empire and send them to the Ministry of Defence. Then she replaced them with Indian handicrafts, and changed the heavy French curtains for raw cotton net curtains, the material that Gandhi's spinning wheel made into the symbol of self-government. She arranged her father's room with a low bed, surrounded with his books and favourite photos. One day she confessed that she would have liked to be an interior decorator, but Destiny had another role for her to fulfill.

If the death of Nehru had deprived the world of a giant – he had been the undisputed leader of the movement of non-aligned countries which grouped together over half the population of the world -; if he had left India without the symbol of its struggle for freedom and without its Prime Minister, and the Congress Party without its head, it had left his daughter Indira in the middle of a huge crater, as though his death had been a bomb that had wiped out everything around it. Nehru had been the dominating force and presence in her life, the light that had guided her steps. Perhaps that passion for her father was the consequence of how much she had missed him as a child, since he spent almost more time behind bars than at home because of his political activism. But when he came home his presence filled the family mansion of Anand Bhawan, in Allahabad, with joy. By then he was already a flesh and blood legend, always relaxed, however much tension there was around him, with a face that seemed sculpted by a chisel, a well- proportioned body, a shy yet inquisitive gaze, an open laugh and natural elegance which he emphasized by wearing a rose in the third buttonhole of his *sherwani*. He was very cultured, with a sharp sense of humour and his gifts as an orator brought him goodwill wherever he was. He felt just as much at ease in high society as he did in the prisons of Her Gracious Majesty. He held talks with everyone from his Cambridge professors to heads of government and Viceroys, from the Emperor King of England himself – and his jailers – to tribal chiefs in Afghanistan.

After his father, the great Motilal, left him on his own at boarding school in England at the age of 13, Nehru spent seven years learning Political Science and reading up on the latest advances of technology. He returned from England in 1912, an English gentleman. He began working in his father's law practice, and Nehru senior became very satisfied with the substantial income provided by his son. The rest of his time he spent in the library of the Law School and the institution that was fundamental to life in colonial India, the club, where he spent many tedious hours sitting in the Chesterfield armchairs in the crowded rooms, discussing legal matters with old members of the British administration. A boring life, according to Nehru himself, which changed because of an apparently insignificant incident, when he received a visit from a group of peasants who asked him for help against some landowners who were using cruel, expeditious methods to expel them from their legitimate lands. Nehru agreed to go to their village with them to clear up the case. It was a three-day journey which changed him from a shy, proud lawyer who, according to his own words, had no idea how most Indians lived and worked, into a revolutionary. "Seeing them with their poverty, overflowing with gratitude, I felt a mixture of shame and pain," he wrote, "shame at my easy, comfortable way of life and all the politics in the cities that ignores this vast multitude of half-naked sons and daughters of India, and pain on seeing so much degradation and unbearable poverty."

In addition to this there came the news that arrived from the holy city of Benares, on the banks of the Ganges. Mohandas Gandhi, the yet unknownlawyer, had caused a real commotion by making an incendiary speech for the poor and against inequality at the opening of the Hindu University. "The exhibition of jewels you are offering us today is a splendid feast for the eyes," he had said to an auditorium full of colonial authorities and Indian aristocrats, "but when I compare it to the face of the millions of poor people,I deduce that there will be no salvation for India until you take off those jewels and place them in the hands of the poor." The audience reacted indignantly. Princes and dignitaries left the university precincts. Only the students applauded Gandhi's words. But the echoes of that speech resounded throughout India, and Jawarlal Nehru wanted to meet him.

"He was like a great breath of fresh air," Nehru would write ofGandhi, "like a ray of light cutting through the darkness; like a whirlwind that questioned everything, but above all the way people's minds worked. He did not come from above, he seemed to emerge from among the millions of Indians, speaking their language and incessantly focussing attention on them and their urgent needs." His strength was summarized in a concept he articulated in 1907, whose name is derived from the Sanskrit, *satyagraha*, which means the strength of *truth*, and whose purpose implied the idea of a powerful but non-violent energy for transforming reality. For the Indian masses, *satyagraha* represented an alternative to fear. It was the Bengali poet, Rabindranath Tagore, Nobel Prize for Literature, who gave Gandhi the title by which he would be known. Tagore called him Mahatma: "greatsoul".

But the great soul needed a great second in command. And his disciple and friend Nehru became just that, and even though they had nothing in common, the combination of strengths that emerged from that intense friendship would end up changing the world. Because Gandhi was a man of faith and religion; Nehru was a rationalist, a sophisticated product of Harrow and Cambridge who hardly spoke the native languages of India. His years in Europe made him see the customs of many of his fellow Indians as ridiculous, such as not going out of the house on days that were not considered auspitious. In the most religious country in the world, he was an atheist who despised holy men and yogis. In his eyes they were responsible for the backwardness, the internal divisions and the domination of the foreign imperialists. Gandhi found him to be too much of a gentleman for his taste and did to him what he did with other members of the upper classes. He sent them out to the villages to recruit new members for the Congress Party and to get to know the real face of their homeland at the same time. Most of them had never seen the poverty of their fellow Indians. But that was the beauty of Gandhi's movement: he put the upper classes in touch with the lowest classes, and these began to exist in the eyes of the rest of society. For the first time, India was subject to a wide people's movement which rejected the way of life imposed from faraway London.

For thirty years, Nehru went round India on foot, in oxcarts and by train, galvanizing the population. But if Gandhi dreamed of an India of villages living in self-determination, an India without caste discrimination but deeply religious, Nehru dreamed of an India freed from its myths and poverty by industry, science and technology. For Gandhi, those were precisely the misfortunes of humanity. For Nehru, they were its salvation.

Their differences of opinion and vision had never put their friendship at risk, or the deep respect each man professed for the other. They were in agreement about the basics: achieving a united and independent India without any bloodshed. Nehru was convinced that, apart from being a saint, Gandhi was a genius. He valued his extraordinary skill in politics, his artistry at speaking with gestures that touched the people's soul. When they met up with each other again, they would talk for a long time, exchanging points of view, assessing the latest progress in the struggle, or the latest setbacks. They would discuss strategy, get angry, then laugh, or they would simply meditate. Gandhi always made it clear that the torch of his struggle would one day come into Nehru's hands, and he helped him into the presidency of the Congress Party on three occasions.

Indira was brought up in that environment where the border between family life and political life was non-existent. She used to tell Gandhi all her little girl's confidences, explaining how much she missed her father, and telling him about her loneliness and her complexes for being an unattractive, sickly little girl. Nehru spent a total of nine years locked up, interrupted by short periods of freedom. His family life was so badly affected by it that once Indira had to tell a visitor, "I'm sorry, but my grandfather, my father and my mother are all in jail."

Since Nehru's death, Indira remembers things from her distant childhood, such as when she dressed up as Joan of Arc and imitated her father saying, "One day I shall lead my people to freedom," as she harangued an imaginary crowd. Or like when she committed her "first political act" as she would later call it, which was to hit an English policeman who burst into the Anand Bhawan house to seize objects and furniture because her father and her grandfather, just like all the members of the party, refused on principle to pay bail when they were arrested. She wanted to join the Congress Party when she was twelve, but she was rejected as she was not old enough. She reacted in her own way, as she would do later in life, taking the bull by the horns. She gathered several hundred local children in the gardens of the mansion. Indira addressed them as her father would have done, calling on them to fight for the freedom of their country in spite of the dangers. In this way she created the "Monkey Brigade", which consisted of children who acted as spies, put up posters, made banners and infiltrated police lines to pass messages on to party members. Her "army" came to consist of several thousand children who gave substantial support to those fighting. How happy she felt when her father was proud of her ...!

Their relationship was always marked by suffering because of the distance that separated them, which only letters could mitigate: "I want you to learn to write letters and to come and see me in prison. I miss you a lot," Nehru wrote to her when she was barely six years old. For her thirteenth birthday, Nehru wrote, "What present can I send you from the prison in Naini? My presents cannot be anything material or solid. They can only be made of air, mind, and spirit, like those a fairy might grant you, things that not even the high walls of a prison could hold back."

Indira delved deep in those letters – there were hundreds of them, interesting, emotional correspondence, because both of them wrote very well

– to prepare the commemorative exhibition, the one she was

coming to London to inaugurate. She wanted to emphasize the compassionate side of her father as well as his incredible bravery and integrity, with the help of photos and objects, and put captions to them with phrases taken out of his writings and speeches. Of all the projects she had undertaken as Information Minister she gave herself to this one with special devotion. Not only out of sentiment, but because she thought that spreading and exalting Nehru's memory was important for the world and for India in particular, a nation that needed the example of leaders that forged its unity.

*   *   *

Rajiv accompanied Sonia to visit the Nehru exhibition. It was a way of introducing the young Italian girl into the complex history of his country, and also a way of explaining who he and his family were. Sonia stood for a long time in front of the wedding dress of Rajiv's grandmother, Kamala, and noted the ritual objects used in weddings in Kashmir. The caption under the photo explained that this woman had also been in prison and that she died of tuberculosis at the age of 36 ... Sonia thought of Indira: with a father in jail and a sick mother ... What kind of childhood had she had?

"Sad," Rajiv told her. "My mother was also ill with tuberculosis. She was shut up in a sanatorium for long periods, and they advised her not to get married or have children ..."

"Thank goodness she didn't listen ..." she said with a smile.

"She was saved thanks to the discovery of antibiotics. She was luckier than Grandmother ..."

There was another sari on exhibit, a pale red one, with a silver border. "That is the sari my grandfather wove in prison for my mother's wedding ... I hope you will wear it one day …" he told her jokingly.

Sonia laughed, not very convinced. She could not imagine herself wrapped in that piece of cloth, which had been made inside a prison cell that had been reconstructed right there for the occasion, from enlarged photos: you could see the camp bed, the notebook in which you could read phrases from his prison diaries, the spinning wheel with which Nehru had spun the sari in a gesture that brought together his love of his daughter and that of his country … Gandhi had made the spinning wheel into a symbol of the struggle for independence. The English had ruined the rich Indian textile industry by putting outrageously high taxes on Indian products, and then selling industrial cloth woven in England. The spinning wheel was a symbol of rebellion, a way of saying that it was not necessary to purchase imported textile products because everyone could weave their own cloth. There was a letter which Sonia read. It was written by Nehru from prison to his daughter who was going to get married: "At first, weaving is very boring but as soon as you get into it, you discover there is something fascinating about it. I spend half an hour a day on it. As that is not very long, I don't produce very much, even though I am quite fast. Since I began, seven weeks ago, I have spun almost ten thousand metres. I understand you need thirty thousand for a sari. In four months time, I may have a sari for you!"

That sari was not only a wedding dress, it was also a flag. For Sonia, a wedding dress ought to be white, with a veil, like those she saw on Sundays in the springtime on the brides getting married in the church of St John the Baptist in Orbassano. Sometimes she forgot that Rajiv was Indian.

Films were being shown of the independence celebrations, and you could see the last parade of the Viceroy, Lord

Mountbatten, and his wife Edwina, aboard a carriage literally besieged by the crowd. "It's raining babies!" said an astonished Pamela, the Viceroy's daughter, because women were throwing their babies up into the air to avoid them being crushed by thecrowd. Rajiv told her that his mother saw how a woman decided that her baby would be safer with Lady Mountbatten and passed it to her. Edwina held it in her arms for a long time. You could see Nehru literally walking over the crowd, shouting for them to raise the yellow, green and white flagof the new nation which included an unusual symbol in the centre: a spinning wheel. Mountbatten struggled to push aside children and young people half-fainting from the confusion and get them to safety. The flag was welcomed with a tremendous roar of joy. A cannon shot could be heard, and then, as though by magic, a rainbow appeared in the sky, giving rise to all kinds of colourful interpretations of the meaning of that "act of God".

But there were also photos and film clips of the tragedy that went with independence. Rajiv told Sonia that Nehru was heartbroken when he made his famous independence speech. A recording reproduced his voice on the night of August 15th, 1947: "Long years ago, we made a tryst with destiny and now the time comes when we shall redeem our pledge ... At the stroke of midnight, when the world sleeps, India will awake to life and freedom ..." Listening to Nehru's voice like that made Sonia shiver. Rajiv explained to her that his grandfather knew that while he was announcing the greatestnews in the history of India, the city of Lahore, the ancient capital of the Mogul Empire and the most cosmopolitan city in the sub-continent, which now belonged to Pakistan, was burning in an orgy of violence. It was the beginning of a tragedy of gigantic proportions known as Partition. The independence of both countries unleashed a movement of ethnic and religious cleansing unparalleled in history. The Hindus, who had lived for generations in what was now Pakistan, were forced to flee. Inversely, the Moslems in India fled in the opposite direction. The film clips of those columns of refugees and the accounts of the atrocities committed – whole families burnt alive in their homes, women thrown off moving trains because they were of the wrong religion, daughters raped in front of their parents ..., left Sonia horrified.

"And what about non-violence?" Sonia asked timidly, seeing that her pre-conceived ideas about the peaceful nature of Indians were collapsing.

"Gandhi managed to stop a lot of the violence with his fasting ..." Rajiv answered, "but in the end not even he could escape from religious fanaticism."

Then he told her that when he was four his mother took him to visit Mahatma Gandhi one day at the home of the Birlas, a wealthy family that gave Gandhi lodging and support every time he came to Delhi. Gandhi was very depressed about the declarations of Hindu extremists who accused him of treason for having defended the persecuted Moslems, and for all the tension the country was undergoing, although the violence of partition had stopped by then. "I cannot go on living in this madness and this darkness," Gandhi had said to the photographer Margaret Bourke-White that very morning. Gandhi, who was like a member of the family, was very affectionate towards Rajiv. While the adults chatted and tried to relax the atmosphere with a joke or two, little Rajiv played with some jasmine flowershis mother had bought for Mahatma. In a photo you could see how the little boy twined them round Gandhi's toes.

"He stopped me with a gentle gesture of his hand," said Rajiv. "'Don'tdo that', he said to me, 'we only put flowers on the feet of the dead.'"

He went on to tell her that that same afternoon, while he was going to prayers in the centre of the garden, a man came up to Gandhi and putting his hands together, he greeted him *"Namaste!"*, he said, then he looked him straight in the eye, pulled a Beretta pistol out of his pocket and fired three shots at him at point-blank range. He was a Hindu fundamentalist.

The exhibition showed pictures of the chaos that followed the attack. Perhaps the most dramatic was the photo of Nehru standing on a car roof, calming the population with a megaphone in his hands. Everyone wanted to get near to say farewell to the "great soul". A loudspeaker reproduced the words that Nehru addressed to the nation on the radio that terrible night: "The light has gone out of our lives and there is darkness everywhere. Our beloved leader, the father of the nation, is no more. The light has gone out, I said, and yet I was wrong. For the light that shone in this country was no ordinary light. In a thousand years' time it will still be shining. The world will see it and it will give solace to innumerable hearts." Sonia felt a shiver when she heard that voice that seemed to come from beyond the grave.

"My grandfather was always obsessed with the idea of keeping India united and secular," Rajiv explained to her. "He used to say that the nation could only survive on those two values … and I think he was right."

Other photos showed Nehru with Gandhi, some smiling and obviously in agreement, others serious and disagreeing; Nehru with Chinese, Soviet, and American leaders; with scientists like Einstein, with writers like Thomas Mann and Pearl S. Buck … In the end, Sonia stood for a long time in front of the photos of the whole family gathered together in Anand Bhawan, looking for likenesses. Rajiv was finer than his father Firoz; he had the elegance of his mother, she thought. The patriarch Motilal looked like her own grandfather, Stefano's father, with his broad face with its strong, square jaw and a moustache just as thick. She did not notice the caption of the photo that spoke about the eternal dilemma of the Nehrus, torn between political duty and personal need, and that in that conflict, duty had always won. Although Sonia was visibly affected by everything she had just seen, she could not measure the scope of those words or imagine that some day their meaning would pursue her.

7

The happy life of the lovers in England left a victim: Rajiv's studies at Trinity College. He failed all his subjects that year. He would never be a scientist. He had already warned his mother that his studies were too hard and that his results would be catastrophic. Indira did not reproach him; after all, she too had failed at Oxford, although the circumstances had been very different: she had never had a proper schooling, and as a young girl she was always ill. Of the members of the family, only Nehru had shown genuine academic ability. His grandson Rajiv was not a great student, or a great reader or an intellectual like his grandfather either. He had always liked practical things, technical matters, understanding how a machine works, attempting to fix it if it breaks down. He was able to set up his own loudspeakers to listen to music, or pull apart a radio to fix it. He was good with his hands, a quality he had inherited from his father.

Rajiv had to leave Cambridge and fall back on Imperial College in London, taking more technical classes in engineering and mechanics. But now he had a clear idea of what he wanted. He had spotted an advert from the flying school in Wiltshire at Thruxton, an old RAF base near Southampton that had been turned into a school for pilots. He wanted to take advantage of the summer holidays to start taking flying classes. Becoming a pilot had an advantage added to the sheer pleasure of flying: it was the fastest way of earning a living, an essential requirement for marrying Sonia. Much faster than a university degree. As he did not want to ask his mother for money, he decided he would work to pay for the hours of flying time and the instructor until he passed the first exams.

In July 1966, Sonia went back to Italy with the certificate of Proficiency in English from the University of Cambridge under her arm. The postman again became the person who most frequently visited the family home on Via Bellini to the exasperation of the Maino parents who, in spite of having permitted the meeting with Indira, were still opposed to their daughter's romance with Rajiv. She said openly that one day she would marry him. Her parents tried to dissuade her. Stefano suggested that she should wait until she came of age before she made any decision: "It's only another year," her mother added. "A decision like that cannot be taken lightly. You might regret it later for the rest of your life."

"While you are our responsibility," her father went on, "I cannot allow you to marry that boy. We are sure he's a nice young man, it isn't that... but I would not be doing my duty as a father if I were to say: go ahead, go off to India, marry him. Don't you understand? Just wait a little longer."

It was a reasonable proposition, but love understands few reasons. At the age of twenty waiting is torture. Post Office strikes, so frequent in Italy, became Sonia's greatest enemy that year. Rajiv continued to write everyday, telling her how happy he was learning to fly over the English countryside. He was flying in a bi-plane, a Tiger Moth, a model from the thirties, an agile, responsive plane that provided him with hours of intense pleasure. The goal was to fly solo, and to achieve that he had to accumulate a minimum of forty hours with an instructor. That was the basic requirement for then taking the "civil pilot's" exam, and after that going on up the ladder until he managed to become a commercial pilot.

Rajiv had thought about making a visit to Orbassano. He wanted to convince Sonia's father to let her travel to India. "I want you to go to India," he wrote to her, "and stay with my mother, without me, so that you can see things as they really are, and, as far as you are concerned, in their worst light because I will not be there and you will not have anyone to turn to. That way you will get to know the country and the people ... I do not want to drag you into anything without you knowing what it all implies. I would feel responsible if, later on, something turns out wrong and you feel hurt in some way – in your feelings or in something else. I do not want to have to call anyone to account, except myself, and that is why I do not want to lie to you or deceive you." The letter showed a certain moral stance and Sonia was moved, although pessimistic about the probability of her father approving of the plan.

In order to pay for the trip to Italy, Rajiv was forced to lay his hands on more money. "I'm sorry I haven't been able to write before now, but I've managed to get a job as a bricklayer on a building site," he said in another of his letters. "I've been working up to ten hours a day, plus an hour and a half travelling, so when I get home I'm exhausted. I'm so stiff I can only write slowly." These were letters full of love and of hope for the future, although the last ones revealed a great fear. Rajiv was worried about the news reaching him from India. The Prime Minister had died from a heart attack while he was on an official visit to the Soviet Union to sign a peace treaty with Pakistan, after a short war. "India is going through a very turbulent situation, a very bad time ..." he wrote to Sonia. "I have the feeling that many people are going to want my mother to be Prime Minister. I hope she does not accept: it will end up killing her."

*   *   *

Rajiv was right. The faction that controlled the Congress Party wanted his mother as Prime Minister: "She knows all the world leaders, she has been round the world with her father, she was brought up among the heroes of the struggle for independence, she has a rational, modern mind and she is not identified with any caste, state or religion. But above all, she can make us win the 1967 elections," wrote one party leader. There was another even more powerful reason: they wanted her in that role because they thought she was weak and would be malleable. The old party bosses were convinced that they could go on in the key positions, enjoying the privilege of making decisions without the responsibility of making them. The best of all possible worlds. Actually they did not know Indira Gandhi. At 48, she did not know herself yet either.

The day before her election as head of the government, the highest authority in the second most densely populated country in the world, Indira had written a letter to Rajiv saying that she could not get a poem by Robert Frost out of her head. For her it summarized very well the crossroads at which she stood: "How hard it is to keep from being king when it is in you and in the situation." She also told him in the letter that on that day, at dawn, she had visited Mahatma Gandhi's mausoleum to bask in the memory of the man who had been another father to her. Then she went to Teen Murti House, now a national museum, and stayed for a long time in the room in which Nehru had died. She needed to feel his presence. She remembered one of his letters when she was 15: "Be brave, and the rest will come on its own." Well, the rest had come. She was going to cross the threshold of her new existence, a life for which, deep down, she had always been preparing herself, even if she did not admit that consciously.

After her father's death, she had dreamed of withdrawing from the world. She toyed with that idea for a while, and even thought about renting a little flat in London and finding a job there, doing anything, perhaps as a secretary in some cultural institution or other. To flee from herself, that is what she was seeking. But soon reality overtook her, and she could not go on dreaming of her own freedom. She had to solve specific problems. She had been left without a home and from her father she had inherited his personal possessions and his rights as an author, and not much else. Nehru had been using up his capital, because his salary as Prime Minster was not sufficient to cover his public expenses, and he was not one to dip into the coffers of the Treasury. It is true that Indira inherited the old mansion of Anand Bhawan in Allahabad, but that had so many expenses that keeping it up was a heavy burden. Besides, she had two sons studying in England. How could she pay for all that? By retiring from the world? She realized it was a pipe-dream, a fancy. Her life had been too dominated by politics for her to be able to retire so young. People came to see her every day, people of all classes and conditions, as they had done when her father was alive. The same crowds that thronged Teen Murti House now came to see her. They came to greet her, to set out their complaints, for her to listen to them, to say a few words to them and show interest in their problems. They were the same poor people, the poor of eternal, ancient India, the poor in whose name Gandhi and her father had fought. Indira was not going to abandon them: that would have been an insult to Nehru's memory. On the contrary, she received them and listened carefully to what they wanted to say to her. It was they who really comforted her wounded heart. From them she gained the strength to move on, to find a meaning to her life. Those poor people made her realize that what she had really inherited had been her father's power.

She also felt Nehru's presence when she went in and out of the Parliament building in the landscaped centre of New Delhi, a gigantic, circular building of beige and red sandstone with a verandah full of columns. Inside, under a thirty-metre high dome, the representatives of the people elected her by 355 votes against 169. Her party voted for her en masse. In her short speech she thanked them. "I hope not to betray the trust you have placed in me." She was radiant, very aware that her appointment with destiny had arrived. She was going to take possession of that "vast spread of Indian humanity" according to Nehru's description.

The residence assigned to her was in the same district of New Delhi as the old palace-like mansion. Number 1, Safdarjung Road was a typical colonial villa with white-painted walls, surrounded by a nice garden. It had four bedrooms of which she turned two into an office and a reception room. She made it clear that every day between eight and nine in the morning, the house would be open to all comers, without regard for their position or social status. These were the same hours that Nehru had set aside for the same task.

Indira explained to Rajiv the reasons that had forced her to accept the candidature. During her months in charge of the

Information Ministry, she had found herself pushed into dealing with a grave national crisis that was not within the jurisdiction of her own ministry. The crisis caught her on holiday in Kashmir, the beautiful region the Nehru family came from. As soon as she arrived, she found out that Pakistani troops, disguised as civilian volunteers, were on the verge of capturing the capital, Srinagar, in order to encourage a pro-Pakistani revolt among the population. Indira disobeyed the Prime Minister's orders to return to Delhi immediately. Not only did she remain in Kashmir, but she flew to the front when hostilities broke out. "We shall not give an inch of our territory to the aggressors," she proclaimed on a tour of the northern cities. The Press praised what she had done: "Indira is the only man in a government of old women," the headlines read. The correspondents who followed her were astonished to witness how Indira was welcomed everywhere by huge crowds shouting their enthusiasm. The Pakistani army was defeated. India, and Indira, emerged victorious, giving rise to the idea that later would take hold of the people's imagination: "India is Indira; Indira is India."

All this occurred while eight thousand kilometres away Rajiv was learning to control his Tiger Moth in the skies over England. "... If my mother does not stand as Prime Minister, everything we have achieved since independence will be lost," he told Sonia in a letter that seemed to contradict the previous ones. And the fact is that in his own way Rajiv was experiencing his mother's conflict, which was the whole family's conflict, from duty to the nation and the inheritance of their father and grandfather, to the demands of a private life. When Rajiv heard that his mother had been elected Prime Minister, the letter that Sonia received was full of the anguish this new situation created for him. "If anything happens to my mother, I won't know what to do. You cannot imagine how much I depend on her, on her help in any situation, especially with you. It's going to be much harder for you than for me. For you, it will all be new and she is the only one who can really help you. I don't know what I would do if I ever lost her."

His mother's photo was on the front pages of the international press. At a newspaper stand in Thruxton, the village near the airbase, Rajiv bought a copy of *The Guardian* newspaper: "No other woman in history has taken on such a responsibility, and no country of the importance of India has ever handed over power to a woman under democratic conditions," said the report. The photo of his mother was also on the cover of *Time* magazine: "Turbulent India in the hands of a woman," said the headline. Although she claimed she was not a feminist, the whole world was curious to know how a woman with so little experience in administrative matters was going to face up to the immensity of the problems that awaited her. As immense as the nation she was to govern, made up of a complex mosaic of peoples who shared races, religions, languages and cultures of enormous diversity. A country with a Hindu majority, but with over a hundred million Moslems, which made it the second largest Moslem country on the planet. Not counting the ten million Christians, seven million Sikhs, two hundred thousand Parsees and thirty-five thousand Jews whose ancestors had fled from Babylon after the destruction of Solomon's Temple. A land in which 4,635 different communities lived together, each with its own traditions, and languages as ancient as they were diverse, such as the Urdu of the Moslems, which was written from right to left, or Hindi, which was written from left to right, like the Latin alphabet, or Tamil which could sometimes be read from top to bottom, or other alphabets that were deciphered like hieroglyphs. In this Babel, 845 dialects were used and 17 official languages. But English, the language of the colonizers, was still the common language after the imposition of Hindi was rejected by the southern states. A country that still suffered striking inequalities, with corruption ensconced in all levels of society and a paralyzing bureaucracy. A country known for its high spiritual achievements and at the same time for its dreadfully poor levels of material welfare, a country where man was more fertile than the land he worked, a country constantly hit by natural calamities, and yet believing in 330 million gods and goddesses. Perhaps the greatest achievement of that nation forged by Nehru and Gandhi is that it was still free, in spite of the string of curses and overwhelming problems inherited from the British colonists. In spite of what an English general had predicted at the moment of independence: "No one can make one nation out of continent of so many nations."

But the continent-nation that his mother was to govern was worse than it had ever been under Nehru or his successor. Several years of drought had caused a shortage of food and unleashed prolonged famines. The state of Kerala was shaken by violent disturbances connected with the distribution of food. The economy was the victim of galloping inflation. The region of the Punjab was suffering unrest because it called for Punjabi to be used there exclusively; one Sikh leader threatened to set himself on fire if this request was not granted. The Naga tribe in the northeast fought for secession. To cap it all, the Hindu holy men demonstrated naked outside Parliament, with their bodies covered in ashes, right under Indira's nose, to demand it be prohibited to kill cows anywhere in the nation. A claim that went against the secular Constitution of India, which called for respect for the rights and equality of all religions. In such a poor country, beef was an essential source of protein for minorities like the Moslems or the Christians. The protests degenerated and there were deaths when the police fired on the troublemakers. "I am not going to let myself be intimidated by the cow- savers," Indira declared defiantly. Decidedly, India was not like any other country. In 1966 it was a gigantic pressure cooker about to explode, as though independence had given rise to the outbreak of millions of little rebellions, the result of centuries and centuries of the exploitation of some minorities by others, of some castes by others, of some ethnic groups by others... The Congress big fish had not done Indira any favour by pushing her to the top.

For Indira there was a clear priority, the same one that her father or Gandhi would have identified: to put an end to the famines and thus avoid the deaths of the poorest people. If to do that it was necessary to ask international bodies and the richer countries for assistance, she would need to swallow her pride and hold out her hand. Twenty years after independence India, much to her dismay, had gained the unenviable status of international beggar. Indira was ashamed at having to ask for aid, but she knew there was no other option. And yet she was determined not to beg for anything: "The weaker our position is, the stronger we must appear to be."

She immediately accepted the invitation of President Johnson to go to Washington and she prepared for the journey meticulously, since the lives of millions of her countrymen would depend on the result, and perhaps her political future too. She worked out her speeches punctiliously and corrected them, consulting her book of quotations that went everywhere with her. She sought simple ideas and turned her back on complicated concepts. She chose her clothes with the same care as she prepared her addresses: a sari, abodice, a shawl and shoes for each reception. To crown it all she wanted her two sons to go with her. Rajiv had to interrupt his flying classes and travel to Paris to meet his mother. There, after General De Gaulle gave a lunch in her honour, they boarded a Boeing 707 which the White House had placed at her disposal. When De Gaulle was asked what he had thought of Indira, the old statesman said; "Those fragile shoulders on which the gigantic destiny of India rests ... don't seem to sag under so much weight. That woman has something inside her, and she will make it."

In Washington, B.K. Nehru, Indira's cousin and Ambassador to the United States, received a phone call at an early hour. It was President Lyndon B. Johnson, a giant from Texas. "I have just read in the New York Times that Indira doesn't like to be called 'Madame Prime Minister' ... How should I address her?"

"Let me find out, Mr President. I'll call you back as soon as I get instructions."

He immediately rushed into Indira's suite.

"Let him call me whatever he wants ..." she said, and before her cousin had left the room she added, "You can also tell him that some of my ministers call me 'Sir'. If he likes, he can do that too."

President Johnson succumbed to Indira's charms. He unblocked American aid which had been interrupted because of the short war with Pakistan, and he got the World Bank to lend India money. The only point of disagreement during the visit was when Johnson asked her for a dance after the official banquet. Indira refused; she did not want even to think about the reaction of the Indian Press to a photo of the "Socialist daughter of Nehru bejewelled and dancing with the gringo President." She explained to Johnson that it could make her very unpopular, and he understood. "I don't want anything bad to happen to that girl," he told his Chief of Staff in his strong Texan accent that made him sound as though he had a permanent cold, before promising Indira three million tons of foodstuffs and nine million dollars of immediate aid. That journey was the first big success of the new Prime Minister, although she confessed to one of her advisors, "I hope I never find myself in a situation like that again."

Sonia experienced all this from a distance, with a certain apprehension because they were spectacular, widely publicized changes. The Italian media gave out the news of Indira Gandhi's rise to power, and the Maino family could see the face of their daughter's suitor's mother close up on television from their sitting room in Via Bellini. But the fact that she was now Prime Minister did not seem to soften their resolve. Quite the opposite: it gave Stefano a sudden fright. For him, that increased the risk and made the whole thing more senseless. Everything around that lady was in danger, he could see that clearly. They had killed Gandhi himself, hadn't they? Those countries were too unpredictable ... Paola, however, could not hide a certain satisfaction. Her daughter had not fallen in love with just anyone. In some way, Sonia had wiped away their *paesani* veneer and had "ennobled" them, although she was not prepared for this love story to prosper just because of that. Neither did she want to lose her.

Rajiv returned from his trip to the United States satisfied, although it was too short and it was too full of official engagements for him to enjoy it as he would have liked. Since he was a little boy, politics had always meant the same to him: interminable photo sessions with his mother, having to listen to boring conversations over lengthy dinners, always being very well- behaved, wearing a tie, saying yes to everything. He was more and more convinced that his was to be a life far away from all those goings-on, a quiet, discreet existence beside the woman of his dreams. He also wanted to get away from himself, from his roots, from the weight of the family tradition which, he felt, could one day crush him. He secretly trusted that the destiny drawn up for him by his name would never catch up with him.

In October 1966, he asked to borrow his brother's car to go and see Sonia; the old Volkswagen had deteriorated so much that he had sold it for four pounds. Besides, Sanjay's car was more appropriate for such a long journey. It was an old Jaguar, a model that his brother had acquired for an exceptional price because it did not work, thanks to his contacts at Rolls Royce. Sanjay had worked on it patiently until he got it to start again. Unlike his brother, Rajiv did not like to show off, and going to Orbassano in that car made him feel embarrassed, but on the other hand he thought it was better to turn up like that, like someone of means and not like a backpacker. In that way he stood a better chance of impressing Sonia's parents favourably.

She was excited that he was coming; she had not seen him for months and the waiting seemed to go on forever. Her sisters and friends were also nervous. It was not every day that an Indian prince arrived in that dormitory town outside Turin, ready to carry off his Cinderella ... There was enormous curiosity, including on the part of her parents, who had invited him to dinner that very day, although everyone pretended it was nothing special.

Rajiv's arrival in his Jaguar caused a real commotion in the neighbourhood. Who could that rich Englishman be, coming to see the Maino girl? they asked each other in low tones. Their perplexity was even greater because his looks did not match his car. "He looks Sicilian," joked one of Sonia's friends. "With a car like that, he could be a *terrone* from the Mafia," another commented. Rajiv arrived untidy and with several days' growth of beard because he had slept in the car in order to save on hotel bills. Sonia did not know whether it was tiredness or the prospect of the dinner, or the recent events which had catapulted his mother on to the international scene, but she noticed he was worried when she was finally able to hug him in an empty street in Orbassano where they had agreed to meet on the morning of his arrival.

"I'm going to have to go back to India," he confessed to her as soon as the passion of their meeting had calmed.

"What about your pilot's licence?"

"I'll get it there. Anyway, I haven't the money to get it in England.

What worries me is being so far away from you."

There was another reason, which was that his mother had asked him to come home.

"She's very lonely. She has huge problems," he told Sonia.

He explained to her that no sooner had she returned from the United States than the opposition attacked her ferociously, accusing her of having fallen under the influence of the Americans and of abandoning her father's non-alignment policy... But not only the opposition: those who had elected her for the position of Prime Minister, the leaders of her own party too. They were bothered by the way Indira faced up to problems, directly, skipping over the party hierarchy, as in the case of the skirmishes with Pakistan. An old colleague of Nehru's had launched a harsh diatribe against Indira in Parliament, questioning not so much the aid but the conditions which the Americans had imposed before handing it over. Among these was the devaluation of the rupee, a very unpopular measure which Indira took in spite of having the whole country against her, thus showing that she was not an imitation of her father, that she was able to administer bitter medicine to the nation if she really believed in it, and that she owed nothing to anybody. But the result was that her popularity fell to its lowest point, while the predictions about India's future became gloomier and gloomier. The idea prevailed that only the personality and example of Nehru had managed to keep India united and democratic, but that now, with the successive droughts, the innumerable little ethnic rebellions, the tension with Pakistan and Indira's leadership, the country was on the verge of disintegration.

"And they blame my mother for it," said Rajiv. "As though she were responsible for the fact there have been three years of drought and the people are dying of hunger ... The fact is, I have the impression I am abandoning her, and I don't like it."

Listening to Rajiv talk about his mother became Sonia's special initiation into Indian politics. She was not aware of it, but she was coming into contact with concepts and ideas that had always seemed very distant and incomprehensible, and that soon would become as familiar to her as at home when they commented on the Juventus results or the Milan fashion week. She was beginning to realize that you cannot live close to someone like Rajiv's mother without it affecting the lives of everyone around her, including Sonia herself. But it was still something too nebulous and faraway to upset her. Each battle in its own time. The battle now was to overcomeher parents' resistance.

Sonia accompanied Rajiv to the house of a friend who had offered to put him up, and then she showed him the town. They had a *cappuccino* each at Nino's bar, walked around the streets in the centre and then stopped at Pier Luigi's bar. Apart from running his establishment, Pier Luigi was aradio ham in his free time, a hobby on which Rajiv also wanted to spend some time. He had discovered it during his flying studies and, apart from theattraction to the magic of electronics, he also saw it as a way of communicating with Sonia when he was far away. The desperation of one day finding himself so distant from her made him dream about any possibility of filling that void.

Sonia left him to rest and arranged to pick him up that night to take him to dinner at her parents' home. Meanwhile, she would go to the annual meeting of ex-pupils at her school in Giaveno. "I remember that day as if it were yesterday," Sister Giovanna Negri would say. Sonia was 20. After the meeting of ex-pupils of the school, Sonia announced that she was leaving.

"Why don't you stay and have dinner with us?" I said to her. "You've been away in England for a long time and we've hardly seen you."

"I can't stay," Sonia replied. "I have a guest coming for dinner tonight."

"And who is it ...?" asked Sister Giovanna, joking.

Sonia blushed, displaying the dimples in her cheeks. In the end she let it out: "My boyfriend."

"Your boyfriend? What a surprise! Tell me all about him ... Who is he?"

Sonia was reluctant to answer, which sharpened the nun's curiosity even more.

"He's Indian ..." she said shyly.

"Indian?" the nun repeated in astonishment.

Sonia put a finger to her lips so she would lower her voice. Then she said, almost in a sigh, "He's the son of Indira Gandhi."

"I was puzzled," Sister Negri would recall years later.

That dinner was a little like the Italian version of the famous film with Katharine Hepburn and Sidney Poitier. Except that it was not fiction and there was no happy ending, although the reactions of Stefano Maino and Spencer Tracy might be similar. Rajiv talked about his studies. He had just obtained his certificate as a private pilot and he thought that in a year and a half he would get the commercial pilot's licence. He wanted to find a job as soon as possible. He had a powerful reason for it: "I have come with a very serious proposal," he told Stefano Maino. "I have come to tell you that I want to marry your daughter."

Sonia did not know where to put herself because she had to translate. Her mother, all nervous, began to put drinks on the coffee table in front of the sofa. Her hands were trembling. The patriarch remained cordial, but firm: "I have not the slightest doubt as to your sincerity and honesty," he told Rajiv, looking at Sonia to get her to continue translating. "I only need to look you in the eye to see what you are like. I do not doubt you. All my doubts have to do with my daughter. She's too young to know what she wants ..." Sonia looked at the ceiling in exasperation. "Quite frankly, I don't think she'll be able to get used to living in India. The customs are too different."

Rajiv suggested that Sonia should go there for a short holiday. He explained the idea that she should first go alone, before he arrived, so that she could judge for herself. But Stefano was categorically opposed to the idea.

"Until she is over 21, I cannot let her go."

It was a hard nut to crack, and Sonia knew but she could not let the atmosphere of the meeting degenerate. Her father's silences could be cut with a knife. The man was as immoveable as a rock, and he only made one small concession: "If at that time you still feel the same towards each other, I will let her go to India, but that will be in a year's time, when she is of age," he said before turning to his wife and adding, "If things work out badly, she won't be able to reproach me for helping to ruin her life."

But Stefano still believed and hoped with all his heart that things would get back to normal and that in view of the difficulties she would find, Sonia would end up by throwing in the towel. He was tormented by the idea of losing his daughter.

8

When Rajiv told his mother about his meeting with the Mainos in Orbassano, Indira was in agreement with the condition the Italian patriarch had imposed. Testing the feelings of the young people was the only way to know if their romance had a future. They had to gain time; she too would really have preferred Rajiv not to have chosen a foreign girl. But if time proved that they loved each other, Indira was not thinking of opposing her son's decision. She had suffered too much with her father's rejection of her own marriage to inflict the same on any of her children.

"Marriage isn't everything. Life is something much bigger," Nehru had told her when she went to see him in Dehra Dun Prison to tell him she wanted to marry Firoz. Nehru advised her to get her strength back before she made any decision. She had been very ill and her father reminded her that the doctors had advised her not to have children. Furthermore, what Indira wanted seemed trivial to him, because it meant throwing "inheritance and family tradition" out of the window in order to marry a man whose background and education were very different from hers. Indira did not agree, at least at that time. She told him she wanted an anonymous lifestyle, free from tension, which she had never had before. She wanted to get married and have children. More than one, she stressed, because she did not want her child to suffer the loneliness that she had known. She wanted to take care of them and her husband in a house full of books, music and friends. If to fulfill that dream, she had to defy the doctors and risk even her own health, she was prepared to do it.

Firoz was the son of a Parsee named Jehangir Ghandy, whose official biography attributes him with being a naval engineer, but other sources state that he was a dealer in alcohol, although there was no connection at all to Gandhi. At the end of the thirties he changed the spelling of his name to that of Gandhi, the name of a caste of perfume-makers, a common name among the Bania castes of the Hindus of Gujarat, where Mahatma came from. The reason is not known for that small change, which ended up being of inestimable value to the future political career of his wife.

Following Zarathustra, the Parsee religion is one of humanity's oldest, but Firoz was never religious, rather the opposite. He had come into contact with the Nehrus because of the struggle movement against the English which led him to become a member of the Congress Party. A very active and very radical militant, he knew the texts of Marx and Engels better than Nehru himself. Together they had joined in a protest meeting in France against the bombing of civil populations during the war in Spain. Firoz had tried to convince the anti-Communist organizers of the event to allow La Pasionaria to speak, but without success. Nehru was furious and made a heated speech, hotly defending the right to freedom of expression.

Nehru did not question Firoz as a militant, but thought he was a poor match for his daughter. Both men were opposites in everything. Firoz was short and squat; a little boastful, he talked very loudly and used swearwords left, right and centre. He was neither refined nor an intellectual. He liked to eat and drink well and he was interested in cars and electrical and mechanical gadgets, passions which Rajiv and Sanjay would inherit. He had been a very poor student, although he liked classical Indian music and flowers, like Indira. But without a university degree or a profession, or the prospect of earning his living, and with a solid reputation as a womanizer, it was logical that the Nehrus should look askance at this nobody who was trying to get into the first family of India.

"You were brought up in Anand Bhawan, surrounded by luxury and servants," her grandmother told Indira in an attempt to put pressure on her. "Firoz has no fortune, he's from another background and another religion."

"We don't care about religion because neither of us is religious," Indira answered. "I am austere, like my mother, and even though I have lived in Anand Bhawan, I can be equally happy in a peasant's hut."

Sonia said more or less the same to her parents when they talked about how difficult it was to live so far away, in a country that was so different. For Sonia, India was an abstraction. She was not in the least afraid, in spite of all she had heard. If Rajiv had been an Eskimo, she would not have minded following him to the North Pole. "When you are in love," she wrote, "love gives you great strength. Armed with that strength, nothing can scare you. You only want the person you love. I only wanted Rajiv. I would have gone to the ends of the Earth with him. He was my greatest safety. I could not think about anything or anyone else, just him."

*   *   *

If Nehru finally gave his consent for Indira's marriage to

Firoz, Indira agreed to her son's request when he asked her to write to Sonia's father toget him to allow her to go to India. A year had gone by, the period of time Stefano Maino had imposed, and the young people's passion showed no sign of cooling. Neither Sonia nor Rajiv was prepared to live without the other; their separation was becoming too painful. Indira understood that they were serious about each other. Actually she would have preferred to follow the traditional line and choose the daughter of a good Kashmiri family to marry her son, according to the tradition, just as her grandfather Motilal had done by choosing Kamala, her mother. Arranged marriages were common, and love marriages were the exception. The first type usually worked better; the divorce rate among these kinds of marriages is surprisingly low because the parents look for candidates for their children in similar social and cultural backgrounds, which really is an advantage when they start living together. The second type were a lottery. Indira had not been lucky. Perhaps Rajiv would, although he had the handicap that his fiancée was a foreigner. In traditional society, foreigners did not even merit a place on the scale, they were considered "casteless". New Delhi was not deepest India, but even so Indira was perfectly aware of how difficult it could be for a Western girl to adapt to life in this country, although she was prepared to make it as pleasantas possible because she liked the girl.

Indira Gandhi's letter inviting Sonia to spend a holiday in New Delhi was a worry for Stefano Maino, but he was a man of his word and he had no alternative but to keep his promise. They discussed it at home and as there was no way out, they agreed that Sonia should go to India, but only for one month, and then she would come home finally convinced that she could never live there, thought her parents. Here, she not only had her family, but also a future. She had been working all year in Fieratorino and she had more and more opportunities to earn a living with the languages she had learned. If she did not like Orbassano because it seemed too small and suburban to her, she could always go and live in Turin. Her parents still dreamed that some businessman would meet her at one of those fairs and would end up marrying her. Sonia made as if she was listening carefully to all these suggestions, but her mind was already far away, eight thousand kilometres away.

On January 13th, 1968, exactly thirty-four days after she came of age, Sonia landed at Palam Airport, New Delhi. Her stomach was in knots. Her parents and sisters had gone to see her off at Milan Airport and not even tough old Stefano had been able to hold back the tears.

"If you don't like it, you come straight back, eh?" he had told her while her mother put even more medicines in her handbag, as though she were going to the jungle.

Sonia did not sleep during the flight. Now that she was alone facing her destiny, a kind of anguish came over her. The excitement of seeing Rajiv became a vague fear. They had been a year without seeing each other. What if he disappoints me? Or I disappoint him? What if he behaves differently in his own surroundings? What if he isn't the same as I think he is? They were inevitable questions, the normal reaction of someone who has put all their money on one card. Now was the moment to turn the card over.

From the air, the tangle of avenues and roundabouts of New Delhi suggested the star-shaped marble geometric figures that decorated the Mogul palaces. The plane landed in the morning. The climate could not be more different from the cold winter she had left behind. The temperature was delightful, the sky was blue, and as soon as she left the plane her sense of smell was filled by a very characteristic odour, which she would later identify as the smell of India: a mixture of burnt wood and honey, of ash and rotten fruit. And a sound: the cawing of the crows, those ever-present crows, dressed in grey or black, croaking insolently and familiarly from the banisters in the arrivals lounge, from posts and window ledges. Rajiv was waiting for her there. "As soon as I saw him," Sonia would say, "I was overcome by a deep feeling of relief." His brother Sanjay was also there and a friend called Amitabh, the son of a couple, the Bachchans, that the Nehrus had known for a long time. The father was a famous Hindi poet and a Member of Parliament and Indira had asked them to put Sonia up for the duration of her stay.

The fears she had felt during the flight suddenly disappeared, as if they had never existed. In fact now she was sure that she had done the right thing by following the dictates of her heart in spite of the difficulties. "I was at his side again and nothing or no one would separate us again," wrote Sonia, remembering her arrival.

New Delhi was not the India she had imagined, at least the part where she lived, with its wide avenues lined with tall, ever-green trees, many of them in flower. The home of the Bachchans was in Willingdon Crescent, the avenue of the banyans. The English town planners who made New Delhi into a pleasant garden city wanted each avenue to have its own species of tree. Janpath, formerly Queen's Way, had neems, sacred trees known for their medicinal properties; Akbar Road had tamarinds, and in Safdarjung Road, where Indira Gandhi's residence was, there was a profusion of flame trees with their shiny green foliage dotted with orange flowers. The small amount of road traffic was composed of cyclists, carts pulled by donkeys or camels, wagons with yellow tops, backfiring motorcycles, old Ambassadors, replicas of the 1956 Morris Oxford III which were made under licence in Bengal, all of them avoiding the cows that wandered freely around in the middle of the road. It was not unusual to come across an oxcart, or even an elephant carrying merchandise, waiting at the traffic lights. It was a quiet city of three million inhabitants, without large department stores or shopping centres, and with a single luxury hotel in the heart of the diplomatic quarter.

Sonia was welcomed with all the warmth that could be expected from an Indian family, although Rajiv could not be with her as much as he would have liked because on 25th January he was going to take the commercial pilot's exam and he had to carry on accumulating flying hours and studying. But his cousins and friends, and even Indira Gandhi, did their utmost for her stay to be as pleasant as possible. Although she was sleeping at the Bachchan house, she spent a large part of the morning at her fiancé's home. At that time, the Prime Minister lived with hardly any security measures. She received people every morning at the doors of her home with just one guard present. Neither did her sons have escorts, except for certain events that were considered to be risky.

Friends and members of the family took turns showing Sonia the city, full of parks, ancient monuments and magnificent buildings that had been put up by the English in 1912 when they decided to change the capital from Calcutta to Delhi. They designed a new city in which they planted thousands of trees. From time immemorial, plants had been the obsession of the rulers of Delhi. Gardens enhanced mausoleums and tombs with the idea that the dead might feel happier and more at peace; others had been conceived as acts of charity for the people, and yet others had been planted by kings for their own use and enjoyment. Rajiv particularly liked to walk around the Lodhi gardens at dusk, with their ponds and lines of gigantic palms that surround the tomb of Mohammed Shah, a beautiful monument of Indo- Mogul style which still conserved the remains of the turquoise tiling and original calligraphy that decorated it. It was a popular place where couples in love could enjoy a moment of peace and quiet and a certain amount of privacy. On his Lambretta scooter, he also took her around imperial New Delhi, and showed her the spectacular views that the British architects had conceived to impress and intimidate the local population. The one Sonia admired from the archway of the Gate of India, where a perpetual flame burns in memory of the Indian soldiers killed in the two world wars, was grandiose. As was the imposing South Block building, a mixture of the Mogul and Neo-Classical styles where, on the other side of the façade adorned with bas-reliefs of lotus flowers and elephants, Indira Gandhi's office was, and above all the Palace of the Presidency of the Republic, formerly the palace of the British Viceroy, an elegant building of beige and red sandstone crowned with a vast copper dome of exquisite proportions, considered by many as one of the most beautiful buildings of the twentieth century.

And where was the India she had been told about? Sonia asked. The India that her parents were terrified of? The other India? It was not necessary to go far from there. It was enough to follow wide Rajpath Avenue, formerly King's Way, and get to old Delhi. That was another world. Around the Red Fort, another spectacular monument built by the Emperor Shah Jehan, the same one that who erected the Taj Mahal in honour of his wife, swirled a colourful, noisy crowd that seemed to be taking part in a huge carnival of snake charmers, jugglers, fortune-tellers, musicians, sword-swallowers and fakirs who pierced their cheeks with daggers. This was eternal India, the same that took over the alleys around the Great Mosque, with clothing stalls full of brightly coloured cloth, fruit vendors, people selling sweets, torches, shoe polish and batteries, bootblacks, street barbers, dark workshops where children wove carpets and others made precision instruments ... An explosion of life, an exotic, riotous chaos that left her drunk with the colours, noises and smells. And everywhere, at the back of a street, at the end of a garden, you could see an old tomb or cenotaph, a Moslem or Hindu monument that went back to the dawn of time, as a reminder of how ancient India is. Nehru had once described his country as "an ancient palimpsest in which layers and layers of thought and reverie have been engraved, without any of them having been able to erase or hide what had previously been written."

And then the spectacle of poverty, which she saw from her place on the back of the scooter when they drove through certain districts: naked children running around the streets, old people making their bowls clink, people who washed and relieved themselves on the pavements. It reminded Sonia a little of the poor of Lusiana where she was born, back in the fifties when she was a little girl, those naked children in winter, those families going hungry that her mother felt so much for, those cripples in the squares, former soldiers who had returned wounded from the Russian front ... But what she had never seen before were deformities like those of some New Delhi lepers who waited for the cars to stop at the traffic lights. In 1968 India had as many lepers as Portugal had inhabitants, enough beggars to populate a country like Holland, eleven million holy men, ten million children under the age of fifteen who were married or widowed. Forty thousand babies were born every day, a fifth of whom died before they reached the age of five. Even so, the figures were better than when independence had come, twenty years before. The improvement in sanitary conditions, although slight, was creating an even bigger problem, and the reproductive age of Indians was growing. As a consequence, the birth explosion was becoming the country's biggest problem because they were literally "eating up" economic progress. Each year the population of India increased by a figure equal to the entire population of Spain.

For Sonia everything around her was new and strange: the colours, the tastes, the people. "But strangest of all were the eyes of the people, that look of curiosity that followed me everywhere." Sonia was becoming initiated into the world of India, discovering how curious and inquisitive the inhabitants could be, especially in those days when there were practically no tourists. If a simple foreigner attracted attention, a woman did even more, and if she was pretty and wearing a miniskirt, which was the fashion in Europe, then she immediately became the centre of attention. Or the object of criticism. Sonia had to learn to control her gestures, her movements and her way of dressing, but it was not always easy: "The absolute lack of privacy, the need to control myself and not show my feelings openly was an exasperating experience." Signs of affection in public were frowned upon, not only in the streets, but also in daily life. She could not kiss Rajiv if there was anyone else present, or even hold his hand without causing a scandal. She was discovering that India was the primmest country in the world, an inheritance from Victorian England. Then there were things that were difficult for an Italian girl: the food for example. Sonia could not get used to the hot spices and felt that they cancelled out the flavour of the food. Or sauces that were so spicy, or the sweet-sour taste of certain dishes. Or the custom of society dinners, where people talked and drank a lot for an interminable time, quickly had dinner and then there was no after-dinner conversation and everyone went home in five minutes.

She did not take long to realize that the eyes that gazed at her so insistently were not doing so just because she was a foreigner, or strange- looking, or a very pretty girl. She was seen as a new member of a familywho had lived for years in the public eye. Everything they did or said, or the opposite, what they did not do or say, was scrutinized minutely, analyzedand judged. How can you live like that? she asked herself, overwhelmed.

But, in spite of everything, Sonia could not see herself back in Italy. This was a very different world, and there was a lot more to see and to explore. At Rajiv's side it was a fascinating journey, in spite of the hidden dangers. Furthermore, she was surrounded by affection from everybody. Sanjay treated her like a sister, half protective and half amused at seeing her adapting. Amitabh and his family too. She felt protected and loved. For both of them, the idea of separating again was simply inconceivable. Why waste more time, why go back to Italy and wait again, even more agony, until they could meet up again here or there? Rajiv could not contemplate going to live in Europe; he was thinking of joining Indian Airlines as soon as he had got his commercial licence. Then they could go and live in a flat. Here in Delhiit was easier; life together was within their reach. Sonia was the one who hadto take the step and take a risk because she had to leave her country and her family behind for an indefinite time. She had come to get to know India and its customs, but she did not need to know anything further because beforeshe got on that plane she had really already made the decision to follow her heart. Even if that meant doing something that went against the grain. She did not want even to imagine her father's face when she told him she was not going back, that she was getting married.

Indira was surprised when she heard that Sonia was prepared to stay and that they wanted to get married soon. They had met exactly three years ago in Cambridge. They had complied with all the deadlines set, they had done everything they had been told to do, and now the moment had come to make the decision. Indira was aware that Sonia's arrival had caused a minor revolution in New Delhi social spheres, although neither Sonia nor Rajiv hadsought that, rather the opposite. Just her presence, because she was the fiancée of who he was and because it was the first time a Nehru was going to marry a foreigner from another continent, had given rise to all kinds of conjecture. Although it was the capital of a country with seven hundred million inhabitants, society was small, conventional, and all the important families knew each other. In their gossiping, most of the comments were full of praise – "How pretty she is!" But others alluded to her lack of "pedigree" – "She's a nobody" – or worse – "She's low caste". Others referred to her way of dressing – "She wants to attract attention" - ; others to her mere presence – "What can that boy see in her?" - ; others to a feeling of national outrage – "Couldn't he have found a better girl here?" Without wanting to she had set a large number of pretty girls in high society against her, as well as their mothers, who saw her as a foreigner, and on top of that, an intruder, who was carrying off one of the most eligible bachelors in the country.

"After a week," Usha Bhagat, Indira's secretary, would say,

"Mrs Gandhi realized that the two of them were very serious about each other and that it would do no good to wait any longer. The fact that they were going out and about in New Delhi encouraged the gossip and the best way to put a stop to it was to let them get married." But when Rajiv suggested to his mother that they should move to a flat of their own as soon as he had a job, Indira imposed a single condition on him: "One thing is to get married outside your community. But to live apart is totally against the Indian tradition of the joint family. They would call us Westerners, they would accuse us of abandoning all our traditions." If Rajiv had been European or a Westerner he would probably have disobeyed his mother and gone to live with his wife. But he was Indian, and in India, sons follow the tradition. Especially when an example has to be set. The solution to the conflict she was in came about because Sonia accepted a condition that most Western women would have considered inadmissible. But Sonia needed to adapt to India, it could not be the other way round, and in India marriage is a family affair more than individual, where harmony among its members is valued above individual fascination. That meant becoming part of the husband's family. She would have to live in the family home, Indian-style, sharing the same roof as her mother-in-law, her brother-in-law and his family if he got married one day. Everyone at number 1, Safdarjung Road. Sonia agreed because she was blinded by love. Besides, living with the family was not something to scare an Italian girl who had lived all her childhood in a town where the Mainos were a clan. She also convinced herself that by not being on her own she would be more protected and that would allow her to adapt better. She saw the positive side to everything - one of the advantages of love, which acts like a drug.

They decided to set the date of February 25th for the

wedding. Everything very fast, but it was better like that. Indira wanted to avoid her son's marriage becoming a national affair, as had occurred with her own marriage. She told Sonia and Rajiv how the whole country had been against it as though every single inhabitant of the nation had felt he had the right to an opinion. Thousands of letters and telegrams had flooded into Anand Bhawan, some insulting, the majority hostile, some congratulatory. There was an explanation, and it was that Firoz and Indira had transgressed two deeply-rooted traditions: they had not submitted to a marriage arranged by their families and they were not marrying "within the same faith". This last had infuriated the orthodox Hindus. And now history was repeating itself. As though the children inherited from their parents not only their physical characteristics and skills but also their conflicts, their contradictions and the situations in their lives.

"Dear Father and Mother," Sonia wrote. "I am very happy. I am writing you this letter to tell you that Rajiv and I are getting married. We expect you all here for February 25th ..." Sonia did not suspect that by the time her letter arrived the announcement of her wedding had already been given out by the worldwide media. A journalist from the *La Stampa* newspaper in Turin went to visit the family at number 14, Via Bellini. "The parents and sisters are going through an extremely tense time," he wrote. "The phone does not stop ringing and journalists and photographers are lining up outside the gate. The father, aged 53, is a man of few words: 'All my life working to get a future for my daughters ... as for the wedding, it's better to talk about it once it's over, or it would be better not to ever have to talk about it,' he declared in a tone that allows the listener to glimpse the fact that he is hurt. His wife, Paola, aged 45, cannot hold back her tears. 'I'm terrified at the idea of my daughter going to live so far away,' she said. When asked about the groom, they added, 'He's a quiet young man, well brought up and serious,' and to the question whether they would be going to the celebration, the father replied, 'Only my wife will go, I have too much work and I cannot waste any time. I will be with my daughter in my thoughts.'"

It was going to be a civil wedding, since it could not be a religiousone. A simple wedding, not a lavish one, "Indian-style" which would last several days. Indira was against the pomp and wasteful showiness of Indian weddings, done like that to proudly display relationships, power and money. The Nehrus did not need to show off. But they did need space in which to live. The colonial villa which the government had assigned Indira when she was named Prime Minister was too small, so much so that the secretariesand assistants worked under lean-tos in the garden. By giving the new couple a bedroom and a small living room at the back, with an independent way out to the garden, they would be even more squashed together. So Indira was in talks with her cabinet to have the house made bigger. Soon the builders started their work.

The fuss of the preparations suddenly absorbed all the members of thefamily, especially Sonia. She did not at all like having to exchange her tight trousers for a sari, an item of clothing in which she felt ridiculous. She couldnot get to feel comfortable because she was always afraid that at any moment the six metres of cloth wrapped around her might fall down. Shefelt like those tourists with very white skin who paraded around wearing garish saris. Of course for them it was just a game, dressing up for a photo toshow when they got back home; for Sonia the sari was much more. Itmarked the first step in the process of her indianization. Sooner or later, she would have to get used to it.

A mass of details had to be dealt with: drawing up guest lists, designing invitations, trying out hairstyles and makeup, etc. Sonia's head was spinning, because in addition she did not understand the Indians' English very well, as they had a strong accent. Deep down she was wishing it would all be over as soon as possible. Her proverbial shyness prevented her from feeling comfortable as the centre of attention, although she could do nothing to prevent it. She was literally besieged by photographers the day she went out with the family as Rajiv's official fiancée, to attend a Pierre Cardin fashion parade at the Ashok Hotel in New Delhi. A lengthy report dealt with the event in the *Femina* magazine. Sonia looked very pretty, with her straight hair falling on to her shoulders, covered by a printed silk sari. She sat between Rajiv and Sanjay while she talked to Indira. A photo that suggested perfect family harmony. On their way out, Sonia answered an insidious question from a reporter: "I am going to marry Rajiv the person, not the son of the Prime Minister." It was inevitable that many people should see her as an opportunist, an ambitious woman who had made a big catch. And that made her feel deeply sad and indignant. When another reporter asked her what she thought about staying to live in India, so far from home, Sonia looked up at Rajiv and giving a shy smile, she said, "With Rajiv I would go to the ends of the earth."

And was India not actually the ends of the earth in those days? For the Maino family it was, and they hardly had time to get organized. In the end, only Sonia's mother came, with her sister Anushka and her uncle Mario (her mother's brother), who would act in lieu of her father and give away his young niece. They arrived the day before the wedding when the *mehendi* ceremony was being celebrated in the garden of the friends where Sonia was staying. This was the equivalent of the bride's hen party. Although traditionally neither the groom nor his parents should attend, on this occasion an exception was made and both Rajiv and his mother were present because they wanted to greet the members of the family who had come from Italy. Indira was warm and extremely attentive to Paola, who felt intimidated and impatient to see her daughter. She looked all over for her. When they pointed her out, she exclaimed in shock: *"Oh mamma mia!"*

She almost burst into tears. She had not recognized her because Sonia's head was covered by a red and purple veil, she was dressed in a full-length red skirt, typical of Kashmir, and an embroidered red bodice. She was wearing bracelets, necklaces and a tiara made out of lily and jasmine petals threaded together – they called it floral jewellery – and on her forehead a *tilak*, the red dot that symbolizes the third eye which is able to see beyond appearances. Her hands, arms and feet were totally covered in curious tattoos done in henna, a paste extracted from the ground-up branches of a bush, tattoos that drew graceful arabesques and intricate designs. When she had got over her shock at seeing her daughter like this, her mother hugged her. "Thank goodness your father hasn't seen you dressed up like this!" she said, full of emotion. Poor Stefano, eight thousand kilometres away, was sad. He confessed to Danilo, his best friend, the mechanic, his fear for Sonia: "She'll be thrown to the tigers!" How right the former shepherd from the Asiago mountains was.

Young girls immediately surrounded Anushka and Paola and offered to paint their hands for them. As they applied the henna, they explained the tradition to them: the darker the drawings came out on the bride's hands, the more love there would be in the marriage. And the longer they took to fade, the longer the passion would last. Paola and Anushka looked at the arabesques on Sonia's hands: they were as black as if they had been drawn in Indian ink.

The wedding proper took place the next day, at six in the evening at number 1, Safdarjung Road. Indira had gone through all her wardrobes for the sari she wanted Sonia to wear, the same one she had worn, the one Nehru had woven during his long hours of imprisonment, once he had accepted his daughter's decision to marry Firoz. Sonia recognized it as she had seen it at the exhibition in London and she remembered Rajiv's words: "I hope you will wear it one day!" At the time she had taken it as a joke. She had still dreamed of getting married in white. Now she took it as an honour and a sign of affection, not suspecting for a moment that when she wore that pale red sari she too would become part of the history of India.

One small incident infuriated Rajiv, when he discovered that there were two reporters among the guests. This was his celebration and he did not want any interference or publicity. That day he just wanted to be Rajiv, not the son of the highest authority in the country, which was really ingenuous of him. He refused to come out of the house until the paparazzi had been expelled. Indira had to calm him down very patiently. When Mendelssohn's Wedding March announced the arrival of the bride, he quietened down. Rajiv went out to welcome Sonia in the garden where there were some two hundred guests, friends and acquaintances of the family. When he saw her come in, on her uncle Mario's arm, his face changed. Sonia was resplendent. She was the living picture of elegance with her hair pulled back in a bun held in place by a brooch of jasmine petals. Her skin gleamed from the turmeric mask that had been put on her a few hours before. She had a simple silver bracelet on her wrist, her eyes were painted with kohl and her face was framed by flower earrings. They made a fine couple. He was wearing tight white trousers, a long cream-coloured jacket buttoned up to the neck, a salmon pink turban, and slipper-type shoes, with upward curving tips, like a prince out of the *Arabian Nights*. After the ritual exchange of garlands, they moved towards a corner of the garden where the closest members of the family were gathered round a table sheltered by a huge screen also made of flowers threaded together on hanging strings. They signed the civil register and exchanged rings. Sonia struggled to control her emotions. Every time her eyes met those of her mother, she felt like crying. So she preferred to look at Rajiv in order to gather her strength. Uncle Mario looked lost; he looked at his niece with affection and indulgence. Paola kept calm, although deep inside that wedding without a priest made her feel infinitely sad. Rajiv's words as he read some verses from the Rigveda chosen specially by his mother, brought the ceremony to an end:

Sweet blows the wind, Sweet flow the rivers.
May the nights and days bring us happiness, may the dust of
the earth yield us happiness, may the trees make us happy
with their fruit, may the Sun endow us with happiness …

And that was all. The young couple came out of the enclosed area to find a shower of rose petals and the noise of fireworks carefully orchestrated by Sanjay. The ceremony could not have been simpler. That is how Indira wanted it, without the fuss of having to kowtow to the orthodox Hindus, who called for a complete religious ceremony. When she got married, Nehru had asked her to agree to do it according to the Hindu rite, walking seven times round the sacred fire and listening to interminable mantras, because hedid not want to make enemies out of them. She had agreed, but now she was taking her revenge. Indira was tougher than her father. In fact she had not wept during the ceremony of her own wedding. Nehru had; his eyes had become damp.

9

In the afternoon Sonia had moved all her things from the house where she had been staying to her new home. The building work done had extended the main sitting room, which Indira had furnished in pastel pink tones and moss green; a sliding door gave on to an area with enormous trees and bushes amongst which fluttered birds and butterflies.

After the celebration, she went into her new quarters, a large, comfortable room that had been added at the back of the house and which still smelled of damp plaster. Her mother had brought her clothes from Italy, a few books and records and the newspapers from the plane because she wasworried her daughter might feel homesick. Sitting on the bed, Sonia glanced at the headlines. "Wind makes Tower of Pisa shake", "Lucia Bose asks for custody of her children" and an interview with the first man to live two weeks with a heart transplant, a South African called Blaiberg. To her it seemed like news from another planet. News from a world that was no longer hers. As Rajiv removed his flamboyant turban standing in front of the bathroom mirror and several servants came in and out looking at her out of the corner of their eyes, Sonia felt dizzy to think that there was no going back now. The die had been cast. How had she come this far? She was surprised at the strength she had garnered to get what she wanted. She, who had

Javier Moro

always been against confrontation, had had to put pressure on
her family and she would never have believed herself capable of
going to such an extreme. Added to the happiness of having
achieved her goal and the joy of feeling Rajiv's presence so close
to her, there was a deep feeling of surprise and also of sorrow.
Sorrow for her father. Sorrow at not being able to share the
most important time of her life with all those she loved, with
her friends from the neighbourhood, with her old teachers, with
her classmates... Sorrow at having to say goodbye to her
childhood, to her parents, her town and her country. Sorrow for
her mother, because Sonia could guess from looking into her
eyes at all the things that would torment her, from the "exotic"
customs to the fact that she was living like that, in the family
home, with her mother-in-law just down the corridor, however
much she was Prime Minister. By having forced the situation,
the harmony of the Maino family had been destroyed, and
Sonia felt she was to blame. But life had put her in that
position, and since the moment she had clung to Rajiv's hand
in response to his shy advances, back there in the gardens of
the cathedral at Ely, she was consistent with herself. No one
was surprised at her state of melancholy because Indian
tradition sees the departure of a daughter from her father's
house for the home of her husband's family as a moment of
great anguish. Most Indian brides cry and their friends and
relations become very sad. Sonia was not going to cry, but her
heart was full of grief, although events were moving ahead too
quickly for her to feel sorry for herself.

The next day in the afternoon there was a reception at
Hyderabad House, an Anglo-Mogul-style palace which the
Nizam of Hyderabad had had built in 1928 as a gift for one
of his mistresses, and which now, under the control of the

government, was used as a residence for foreign dignitaries.
Great media events or press conferences were also organized
there. Around a thousand people turned up – family friends,
party colleagues, politicians, diplomats, journalists, artists, etc. –
all of them presenting the gilt-edged invitation they had
received from the Prime Minister's office and anxious to see the
foreign bride close up so they could judge for themselves
whether everything they had heard was true, since it was all so
inconsistent and so twisted by gossip. Dressed in another
magnificent sari, Sonia felt like an animal in the zoo. It seemed
to her as though the women were piercing her with their eyes,
trying to find out what she was made of. Most of them had
travelled abroad and were aware of how different India was
from Europe. Some of them looked at her with pity, others with
envy, yet others with genuine sympathy. The time came for
dinner, served on the floor, Kashmir-style. To the sound of a
small orchestra of classical Indian music, the guests enjoyed
succulent typical dishes with the aroma of cinnamon,
cardamom, saffron and cloves: lamb with turnips, chicken with
spinach, fish with lotus root... There were also potatoes in
yoghurt sauce or fried soft cheese for the vegetarians. The
members of Sonia's family were able to have Italian food, and
Rajiv's uncles and aunts, Parsee food. The delicious green tea
from Kashmir, *Kavha*, was served at the end. But it was not an
ostentatious reception. "The budget was small," Usha, Indira's
secretary, would confess.

Neither was there the money or time for a proper
honeymoon. But Rajiv wanted to show Sonia's relations a
little of India, so they all went off to Rajasthan, romantic
India, the land of the old feudal lords, the most spectacular
region in the sub-continent. It seemed incredible to them

that mediaeval villages could exist so close to a city like Delhi, with no light or running water, but dazzlingly beautiful, where all the trades in India rubbed shoulders in the market square: vendors of second-hand clothes, street dentists, peasants squatting next to their vegetable stalls, tailors, blacksmiths, carpenters, jewellers... Goats, cows and camels swarmed among the mounds of essences of all colours – ochre saffron powder, yellow turmeric powder, ground red chilli peppers - . On the way to the Ranthambore national park, they saw blots of yellow, red, purple and pink in the fields, which were the turbans of the farmers and shepherds walking in the ochre-coloured dust kicked up by their flocks. Their wives were dressed in the same hues: they wore jewels of old silver and semi-precious stones and looked like princesses instead of peasant women.

Ranthambore was a natural park created in 1955 in a semi-jungle area to ensure the survival of the tiger. An immense fort, which held ruined temples, palaces and cenotaphs imprisoned by the roots of gigantic banyan trees, dominated the park from the top of a promontory. Below, among the hills covered in vegetation and lagoons of silvery waters, you could see deer, antelopes, bears, jackals and wild boar. And if you were lucky, the occasional tiger at dawn. Rajiv liked this place because it brought together two passions of his: his love of animals and his fondness for photography. Besides, he thought that his wife's family would take away wonderful memories of India because in the jungle you could not see the humanmisery. Rajiv told them that he and his brother had been brought up surrounded by animals, enjoying a real zoo in the gardens of Teen Murti House. Many of those animals were gifts that heads of state or Indian politicians had made to his grandfather. They had had parrots, doves, squirrels, a crocodile and a panda from the

Himalayas called Bhimsa, a present from the state of Assam for his grandfather. They had also had three tiger cubs. Rajiv adored them and one of his big upsets as a child was when his grandfather decided to get rid of one and give it to Marshal Tito.

On the way back to Delhi they stopped in a village where a wedding was being celebrated. It was a real Hindu wedding, full of colour and noise. The groom, with his face hidden by a little curtain of flowers, appeared riding on a skinny white mare covered in a velvet rug embroidered with gold. To the sound of drums and tambourines, he pranced towards his bride, who was waiting for him under a canopy. The families were proud that some strangers were attending the ceremony and immediately brought them tea and sweets, while the young man dismounted. Then the priest invited the bride and groom to meet each other officially. Slowly and shyly each of them pushed aside the other's veil with their free hand. The boy's happy face appeared in front of the shy gaze of the bride, a girl who could not have been older than twelve, as fragile and frightened as a little bird. Her family watched her with ill-contained emotion. Rajiv acted as interpreter, not only for the language, but also for the customs. That simple wedding, which seemed so innocent and inoffensive, hid several of India's evils, real social scourges. Child marriages like this one risked girls becoming mothers, with the subsequent rate of mortality and health problems for mother and child. Furthermore, the bride's parents, who looked like peasants, had probably got into debt for many years in order to pay the dowry, an indispensable requirement for marrying off a daughter. Yes, that was all very pretty and picturesque, but those customs kept the poor trapped in the mire of poverty. It was there that Sonia first heard of the custom of *suttee*, which was still practised sporadically in this region. The guests commented on a recent case, not very far from where they were, which had been a national scandal. A young widow had hurled herself on to her husband's funeral pyre. The police had investigated the case without managing to find out the truth. The opinions of the guests at the wedding were very divided: some said that the widow was a saint for having had the courage to become *suttee*, others said that she had been drugged and forced to leap into the blaze so that she would not inherit any of her husband's goods... Rajiv inclined towards the latter version. How could you get this country to modernize? he seemed to be asking himself, thinking about the enormous task that had fallen to his mother, as he drove the car back to Delhi.

Then it was time for Sonia to say goodbye to her family. She went to the airport with them. After embracing her mother Sonia broke down and burst into sobs, perhaps because she guessed the sorrow she was feeling at leaving her daughter. For her mother, that was the real farewell: some were going back home, to their real home; Sonia was remaining in that strange land, alone and without them. Never more than at that moment had reality appeared so crudely, so much so that it hurt. Both of them were in floods of tears, and they did not normally cry much, which made the scene even more heart-breaking.

"Write to me a lot, call me often..." "I promise, *mamma*."

In the car that was taking her back home, Sonia dried her face as flashes of happy moments from her childhood in Lusiana came to mind. She remembered going out to milk the cows with her father and mother, or when friends and cousins came to celebrate their birthdays with lots of presents. How far away that life seemed! By staying in India, she realized now thatshe was starting from zero. All that tension and all that hustle and bustle had left her feeling exhausted and depressed. She needed to see Rajiv as soon as possible. Only he could comfort her because he was the justification for all her anxiety.

But Rajiv was not at home, he was at his classes, at the flying club. Sonia went to her room. If her husband was not there, then she preferred to be on her own, to lie on the bed and weep all those tears, and try to cast off the melancholy while she waited for him to come back. But as soon as she opened the door, she saw an envelope on the bed, with the heading of the Prime Minister's office on it. She opened it. It was a note from Indira which said, "Sonia, we all love you very much." Then her face lit up. Her melancholy evaporated like magic, she smiled and went out of the bedroom.

10

Everyday life in the Gandhi household began early, almost at dawn. When Sonia woke up, Indira was already at the end of the garden at her daily conversations, surrounded by the poor who came to have her darshan. Then she got into her official car which took her to her office in South Block, where she spent the whole morning. In the afternoons she usually went to work in her personal office, which acted as the Congress headquarters, and was very close to her house, at number 1, Akbar Road, only about fifty yards away. It was a pleasant walk through the garden, always green and with flowerbeds full of flowers and sweet-smelling plants. The government had just given this house over to her so that they could all fit into hers.

Rajiv too usually left early for his flying lessons. He passed the commercial pilot's exam with no difficulty and was now doing practice flights for the national airline, Indian Airlines. He was flying a DC-3, the famous Dakota, the plane of his childhood dreams. His brother Sanjay was absorbed in the task of designing an Indian car, adapted to the roads of India. Each member of the family led a separate existence, but Sonia spent a lot of time alone. A time that allowed her to observe the hustle and bustle of a large Indian house and get used to the heat, which soon came. A dry heat, intense and scorching, which rose inevitably day by day, and would go on rising until the rains in June, that is if they arrived on time this year. She did not like the air-conditioning because she was worried it would bring on an attack of asthma; she preferred to stand under the blades of the ventilators that hung from the ceiling. She understood why the domestic staff moved so slowly. At first she thought they were just lazy; now she understood that the heat, similar to the *ferragosto* in Italy, except they were in March, debilitated your muscles and weakened your willpower. There were not many domestic servants for a house like this. Normally there would have been a minimum of ten or fifteen, each in charge of a task specific to their caste. Although Nehru and Gandhi had officially banned castes in the Constitution of the new independent nation, the reality is that they still influenced people's behaviour, especially in the lower levels of society and in rural areas. In none of the Nehru homes had they been able to fight that hierarchical structuring of domestic life, however much they had tried. It was no easy thing to wipe out thousands of years of history at one stroke. So the tradition continued, and the person that served the table was not the same as the one who cleared it; the chauffeur drove the car but did not wash it; the cook cooked, but did not wash the dishes; the ones who swept the floor did not clean the bathrooms, etc. The Nehrus managed with fewer servants than usual, but even so Sonia was not used to their eternal presence, as they slipped noiselessly along the corridors, and gave her terrible frights. Perhaps what bothered her most is that she seemed never to be out of view of indiscreet eyes, even in the privacy of her own quarters. More than once, after locking herself in her bathroom, she had jumped when she discovered the man in charge of cleaning, a bony, very dark-skinned figure, squatting with a rag in his hand, trapped in the corner. Little by little she learned what the wives of diplomats living in India had to learn - to live alongside that swarm of people, to know how to control them, to have patience with the sweepers, who only moved the dust from one place to another, to address each of them according to his rank or his religion so that at no time do they feel they "lose caste", to take them to the doctor if they fall ill because there is no social security, etc.

Not even the house of the Prime Minister escaped the bustle of everyday life in Indian cities. At mid-morning, Sonia would hear the picturesque street vendors calling out their wares from the street in sing-song voices. Some of them pushed little carts overflowing with fruit and vegetables; others carried boxes full of sweets; others brought milk, or the newspapers... From time to time a man with a dancing monkey and some bears called from outside, offering his show. Cloth vendors also came with their bundles of tablecloths and placemats, hand woven, plain or patterned, made of the finest cotton or raw silk, multicoloured or white. The tailor sat on the veranda sewing all morning, while Sonia looked in fascination at the bracelets of polished glass that a street vendor was offering her and whom the servants had allowed in thinking it would amuse her. The doors and windows that were open to the garden allowed in the perfumes of the flowers and the smell of the freshly cut, damp grass that went yellow as the days went by.

Sonia often appeared in the office where her mother-in-law's two private secretaries were working. One of them, Usha, would remember that she used to come to see her to ask her about all kinds of Indian things. How do you adjust a sari? How are birthdays celebrated? What present do you take to the party for a baby's first haircut? How do you say "shut the door" in Hindi? etc. They teased her saying that she did not have only one mother-in-law, but three. She hardly saw the real one because she was so busy, although her presence was always felt. She was the central person in the family. One day Sonia went into Usha's office very upset. She was holding a note that Indira had left her expressing her point of view about certain things, mostly critically, such as the fact that Sonia refused to learn Hindi or was so shy with people she did not know. "Why doesn't she tell me in person instead of writing me a note?" asked the Italian girl on the verge of tears.

"Mrs Gandhi finds it hard to express herself," Usha answered, "she's a rather introverted lady. But don't worry about the letters, she also used to communicate like that with her husband and her father."

Sonia's shyness and perhaps a certain complex began to hold her back so much that it became a problem when it came to dealing with important visits, or simply socializing. Apart from her husband's friends and those of her brother-in-law, with whom she was on very friendly terms, it was difficult for her to break the ice and open up to people. Inside she was still a little peasant girl from the Asiago mountains, the provincial Italian student transplanted on to another planet, the home of a Prime Minister, where people of all classes and conditions came and went. "For a long time, Sonia was very timid," Usha would say. "It was a complicated task to persuade her to do something." In spite of how busy she was, Indira never lost sight of what was happening in the house and tried hard to get her daughter-in-law to come out of her shell. "It would be wonderful if you could convince Sonia to come tonight. But don't force her if she really doesn't want to," she said in one note to her secretary. Both Rajiv and his mother were rather reserved by nature, so they understood that Sonia might need to take her time to get used to this new life. They tried to put as less pressure on her as possible, because they could see she was having difficulty adapting. Here she could not do simple things, like going out with a girlfriend for a walk, for example. The wide avenues of New Delhi were not made for walking: the distances were too great to be covered on foot. Besides, that part of the city was purely residential, and there were no shops or businesses. The restriction on her movements, the food, the heat, and the distance from her family caused attacks of homesickness that the magazine *Oggi,* sent punctually by her mother every week, could barely manage to alleviate. She was between two worlds, but not standing firmly in either of them. She remembered her father, and his warnings, and there were times when she would have liked to pick up the phone and talk to him, but Sonia was strong and knew she had to put up with it. Rajiv's presence, in the evenings, calmed her anxieties.

In May it was so hot that, thinking that it would do her good to have a change of air, Indira invited Sonia to go with her on an official visit to the kingdom of Bhutan, a small country in the foothills of the Himalayas which was totally isolated from the world. To accompany her, she also invited the daughter of the Foreign Minister, Priti Kaul, who was the same age as Sonia. It was only a two-day trip, but they had great fun. As soon as they got off the helicopter, they were greeted by King Dorje Wangchuk, a very affable man and a devout Buddhist. He was an absolute monarch who kept his kingdom closed to the outside world. The temperature was perfect; it made you feel like drinking in the crystal-clear air. What a relief! thought the Italian girl when she felt the cool breeze from the mountains caressing her face, just like when she went on a trip to the Alps. Here there were no ski-lifts or restaurants, just prayer flags that floated in the wind, sending out Buddhist prayers towards the chain of the Himalayas, which showed its steely peaks against an intensely blue sky. There was nothing here that could be considered "modern". There was practically no road traffic except for a few motorbikes, and the people wore the traditional clothes with a kind of coloured apron that looked very picturesque. They were on horseback or in carts pulled by oxen similar to yaks. The retinue came to the imposing monastery of Tashichhodzong, which dominated a bright landscape of white-crested mountains on whose slopes there were golden terraces of barley that came down towards the valley like a gigantic stairway. It waslike a journey into the Middle Ages: there was no television, there was no jail or delinquency and the only concession to modern times was electricity, but only for two hours a day. The king accompanied them to their rooms himself. They had three rooms and a bathroom, all quite modest, and he explained that they were his own rooms. At that time there was no hotel infrastructure in Thimpu, the capital, which seemed more like a small town, so he gave his guests the best he had. After the banquet, at which Indira and the monarch talked about how to democratize the kingdom and at the same time preserve it from the negative influences of modern times, the girls went back to their room. Sonia discovered a trapdoor in the floor, under a carpet. Dying with curiosity, the two of them lifted it and saw a simple room with a narrow bed, similar to a monk's cell. Suddenly a torch shone and they saw the king, scantily dressed, getting ready for bed. They shut the trapdoor feeling really embarrassed. They told Usha, who in turn told Indira, fearful that the incident might lead to a diplomatic conflict. Indira just laughed.

The next day they flew by helicopter from Thimpu to the state of Sikkim, on the frontier with Tibet. They were welcomed by the local king and his wife, a delightful New Yorker called Hope Cooke, in their palace. At night, when Indira had already gone to bed, the American woman came to the girls' room with the delicacy that Sonia liked the most: smoked salmon. It reminded her of her time in England, where she had discovered it.

It was a short parenthesis of coolness in the middle of the extreme heat that was scorching the north of India. When they came back to Delhi, down on the plains, the thermometer marked 43° at eleven in the morning. The asphalt was melting. The trees looked as tired as the people who walked along with their umbrellas open to protect themselves from the sun. The rickshaw men waited for clients lying in any patch of shade they could find. At home the flowers in the garden had withered and the lawn was like dry straw. The servants sprayed water on the front of the house. Sonia had to learn to limit her movements to the minimum in order to save her energy. The temperature at night became so intolerable that she had to give way and have the air conditioning on. They advised her not to go out at midday because the sun was too fierce. This heat was nothing like the *ferragosto*. The air was so thick you could cut it with a knife, and the temperature went up to 46 degrees a few days later. It was a cruel and pitiless climate. Sonia waited anxiously for Rajiv to return, lying on her bed and dreaming about the bucolic countryside of the Veneto, remembering the squeaking of her Wellington boots in the freshly fallen snow, the icy water she drank directly from the streams, the smell of the countryside after the rain, the green meadows dotted with poppies in spring ... But then her husband was there and they waited for evening to come in order to go out for a ride on the scooter and have an ice cream in one of the few places that served them in hygienic conditions. You had to be careful what you ate outside the house, because the heat affected the conservation of food.

The tension at home increased in proportion to the heat, not because of how uncomfortable it became, but because of the political repercussions. After all, that was the house of the Prime Minister, and her work and her future depended largely, that year, on whether or not the monsoon rains came on time. Indira's greatest concern was to continue the fight against hunger. She was clear that the shortage of food could be fought by introducing new methods of agriculture which had proved their efficiency in other parts of the world, and by encouraging the building of fertilizer factories. To achieve a real green revolution, to make India become self- sufficient, that was her main priority and she worked on it unstintingly. Everything else - and there was a lot more - could come later: health, education, improving the status of women, etc.

The problem is that her ambitious programme needed time to produce results. Meanwhile, people had to eat. And it was such bad luck that India had suffered three consecutive years of drought. If the rains did not come that fourth year either, it would be disastrous. Added to that was the fiasco of American aid. In spite of all the indications, President Johnson had wanted to use the food aid as an instrument to make India fit in with his policies. Although Indira was prepared to make some concessions (facing a storm of protests at home), she never had any intention of abandoning her father's non-alignment policy. In reprisal for a criticism that the Indian Foreign Minister made of Israel for its attitude towards the Arab countries, Johnson began to delay the shipments of foodstuffs. He asked for the reports on the grain shipments to pass through his office before the final go-ahead. Indira had a map of India on the wall in her office in South Block, where she tracked the movements of each shipment of food. The slowness was exasperating.

"These Americans don't understand that every day that goes

by means the death of many people!" she said at home in indignation, one day when Sonia had prepared a dish of pasta. "Don't take this wrong, it's nothing personal," she went on to say to Sonia, pushing aside her plate, "but I have decided - and I have just announced this in Parliament - that I am going to stop eating wheat and rice in protest."

The session in Parliament had left her exhausted and she hardly had any dinner. She complained of having a bad migraine. None of the doctor's prescriptions had managed to get rid of the persistent headaches that she had been suffering for several days. India's problems were the cause.

"If the rains don't come, there'll be another famine."

"I'm going to make a home remedy for you, which my parents taught me as a cure for headaches."

Sonia made an infusion of camomile and dipped some gauze in it and applied it to her mother-in-law's forehead. Indira continued talking. She wasworried that another drought would show her agrarian policy in a bad light and it was the pillar of her government's action, which had begun to show such promising signs. "She began to calm down and feel better," Sonia would remember, not understanding the nuances or details of the hugeproblems her mother-in-law was facing, but clearly aware of their importance and scope. Suddenly, Indira changed the subject.

"How are you getting on with your Hindi?" she asked unexpectedly."Badly," answered Sonia.

Indira wanted Sonia to learn Hindi at all costs. Apart from political reasons, because the Nehrus had always been accused of being too "British" or "Western", Indira thought it would be a genuinely good thing if her daughter-in-law could express herself in the language of the people becauseit would open up contacts to her and also the gateway to deepest India. Was language not the soul of a culture? But Sonia did not understand why shehad to learn a language only spoken by the servants, as English was what their friends and guests always used. They had given her a private teacher who had been determined to teach her the language from an academic point of view, with lots of grammar.

"The classes are really boring," Sonia told her, glad to have succeededin relieving her pain.

Indira did not insist, but a few days later she left a note for Usha, her secretary: "It looks as though Sonia's progress is non-existent. The teacher'smethod is not working. The more Hindi conversation you practice with her, the better, please."

Certain habits in that house would have been difficult to understand for anyone. For example, they had always spoken Hindi at lunchtime and English at dinnertime in the Nehru household, and every day one of the meals was Indian and the other Western. Sonia did not understand why each person could not eat whatever they wanted and speak the language they wanted. But as she was tractable, she did not dig her heels in. And she was intelligent enough to know that she had to find her place in that family even if she had to bow to demands that she did not really understand. She accepted that that was part of her process of adaptation.

June seemed to go on forever. It was as if the whole city was looking up at the sky seeking signs of rain. The front page of the newspapers showedthe record temperatures in large, black lettering: 46 degrees at India Gate on Rajpath it predicted on 15th when the monsoon should already have arrived. A photo showed groups of children bathing in the public fountains. The burning, parched air dried out your throat. Your eyes stung as though they had grains of sand in them. A layer of grey dust, which the wind had brought from the deserts in Rajasthan, covered the garden at number 1, Safdarjung Road. For Sonia, it was something new to experience how extreme the climate was. In Europe the climate was very regular, and forecasts were used especially to know whether or not there would be snow in the mountains or sun at the beach the following weekend. Here the climate was much more dramatic because of its intensity and its importance for the life of the country, which was eminently agricultural. The failure of the rice crop could mean death for a million peasants. For that reason these crucial days in the life of India were paid so much attention by the people and by the media.

Finally, at the end of the month, a deafening crash followed by a whirlwind of scorching air, which lifted up clouds of dust and ripped the leaves off the trees, announced the first storms. As though night had suddenly fallen, thick black clouds covered the sky and the dry wind gave way to heavy drops of rain which hammered down on the roof of the house. The domestic staff seemed to revive after so much drowsiness. They went outside and got soaking wet and smiles lit up their faces again. It looked as though the tall palm trees at the roundabout also quivered with emotion. The television showed pictures of the euphoria which was taking over the country. People of different religions and castes leaped and danced together in the streets like children, splashing in the water, taking showers under the gutters from the rooftops. It was like a big party where the monsoon had made the differences between men vanish.

But the intensity of the heat was followed now by the intensity of the downpours. The water fell with such force that, inside the house, the noise was deafening. The temperature suddenly dropped a few degrees, and a gentle breeze brought a touch of coolness. In the garden, the frogs went croaking across the grass that regained its greenness as though by magic, buttwo days later the garden was so flooded that it looked like a lake. If many slum areas literally disappeared with the rains only to be rebuilt later, the districts of New Delhi were not immune to the consequences of the downpour. The elegant roundabouts of the embassies' neighbourhood were flooded, as well as the tunnels, and many vehicles were stuck like dead things, taxis, rickshaws with their engines flooded giving their dying belchesunmindful of the efforts of their owners to get them going again. Although the heat became less intense, the feeling of sultriness was unpleasant. Sonia had the impression that her hands were always damp; she changed herclothes several times a day because they were soaked in sweat. She was astonished that it did not stop raining for days, as if the gods of the climate were taking revenge for the burning, dry heat of the previous months. Now she understood why the facades of so many buildings seemed dirty and stained, why there were so many potholes, and the answer was that the climate washed everything away and made any maintenance work too expensive for such a poor country.

The positive part is that the rains brought the joy outside into the house, as though the happiness of a whole, gigantic country slipped in through the windows and invaded every corner. A country which, by not dying of hunger this year, might perhaps keep going and not face those terrible famines of the past again. Very in touch with the feeling of the people, Indira seemed infected with that joy. In spite of so many otherproblems, she was a radiant woman once again.

11

Perhaps because she did not see Sonia's shy behaviour as a threat, in a surprisingly short period of time Indira, who was of a rather suspicious nature, came to be really fond of her daughter-in-law. She was a discreet, direct person, two qualities which had won her immediate sympathy. But she was also home-loving and she liked to lead a family-oriented life. She did not push Rajiv to live with her as a couple apart from everyone else, as might have been thought at first. On the contrary, she insisted that they should go on respecting the age-old traditions, such as having meals together, a custom that went back to the times of Teen Murti House. Independently of where each member of the family was, they all tried hard to get home to have their meals together, unless there was some official act or other. Since the time they were children, Rajiv and Sanjay had got used to leaving whatever they were doing in order to have lunch with the rest of the family. Sonia thought this was a very good idea because conversations at table were always very lively, except when Sanjay started talking politics with his mother. The usual thing was an exchange of points of view, jokes and personal experiences. If Rajiv and Sonia were going out at night with their friends, they waited for Indira to finish having dinner and kept her company. Indira had a great talent for conversation; she was quick in her observations, clear in her descriptions and she had a sharp sense of humour. Her interests were not limited to politics, but also the arts, advances in science, people's behaviour, books, nature... There were surprising things within her, which were only revealed with time. For example, she was able to recognize a bird from its song, as in the fifties she had been a member of an ornithological society and had learned a lot about birds. She could also tell many tales about her trips abroad. In Santiago de Chile the wife of a politician greeted her by saying, "Ooh, how slender and delicate you look. I was expecting to see a kind of Golda Meir..." Sonia used to burst out laughing at those stories. Like the one in the Kremlin, after a banquet which Brezhnev and Kosigin gave in her honour, at coffee-time when the Russian custom of separating men and women was observed, to her great surprise, Indira found herself in the men's group... Or when Indira went to see Gandhi to talk to him about her marriage with Firoz, and, instead of encouraging her to have a family, the old holy man suggested that she and Firoz should become adepts at his ideal of marriage and stay celibate after they were married. Then why get married? Indira had snapped at him, annoyed. Sonia, who laughed easily, was enchanted by all these anecdotes.

When the Italian girl had understood the basic workings of an Indian home, she began to replace Usha in domestic matters. Feeling useful and being occupied was the best weapon against homesickness. "Sonia was an organized type of person and she was strong, although she kept a low profile, but she knew what she wanted," Indira's secretary would say. The Italian girl behaved as she really was: affectionate, always wanting to please, turning her back on confrontation, even a little submissive in the face of the tremendous sense of authority coming from her mother-in-law. "I understood that I had to give my mother-in-law some time to get used to the new situation in the family too, although she was not especially possessive about Rajiv. In those days, I was always with her, ready to support her," she stated in an interview published in the *Weekend Telegraph* years later.

In that house with its Indian but also Kashmiri and English customs, Sonia made her contribution in a subtle way. And she did it with a powerful tool, which she handled decisively. Sonia had learned the secrets of Italian cooking from her mother, and soon the Prime Minister's house was redolent with the aroma of *lasagna al forno*, with *pesto* sauce with basil picked fresh from the garden, and even with *ossobuco*, Milanese style. In those years it was impossible to get hold of cheese in New Delhi, but there was always a friend coming from Europe who would bring her vacuum-packed mozzarella or grated gruyère. There was often some joker who said that instead of Indianizing Sonia, she was Italianizing the family... The joke was repeated inside the house only, because if a comment like that reached the Press, they knew that the opposition would use it viciously. The truth is that in the Gandhi-Nehru home there was room for everything, just like India itself, the melting-pot of cultures and traditions, always ready to take in foreign things and make them its own. If Sonia adapted to the existing culture, she also fought her own, silent battle to leave her mark, pan in hand, in that cosmopolitan house.

Later, she began to learn to recognize Indira's tastes and preferences, such as her fondness for flowers, for example, and she always made sure there were splendid bouquets on the tables. They both especially liked the smell of lilies, a balm that invaded every corner of that house decorated with almost spartan simplicity, but with taste. The curtains were of raw cotton, the carpets came from several places in the north; there were tribal objects, paintings by Indian artists, some antiques such as a beautiful screen, and Colonial English-style pieces of furniture. Sonia understood that simplicity and economy were the keys to her mother-in-law's personality. Indira did not like to throw anything away; quite the opposite, and she kept plastic bags folded up carefully so they could be used again. Sonia learned to pack suitcases the way Indira liked, using the tiniest space, without wasting an inch. If Indira needed anything for the house, Sonia took charge of obtaining it. The sales assistant in The Shoppe in Connaught Place would remember that she saw her come in one day, dressed in leather trousers and with her lovely long hair falling on to her shoulders. She had come to buy a cotton tablecloth as a present for her mother-in-law on her birthday. The only thing that Sonia did not share with Indira was the intricacies of Indian politics, which were of no interest to her and which she made no attempt to understand.

But in that kitchen which Sonia turned into the nerve centre of the home, where everyone came even if only to ask what surprise she had in store for them to eat, they inevitably talked about everything.

"The family of the Maharaja of Jaipur have stopped talking to us," Sanjay came home saying scornfully one day. "The Kotas and Travancores too. Don't expect them to invite us to any of their parties."

In this way Sonia found out that her mother-in-law had abolished the last privileges of the maharajas. Rajiv told her that when their states joined the Indian Union, the maharajas received the constitutional guarantee that they would be able to keep their titles, their jewels and their palaces; that the

State would pay them an annual sum in proportion to the size of their kingdoms; and that they would be exempt from paying tax and import duties.

"But with so many Indians and so many of them poor, my mother and her government think that those privileges are anachronistic and out of place," he told her. "The fact is that the maharajas are out for her blood. The Maharani of Jaipur, who is the local leader of a party on the Right, has given instructions to her followers to break up one of Mother's rallies. But she has confronted them. Do you know what she said? 'Go and ask the maharajas how many wells they dug for the people when they governed their states, how many roads they built, what they did to fight the slavery we suffered under the English!' The result is that Mother has ended up winning acrossthe board, as usual."

Indira had done it because she had had to veer to the left in her policies on seeing that the Americans had left her in the lurch. In order not to go on losing support within her party, she had signed a treaty with the Soviet Union calling for an unconditional end to the American bombing of Vietnam. Furious, Johnson had delayed the shipments of food even more. The poor were dying of hunger, not suspecting that they were the price their country was paying in order to keep its independence against the strongest power in the world which wanted to use them as pawns. The maharajas had not been the only victims of that change of policy. Indira's programme made the most liberal shudder, the industry bosses, the businessmen, the aristocrats and definitely the elite of the country because she also announced the nationalization of banking and insurance companies. Sonia witnessed the euphoria of the common people at these measures. Shop assistants and civil servants, taxi drivers and rickshaw men, the unemployed and those that had never been inside a bank danced in the street outside the house. These were daring, popular measures which brought Indira huge political success because the government was taking away financial resources from the capitalists and giving them to the people. The peasants, the small businessmen and dealers were also happy because they were going to benefit from credit under better conditions in the nationalized banks, and all the parties of the Left stood firmly alongside Indira.

*   *   *

During the early months of 1969, Sonia began to feel ill. At first she attributed it to food poisoning or some local virus, but the doctor quickly put her right. She was pregnant. The news filled the family with joy. Indira felt very happy and redoubled her care for her daughter-in-law. She was euphoric at the idea of being a grandmother. Children had always been a weakness of hers. Now she left notes like: "Tomorrow is *navroz* (Parsee New Year), but I'm going away early in the morning. Can I give you a kiss now?" Indira was deeply grateful for the stability that Sonia was bringing into her life. She no longer came back from her exhausting tours or from long sessions in Parliament to the solitude of an empty house, but to a home full of life. And that happiness was increased by this news that, more than any other news, was the reason for deep, personal satisfaction in Indira. Her new agricultural policy was beginning to bring results. The grain harvest for the current year was double the usual thanks to the abundant rains of the last monsoons. The greatest production was recorded in the Punjab states, in the north,

155

the land of the Sikhs, a well-organized, hardworking community whose peasants had planted new varieties of dwarf wheat developed by Indian scientists from Mexican stock. The new varieties of rice, cotton and peanuts had also shown spectacular results. The increase in production was so promising that it augured that the endemic shortages could soon become a thing of the past. How happy Indira would be to get the thorn of Lyndon Johnson out of her side...

However, Sonia did not join in that euphoria. Her happiness was tainted by a new feeling, which she had never experienced before, and which rose up out of the depths of her being. It was a vague, yet intense, atavistic fear. Fear of giving birth so far away from her family, fear of catching a strange illness, a tropical infection, fear that the child might be born with some problem... She once again felt homesickness and even thought about going back to Italy to have the baby, but no, that was impossible because how could she be far away from Rajiv at a moment like that? What would the politicians here say? That Indira's daughter-in-law did not trust Indian medicine (which was perfectly logical at the time)? That what was good for the people was not good enough for Indira's *bahu*? Whether she wanted it or not, politics was interfering in her private life. But Sonia was sufficiently clear-thinking to accept it and to understand that the hormonal changes in her body were upsetting her, and that her state of mind would improve with time.

* * *

But five months into the pregnancy she was still feeling constantly sick. Her morale was also affected. Sanjay paid lots of attention to his sister-in-law. When he knew his brother was flying, he did not leave the house without checking to see if Sonia wanted to accompany him for a drive, to have an ice cream at Nirula's, one of the few establishments similar to a Western café, or to visit a friend. But Sonia did not feel like going out. She preferred to stay at home, spending hours stroking the dogs *Putli* and *Pepita*, two Golden Retrievers, favourites of Nehru's from the times in Anand Bhawar, and a mongrel called *Sona* that Rajiv brought home from an alley in old Delhi when he was a boy. When her husband came home again, they spent hours listening to music. At home Rajiv was making a large collection of records that he had put together over the years and which he treated with great care. He did not want anyone to touch the equipment or records without first checking that it would be done as scrupulously as if he did it himself. From time to time they attended concerts of classical Indian music, where Sonia learned about *ragas* (a classical melody) and *ghazals* (poems sung in Urdu) and to distinguish instruments such as the *sarangi* or the *tabla*, precursors of the guitars and drums of the West. Very often Rajiv recorded the recitals of great masters like Ustad Ali Khan or Ravi Shankar and then added them to his collection, which he classified methodically. But if they did not usually go out much and they were not very fond of parties, now that Sonia's health was fragile, they went out even less. They had never wanted to become part of the New Delhi jet-set or to belong to any group. Rajiv felt comfortable with friends of very varied social rank, from a mechanic at the flying club to his old classmates at Cambridge who came to Delhi with a certain frequency. Sonia, feeling dizzy and sick, only agreed to go out on Sunday mornings to Khan Market, where the best-stocked record and book shops in the city were. It was a short ride, which the Italian girl took advantage of to buy fruit and also some European products in one of the shops there, frequently visited by diplomats. At five months, the gentle curve of her belly, which she could proudly see reflected in the shop windows, was the object of the gossip of the people she met that knew her, because in a way New Delhi was like a big village.

Five months is a length of time after which it is considered that a pregnancy has passed its most critical period. In Sonia's case, it was not like that. In the middle of one hot night, she felt shooting pains in her belly and realized she was losing a lot of blood. The pains were so sharp and there was such a strong feeling that she was emptying from the inside that she thought she was dying. Rajiv organized transport to the hospital in his mother's car. He saw Sonia was so pale and weak that he was scared he was going to lose her. After the transfusion, when she was feeling better, they told Sonia that she had lost a lot of blood, but that now, once she had had a little operation, she was going to feel better. "What about the baby?" she asked, terrified because deep down she knew what had happened. Rajiv's eyes, looking down at the ground, said it all.

It was the hardest moment in Sonia's life. Five months into the pregnancy she did not considered that she had had a miscarriage, but that she had lost her baby. Added to that deep grief was a bitter feeling of personal failure. It seemed to her as if she had failed her husband, Indira, her own family and the whole world. It seemed as though she were paying now for all the happiness that life had given her, as though she had to expiate the sin of her extraordinary love story. The doctors' explanations which assured her that what had happened was relatively common in a first pregnancy and that it did not mean that the same would happen again the next time they tried, did not manage to lift her out of her profound melancholy. Furthermore, there were comments from the domestic staff about such an event being an evil omen, or the rumour on the streets that attributed responsibility for what had happened to Indira "because she forced her daughter-in-law to move and walk, obsessed with the idea that she should keep fit and not get too fat during the pregnancy". In certain areas of gossip in the city, after everything that had happened with the nationalizations and the abolition of the maharajas' privileges, it had become fashionable to call Indira a monster. As was to be expected, the family reacted as one and everyone surrounded Sonia with attention and affection. Indira was very upset. This had reminded her of a similar event, when her second son was born on December 14th, 1946. The birth pains had begun at night, totally unexpectedly. She was taken to hospital as an emergency where the English doctors came to fear for her life because she was bleeding to death. Right from the start that baby had been a problem. Nehru arrived when the bleeding was finally under control. A baby boy was born in the early hours, which Nehru named Sanjay, as a tribute to a visionary priest who describes the great battle against the blind king in the *Mahabharata*, the great epic of Hinduism. Firoz, her husband, did not come until a few days later. He was working in the city of Lucknow, and Indira had just found out that he was having a love affair with a Moslem woman, the daughter of a prominent family in the city. Therefore, the arrival of the baby had not been as happy an event as that of their first child, Rajiv. And Indira, subconsciously, blamed herself for it. She must have thought it was unfair and that she had to make up for it. All her life she felt she owed Sanjay something.

159

Little by little, Sonia emerged from the ocean of sadness in which she was submerged, although she never smiled until she became pregnant again, a few months later. This time, her gynaecologist was strict: no walking or effort. The more time she spent lying down, the less risk of another miscarriage there was. Determined this time to complete the pregnancy, Sonia prepared to spend nine months in bed. Her inspiration came from another world-famous Italian, Sofia Loren, who had just gone through the same thing, with a happy ending. It was a tough experience, but Sonia took it as a test that she had to pass. She had the support of Rajiv, who spoiled her and cared for her with great devotion. Fortunately, he was not like Firoz, his father: he was home-loving, affectionate and totally faithful. He was still as in love with Sonia as the first day. Or more, because now a deeper feeling was added, one which is born from togetherness, from looking at everything through the other's eyes, of a life together fully accepted and enjoyed.

Indira was delighted again and took care of the baby's layette with an eye for all the details. "You're always boasting about the joys and 'superior status' of being a grandmother," she wrote to her American friend Dorothy Norman from a plane that was taking her to the south of India to celebrate the fourth centenary of the synagogue of the Jewish community in Kerala, "and that is why I am letting you in on a secret: I am also competing for that status. Sonia is expecting a baby at the end of May. Isn't it exciting? Although when a daughter-in-law is from another continent, there are many complexities too." She was referring to Sonia's fear of giving birth in Delhi, and to the new demands of her daughter-in-law, which arose as a reaction to the pressure around her. Suddenly Sonia declared that she did not want either a wet nurse or a servant to take care of the baby, and that she would do it all herself. To say that was a little naif, a way of affirming herself by making it understood: "I am European and in my private circle I will do things my way." Indira and Rajiv took it like that, and did not insist, convinced that her stubbornness would pass once the baby was born. Reality would ensure that things fell into place. It was going to be very hard for Sonia to do without help bearing in mind that she would have to be available to accompany her husband or Indira on official visits. But, in general, the joy of welcoming a new member of the family compensated for the domestic friction. When Rajiv was working, his mother or his brother tried to take turns to be with Sonia at mealtimes. They did not want her to feel lonely at any time or for her to lose heart. Now Rajiv was flying as co-pilot on Indian Airlines Fokker Friendship turbo-propellers, high-winged aircraft with room for some 40 passengers, worthy successors to the DC-3.

Sonia spent a lot of time with both brothers, who shared friends and interests in common, although Sanjay was to be seen less and less. He was obsessed with his project to build an "Indian Volkswagen". With a friend he had opened a workshop in the outskirts of the city and there, surrounded by rubbish dumps and open sewers, he was chasing his dream of becoming a local "Henry Ford" amid pieces of metal and rusty iron. The project to build a working class car produced for the masses had been under discussion for more than ten years in government offices, and finally the decision was made to hand production over to the private sector. Until then, only two models were made under licence in India: the famous Ambassadors, replicas of the Morris Oxford which served as taxis in post-war London, and which are still made at the Hindustan Motors factory in the state of Bengal, and the Fiat Padmini, which would become the only model of taxi in Bombay (in Europe they were known as the Fiat 1100). The car that Sanjay wanted to make had to be completely Indian, it would be cheap, able to reach the speed of 50 kilometres an hour and would consume only five litres per one hundred kilometres. The name he had chosen was Maruti, an allusion to the son of the wind god in Hindu mythology.

At that time Indira was not looking beyond her own career. She did not imagine a family dynasty, just like her father before her. In numerous interviews she repeated that her sons had no interest in politics and that she would do whatever she could to keep them away from the world of politics. She showed no desire to pass on the family "burden" to them. Indira did not like in the least to mix politics with her private life.

But her son Sanjay, determined at all costs to make a success of his project, was going to cross that line that his mother had so much interest in keeping. Why didn't he have the right to manufacture a genuinely Indian car? he asked himself. It did not seem fair to him that just because he was the son of the Prime Minister, a venture like this should be closed off to him. Indira was in a difficult situation, torn between her feelings as a mother and her duty as the leader of the country. She had asked Sanjay not to present his project to the Ministry of Industrial Development, but he had paid her no attention and had formally asked for the licence, in spite of the fact that he had not even completed his training as a Rolls-Royce apprentice and was not a businessman or a car manufacturer. In fact his love affair with cars had been a constant headache to his mother. As an adolescent, more than once the police had brought him home after having found him with a friend, abandoning cars they had previously stolen from a car park in order to go for a joyride. These spoilt-boy games took on different aspects as he grew up. In England Sanjay had caused several accidents without physical damage, and several times he had been arrested for speeding at the wheel of his old Jaguar or for not having a valid driving licence.

Unlike Rajiv, Sanjay was aggressive in his way of fighting for what he believed in and he exerted considerable pressure on his mother to get the licence granted. Indira presided over the cabinet meeting at which the Industry Minister granted Sanjay a permit to produce fifty thousand cars a year, made entirely out of Indian materials. And that was in spite of the fact that Sanjay had no qualifications and could not present the results of any previous projects. It was clear that if he had not been the son of the Prime Minister, they would never have given it to him. For once, Indira broke her sacrosanct principle of placing duty before personal desire, an exception that would cost her dearly. A scandal and a general protest accompanied the birth of the Indian car project. Indira was accused by the Press of the worst kind of nepotism. An opposition Member of Parliament called the concession "a disgrace to democracy and Socialism." Others spoke of "unlimited corruption". Her own allies, the Bengal Communists, joined in the storm of criticism. Indira replied in an unconvincing manner, "My son has proved he is an entrepreneur... If we do not encourage them, how can we expect other young people to take risks?" In fact Indira believed blindly in her son and probably thought that the Maruti was a golden opportunity for Sanjay to make his way in life and prove his worth. She knew he was young, immature and impetuous, but she believed he was skilful and strong. She thought that he would learn and that he would be able to control it all. She also knew that this meant exposing him to the public eye. In the long term it meant that, in spite of repeating that she did not want her sons to go into politics, Indira already saw her younger son as a worthy successor of the Nehru-Gandhi lineage. It was perhaps a way of feeling a little less lonely in the exercise of power.

In that struggle against the feeling of loneliness that had come over her since her earliest years, the birth of her grandson, on June 19th, 1970, filled her with joy. Just as in all homes all over India, the birth of a son was an extremely important event. Rajiv was present at the birth, which was unheard of in the India of the time, and he did so camera in hand to record the first tears of his son, who had been born a little premature. Sonia was exhausted, but her husband helped her a lot, changing the baby and getting him to sleep between feeds. They behaved like modern parents, although eternal India was already waiting at the gates of the house when they came home from hospital and a holy man was waiting for the baby to draw up his astrological chart. The name chosen was Rahul, suggested by Indira. She explained to Sonia that it was the name she had originally chosen for her first son, although in the end she called him Rajiv to please her father. Nehru had been receiving suggestions for names in prison, and had chosen Rajiv because in Sanskrit it meant "lotus", the same meaning as Kamala, the name of his wife who had died eight years before. In the same way as Indira gave way to her father's wish, Sonia gave way to Indira, and by doing so became a little more Indian. Rahul was the name of a son of Gautama Buddha and in Sanskrit it meant "he who is able". Although the family was not religious, the strength of custom caused the child to be welcomed with the corresponding Hindu rites. The ceremony of the first haircut took place three weeks after the birth, and all the couple's friends gathered at the house. They shaved the baby's head, leaving only one lock of hair which, according to the tradition, would protect his memory. Shaving his head had the symbolic meaning of freeing him from the remains of his past lives and preparing him to face the future.

Indira was absolutely captivated by the baby. She tried to come home between sessions in Parliament just to see him and hold him in her arms. The woman who was grimly pursuing the aristocrats of India, who had just stood up to her party to remain in power, who expelled colleagues who had not voted for her, was a grandmother who melted when she was with her grandson. "How much he looks like Rajiv!" she said, without anyone else being able to find any similarity whatsoever yet. However this was no compliment because she had said thousands of times how ugly Rajiv had been when he was born. But the baby touched a sensitive spot inside her and reminded her of the time of her own motherhood. Indira had given birth to Rajiv on August 20th, 1944, not in a hospital but at the home of her youngest aunt, in Bombay, in difficult conditions. She had become pregnant in spite of her history of tuberculosis, the doctors' warnings and her father's opposition to her marriage, so that birth was seen as a real triumph over adversity. Indira wanted above all that Nehru should know his grandson. It was still three years until independence and he was locked up in a British jail on what would be his ninth and last imprisonment. When she heard that he was going to be moved, Indira turned up at the gates of Naini Prison in Allahabad, and in the short time between the prison gates and the prison van, she held little Rajiv up in her arms. "In the dim light of a lamp post, my father discovered his grandson for the first time, and was looking at him for the short time he was allowed," Indira said.

When Sonia had recovered, they travelled to Italy with the baby. Sonia had often dreamed of this moment during her long convalescence. The smell of delicious coffee as soon as they got to the airport, the silence of the big public areas, the biting cold, the comfort and speed of the cars, the water you could drink from the tap, the supermarkets that sold everything … those simple things she lacked in India seemed marvellous to her. It was as if it was the first time she was in her own country. It was a moment of intense joy to meet her family, in their town. She hugged her father and they did not say anything to each other, it was not necessary. Stefano Maino suddenly found himself with little Rahul in his arms and the only thing that mattered was the baby's wellbeing. Was that moment not worth all the grief of the past? Sonia seemed to ask herself. Finally, she was under the same roof with all those closest to her heart.

12

They soon came back to New Delhi, to get on with their quiet family life, although this was a false calm because it was always under threat from the ups and downs of politics. In spite of how much Indira loved her grandson, she hardly saw him because she was so busy. She spent many hours in her office in South Block, and when she came home she was always tired and worried-looking.

"What's going on?" Rajiv asked as soon as they arrived back. "They say there's going to be a coup," Sanjay answered. "Who says so?"

"Everyone. At parties, at cocktails, at dinners. People are talking about nothing else. Mother knows, and she fears the worst."

Indira had made herself many enemies with her attacks on the wealthy, who accused her of turning India into a Communist country. All of the Right had turned against her, the employers, the owners of the media, the maharajas and their descendents, etc. and, like a large part of the country, she feared a violent reaction. But she did not want to make India into a Communist country like those she had known on her travels behind the Iron Curtain. Quite the opposite: she was making great efforts to reassure the wealthy that their interests were not endangered. She had compensated the great financial families with generous indemnities for the nationalization of their banks. Freedom – individual, collective and national – was a supreme value that she was not prepared to sacrifice on the altar of Socialism.

But the rumour that the military were preparing a coup had spread like wildfire in the big cities, Bombay, Delhi and Calcutta. The idea that India would not be able to survive either as a democracy or as a unified country was taking root among the elite sectors of society. The figures of Nehru and Gandhi were beginning to be seen as relics of an idealist past which no longer had much to do with reality. More and more isolated at the height of power, Indira began to feel paranoid. And she had good reason. General Sam Manekshaw, a Parsee who was Commander-in-Chief of the Indian army, was asked the same question wherever he went: "When are you going to seize power?" He refused to answer. What shocked him most was that among those asking him the question, there were ministers in Indira's cabinet.

Tired of so much rumour, which had even filtered into her own home, Indira called General Manekshaw to her office in South Block. They were old friends; Indira had been married to a Parsee and that always added familiarity to the relationship. Sam found her seated on the other side of her kidney-shaped office desk, with her elbows resting on the table and her head in her hands. After greeting him she said in a tired voice, "Everyone says you're going to replace me... Is that true Sam?"

The soldier was shocked, but reacted after a few seconds: "I took a few steps towards where she was sitting. She had a long nose, and mine was also prominent, so I brought my nose close to hers and asked her, looking her straight in the eye: 'What do you think, Prime Minister?'

'You can't do it,' she answered.

'Do you think I'm so incompetent?'

'No, Sam, I didn't mean that. I mean you won't do it.'

'You're absolutely right, Prime Minister. I do not interfere in matters of politics. My job is to run the army and make sure it's maintained in first class condition. Yours is to run the country.'

'My ministers say a coup is being prepared. Even my sons have heard that.'

'Those ministers, you named them. Get rid of them. You must trust me.'

The general had never seen her so worried and so low as that day. "She had many political enemies," Manekshaw would remember. "They were constantly plotting against her. But she was a clever girl. She came to me and said, 'Sam, if you're thinking of doing anything, just be aware that I know all about it.'

It was a turbulent Christmastime. Although behind closed doors Indiradid what she could to keep her worries to herself, it was impossible to be immune to the tension in the streets. Sanjay was the one who asked her most often what she was going to do, but Indira would answer with one of her famous silences and would pick up little Rahul, as if she sought the answer to complicated matters in that simple gesture. What would her father have done in the same circumstances? she asked herself. In 1951, Nehru had found himself in a similar situation, although not so extreme. And he had decided to ask the people. Indira would do the same. She felt that her government, only dependent on the support of the parties of the Left, would not survive the attacks of the powerful forces that had banded together against her. She had the intuition that if the people were consulted, they would back her.

But this time she would separate the general elections from the state ones. Until then, they had always been held at the same time, with the result that local considerations of caste and ethnic origin became mixed up with larger, national matters. Now she wanted to make sure that they would not be connected. She wanted to present a real national program to the electorate.

On December 27th, 1970, at eight o'clock in the morning, after her daily meeting in the garden, Indira had a cup of tea with Sonia.

"I won't be back for lunch today," she told her. "I'm going to see the President of the Republic and I'm going to ask him to dissolve Parliament. It's going to be a very heavy day. Tell Rajiv that I'll be speaking on the radio tonight."

In effect, that same night she addressed the nation to announce thatthe general elections would be brought forward a year. Sonia heard her from the kitchen at home: "Time will not wait for us," Indira said in a somewhat apocalyptic tone. "The millions of people who are calling for food, housing and work are in a hurry for us to do something. The power in a democracy isheld by the people. Therefore we are calling on the people to ask for a new mandate." A short time after the announcement, a *Newsweek* journalist asked Indira what the central issue of her campaign would be. Without hesitating for a second, Indira said: "I am the issue."

For the next ten weeks, she was hardly at home, and when she was it was just to change her clothes and go back out. Sometimes that happened at one in the morning, and on hearing her, Sonia woke up, ready to help her look for a sari or to make her some tea. She gave her news of the baby, and Indira talked to her about the campaign. She was hopeful: "I like being with people, with ordinary people. I don't feel tired when I'm with them," she said as they both looked back on the day. "You know, Sonia, I don't see them as a mass, I see them as many individuals together..." She was happy because the great alliance that brought together opposing parties – from parties on the Right to Socialists – and who were her adversaries, had committed the mistake of choosing a slogan that reflected their deepest wish: "Let's get rid of Indira".

"I have proposed another slogan: "Let's get rid of poverty!" Don't you think it makes more sense?"

Sonia nodded. Indira went on, in a low voice in order not to wake the baby. "That slogan gives our party the moral high ground and an image of progress against a reactionary front. After all, the poor are the greatest majority of the electorate..."

"They'll see you as their saviour..." "I hope so."

The campaign she carried out in January and February, 1970 was very intense. Having frugal habits – she did not eat or sleep very much – helped her in her efforts. More than thirteen million people attended her rallies and another seven million greeted her at the sides of the roads, according to official statistics. "In the 43 days I had available," she wrote to her friend Dorothy Norman, "I travelled over sixty thousand kilometers and spoke at some three hundred rallies. It was marvellous to see the light in people's eyes." What was even more marvellous was to see that the type of poverty that existed twenty years before was no longer visible, except in certain areas inhabited by untouchables and tribal communities. You no longer saw terrible deformities like you used to, or children with their bellies distended from malnutrition. "Perhaps they don't all have a roof and a job, but the people seem healthy. The children's eyes shine," she told Dorothy.

That was a great source of pride for her, backed by statistics.

In five years, the annual production of wheat and rice had doubled. "For the first time, I do not have the impression that the economy depends exclusively on the success or failure of the monsoons," wrote a British journalist who travelled regularly to India. The Indian media, mostly in the hands of the opposition, did not talk about this, but the people did speak up in the greatestcall to elections to date in the world.

On the night the results came out, the whole family was together at home. Sonia had made sure there were sweets and flowers everywhere. The house was lit up outside, and inside the atmosphere was of contained enthusiasm. As the Electoral Commission gave out numbers and results, the euphoria grew. Two hundred and seventy-five million people had voted in this fifth call to elections since independence. Not a single person had had to walk more than two kilometres to place his vote. Almost two million volunteers had acted as electoral agents. Sixty-six attempts at fraud had been detected, an insignificant number in such a huge country. The tendency of the results was clear: Indira's party was winning in all constituencies. One after another, cars began arriving at the house. A victory like this came accompanied by an unavoidable circle of flatterers. People who did not hesitate to bow down and touch her feet, a traditional way of greeting which the Nehrus had always seen as a sign of servility when the people doing it were wealthy. Her ministers, the same ones as had talked behind her back about a military coup, were the first to arrive and prostrate themselves. Sonialearned then to recognize these toadies with their honeyed words who changed their coats according to the political temperature. That was the time when her obsession was born to identify them and keep them at bay, an obsession that would never leave her. Sincere friends also arrived to congratulate Indira, who came in and out of her study packed full of party colleagues sitting cross-legged on the floor. Another room, near the entrance, was suddenly filled with more people. The telephones rang non- stop. The dogs also joined in the general excitement and slipped in and out of the legs of the visitors, whom Sonia welcomed with little Rahul in her arms. Indira tried to hide her jubilation, but in fact she had achieved a comfortable two thirds majority for her new mandate. A victory that made her the most powerful Prime Minister since independence. The person most venerated, most feared, most loved and in certain spheres, the most hated.

But it was also a victory for India. The elections showed they were a real unifying force in the nation, over and above the differences and diversity. Democracy was confirmed as the new religion in this country so ancient and so peopled with gods, a religion that helped to clear the path towards the future.

*   *   *

Indira did not have much time to savour her triumph. Two weeks after the announcement of her fantastic victory, the Pakistani army launched a fierce attack on the Bengali citizens of East Pakistan. The pictures on television showed a human tide, made up of millions of refugees, mostly women, children and old people. They crossed the border seeking refuge in the Indian province of West Bengal, already very densely populated, and whose capital was Calcutta. Neither Sonia, nor Rajiv, nor Sanjay missed a news broadcast. That flood of refugees reminded them of the tragic events of Partition. They knew that Indira was facing a crisis of enormous proportions. How could a country as poor as India take in so many refugees? they asked themselves anxiously. Would it be necessary to intervene in East Pakistan to stop the flow of people arriving? What will Mother do?

"Is it civil war?" asked Sonia.

They explained to her that it looked like that because it was happening within the same country, Pakistan, but it was a country made up of two parts separated by over three thousand kilometres of Indian territory, the product of the partition of the sub-continent according to the doubtful religious and community criteria used when independence came from the English.

Actually, there was no real unity between those two nations, whose western part had just declared war on the eastern part. The inhabitants of West Pakistan spoke Urdu and were rather tall and fair-skinned. Those of East Pakistan were short, dark-skinned and spoke Bengali. The only thing they shared was Islam, but this was not enough of a basis on which to found a nation. Above all because, in spite of the eastern part being more densely populated, most of the resources – healthcare, education, electricity – were systematically diverted to the western part. Those in the west were unashamedly exploiting those in the east, who were calling for autonomy.

In contrast with India, where democracy had survived political upheavals, famine and war, Pakistan had been under military rule for thirteen years. Its President, Yahya Khan, known for his fondness for alcohol, had promised to celebrate the first free plebiscite in the country's history in December 1970. He could not foresee the consequences of those elections, which uncovered the contradictions and fragility of that political entity known as Pakistan. In the west, Zulfikar Ali Bhutto won, a lawyer educated in England who had gone into politics when he went back to his country and who was the leader of the PPP (Pakistan People's Party). In the east, a party won overwhelmingly, led by a charismatic character, Sheikh

Mujibur Rahman, a friend and ally of Indira's, who had run a campaign denouncing the colonialism exercised by West Pakistan over the easternpart. He gained such a massive victory that he achieved the majority in the Pakistan National Assembly. According to the logic of the results, he should have been named Prime Minister. But the general in power had no intention of the eastern part taking over political power. In view of the movement of civil disobedience launched by Sheikh Mujibur Rahman all over East Pakistan, calling an indefinite general strike, the dictator Yahya Khan decided to crush the rebellion by force. Suddenly and with no warning, he sent forty thousand soldiers from West Pakistan to invade the eastern part. Press reports spoke of a brutal, merciless attack. Many officers, boasting that they intended to improve the genes of Bengali children, raped thousands of women, sacked and burned homes and businesses, and murdered thousands of innocent people. Anyone suspected of dissidence was tracked down and eliminated, especially if they were Hindus: students, university professors, writers, journalists, professionals and intellectuals, no one escaped the terror of those tall, strong, well-equipped soldiers who cut people's throats without mercy. Not even children escaped the brutality: the lucky ones were murdered alongside their parents, but thousands of others would have to spend the rest of their lives blind or with horribly amputated limbs. Sheikh Mujibur Rahman was arrested and sent to West Pakistan, where he was jailed.

"Are you going to declare war, Mother?" Sanjay asked her at dinnertime, like someone asking if she were going away on holiday or on a shopping trip.

"If I can't find another way to fix the problem, I'll have no option.

Anyway, tomorrow I'm talking to General Manekshaw."

Indira knew that if the Pakistani dictator had acted so confidently, it was because he had the backing of his main ally, the United States. The other ally was China, who had declared war on India in 1962, and had, in a lightning attack, annexed border lands in the Himalayas. That had been humiliating for India, and a mortal blow to Nehru's old idea of solidarity among the non-aligned nations. It had also marked the beginning of the end for Nehru. His health began to fail, and more than one observer attributed his death to the sadness caused by the attack from the neighbours in the north.

*   *   *

"You know what's happening in East Pakistan?" Indira asked her old friend Sam Manekshaw, Commander-in-Chief of the army, as soon as she got to a meeting of her government.

"Yes, there are massacres," replied the general.

"Telegrams are pouring in from the border states," Indira continued. "They say the refugees keep on coming. Sam, we have to stop the flood any way we can. We have no resources to deal with any more people. If we have to go into East Pakistan, do it. Do whatever you have to, but stop them."

"You know that means war."

"I don't care if there is a war," the Prime Minister cut him off.

The general went on to explain the dangers of an invasion. The monsoon rains were about to fall, troop transport would have to be carried out by road because the fields would be flooded. The Air Force would not be able to act under those circumstances. He told her frankly that in that situation they would not be able to win a war.

"The harvest has begun in Punjab and Haryana," added the careful general. "If the country goes to war at harvest time, I'll need all the roads available, and that is going to cause problems in food distribution, and maybe lead to famines. Then there's the problem with China. The Himalaya passes will be open in a few days... Will they stand there with their arms crossed, if they're allies of Pakistan? What shall we do if they give us an ultimatum?"

"They won't," said Indira. "Let me tell you that we're about to sign a pact of cooperation and mutual defence with the Soviet Union. A pact forthe next 20 years."

Such was Indira's fury, the general remembered, that her face got redder and redder. She decided to break off the meeting and carry on in the afternoon. The ministers left the room, but Indira asked Sam to stay. When they were alone, the general felt it was obligation to tell her, "My duty is to tell you the truth, Ma'am. But in view of all I have told you, if you want me to present my resignation, I am prepared to do that."

"No, Sam. Go ahead. I have the utmost confidence in you."

From then on, the Prime Minister and the Commander-in-Chief worked in perfect harmony. Indira never allowed anyone to stand between them. Sam had convinced her that the military option should be the last resort, and then only if they were forced into it. The strategy now was togain time, at least until winter came back to the Himalayas and froze the mountain passes, an essential requirement if the Chinese were not to be tempted to become involved in the conflict.

The tide of refugees was unstoppable. As many as 150,000 werecrossing the border every day. They arrived in lorries, oxcarts, rickshawsand on foot. Sonia saw how upset Indira was when she came back from a visit she had made to Calcutta.

"I visited camps in the torrential rain," she said at home,

sitting at the table, but not eating a thing because she had no appetite. "I thought that after the experience of the refugee camps during Partition I would be prepared forwhat I was going to see. But I wasn't. I've seen men and women as thin as toothpicks, skeletal children, old people being carried on the backs of their children walking over the flooded fields... They stood for hours in the mud because there was nowhere dry to sit. The people with me expected me tosay a few words, but I was so upset that I couldn't speak."

In eight weeks, three and a half million refugees had come into India. Although the majority were Hindus, there were also Moslems, Buddhists, Christians... People from right across the social spectrum and of all ages. Whatever it cost, Indira repeated, she would not leave them to their fate. She and her advisors planned the organization of the refugee camps meticulously. She wanted her government to do its best to house them, feed them and protect them from epidemics. If once again she had to go round theworld asking for money to cover the cost, she was prepared to do it.

Sonia was a little frightened at the turn events were taking, but she didnot show it. She had blind faith in her mother-in-law. The Press insisted that the atrocities were still going on, and the flow of refugees did not sloweither. Where will it all end? they asked themselves at home, glued to the television at news time. Everywhere the same call could be heard for the government to send in the army. But in spite of all the frantic calls, Indira kept her cool. As always in times of crisis, she remained in total control of the situation. The family atmosphere at her home in New Delhi helped her to relax. Seeing her grandson Rahul growing was like a balm to her. Decision- making, especially when it affected a sixth of humanity, could easily become mental torture. Staying clear-headed and calm was fundamental, for her, for the country and for the world. In that she found Sonia to be of great help. "Your daughter is a treasure," she wrote to Paola. In public, she complimented her all the time. She told one veteran reporter, "Quite simply, she's a wonderful woman, a perfect wife, a perfect daughter-in-law, a great mother and a fantastic housewife. And the most incredible thing of all is thatshe's more Indian than any Indian girl!" One day the whole family attended the screening of a documentary that a friend of Indira's, the journalist Gita Mehta, had filmed about the refugees, and which was going to be shown in the United States. Sonia was deeply moved by the pictures. The documentary showed and interviewed women that the Pakistani soldiers had held captive in the trenches. One of them, aged about fifteen, must have been raped about two hundred times. She could not cry; she was in a state of catatonic shock. Pictures of old and young people could also be seen, returning to the wreckage of their homes, pictures of fields burned and devastated. When it was over, Sonia realized that Indira was crying.

13

Indira was ready to burn all the bullets to avoid a war, or at least to delay it. She thought that only intervention from the rest of the world could achieve a peaceful agreement to stop the bloodshed. The world press reported the atrocities committed in what they were beginning to call Bangladesh. The editorial comments were critical about President Nixon's support for the Pakistanis. The American elite seemed united in its strong condemnation of General Yahya Khan. In France, André Malraux proposed sending weapons to the Bangladesh resistance. The ex-Beatle, George Harrison and the Indian sitar master Ravi Shankar organized a massive concert to raise funds for the refugees. Allen Ginsberg, the poet Indira had listened to in London when she went to inaugurate the exhibition about her father, sang of the suffering in the camps.

Indira had no option but to go off on tour around the United States and Europe, trying to galvanize worldwide public opinion.

"If people in the West could see the pictures in the documentary that we saw the other day," she told Sonia, "I am sure they would mobilize."

She intended to spend several months travelling round the world. She went with the certainty that the domestic front was well looked after, which gave her some very necessary peace of mind. That is what she told an Arab journalist on one of her stopovers. "I have no concerns about the family when Sonia is at home." Before she left, her daughter-in-law had given her some more good news: she was pregnant again, and this time it did not look as though she would need to spend another nine months in bed.

*   *   *

The tour began badly; her meeting with Nixon was a huge fiasco. Decidedly, Indira was accumulating bad experiences with American presidents who considered her too far to the Left, although Nixon seemed a hundred times worse than that brute of a Johnson. Their discussions were tinged with mutual distrust and antipathy. Indira and Nixon met sitting in wing-back armchairs on either side of the fireplace in the Oval Office at the White House, while her advisor and Kissinger, like a couple of seconds at a duel, listened to their bosses' dialogue while sitting on the edge of sofas.

Nixon refused to recognize the dimension of the human tragedy that had been unleashed on East Pakistan. He also refused to accept Indira's suggestion that he convince General Yahya Khan to free Sheikh Mujibur Rahman and set up direct negotiations with him and his party, the only serious chance of putting an end to the conflict. Nixon did not feel sorry for the fate of the refugees or Sheikh. Indira's words seemed to slide off him. "It was a dialogue between two deaf people," declared Kissinger when they came out. Then he made the comment that Nixon had said things "that were unprintable". Years later, when the documents of the time were declassified, it became known that Nixon based all his policies in that corner of Asia on his personal sympathy for the dictator Yahya Khan – "a decent and honourable man" – whose loyalty towards the United States should be rewarded by helping him to repress the rebellion in East Pakistan, and his aversion towards the Indians – "those bastards" – as he called them. Both were sure they would not go to war. They were too poor even for that, they thought.

The next day, Nixon made Indira wait forty-five minutes in the antechamber of the Oval Office. The Prime Minister was full of repressed anger when they sat down to talk. She was the head of a country of poor people, but it was a great democratic nation with a huge population and an age-old civilization, and she did not deserve such treatment. In front of her she had a person who did not seem human, a man who, according to her advisor, "lacked all moral principles". And a Kissinger who was "an egomaniac who thought he was Metternich". Why waste any more time with that kind of negotiators? The fate of the refugees and the financial burden that India had to bear had left them cold. "It would have been a mistake to shed tears over what that old witch was telling us", Nixon had said in private to his advisor. They were clear allies of Pakistan, and Indira realized that she was not going to change that on that visit. So at their second meeting, Indira paid back his rudeness with subtlety. She made no reference to the problem with Pakistan, as though Southern Asia were the most peaceful part of the world and, instead, she asked about Vietnam and American foreign policy in other parts of the planet. Nixon took it as an insult. "That old bitch" he called her in private.

In spite of how full her agenda was, Indira managed to take a couple of afternoons free for her private activities. Her friend Dorothy Norman found her exhausted. The tension of the meetings with Nixon and the continual journeys, the effort of having to keep a tight control of herself and stay reasonable in the face of provocation were beginning to leave their mark on Indira's face. Dorothy had bought tickets for a performance of the New York City Ballet. It was a work by Stravinsky, choreographed by Balanchine: just what her friend would like. At the last moment Indira told her she could not go. "She seemed sad and jumpy", Dorothy would remember, not understanding what was wrong. Indira tried to explain herself. "I can't Dorothy. It would be too beautiful. I can't bear it."

She was on the verge of bursting into tears. Dorothy was worried, but the next day she was relieved to see that Indira "had recovered her poise".

In the other countries Indira came up against the same message. They asked her to be patient, to accept the presence of UN observers and to find a peaceful solution. "The biggest problem I have come up against," she told the Press, "is not the confrontation on the border, but the constant efforts of people from other countries to divert attention away from the basic question." On English television she appeared as a Prime Minister who measured up to the circumstances. She had lost weight, and on her face her father's features were appearing, the same imperious manner, great dignity and a fiery look. When the interviewer talked to her about the need to be patient, Indira exploded: "Patience? Patience for the massacres to go on? For the rapes to go on? When Hitler was killing everyone … did you just stand there doing nothing? Did you let him kill all the Jews? How can an exodus like this be controlled? If the international community had recognized the situation, the problem would already have been solved." She was not only addressing the interviewer, but also all the world leaders who were ignoring her.

When she returned to India she found that the number of

refugees had risen to ten million. Now she was convinced that war was inevitable, but she did not say anything at home. Omitting all the tensions of the journeys and what was looming on the horizon, she told them she had managed to get the time to see the opera *Fidelio* in Vienna, where she had also seen a spectacle she had liked a lot, the Spanish Riding School. In Paris she had dined at the home of some friends where she had met Joan Miró and a politician named François Mitterand who had made a very good impression on her. It was as though she was returning from a pleasure trip instead of an exhausting and frustrating international tour. But Rajiv and Sonia were not deceived. They knew perfectly well the level of tension she was putting up with and in the end Indira could not hide the truth from them: there would be war. Sanjay did not seem to be affected by the news, but Rajiv and Sonia were worried. Little Rahul grizzled in his cot.

"You'll have to get used to going out less and to having more protection around you, at least while all this lasts," said Indira. "The whole country is calling for fast and efficient action. Time's running out."

That night, her friend General Sam Manekshaw came, and Sonia and Rajiv could hear fragments of the conversation, in which the general talked about the army's preparations, bases for operations that he had set up inside Bangladesh, and how he had protected the border with West Pakistan with defence units.

"I'm afraid we have to go to war, Sam," they heard Indira say.

"If we do, it has to be now, taking advantage of the full moon on December 4th. That day, we can attack Dacca."

Indira remained pensive for a moment. She never thought that one day she would have to start a war. But if the world ignored the problem and the situation became untenable, she had no option but to take matters into her own hands. She remembered some words her father had said to her one day: "Be mistress of your own life, of your present and your future, consult me if you need to, but decide for yourself." She could not consult him, but she could decide. She turned her head towards her old friend and said, "Go ahead, Sam."

At home, she tried not to let her worry show. In fact they all made the same effort. They were afraid for Sonia, who was in the advanced stages of her pregnancy. The Nehrus were used to hiding their feelings when things were going badly. In that, they were very British. What if they went to Italy for a while? The suggestion had come from a friend, but Sonia rejected it. She had no intention of leaving Indira on her own in that situation. That did not fit in with her concept of loyalty. Sonia knew her mother-in-law well enough to guess that now more than ever she needed the warmth and companionship of her family. Besides, both she and Rajiv had confidence in life, in the future, in Indira and in India, and it never occurred to them to think about the consequences in case of defeat. That eventuality simply was not considered.

What they did was to surround Indira with affection, without asking too many questions and trying not to wear her out more than she already was. They were very loving towards her and when they saw she was especially worried, Rajiv would give her a big hug.

Indira travelled to Calcutta on December 3rd, 1971, one day before the planned attack. On the great esplanade in the centre of what had been the British Empire's capital, she addressed a crowd of half a million: "India wants peace, but if war breaks out we are prepared to fight, because it is as much about our ideals as our security..." Just as she pronounced these words, an aide came on to the podium and passed her a note: *"Pakistani fighters have bombed nine of our airbases in the northwest, the north and the west, including those in Amritsar, Agra and Srinagar in Kashmir."* Indira hurriedly finished her speech, without announcing what she had just read. As soon as she left the rally she told her aide: "Thank God, the Pakistanis have attacked first!" The third Indo-Pakistani war had broken out. And Pakistan was the aggressor.

That night Indira flew back to New Delhi, and her plane was escorted by Indian fighters. There was the danger that the Pakistani Air Force might locate the plane and shoot it down. But Indira did not seem to be affected by the speeding up of events. Quite the opposite: she took out of her bag a book by Thor Heyerdal about the Ra expedition and read during the entire flight. There was no point in getting upset: the die was cast. When she landed, the capital was shrouded in utter darkness, the result of the power cut ordered by the military authorities. Indira went directly to her office in South Block where, in the map room, she was informed of the damage inflicted by the Pakistani planes. Then she met with members of the opposition to inform them that she had given orders for the Indian army to invade Bangladesh. They described her as "calm, serene and confident". It was past midnight when she addressed the nation on the radio to announce the Pakistani attacks and warn of the great dangers that were threatening that part of the world. That day she did not sleep at home. She stayed up all night monitoring the escalation in the military situation. The following morning, in Parliament, she announced to the representatives of the people that they should prepare for a long fight.

About to go into labour when the conflict broke out, Sonia was more worried about the birth than a war that she saw as far away, in spite of having to spend the recent nights in darkness because of the power cuts. If she felt anxiety, she did not show it at any time. Life went on as usual, apart from extra army reinforcements to protect the house and the fact that now General Sam Manekshaw came for breakfast every morning to inform the Prime Minister about how the conflict was going. Sonia liked to serve tea for the general, a pleasant, courteous man, known for his fondness of British military traditions. Every day, as soon as he got up at 5.30, he liked to have a shot of whisky, listen to the news on the BBC and take care of his garden for a while before he went off to work. The same serene, confident behaviour as Indira, which inspired calm in everyone around her – colleagues, military men, soldiers – also had an effect at home.

On the sixth day, Sam arrived with a serious look on his face. Sonia heard him say that several units of his army had become stuck in swamps near Dacca, the capital of Bangladesh. They were losing crucial hours. The general informed Indira of the precise number of losses and planes shot down. He seemed very upset. She asked questions, always calm and positive. "Sam, you can't win every day," she told him by way of consolation. Sonia saw them go out on to the porch. There was not the slightest trace of anxiety in Indira's face as she shook hands with the Commander-in-Chief. General Manekshaw said that Indira's courage was an inspiration to everybody. Sonia was able to verify that when she heard the people shouting victory from the other side of the gate.

Not even that day did Indira lose her interest in family matters.

When she came home after an exhausting day in Parliament and her office in South Block, she shut herself up with Usha to deal with matters that deserved the same importance as those she had discussed during the day: how to organize national Republic Day without knowing the result of the war, for example, or what to give Sonia on December 9th, her birthday, and drawing up a list of presents for the coming Christmas.

Perhaps the commotion was inside her and Indira was not as sure of herself as she wanted to seem, because at that time she began to ask for the services of astrologers and palm-readers. That night her yoga teacher arrived, a guru called Dhirendra Brahmachari, a good-looking man, with long hair and a beard, always dressed in an orange kurta and sandals. He locked himself in a room with her for a long time. At nine o'clock, while Usha, Rajiv and Sonia were watching the news on television about the Indian troops stuck in the swamp, Indira came into the living room, with a worried look on her face. She had just said goodbye to the visitor. "He thinks we're going to have a hard time of it until February," she said, somewhat perturbed.

On December 6th, while the Indian army was getting out of the swamp and advancing on Dacca, in Parliament Indira announced official recognition of the new nation of Bangladesh. A loud ovation welcomed her words. She received unconditional support from all sides. The opposition and all sectors of society had come together as one under her leadership. The people began to identify her with Durga, the goddess of war who rides a tiger and defeated the demons after they had ejected the gods from heaven.

Sonia would not forget that December 9th when she

became 25, and was eight months through the pregnancy. Indira called mid-morning to say that she would not be attending the family's celebratory lunch because something serious had come up. It had to be very serious for Indira not to be present at her daughter-in-law's birthday, those that knew her thought. The news, which came from the United States, shook everyone. Nixon had decided to send the Seventh Fleet to the Bay of Bengal, led by the nuclear aircraft carrier, *Enterprise*. This was utter provocation which could lead to a worldwide holocaust.

While some friends celebrated Sonia's birthday in the intimacy of her home, Indira, worked up, was giving an incendiary speech on the esplanade of Lila Ram in New Delhi, in front of a crowd of hundreds of thousands. Some Indian fighter jets flew over the place to prevent any surprise attacks by the Pakistani Air Force. Indira had not listened to the advice of her security staff to speak on the radio instead of in public. She was brave; it seemed she was afraid of nothing.

At night, she met with General Manekshaw and her advisor. Undaunted by the American provocation, Indira confirmed her decision to continue with the war. She thought that Nixon's gesture was a bluff because the Americans would not be so crazy as to open up another front in Asia after the one in Vietnam. But also it was true that anything could be expected from a person like Nixon. She turned to General Manekshaw: "Sam, now it is imperative that we capture Dacca before the Seventh Fleet arrives in Indian waters," she said. "Do you think that's possible?"

"Yes," replied the general without hesitation, "unless the Chineseintervene."

Indira's advisor stepped in: "They are upset at the situation, but they have not made any direct threats," he said.

"Well then," Indira went on, "tomorrow I'll send the Foreign Secretary to Moscow to activate the treaty we have with the Soviets and to make sure of their support if there's an American or Chinese attack. My opinion, let me repeat, is that we have to go with the war. Do you agree?"

They both nodded.

The visit of the Indian Foreign Secretary served to get the Russians to send a fleet to the Bay of Bengal. In a few days it was following in the wake of the American ships. The situation had reached a critical point. From the White House, Nixon launched furious attacks against "Indian aggression". His administration announced a halt to economic and military aid to India, but continued to send war material to Pakistan, something which was denounced even in the American Press. Indira wrote him an emphatic letter: "This war could have been avoided if the nations, especially the United States, had used their influence, their power and their authority to find a political solution. As President of the United States and representative of the will, aspirations and idealism of the great American people, at least let me know exactly where we have gone so wrong that your representatives and spokesman treat us with such harsh language." Indira spent the day wondering whether or not to send the letter. At night she decided she would. The American President would have yet another reason to hate her even more.

On December 13th, when his army was at the gates of Dacca, General Manekshaw sent an ultimatum to his Pakistani counterpart in which he gave him three days to surrender. At five in the afternoon on 16th, Indira wasbeing interviewed by a reporter from Swedish television who was more interested in finding out what clothes she liked to wear and what her childhood had been like than in the progress of the war, when the phone suddenly rang. It was Manekshaw: "Ma'am, we have beaten them. They've just surrendered. Dacca has fallen." Indira shut her eyes and squeezed her fists.

"Thanks, Sam," she said.

She finished the interview in a hurry and went to Parliament. Before the assembly of expectant MPs, she began saying: "Dacca is today the free capital of a free country..." But a warm ovation mixed with cries of jubilation drowned out the rest of her speech. "We've won!" even the opposition MPs shouted. "Let's crush the enemy forever!" said others. "Long live Indira Gandhi!" cried the people.

Later she met with the army chiefs. The balance for the Indians was 42 planes and 81 tanks destroyed; the Pakistanis had lost 86 planes and 226 tanks. The greatest difference lay in the number of prisoners. The Pakistanis had taken a handful of prisoners in the fighting in the west. India held 94,000 Pakistani prisoners. Indira attempted to calm down her generals, who were not in agreement with the unilateral ceasefire that she was calling for. The high command echoed a large part of public opinion: to go on collecting victories "until the enemy is totally defeated". But Indira was pragmatic: "We have to stop once we have achieved our aims, we cannot give either China or the United States excuses to intervene. We must hand back the prisoners and put a stop to the conflict now." The generals cleared their throats, except for Sam, who listened imperturbably, with his long nose pointing at each person as they spoke. Indira explained that her position was based on a political appreciation of the situation and that she spoke with the authority provided by the support of a unanimous cabinet. Once she had finished, the generals got up, saluted and said they would carry out the government's instructions. "This is something that could not have happened in many countries, and not only in the Third World," Indira would remember.

Indira's strategy of gaining time, her perfect sense of opportunity, the excellent relationship she had with General Manekshaw, and her almost maternal way of speaking to the troops were qualities recognized unanimously by all sectors of society. The international Press spoke of her in grandiose terms. The goddess Durga had become the "Empress of India".

Indira had called Nixon's bluff. She was right that the Americans could not rush to save their ally the Pakistani dictator because they could not afford to open up another front in Asia. Nixon was furious with the outcome of the war. "We've been too soft on that damned woman," he told Kissinger. "Look how she's done that to the Pakistanis when we'd warned that old bitch not to get involved." These were his exact words. Kissinger was annoyed with himself for having underestimated the military strength of the Indians. "The Indians are such poor pilots that they don't even know how to get their planes off the ground," he had told his boss during Indira's visit. A comment that Rajiv would not have found at all amusing. But the opinion of the American people, and of the American Press, disagreed with its leaders. In an opinion poll, Indira Gandhi was classed as the most admired person in the world.

Indira's decisive action saved the life of Sheikh Mujibur Rahman, who had been condemned to death in Pakistan. One of the conditions of the armistice agreement was the immediate liberation of the leader of the new Bangladesh. On January 11th, 1972, Rahman made a stopover at Palam Airport, New Delhi, on his way back to Dacca. He had come to thank Indira, and they both gave speeches full of emotion: "His body was locked up, but no one could lock up his spirit, which continued to inspire the people of Bangladesh..." she said. "Indira Gandhi is not only the leader of a country, she is a leader of mankind," declared Sheikh Mujibur. It was a moment of intense euphoria after the tension accumulated over the recent months.

In the following days and weeks, thousands of baby girls born in India were named Indira by their parents. One of them, however, born a day after Sheikh Mujibur Rahman's triumphant visit to New Delhi, was not called that. Her parents, Sonia and Rajiv Gandhi, gave her the name of Priyanka, which in Sanskrit means "dear to the sight".

ACT II

THE EXTERMINATING ANGEL

What can the river do against fire,
the night against the sun, the dark against the moon?

Sanskrit aphorism

14

Usha phoned Indira, who was on tour in the state of Bihar, to tell her the good news. A year and a half after the birth of Rahul, they were proud to have a new member of the family. The Prime Minister was radiant. What more could she ask for? She was the undisputed leader of the country, her position was unassailable, and on top of everything life was giving her the gift of a granddaughter, like a coronation. She was ready to spoil her a lot, and she always kept herself informed of her needs. In line with her style, she sent messages to Sonia from the most unexpected places with questions like: "How did the baby sleep last night?" or "Has Rahul still got a runny nose?" That moment of joy reminded her of another, equally intense moment, when she had decided to get married to Firoz. "I feel a serene happiness deep inside which nothing or no one can steal from me," she had written to her father. Nehru had written back to her from jail, tempering his daughter's enthusiasm from the height of his years and experience: "Happiness is something rather fleeting. Being fulfilled is perhaps a more lasting feeling." Nehru knew, and Indira had already learned it, that happiness is as fragile as the finest of porcelains. It is better to preserve it and enjoy it while it lasts, because it can be broken – or stolen.

Indira certainly felt fulfilled, and in full possession of her faculties. She had become used to power, not because of what she got out of it in material terms, because her few needs were amply covered and she lacked ambition in that sense, but because of the feeling of plenitude it gave her.

The feeling that she was true to her destiny because she belonged to the family into which she had been born. The deep conviction that she wasdoing her duty, which did not arise out of personal choice, but from the moral legacy she had received from her father, and he from his father before him. In the end, the Messianic feeling that Nehru had instilled in her had filtered down to the depths of her spirit.

But Indira had also learned that power, fame and popularity do not last forever. How could she go on rising when she had reached the top? Or was it that once at the top, the only direction left was down? These were thoughts that came to her more and more frequently at difficult moments. "I feel like a prisoner," she wrote to her friend Dorothy Norman in June 1973, "because of the security team, who think they can hide their incompetence by surrounding me with more and more people, but above all because I realize that I have come to the end of a road, and that I cannot grow any more in that direction." In fact, she would have concentrated exclusively on questions of international politics if she could have, because that was what she really liked. She felt she had the soul of a statesman: great matters and great challenges inspired her. She had signed an agreement with Bhutto which guaranteed long-lasting peace with Pakistan; she wanted to solve the conflict over Kashmir, the land of her forefathers; she was seeking normalization of relations with the Chinese. On the other hand, internal politics, the squabbling between parties, the betrayals, the forced alliances, the hustle and bustle of public life in India weighed heavily on her. "There are no normal days for a Prime

Minister of India," Sonia heard her say as she served tea to Indira and her friend Pupul. "On a good day, there may be two or three very urgent problems. On a bad day, there might be a dozen. After a time, you manage to live with it, although you never really get used to it. If you do, then it's best if you leave the job. As Prime Minister one must always feel a little uncomfortable, always seeking to find one's balance."

On a personal level, the goddess Durga went on living in her austere way. She hardly wore any jewels, a reflection of her frugal personality. Her most highly valued saris were those that her father had woven in prison. However she had a nice collection of saris which she used "politically", in the sense that she wore them according to the place and population she was intending to visit. She had them from all over the sub-continent. Also in her wardrobe there were regional costumes which she wore when she went on tour in the north-eastern territories, to make it clear that the sari was not the only item of clothing that women wore in India.

Sonia learned to recognize all those clothes and helped her to choose them before each journey. During the Bangladesh conflict, Indira had leaned towards the colour red, as though the war had heightened her sensitivity to that colour, which traditionally was not for widows. Indira had confessed during that time that she saw everything as though through a red filter and that this colour had been with her throughout the whole war. But afterwards she went back to her usual tastes, that is, all colours except mauve and violet. She preferred bright tones to pastel tones, especially green. As it was difficult for her to go shopping, Sonia and Usha brought saris home for her. Indira quickly chose the ones she liked. She knew how to wear them with style, and looked as elegant in a simple hand-woven cotton sari as in a heavily embroidered one, made out of Benares silk.

Sonia had become an indispensable presence in that house. Indira loved her like the daughter she had never had. Now that there were more receptions and dinners for foreign dignitaries, Sonia took on with her mother-in-law the role that Indira had taken on with her father when she lived in Teen Murti House. She was very conscientious when it came to choosing the menus, in which beef and pork were never included. Hindu vegetarians did not eat eggs, but they did eat dairy products, and the strictest ones, the vegans, would not eat anything of animal origin. She also prepared halal food for the Moslems and kosher for the Jews. Ensuring that everything was in perfect order was not an easy task, especially when foreigners were coming. It was difficult to obtain essential products for a good Western menu, even in the American Embassy store. Sonia learned to plan the meals with great care, mixing Indian and European dishes according to the availability of the ingredients. The worst thing was that once again there was a shortage of basic foodstuffs. After six years of abundant monsoons, the rains had failed again. The cloud of dust that suffocated New Delhi was so dense that Sonia did not go out without her inhaler. She could see the disorder in the streets from inside her white Ambassador with dark windows. There were demonstrations all over, streets blocked off, people protesting. "Indira isn't getting ready of poverty!" said a man armed with a megaphone in front of a small crowd at a crossroads in New Delhi, alluding to Indira's electoral slogan, "She's getting ready of poor people by starving us to death!" The victory had not let the winner off the hook, and India was wounded. Dealing with the refugees had emptied the country's granaries. The State's coffers were empty. The worldwide oil crisis had made the price of crude oil rocket, and inflation was out of control. If before it took Sonia twenty minutes to get to Connaught Place, now she had to allow more than double that because of the complicated route she had to take, such was the turmoil in the streets. It was paradoxical to have to go round the city shopping for luxury banquets while the poor were starving in the streets. That was a reality that Sonia could not get used to. Back home, she made sure that every light bulb worked, and that the taps in the bathroom did not drip. She made certain any tall guests would have suitable chairs and that the shorter ones could be sure of a footstool.

When she was at home, whenever she could, Indira continued to use her little study on the veranda, by her bedroom, even though she had a large office available to her at Akbar Road, about fifty metres away. But inside the house, she could feel the presence of her family around her, she could hear the hustle and bustle of domestic life, she could see Sonia walk by with the baby in her arms and that made her life sweeter. For her, work, leisure and family duties were not compartmentalized activities, but flowed into each other. She got more out of herself when she did several things at the same time. "The more you do, the more you find you can do" was her favourite saying. Her mental powers all worked at the same time, and that perhaps was the secret that allowed her to deal with much more work than normal people. Sonia observed that work and rest were not separate periods for her mother- in-law. It was a question of doing something different, even if only for a short time, such as reading, arranging bouquets of flowers, organizing books or clothes, or talking to the family. Sometimes Indira would complete a crossword over lunch, which seemed strange with the number of problems awaiting her. "It helps me to relax and organize my ideas," she would say. At home, she continued with the custom of leaving notes: "Today you missed a nice photo," she wrote to Rajiv one day. "This morning in Akbar Road, two parakeets sat for a long time on the branch of a tree. There was also a pair of woodpeckers fluttering around all the time."

Sonia learned a lot from her, because of the loving relationship they had formed with each other which was getting stronger all the time. Indira's problems, which were largely the problems of India, ended up being discussed at home. They did not talk so much about the routine things in political life as about the large issues: the severe economic crisis that had begun in 1972 and which was threatening to become the most serious of them all, the overpopulation which was choking the country's development, the eternal tension between religious communities, the occupation by slum- dwellers of public areas in all cities or the effects of natural disasters, age- old companions of man's existence in Asia. The love that Indira felt for the common people infected Sonia too, and she was moved by her mother-in- law's role as champion of the poor, an echo of her adolescent dreams of heroic missionaries. Besides, she admired her, not so much because of her successes in political life, but because she was spontaneous and informal, and totally lacking in arrogance. Sonia appreciated "her capacity for loving and giving". "For us, she was someone who generously shared her broad knowledge, her warmth and her presence. When she went away on a trip, she would write to us about the people she met and her experiences. When she was here, she watched over each and every one of us." Indira took very seriously the little events in the day to day lives of her grandchildren, like their first tooth or their first steps. She was amazed at the extraordinary phenomenon, as old as humanity itself and yet always new, of how a child develops his knowledge of the outside world, with that endless sense of adventure, that passion for investigating everything around him… "You will see that very quickly a child goes through millennia of human history, and unconsciously, and in part consciously too, will live within himself the history of his race", her father had once written to her, and she had wanted toshow Sonia the letter. She was touched that in spite of all the pressure from the outside world which Indira received, she was still sensitive to the spectacle, small and grandiose at the same time, of seeing her grandchildren growing.

In spite of keeping a close eye on her mother-in-law's well-being, Sonia kept up her private life with Rajiv. The fact that there might be a dinner in the main dining room did not mean that they had to attend as well. Sometimes they did, other times they did not. They had their family life verywell organized, and it was as stable as their relationship was. "They always loved each other a lot; I've never seen a couple so united since the day they met," Christian would say, the friend who had introduced them in Cambridge. "Our marriage always worked very well, right from the start. Sonia was always very understanding," confessed Rajiv, who had risen to pilot and now flew an English plane, the Avro HS-748, another worthy successor of the famous Dakota DC-3. Among his colleagues in the airline, he was regarded as a good professional, although sometimes they teased him for being too meticulous with flight plans, technical problems andtimetables. He could not stand to make a poor job of anything, and he was always prepared to take over a flight if for some reason a colleague asked him to do him a favour and stand in for him. He was a good workmate, good-natured and indifferent to the hierarchy.

15

The one Indira was worried about was her other son, Sanjay. "Rajiv has a job, but Sanjay does not and he's involved in an expensive venture. He is very like me when I was the same age – with the rough edges too – to such an extent that it makes me feel sad to see the suffering he has to go through." Two years after having won the government licence to manufacture a 100% Indian car, Sanjay's company had still not produced a single saleable vehicle. There was no shortage of help, owing to the privileged position which his mother's increasing success gave him. He had managed to get some politicians and businessmen to invest large sums of money in his company, in the hopes they would ingratiate themselves with Indira. They knew that if they should lose their investment they could ask for political favours. From Bansi Lal, the head of the government of Haryana, a chubby individual with glasses, who was trying as hard as he could to get closer to the party leadership, he got fifty hectares of agricultural land in the outskirts of Delhi. "When you hunt the calf, it is certain that its mother will be following it," Bansi Lal had declared with crushing logic to a friend. When the Press uncovered the fact that it had been necessary to relocate over a thousand peasants in order to build the Maruti Factory, Parliament reacted virulently to what it called another act of "flagrant nepotism". The price paid was suspicious, and the location of the land, near an old army arsenal, violated the government's laws which prohibited the building of an industrial factory less than a kilometre from defence installations. But they were never able to prove there had been any bribery. Indira kept her mouth shut, as though it had nothing to do with her, although her chief advisor, a trusted consultant, had warned her about the ingenuousness of her son's plans and his inexperience with industrial projects.

"Sanjay's failure to produce a car could seriously affect your political position," he told her. "The Maruti may be the crack in your armour that the opposition parties are looking for."

Indira looked up at her advisor for a few seconds and did not answer. She felt a mixture of faith and compassion for her son which prevented her from seeing reality as it really was.

But there was another strong factor that contributed to Indira's blindness: her immense power. The men that Indira chose for important posts acquired enormous power to dispense favours and sponsorship, just because they had been designated by her. They relied on a gigantic source of corruption, which were the measures that the party itself had set in motion to control economic activity as part of its Socialist programme. In order to do any business, to start up any company, to import pieces of equipment or spare parts you needed endless licences, permits and authorizations. A system that people called the Licence Raj, 'the empire of the permit'. There, bureaucrats and politicians had the chance to get rich by exchanging favours for money or other favours. The Licence Raj prepared the way for even higher levels of corruption. And Sanjay decided to fish in those waters.

Indira was aware of the influence that money and power exercised over those who were around her, but she thought that a certain degree of corruption had always existed and was an integral part of the system. The important thing was for it not to get out of control. Besides, closing her eyes to the corrupt practices of her people was also a way of keeping them tied down. It was true that Indira was not the only case – in India or in the world

– of a political leader who was personally irreproachable but who turned a blind eye to the corruption of others. It seemed to her these were matters of little importance compared, for example, to the figures that had just been published that said that less than 20% of Indian women could read and write, and in the state of Bihar only 4%... Or that the population of the country was going to pass the threshold of seven hundred million. Which is to say more than double the population there was at the time of independence... At that rate, in only a few years, the population of India would overtake that of China. Those really were problems that demanded the highest level of attention. As was the wave of strikes, the discontent of the people and the spectre of famine. Even Rajiv and Sonia, who did not go out much, began to notice the corruption from the way the wives and daughters of members of the Congress Party dressed. Now they were wearing saris of imported silk, diamond jewellery and Italian shoes when they attended official receptions.

Very much in spite of his mother's tacit support, Sanjay's project did not take off. All the prototypes had defects in the steering, gearbox, suspension and cooling system. One day he invited Sonia to try one out on the circuit round the factory perimeter. Sanjay tried hard to show that his vehicle was capable of reaching a hundred kilometres an hour, but theground was so full of holes and bushes that Sonia was scared to death and asked him to slow down. Although it was new, the car looked old. The doors did not close properly, the suspension was very rough and the sound of the engine was deafening. But Sanjay could not see those defects. To such an extent that, in May 1973 he thought he could finally present a model before the Press and invited a reporter from *Surge* magazine to try it. The car overheated and lost oil. The reporter noted that there were only five unpainted cars in the workshops and another fifteen in the process of being manufactured. The engines were assembled manually and there was no sign of an assembly line. She realized that instead of being the cheap mass-produced car that the government wanted, the Maruti was a very poor-quality handmade product.

The problem was that Sanjay had raised a lot of money and was burdened with debts. At first, as he could not call the people who could help him with the finances directly, he used the services of one of his mother's secretaries, a man with oily hair brushed back from his forehead and with a broad mechanical smile, whose name was R.K. Dhawan (he had been Nehru's stenographer). Dhawan saw a good opportunity to improve his standing with his boss by cultivating contact with Sanjay. He dealt with calling different businessmen from number 1, Safdarjung Road, and they came running because they did not want to miss the chance to do the Prime Minister a favour, via her son. It is possible that they thought that Indira herself was interested in these deals, but actually she knew nothing at all about her offspring's shady business.

Later, Sanjay asked for a deposit of half a million rupees from each of the 75 dealers that he had designated, in exchange for the promise to hand over the first cars for sale in the next six months. He had also gone to the banks, recently nationalized by his mother and had obtained unsecured loans to the value of eight million rupees. But the car still did not materialize and Sanjay's ineptitude became evident. In order to defend himself from the ever more numerous attacks, he attributed his failure to bureaucracy and the number of administrative stumbling blocks through which he had to navigate. He was partly right, but if anyone was in a position to strugglewith the difficulties and obstacles of the Licence Raj, it was him. Even so, hechose to blame everyone else. But the MPs' protests were becoming very strident and the newspapers began to talk about the Maruti affair, linking Indira and her old enemy, Nixon. The Maruti affair, according to the Press, was Indira's Watergate.

At the end of 1973, anxious at the proportions the affair was takingon, Indira asked her Chancellor of the Exchequer to take a look at the Marutipapers. Sonia could see she was very worried. Her mother-in-law was convinced the opposition was using the Sanjay business to destroy her, and itdid not seem fair to her. She still thought that her son deserved an opportunity. One day she told her that in her youth she had met a Catholic priest who had built a plane in two garages in Bombay and that he used to take his friends for rides over the bay. "If that man could build a plane... Why can't Sanjay build a car?" she asked.

The reasons for her son's inability to imitate the Catholic priest came to light in the interview that took place between Indira, Sanjay and Subramanian, the Chancellor of the Exchequer, who had been the architect of the "green revolution". The minister asked Sanjay for the report on the project.

"There cannot be a report on the project before the project is carried out," answered Sanjay.

The Chancellor went on to explain to him that although he might possibly be able to design a car, he should have a report with the specifications for each component, the way they would be produced and the cost per part.

"That is no longer necessary," Sanjay answered with a touch of arrogance. "Those are the old ways of working."

The Chancellor told Indira that, however dynamic he might be, her son lacked the knowledge required to be successful in an enterprise like this. He promised her he would obtain the help of professionals to advise him, but Sanjay was vehemently opposed to it. He did not want anyone to overshadow him or to lose control of his business. Everything pointed to Indira listening to her Chancellor, but she did not. Caught between her duty as a leader and the blind faith she had in her son, not only did she ignore Subramanian's advice, but she removed the advisors who were most critical of Sanjay. The absolute power that Indira now wielded demanded characterless, malleable people around her. She did not allow anyone to overshadow her or show disagreement or criticism, even if it was friendly. Power, which was poisoning the son and blinding the mother, only accepted submissiveness.

Rajiv had never liked his brother's project, which he saw as a megalomaniac's dream which could harm his mother's reputation, and by extension the reputation of the rest of the family. Both brothers had their first big disagreement as adults when Rajiv, on returning from a trip, found out that Sanjay had convinced Sonia to sign several documents that made her a partner in a new company, Maruti Technical Services, with a salary, bonuses and travelling expenses included. The children, Rahul and Priyanka, also appeared as partners.

"How could you do that?" he asked his brother furiously. "I don't want to end up with mud on my face from your shady dealings, or for you to get Sonia and the children into trouble…"

"There's no trouble…"

"What do you mean? How long do you think it's going to take the opposition to find out about this?"

"It isn't illegal."

"Yes it is. You've forgotten that, by law, Sonia does not have the right to own shares in an Indian company because she's a foreigner."

Sanjay shrugged his shoulders, as if that was not of the slightest importance. Rajiv was also angry with Sonia.

"I agreed just as a favour to your brother," she told him. "He's always been so kind to me, and if he asks me to do him a favour, I'm not going to say no."

"But you've signed that you're going to receive a salary, do you realize that?"

"I signed blind, I didn't know about the salary, and I never had any intention of taking any money, you know that…"

"You'll see how the Maruti affair is going to reflect badly on all of us sooner or later."

Rajiv was furious, as Sonia had rarely seen him. Under the name of a consulting company, Maruti Technical Services was actually a cover for diverting money from the mother company, Maruti Limited, into the hands of Sanjay and those who had invested large sums in the car factory that never produced cars. Now Rajiv wanted only one thing: to distance himself completely from anything that had to do with Maruti.

*   *   *

Both brothers had been brought up in the same home, but since their earliest childhood they had shown marked differences. The primary school teacher who had taught them described Rajiv as a polite, docile child, a decent student. On the other hand, Sanjay was rebellious, destructive, and stubborn, with no interest in school activities, arrogant towards his teachers and very difficult to deal with. He grew up as a turbulent, capricious teenager, messing around with cars and attracting dubious friends. Bothjoined Doon School, the most elite school in India, created in the image of the great British educational establishments such as Eton or Harrow. But Sanjay could not stand the discipline or the pace of studies. He had so little interest in reading that in an interview he gave as an adult he was unable to name a single book that had influenced or inspired him, not even those written by his grandfather. He only liked the metal workshop activities. He was obsessed by cars and planes. In spite of being who he was, he was expelled from school. It was then that, in desperation, Indira sent him to takea course as an apprentice at Rolls-Royce in England. "What he liked most was to talk about Indian politics and to make fun of English politics," his supervisor would say, before adding, "Once, when I told him off for amistake he'd made, he said to me, 'Look, the British have fucked with India for centuries, and now I've come here to fuck with England.'"

Brought up among Prime Ministers that the people adored like gods, Sanjay ended up thinking that India was his personal playground. He never knew privation, unlike his mother and his grandfather. After a life of struggle, Nehru had given free rein to his desire to spoil his grandchildren, asif by doing that he could make up for the suffering he had gone through. Sometimes he gave them eccentric gifts, like a crocodile that became Sanjay's favourite pet until Indira finally sent it to the zoo when it almost bitoff her fingers. Neither did Sanjay inherit from them their immense love for the people of India or their genuine compassion for the poor. He never had to see the skeletal faces of old women weeping for their dead, he never had to look into the eyes of peasants who stared at their fields cracked open from the drought, he never heard the silent clamour of a people who had been crying out for protection for centuries. Sanjay seemed to be annoyed by the backwardness of his country and he did not understand its complexity. He was a rebel against tradition, impatient with laws and rules. He went from being kind and attentive to direct and brutal in a flash, and that brusqueness was shocking in a country where relations between people were steeped in ancient courtesy, like a patina, the product of thousands of years of uninterrupted civilization. For him, life was a game in which you had to win, and the problems of life were obstacles that had to be overcome in order to reach the finishing line. And he was in a hurry. A hurry to change things, to get there sooner, to gather the power that was not his to wield. He was in such a hurry that he did not care about the means to get to the end.

His brother had grown in the opposite direction. Since he was little he had always been more sensitive to the suffering of others. He had inherited his mother's sensitivity to those more unfortunate and her love of India, and that could be seen in the photos he took. As a young man, he visited his parents' friends who were ill, spontaneously, without anyone forcing him to do it. One day, when he was 17, Indira met him when she went to give her condolences to the family of a friend and veteran leader of the Congress Party who had just died. That is how she found out that her son had been visiting him during his last days. Rajiv was the type of person who did not hesitate to stop and offer his help if he saw a road accident, and if necessary, he took the victim to hospital and then was concerned about his progress. In the garden at home, he watched over a robin's nest, and if there was an injured fledgling, he would take it to the Chandni Chowk bird hospital, even at the risk of arriving late for work. Rajiv was happy with what he had, with Sonia, their children, their dogs, and the luxury of being able to spend time doing what he liked to do. He did not ask any more of life, and there, precisely, lay his wisdom. But his mother did not seem to appreciate it: more than wisdom, she saw a lack of ambition, which did not arouse her admiration.

And yet Indira thought that a privileged life did not mean that they had not suffered in their childhood. They had lived in a house that was always full of adults, whose atmosphere was steeped in the seriousness of the discussions and the solemnity of what was decided in the offices, rooms and studies of Teen Murti House. The fact that they had not become fond of reading was perhaps a reaction against that official world of protocol where they were just children, she thought, always seeking excuses for them. When they really had a good time was when they went to visit their father at weekends and for the holidays. Firoz was an extrovert, talkative and affectionate, and gave them his full attention. He knew how to play with his sons and keep them entertained. He taught them to assemble toys and take them apart again, to plant and care for roses, because he was very fond of growing them. Far from the stern formality of the Prime Minister's palace where they lived, in their father Rajiv and Sanjay found a person with an overflowing capacity for fun. Furthermore, he was able to instil in them the feeling that they were very important to him, which made a deep impact on them. Just as in all broken marriages, in the end it is the children who suffer for the tension between the parents, even if they do not understand it. But could Indira explain it to them? Could she tell them that she no longer lived with Firoz because he had been repeatedly unfaithful to her? Because they did not understand each other and she was fed up with fighting? Her sense of dignity prevented her from doing that. The boys could see that their grandfather Nehru had no sympathy for his son-in-law, and they picked it up. Perhaps sub-consciously they blamed their mother that Firoz was away from them and was not part of the Prime Minister's home. After the cremation, a devastated Sanjay threw in his mother's face that she had not looked after their father. He blamed her directly for the heart attack that had killed him.

Indira took it well. She must have felt guilty that her marriage had not worked. And therefore guilty that her children might have suffered because of it. Her weakness for Sanjay perhaps hid her desire to make up for that guilt. It shocked Sonia that she, the strongest woman in India, should be so astonishingly weak with her younger son. Her many enemies did not take long to realize that Sanjay was her Achilles' heel.

Indira, who was completely open with Sonia, often chatted to her. She was perhaps the only person in the house with whom she shared confidences. One day she confessed to her that her marriage had seen many ups and downs, but that she could not have married anyone other than Firoz. He was the only man she really loved. She often talked to her about him, and with affection, because she said that Rajiv reminded her of her husband. They both had their feet on the ground, were sensitive to the beauty of nature and music, and were good with their hands and practical in their way of dealing with problems. She never thought that Firoz would die so soon, so young. It is true, she admitted that she had pushed him aside in recent times, but she had done so thinking that they both had their lives ahead of them and that they would make up for lost time. They had been reconciled in 1958, after his first heart attack. So that he could recover, Indira had organized a family holiday in a houseboat on the lake in the city of Srinagar, the Venice of the East, as the capital of Kashmir is known. Firoz and the boys had a wonderful time, swimming, canoeing and taking photos. Indira took advantage to learn Spanish, a language that had always attracted her.

The spectacle of nature in Kashmir, the land of her ancestors, always filled her with emotion. The sunsets over the sparkling waters of Lake Dal were sublime. There was magic in the air. It seemed as though the kingfishers were tame. One of them flew into the houseboat and perched on Rajiv's shoulder. Then they made an excursion of several days to Daksun, an idyllic place where they caught wild trout in rushing rivers that flowed down among meadows covered in flowers and woods of pines and Christmas trees, framed by the eternally snow-capped mountain peaks. Firoz told her that he had just bought a piece of land in Mehrauli, near Delhi, and they talked about building a house there one day. It would be their own house, so they would not have to live in government-owned houses anymore (as MP for the state of Uttar Pradesh, Firoz also lived in an official residence). It was a wonderful reconciliation for Indira, after such a stormy marriage, with so many fights, betrayals and humiliations, even more painful because most of them had been exposed to the public eye. Now the shadow of the peaks of the Himalayas acted as a balm that healed the wounds of the past. During that time when they were able to enjoy the peace of the mountains, they once again talked about a future together. It was then, in that fleeting yet intense moment of happiness, that Indira decided that once her father had died she would give Firoz all her attention. But on September 8th, 1960, the heart attack came and shattered the dream.

16

Sanjay no longer had a reputation as a womanizer, which he had had in England. Obsessed with the Maruti, his life was just work, work, work. He left home before dawn and came home at seven or eight at night to have dinner with his nephew and niece or to share a snack with Sonia. Rarely with his brother or his mother, because they were both so absorbed in their work at the time that they were rarely at home.

Since his return from England, Sanjay had had two relationships, one with a Moslem woman, which did not last long, and another longer and moreserious affair with a German woman, Sabine von Stieglitz. She was Christian's sister, the friend who had introduced Sonia to Rajiv, and she worked in New Delhi as a language teacher. Tall, blonde, pretty and cosmopolitan, Sabine was culturally more English than German because she had lived almost all her life in England. She was a great friend of Sonia's. They spent many afternoons together, taking care of the children, playing with them or reading them stories. One of them, "The animals in my town", was especially funny because it described the elephant, the monkey, the boa, the raven, the vulture, the crow... as familiar animals. And it was true, they were everywhere. The cawing of the crows was the soundtrack to life in India.

Sonia was a great mother, very meticulous with her children's upbringing. She did not tolerate any fussiness with food, and she knew how to control their behaviour, without being as severe as Stefano had been with her and her sisters. She spoke to them in Italian when they were alone, and in English if they were all together or with Sabine. Actually, Sonia was meticulous in everything, and because of that she wanted to take a course in restoring old pictures. That hobby fitted in well with her discreet, hardworking personality, since she was conscientious and had an eye for detail. She thought of doing it as a job as soon as the children were a little older and needed her less.

Sonia nursed the hope that the relationship between Sanjay and Sabinewould become stable one day and they might end up getting married. But Sabine was getting tired of waiting.

"Sanjay is more in love with the Maruti than with me," she confessed to Sonia one day. "I don't believe he's going to get engaged to me. He only thinks about his business venture, and there's no room for anything else in his life."

"What are you going to do?""I'm going back to Europe."

"What a shame!... It would have been great to have you as a sister-in-law."

"I would have liked that too," she told Sonia, as Rahul and Priyanka fought over a biscuit.

Sonia went to the airport to see her off. What she did not know was that she would see her again two days later.

"What's happened? Weren't you in London?"

Sabine told her that when they got to Teheran, the Air India pilot called her over the P.A. system. Surprised, Sabine went to the flight deck of the Boeing.

"Someone wants to talk to you over the radio," they told her.

It was Sanjay. There, in front of a crew that could not get

over their amazement, they acted out their penultimate love scene. Sanjay asked her to go back to New Delhi: "Let's give each other a last chance," he begged her. Sabine could not resist the man she loved and that is why she had returned. She was a little ashamed at having given in. Sonia was delighted, and once again dreamed that her friend might become her sister-in-law.

But a few weeks later they broke up again, and this time it was for good. Sonia's dream of having her friend close at hand vanished, but only for a while. Sabine did not settle in England. She had become used to living in India. In Europe she missed the warmth of the people, Asian politeness, and the rhythm of life. "I feel the same," Sonia told her. Besides, Sabine had a job that allowed her to live better than if she had gone off to London. So, to Sonia's great joy, they once again spent their afternoons together, and weekends in the surrounding area, like the one that ended in a little tragedy when they got too close to a wasps' nest and went home covered in stings.

Sabine finally met one of the teachers at the Goethe Institute in New Delhi and married him. They lived in the Indian capital for six years. They did not have any children until later, after they had moved to Mexico, but they had dogs that they allowed to run free with Sonia's when they went to the countryside, to the delight of the children. Sabine held on to the memory of Sanjay as a serious young man, with drive, but too egocentric.

For Indira it was better that way because if both of her sons had married Europeans it would not have been politically correct. It would have been like publicly confirming that the Nehrus were going completely Western and were leaving their Indian roots behind forever. By then Sanjay was already involved in politics, not so much out of vocation as to defend himself from the criticisms that were pouring down on him from all sides as a consequence of his appalling management of the Maruti affair.

It was at a cocktail party to celebrate the coming wedding of an old school friend that Sanjay would meet his future wife. It was December 14ᵗʰ, 1973, and the date coincided with his birthday. That day Sanjay was very excited, and it was not because of alcohol because he never drank. But he was aware that he was the most eligible bachelor in India. Handsome, although at 27 he already had a large bald patch, he tried to be careful not to get involved with women that he suspected were only interested in becoming members of the first family of India. The friend that was getting married introduced him to a cousin of his called Maneka Anand, a willowy girl with regular, well-proportioned features. She was freckled and attractive enough to have won a beauty contest, and she worked from time to time as a model for a make of towels. She was pretty and photogenic, with a lively, energetic character. She immediately attracted Sanjay and he spent the evening talking to her. Maneka told him she had dropped out of her Political Science course at Sri Ram College in New Delhi and wanted to become a journalist. She was the daughter of an army colonel, a Sikh, and his wife, named Amteshwar, the daughter of a Punjabi landowner and farmer.

From that day on, Sanjay spent all his free time with Maneka. They saw each other every day. As he no longer liked going out to restaurants or the cinema, he preferred to see her in the evenings at the home of one of the families. Sonia was not very impressed with this new girlfriend. Compared to Sabine, she was an immature little girl who would only last as long as it took Sanjay to see how ambitious she must be. Because now Sonia was infected by the distrust that comes with power or proximity to power. Like her mother-in-law, she thought that anyone who came close to the family did so out of self-interest. Most of the time she was right. She thought that Maneka, just another one of the many girls who courted the golden bachelor of India, would be a flash in the pan.

But at the beginning of 1974, Sanjay invited her home for lunch, a sign that the young man was taking the relationship more seriously than usual. The girl was very nervous because she had to go through the difficult step of meeting the Prime Minister. Sonia understood her perfectly: she had been extremely nervous the day that Rajiv was to introduce her. The difference was that at the time she and her fiancé had been together for a year, and not a month, like Sanjay and Maneka. But she knew her brother- in-law and she knew how impulsive and impatient he was. Also, at that time, in England, Indira was a different woman, more deliberate and without the stress or tension that come from power. Visibly intimidated, Maneka looked at everything like a frightened little bird: the furniture, the pictures, the photos. When she suddenly came face to face with Indira, she did not know what to say. She went red and began to stammer. Indira broke the ice: "As Sanjay has not introduced us, tell me your name and what you do for a living," she said.

Maneka went on to stutter it out as best she could, omitting the fact that she was a model for a company that made towels, which she did not think was worth mentioning.

Indira chatted to her for a while and, as she was used to seeing the girls that Sanjay seduced passing through, she did not think anything special about it, except that she was rather young. Although she would have liked to find a daughter-in-law from among the best families of Kashmir, she did not get involved in her son's love affairs, as she had not done with Rajiv either. Some time ago she had given up the idea of organizing an "arranged marriage", Indian style. That she would leave for another life when she would have more time and more peace of mind...

*   *   *

The months went by and it seemed that Maneka was there to stay. She was not just one more girl in Sanjay's life. He had fallen in love and, true to his impulsive character, he wanted to get married straight away. At first Indira had no difficulty accepting her. The fact that she was from a Sikh family was no problem for the Nehrus, who had always proclaimed equality between the religious communities of the country. But under pressure from her son's haste, she had no time to gather information about the family of her future daughter-in-law. Meanwhile, they set July 29th for the date of the engagement. Both families gathered at number 1, Safdarjung Road where, after a brief ceremony, they all sat down to celebrate with a meal. Indira immediately realized that they were not educated people, or cosmopolitan or even cultured, and she could see the mother was very self-satisfied at having placed her daughter in the most sought-after family in the country. She might have been able to say something similar about Sonia's family, but the difference is that they were simple people, and did not show off at all and were completely lacking in ambition. These were noisy and ostentatious, showing off their jewels and with vulgar taste in their style of clothes. However, Indira was equal to the circumstances. Noblesse oblige. The engagement ring her daughter-in-law was wearing was a present from her. And it was a very special present. It had belonged to Kamala, her mother, and had been designed by her grandfather Motilal. She secretly trusted that one day this young girl would come to understand the deeper meaning of such a valued present. She also gave her a gold and turquoise set, as well as a very fine embroidered silk sari, of Tanchoi style, a mixture of Indian and Chinese styles. A month later, she gave her an Italian silk sari for herbirthday.

The fears about Maneka's family were confirmed by the information that began to flow in after the engagement. Indira found out that Amteshwar, her son's future mother-in-law, had spent ten years in litigation with her brother over their father's legacy. She was a woman with a very basic level of education, and, according to people who knew her, she was envious and scheming. Rumours reached her ears that the other members of the family were rough and loud-mouthed. Other sources said they were social climbers. Just the type of person they had always tried to avoid had slipped into Sanjay's life. Although parents are rarely happy with their children's choice of partner, now Indira had to drink from the same cup as she had given her father when she informed him of her decision to marry Firoz. As in that case, now too it was a matter of families who came from different worlds and did not share the same values. But would it do any good to stand up to her son, as Nehru had stood up to her? Rarely in her life had she suffered as much, so she was not prepared to do the same to him. She could not open up another battlefront. The number of problems she had to struggle with was making her feel depressed. She could not see how to lift India out of poverty, and that made her despair. Her faithful secretary, Usha, would remember that at the end of July, on the way back from a funeral for the eternal rest of an old friend of the family, Indira had told her that she was tired of life. She gave her instructions on how her body was to be disposed of when she died.

"I don't want a funeral, Usha. Write it down… I want them to put my body in a coffin and drop it from a plane on to the perpetual snows of the Himalayas. Perhaps that way I can enjoy the peace that I have not enjoyed inlife."

"Madam, the important thing is to have peace in this life, don't youthink? In the other life it's guaranteed…"

"Yes, I know, but that's out of my hands and I don't think it's possible now."

"It has to be, Madam. But just let me say that no one's going to agree to dispose of your body like that. If it were ashes, maybe… But how do you expect them to throw a coffin out of a plane and for it to smash open on the ground?"

"Well I don't want to be buried or cremated," Indira stated baldly.

In that state of mind, the prospect of marrying her son to a girl of 17 from a family that she considered "vulgar" was not something to raise her morale. The only thing she could do was to delay the wedding. When she heard that on the date set Maneka would not yet be of age, she told her son, "You'll have to wait until she's eighteen. I can't allow you to break the law."

The problem of child marriages was still a thorny topic in India and had been denounced by Gandhi, Nehru and all those who wanted to modernize the country. Thousands of girls ended up being "bartered" by their fathers, married off and turned into servants to the husband's family, with no power to decide on the number of children they would have. Maneka's case was far from that, but Indira was not prepared for Sanjay not to set an example. Besides, by gaining time perhaps her son would eventually think again.

But that did not happen. That summer, Sanjay had to have a small operation for a hernia. After her morning classes Maneka spent the afternoonand part of the night in the private room at the All India Institute of Medical Sciences, the most up-to-date hospital in New Delhi. A few weeks after his convalescence, on September 23rd, 1974, they got married in a civil ceremony in the house of an old friend of the family, Mohammed Yunus. The wedding was proof of the secular India that the Nehrus had always defended: the son of a Parsee and a Hindu was marrying a Sikh girl in the home of a Moslem friend in front of a Catholic daughter-in-law. Indira was generous to Maneka: she gave her twenty-one saris of the finest cloths, some gold jewellery and, most valuable of all, one of the cotton saris that Nehru had woven in prison with his spinning wheel. She did her duty as a mother- in-law down to the last letter. To welcome her daughter-in-law, she assigned the new couple a bedroom that gave on to the main sitting room, near the front door, in the opposite part of the house to Rajiv and Sonia's room. She decorated it and furnished it with great care, placing objects and jars on the dressing table and choosing some bracelets that, by tradition, Maneka was towear on her wedding night and which she left on the bedside table.

Just after the celebration, Maneka came into the home of the Nehru- Gandhis just like Sonia had done with Rajiv six years earlier. "The wedding went off well," Indira wrote to Dorothy Norman that same night, "Manekais so young that I had my doubts about the matter and was not sure if she knew what she was doing. But it seems that she has fitted in, and is livelyand happy."

But Maneka was not Sonia, and although she came from a family that lived only one kilometre away, her adaptation was much harder than her sister-in-law's who came from the other side of the world. In spite of Indira's hopes, the girl found it hard to fit into that household. To start with, she smoked, a habit which was very frowned upon. Sanjay hated tobacco; Indira, who had had tuberculosis, loathed it; and Sonia, who was asthmatic, was allergic to the smoke. A bad start. Furthermore, she was talkative and spoke very loudly. "In my house we were informal and sometimes used bad language," Maneka would say. "The Gandhis are polite to each other, come what may." Sanjay and she had diametrically opposed temperaments and there were many factors that suggested it would become a failed marriage. It is true that it was not always easy to communicate with Indira, an imposing presence. Sometimes, during meals, Maneka would start talking about books she had read or was reading as though she wanted to impress her with her intellectual capacity. Indira would look up, glance at her and go on eating. "She was spirited and intelligent," Usha, Indira's faithful secretary, would say, "but at the same time she was ambitious and very immature." Several times she mentioned that one day Sanjay would be Prime Minister, which made the others feel embarrassed for her. Other times she spoke about happiness with a gloomy face. "I knew she was not referring to a philosophical search," Usha would remember, "but to her own unhappiness caused by Sanjay's absence." What she really liked doing was going out and being seen, exactly what her husband could not do now, busy as he was in leaving his mark on Indian society.

Consequently Maneka was very bored in a house where no one smoked, drank or swore. She killed time in Usha's office asking about her husband's agenda, which was always very full, and trying to discover the keys to that new world in which she was trapped. The traditional world she did not even attempt to get near. When Sonia suggested that she might teach her to cook, even if only to amuse her, because nobody knew better than she did what was happening to her sister-in-law, Maneka replied that she was not interested in cooking or anything else to do with the house.

They all quickly realized that Maneka struck a discordant note. It made Rajiv annoyed to find her lying on a sofa in the sitting room smoking while Sonia was busy with the housework.

"She doesn't do a thing!" he said quietly to Sonia. "Who does she think she is?"

Sonia shrugged, as though to say: that's how things are. Neither did they like her way of treating the servants, shouting and showing no respect, very typical of the wealthy classes in India. Indira too did not like her vulgar, shrill behaviour. The problem was that the only place where she could find protection from the harshness of a life in politics was at home, and even that was disturbed now. Number 1 Safdarjung Road was no longer an oasis of peace and quiet.

17

Indira's mood reflected the mood of India, which was unable to get back on its feet again after the Bangladesh war. Unemployment was rising, and with it numerous manifestations of the people's discontent. The rate of strikes and demonstrations was harrowing, and many of them ended in violent clashes with the police. For Sonia, the task of doing the shopping could turn into a real string of disasters: streets blocked off, arbitrary diversions, stone-throwing, shops closed from shortage of stocks due to a transport strike, etc. There was not a single normal day. It was as if the nation had lost its way and had embraced anarchy. All over the country people talked about nothing except corruption, riots, lock-outs, sit-ins and strikes. Sonia was especially upset at the "sugar" scandal, as it became known, which caused the death of many people, including a lot of children. Some unscrupulous shopkeepers had started selling a mixture of sugar and ground glass. This turned out to be lethal and showed up the lack of control and complete indifference of the administration. Always thinking about her children, Sonia asked herself, horrified, "What if that sugar had ended up in Rahul's playschool?"

In view of the desolate state of affairs in the country, J.P. Narayan, a fragile man of 72, a hero from the liberation movement, as well as an old friend of the Nehru family, was able to unite different groups opposed to Indira. His programme proposed a federation of villages and aimed to launcha "total revolution", a democracy without parties. It was madness, the vague idea of a Messianic idealist, but it served to galvanize the masses against Indira's party, which they accused of corruption. In fact, the seeds of Indira's downfall had already been sown and lay in the immense power she had managed to gather around her and which acted like a poison that infected everything, even her own home, through Sanjay. As there was no legal system of party finance, the Congress Party depended on substantial private donations. Aware of the power granted to them by the fact that they held an overwhelming majority in the national Parliament and in most of the state Parliaments, too many members of the party became greedy and expert at exchanging economic aid for political favours.

JP's movement managed to organize several important strikes, which ended in confrontations with the police. The protests degenerated into widespread rioting when it came to light that a leader of the Congress Party had permitted an increase in the price of cooking oil in exchange for an important donation from the producers. That was the spark that caused the people's fury to explode. Homes and shops were pillaged, buses were burned and government property was destroyed. Rajiv was unable to return home for several days because his plane had not been able to take off when the airports were closed. Incapable of controlling all the swindles and shady dealings of the members of her party, Indira felt threatened. This fear was added to the paranoia that she had been feeling since the previous year, when a CIA-backed coup took place, which overthrew another Socialist, the democratically elected president of Chile, Salvador Allende. She knew precisely who had orchestrated it, and feared that they might attempt to take advantage of the chaotic situation in India to try the same on her. Above all, because Nixon had just been re-elected, and Kissinger was once again at his side.

What was to be done? She was not contemplating resignation, at least not without a fight. She attributed the riots to the malicious manipulation of the opposition, which was determined to oust her from power, and to a murky international conspiracy. She found it hard to believe that the people might be losing their faith in her. But she could not let anarchy go on spreading any longer, like a pool of oil, appropriately enough. So she plucked up courage to face the greatest challenge of her career, a national railway strike that was threatening to paralyze the country. Winning that showdown was decisive for her and for India. She was facing a million and a half railway workers who were demanding, among other things, an eight- hour working day and a 75% pay increase, a concession that it would be impossible to grant. "In a country where there are millions of unemployed and many millions more with unstable jobs," she explained audaciously at a union conference, "what is needed is a fair share-out of opportunities. In this sense the workers should recognize that in our country having a job is in itself a privilege." These words inflamed things even further, and so the strike was on. A million railway workers supported it. They suddenly upped the level of their demands: "What we want is to change the history of India and overthrow the government of Indira Gandhi."

As is usual in these conflicts, the lives of the poorest were at stake. Paralyzing the trains, thus affecting the transport of merchandise, was likely to cause a famine, something that Indira was not prepared to allow. So she applied a recent law (MISA, Maintenance of Security Act), which allowed preventive arrests to be made. An unprecedented deployment of police officers moved on the railway colonies, the old districts created by the English to house the railway workers and which were near the train stations. "It was like an occupied country," a union leader would say, unable to get over his astonishment. At dawn the police went into the railway workers' homes and arrested anyone who refused to go to work. Some families were thrown out of their homes – they were government property – and were forced to live out in the open. Sometimes the arrests were violent – there was one case in which the police set fire to a railway worker's shack – and some strikers ended up being injured. In total, sixty thousand workers were arrested. Indira acted like a general in the heat of the battle. She sent the army and the navy to protect railway facilities from possible acts of sabotage. The military got the signals and telecommunications going, and worked the trains under the protection of armed guards. She was convinced that if she crushed this strike, there would not be another for fifty years.

Indira was very clear-thinking, and fully in control of her faculties, as was usual with her at moments of high tension. She trusted herself. She tried to do several things at the same time, which was her infallible way of relaxing and finding solutions to difficult problems. One afternoon, when she was giving a press conference in the garden at home and she could see her grandson Rahul amusing himself on the grass by playing war games with plastic weapons, she had an idea. She thought the moment had come to give the go-ahead to the scientists who had been waiting for years to set off a nuclear bomb. It had been Nixon's decision to send a nuclear aircraft carrier to the Bay of Bengal that had caused the acceleration in the Indian atomic programme. It was not exactly the idea of a little grandmother, but it was that of a brilliant strategist. She kept it secret until the moment of the explosion, which took place a few days later in Pokhran, in the Rajasthan desert, near the border with Pakistan.

Just as she had foreseen, the news caused great enthusiasm among certain levels of the population who experienced it with real patriotic fervour. The MPs who stood up in the great hall of Parliament to congratulate each other seemed to have forgotten the urgent economic problems and the train strike. Indira had got what she wanted, which was to divert the country's attention. Overpopulated and almost paralyzed, with an income per capita that placed it at number 102 in the world ranking, India became the sixth world nuclear power, largely out of internal political necessity. Criticism intensified abroad. Indira defended herself, "... India does not accept the principle of *apartheid* in any area, and technology is no exception."

It took her 22 days to crush the strike with an iron fist. In spite of condemnation from the Press for the brutality of the repression, the middle class, the people who had always appreciated the punctuality of the trains, praised the firmness of the Prime Minister. The chambers of commerce too, although that did not mean many votes. For Indira it was a bittersweet victory. While the victory in Bangladesh had raised her to the category of goddess, this one left a bad taste in the mouth. The Prime Minister had shown that she could be harsh and even merciless. Her way of repressing the strike left a lasting wake of fear in wide sectors of society. The counterproductive effect of such severity was that the opposition became even more united against her. Even the most favourable political observers had to admit that her popularity was plummeting. In the elections that would take place in 1976, the defeat of the Congress Party now seemed like a real possibility.

*   *   *

On June 12th, 1975, day broke with heavy black clouds in the sky which announced the long-awaited rains, or perhaps forecast fateful days ahead. At that time in the morning, the heat was already intense, but Indira continued her daily routine of doing twenty minutes of yoga exercises in her room. Her granddaughter Priyanka's crying tempted her to interrupt her exercises, but as it stopped immediately, she thought that Sonia had got up and was dealing with the little girl. Then she had a shower and got dressed in five minutes, "something that few men can do", she liked to boast. On her bedside table the books were piling up. With working days of sixteen hours, she had no time for anything, not being with the family or seeing her friends, and of course not for reading, and she missed it.

She was having breakfast on a tray in her room with tea, fruit and toast when her secretary R.K. Dhawan, the one who had been so obliging to Sanjay, knocked on her door. He was bringing bad news. D.P. Dhar, an old friend and advisor of Indira's, had died minutes before an operation to fit him with a pacemaker. This was the man who had been sent to Moscow at the time of the Bangladesh crisis to ensure the backing of the Soviets and who had acted since then as ambassador to the

USSR. Another pillar of trust and friendship had disappeared from her life. Indira went straight to the hospital to comfort his family and to help in organizing the funeral rites.

She returned home about midday, and there was more bad news waiting for her. Her secretary informed her that in the previous day's elections in the state of Gujarat, the Congress Party had been beaten by the Janata Front, a coalition of five parties which included sympathizers of J.P. Narayan, the idealist who wanted to overthrow her. She was not too surprised. The bad thing was that those results forecast defeats in other states. Was it perhaps the beginning of the end? she wondered. Did not all human enterprises follow the same model of evolution as in nature, which is to say a growth stage, a development stage and then an end? She had tried tomake peace with JP, but his Utopian idea of setting up a government withoutparties was unacceptable because it meant the death of democracy. She had expressed this to JP, but he was a revolutionary who still believed in great, abstract ideas. He did not leave off in his determination and he did not become more flexible in his demands.

"You must agree with me that the government in Bihar is very corrupt," said JP in a trembling voice.

"Yes, everybody knows that," replied Indira.

"Then I insist that you dismiss it and call new elections."

"I can't do that, JP. It is a democratically elected government and I have no authority to dismiss it."

There was no reconciliation, just the opposite. Indira ended up accusing him of having backing from the CIA and the United States to overthrow her, and he told her she wanted to turn India into a satellite of the USSR.

However, at the end of the meeting, JP asked to see her

alone, withouther advisors. They went into the sitting room and there, to Indira's surprise, the man made a gesture of personal kindness, in spite of how bitter their political confrontation was. He handed her an old folder that had belonged to his wife and which contained letters that Indira's mother, Kamala, had written to her fifty years before in the clamour of the struggle for independence.

"I had them put away since my wife died," JP told her, "in the hope of giving them to you when I had the chance to see you."

Indira was moved by the gesture of this man who, nevertheless, was determined to destroy her. How strange politics is – she must have thought – that it allows hatred and love at the same time and in the same person. She felt a pang in her heart when she read those letters which brought her mother back to life, so fragile, always so ill, and which now revealed her unhappiness at feeling the contempt of Nehru's sisters who found her too traditional and religious. She thanked JP from the depths of her heart, even knowing that he would keep his promise to intensify his crusade against her.

The third piece of bad news of the day came at three in the afternoon. Still dressed in his pilot's uniform, Rajiv burst into Indira's bedroom. On hisway back from the airport, he had met one of his mother's secretaries who had filled him in on some news that had just come in on the teleprinter.

"The verdict of the Allahabad Judge has just come out..." said Rajiv. "And...?" asked Indira, turning her head slightly, as though she expected the blow she was about to receive.

Rajiv read her the text of the sentence that the secretary had given him. It said that the Prime Minister had been declared guilty of negligence in the electoral proceedings in the 1971 elections. As a consequence, the result of those elections was invalid. The tribunal gave the Congress Party twenty days to take the necessary steps so that the Government could go on working. Furthermore, it prohibited her from holding any public office in the next six years.

Indira sighed and stayed calm. She looked out into the garden. Her grandchildren were playing on the grass. Everything seemed so normal and calm, except for the black clouds that still threatened to unload their rain. How curious life was, she must have thought. The biggest blow of her career had been struck against her in her birthplace, in the same courts where her grandfather Motilal Nehru had given his most brilliant arguments. She turned towards her son: "I believe there is no option but to resign. The moment has come," she said without the slightest trace of emotion.

She had been expecting a guilty verdict, but not one so out of proportion. The opposition had used a legal dodge to corner her. The sentence corresponded to the complaint that a political rival called Raj Narain had made four years previously to the court in Allahabad, having lost by a hundred thousand votes. The accusations were trivial and referred to the improper use of staff and government-owned transport during the previous electoral campaign. In private, everyone, including her adversaries, admitted that the charges against her were ridiculous and that the judges had overstepped the mark. According to the London *Times* newspaper, it was the equivalent of "removing a prime minister from office over a traffic fine". But in the India of 1975, the people came out on the streets to celebrate.

Her friend Siddharta Shankar Ray, head of the Bengal

government, arrived at the house shortly afterwards. He was a trusted man, upright, one of the old guard of unconditional friends. The party was in uproar, he told her. Then he went on: "...What the opposition has not managed to do in the elections, it is trying to manipulate by means of a legal sentence."

"I have to resign," said Indira impassively.

The man took a seat. He looked at Indira: her face betrayed herinfinite tiredness.

"Don't make that decision too lightly. Let's think about it." Indira shrugged.

"Is there any other solution?""We can always appeal."

"It will take months... We know how justice works here."

The conversation was interrupted by the arrival of two ministers, followed shortly after by the president of the party and several more colleagues. The house began to fill with people. Sonia offered them sweets and drinks. With her own eyes, she could see how some were worried about losing their position, while others, on the contrary, were excited because Indira's seat was up for grabs. The rumours, the uncertainty and the heat made the air seem unbreathable. Some talked to Indira, trying to dissuadeher from presenting her resignation; others stood in little groups, weighing up the strengths of different leaders who could replace her. The still Prime Minister listened to them all, in silence. "I believe I should resign immediately," she repeated.

In the evening, Sanjay came back from the "factory". He had heard the news on the radio. Coming into the house, he met his brother.

"What is she going to do?" he asked. "Resign. She has no option."

"No," said Sanjay, "that cannot be."

In a second Sanjay saw his dream of being a great businessman shattered. If his mother gave way to her enemies, he could say goodbye forever to Maruti Ltd. He went into the sitting room full of people, hardly saying hello to anyone, as was his custom, and he took his mother by the arm and asked to speak to her alone for a few minutes. They went into the study in the next room.

"Rajiv has told me you're thinking of resigning." "We're weighing it up. I don't have many options."

"You mustn't do it, Mother. If you give way now and resign because of those paltry charges, when you don't have parliamentary immunity they will have you thrown into jail for any excuse they can make up."

"I have a clear conscience. We're thinking about exchanging jobs. Let the party president take on the post of Prime Minister until my appeal is dealt with in the Supreme Court. Meanwhile, I'll take over the presidency of the party."

"That's crazy, Mother!" said Sanjay, and his shouts were heard in the sitting room next door. "Do you think once he's in your job the party president will give it back to you? He never will. They all seem to be very loyal and great friends of yours, but you know better than I do that their smiles hide their personal ambitions. They all want your position. They all seek power. You must not resign under any circumstances."

Accepting defeat was not an easy thing for Indira. Could she withdraw with her tail between her legs over something so trivial, she who had spent her life in politics and had been Prime Minister for almost a decade? It did not fit in with her idea of dignity. Could she leave her party colleagues in the lurch, when all of them depended on her? The whole country? Did they not say that India is Indira and Indira is India? Was she going to allow J.P. Narayan to kill off democracy and sink the country into anarchy? She was tired, it is true, and sometimes even depressed at not finding solutions to the ills of the country. If she only had to listen to her inner voice, the voice that called for serenity, perhaps she would opt for resignation. For herself, she would do it. But she was not alone. She thought of Sanjay... What would become of him if she lost her job? They would hurl themselves at him like bloodhounds and devour him for having dared be enterprising, or simply for being who he was. What would become of the rest of the family? Power showed itself to be a necessary defence against all the enemies that same power had created over the years. Power protected the family. Without that shield they were in danger.

Indira went back into the sitting room. "I am determined to fight to keep my job," she told her lawyer. They agreed that he would ask the Supreme Court to put off the sentence until the court decided about her appeal. The manoeuvre would allow her to gain some time and to remain as Prime Minister until she could gather forces and support. As soon as she announced her decision, the tension in the house relaxed. To hide their disappointment, those who were already dreaming of taking over from her broke into the most servile praises. Sonia was perplexed. Deep down, she would have liked her mother-in-law to resign, because she missed a more peaceful lifestyle.

18

Over the following days, Sanjay and his henchman, secretary Dhawan, organized demonstrations and marches in support of Indira. They had no qualms about requisitioning the vehicles of the municipal transport company of Delhi to bus in thousands of demonstrators. The whole party apparatus mobilized so that their voices could be heard loud and clear in support of Indira. Specially chartered trains arrived in the capital full of supporters for the rallies.

Now Sonia and Maneka could not go in and out of the house so easily because there was a permanent crowd at the gates calling for Indira's presence. She came out once a day to greet them. Neither Sonia nor Rajiv liked the look events were taking on. She was frightened because the car that took her to Khan Market one morning had been hit by a stone. There was only a scratch on the bodywork, but it had been enough to make her feel afraid. In addition, living with Maneka was becoming more and more difficult for her. And Sanjay seemed like another person. She rarely saw him, but when she did he was no longer as affectionate as before. She realized that Maneka's presence was poisoning relations between the two brothers, and between her and Sanjay too.

"Why don't we go to Italy for a while," she asked her

husband, "until things get back to normal?"

Rajiv thought it was an excellent idea and agreed that it would begood for the children. But he was clearly worried.

"How are we going to tell my mother? Can we abandon her at a time like this?" Sonia remained thoughtful, and did not answer him. For the first time,she was afraid, for herself and for the children. The atmosphere had never been so charged.

On June 20th, 1975, Sanjay had the idea that the whole family shouldattend a solidarity rally that he had organized at the Boat Club in New Delhi.

"It'll be good for the people to see us all together," he had said. "I'd prefer it if you didn't decide for us," Rajiv spat back at him."It's for Mother's sake," his brother answered.

They were in a compromising situation, so Rajiv and Sonia reluctantlyagreed. It was perhaps Sonia's first political act. Being in front of a crowd ofover a hundred thousand made quite an impression on her. Dressed in akhaki sari, she was next to Rajiv, Maneka and Sanjay, behind Indira. From up there it made her dizzy to think about the vast expanse of her adopted country. So many people, so many beliefs, so many religions... When her mother-in-law turned round to them, Sonia smiled at her. She suddenly saw her in contact with the people she was always talking about, that privileged contact that justified all the upsets and which was now not something abstract but utterly real. They were there, at her feet. Sonia was able to see the enormous support of the people, which Indira still enjoyed, and which exceeded by far the mere presence of the supporters paid by Sanjay. She got goose pimples when she heard her mother-in-law tell the crowd that serving the country was the tradition in the Nehru-Gandhi family, and that shepromised to go on serving until her last breath. It was the first time thatIndira had been seen flanked by her family, and the rally was a great success. Sonia realized how much Indira needed to have her family at her side. No, it was not the moment to abandon her.

JP's followers organized counter-demonstrations outside the palace of the President of the Republic and in several cities in the immense country. The journalist Oriana Fallaci was the first to hear from the lips of an opposition leader that they planned to block the entrance to number 1, Safdarjung Road with hordes of people in order to turn Indira into a prisoner in her own home. "We'll camp there day and night," said the leader. "We'll force her to resign. Once and for all. The lady will not survive our movement."

On the morning of June 25th, Indira called Siddharta Shankar Ray, the head of the Bengal government, to her office at home. He was in New Delhi by chance, and when the sentence was made public, he had advised her not to resign. He found her very tense. Her desk was covered in reports from the Intelligence Agencies.

"We cannot allow it," Indira told him. "I have information that at a rally tonight J.P. Narayan is going to ask the police and army to mutiny. It is possible that the CIA is involved. You know that I'm high on the list of people hated by Richard Nixon... What can we do?"

Ray was an expert in legal matters, and had a reputation for honesty and toughness. He still thought Indira should remain in her job. She continued describing how the country was deep in chaos.

"We must be able to stop this madness. I feel as if Indian democracy were a child, and just as sometimes you have to shake a child, I think we have to shake the country to make it wake up."

"Are you thinking about a state of emergency?"

Indira nodded. Actually she was not seeking advice about what decision to make, because she had already made it the day before. Her son Sanjay had mentioned it to her, but the idea had not come from him but from his protector, Bansi Lal, the chubby head of the government in Haryana who had provided him with the land to build the factory. According to Bansi Lal and Sanjay, there were at least fifty politicians in the country that it was necessary to remove from public life. Naturally, the first was J.P. Narayan.

Declaring a state of emergency was a way forwards... But what option did Indira have? Between a dishonourable step-down and the state of emergency, she preferred the latter.

"I want to do it all impeccably from the legal point of view," the Prime Minister specified.

"Let me study the constitutional aspects. Give me a few hours and I'll be able to tell you something."

"Please be quick," she asked.

Ray went away and came back at three in the afternoon. He had spent several hours going over the text of the Indian Constitution, and the American one too.

"Under Article 352 of the Constitution," he told Indira, "the government can impose a state of emergency if there is the threat of aggression from outside or internal disorder."

"J.P. Narayan's call for the army and police to mutiny is a sufficiently serious threat, isn't it?"

"Yes, it is."

"Then by doing that they've fallen into their own trap." "In effect. They've handed you on a silver tray the justification you need to suspend parliamentary activity and to impose a state of emergency."

There was a silence. Indira's eyes gleamed in the darkness. One thing was missing: the signature of the President of the Republic, but he was an ally and Indira did not doubt his loyalty.

"Will you go with me to the President's palace?" she asked Ray. "Let's go."

With the four-line document that the President signed that same night in the splendid Ashoka hall of the old Viceroy's palace, and which ratified the proclamation of a state of emergency, the biggest democracy in the world became a virtual dictatorship. The government of India was now authorized to arrest people without prior authorization, to suspend civil rights and liberties, to limit the right of interference of the courts and to impose censorship.

*   *   *

Rajiv had been away on a flight for two days, and on one of the stopovers of his route, he was very surprised to read in the papers that his mother had declared a state of emergency the day before. No one had said anything to him. The measure went against his peace-loving nature, and although he was not a political man, it seemed to him that it went against the democratic principles of the family tradition. What concerned him above all was that his mother had given way to his brother's insistence. No one knew Sanjay's hold over his mother better than he. For some obscure reason, his mother was incapable of resisting the emotional blackmail to which his brother subjected her. And no one knew Sanjay better than he did - his strong points, his limitations and the danger he could represent. So he was disturbed and alarmed, and Sonia's idea of going to Italy for a while went through his mind again.

"I don't know what we should do," Sonia told him. "I'm very worried about your brother's behaviour. He's getting more and more involved in politics."

She told him that Maneka was in Kashmir, where Sanjay had sent her at Indira's indication, since she was worried that the girl, being so talkative, might reveal her intentions regarding the declaration of the state of emergency, which they had kept a complete secret until it was announced. She went on to tell him that the day before Sanjay had had a meeting in Indira's office with secretary Dhawan and the deputy Home Secretary until very late.

"Do you know what they were doing? They were getting in touch with heads of local governments and they were sending them orders for arrests. They had a blacklist of "enemies". The worst thing isn't that, the worst is that they were doing it in your mother's name."

"I know they arrested J.P. Narayan in the early hours – I heard that at the airport," said Rajiv with a sigh. "A police patrol took him in handcuffs to jail. It seems that Narayan couldn't believe it; it seemed incredible to him that Mother should have taken such drastic steps."

Sonia went on to tell him that at three o'clock in the morning, after having helped Indira to complete the draft of the speech that was going to announce the state of emergency to the people, Siddharta Shankar Ray was getting ready to leave when he met secretary Dhawan in the corridor. Dhawan told him, "The steps have now been taken to cut off the electricity supply to the main newspapers of the country and to close the courts."

"Ray was thunderstruck," Sonia continued, "and he was furious. He asked for your mother to be woken. She was exhausted after such a long day. At that moment Sanjay came out and began to argue with Ray. Do you know what he said? He said: 'You have no idea how to run a country!'"

"As if he knew!" said Rajiv, looking up.

"The fact is that he didn't go until your mother appeared. She was astonished because she didn't know a thing about those orders for arrests. Your brother had given them. She asked him to wait for a few minutes and she went off to talk to Sanjay."

"What Sanjay is after with those measures is to protect himself and his business, making it appear that he is also protecting Mother from the legal actions that have been undertaken against her."

"Your mother may be tough and authoritarian, but she has principles too. Her eyes were red from crying when she came out of the room where she'd been shut in with Sanjay. She told Ray that the newspapers would have electricity and no court would be closed."

"But that's a lie," said Rajiv. "Today there are no newspapers on the street because they've had their electricity supply cut off. Sanjay has got away with it again."

It would have been a great success for Indira if the state of emergency had lasted only a short time, and especially if Sanjay had not grown as a power in the shadows. The first day, when the Information Minister, I.K. Gurjal, a cultivated and respected man with a gentle manner, arrived at his office in Akbar Road, Sanjay ordered that all the news bulletins should be first submitted to him before they were broadcast. Usha, sitting in her office, witnessed the scene.

"That is not possible," the man told him. "The bulletins are confidential."

"Well, from now on it will have to be possible." Indira was in the doorway and heard the conversation. "What's going on?" she asked.

The minister repeated his explanation.

"I understand," Indira told him, "if you don't want to give them to Sanjay, I suggest that a clerk from your ministry brings them to me every morning so I can see them."

The minister left with the firm intention of presenting his resignation, but he was called back in the afternoon to what they were now calling "the palace", which was nothing other than Indira Gandhi's residence. Sanjay asked him to deport the BBC correspondent, a very well-known and well- liked journalist named Mark Tully, for having sent a report that "distorted" the facts.

"It is not the job of the Minister of Information to arrest foreign correspondents," Gujral answered him.

When Sanjay immediately reproached him for the fact that his mother's speech had not been broadcast in its entirety on television, the minister lost patience.

"If you want to speak to me, you'll have to learn to do it politely," he told him. "You are younger than my son and I don't owe you any explanations."

He did not have time to present his resignation. Indira called him that same night to relieve him of his post "because under the circumstances the Ministry of Information needed someone who could deal with matters more firmly."

The new minister announced extremely harsh censorship laws, including prohibiting people from quoting Nehru and Gandhi's declarations for freedom of the Press, which was a cruel irony of history. One by one, the representatives of the international Press were invited to leave.

The only one of her ministers who questioned the need to impose the state of emergency was relieved of his position and replaced by Bansi Lal, the head of the Haryana government, and the first to suggest the need to impose the state of emergency... At the age of 29, just because he was his mother's son, Sanjay was on his way to becoming the most powerful man in India.

The censorship of the Press was harsher than when the British had imposed it during the struggle for independence. At least, at that time, the newspapers were authorized to report the names of those who had been arrested and the jails where they were being held. Now people found out by rumour where their loved ones were, almost all of them members of the opposition. Some one hundred thousand people approximately were arrested without charges or trial. The conditions in which they were held were so tough that 22 detainees died in their dirty, overcrowded cells. If the railwaymen remembered how the strike had been crushed, now no sector of the population was safe. The most talked-about arrests were perhaps those of the Maharanis of Jaipur and Gwalior, former princesses who led parties in opposition to Indira in their respective states and who were locked up in the infamous Tihar jail in Delhi, alongside criminals and prostitutes. Gayatri Devi, the elegant Maharani of Jaipur, did not complain about the filth, or the promiscuity or even the stench. She only complained about the noise the other prisoners made and asked a friend to send her some wax earplugs.

Meanwhile, Parliament granted Indira the same immunity as the President of the Republic and state governors enjoyed. The Prime Minister was retroactively absolved of all the charges of electoral fraud that she faced and which had been what triggered the current state of emergency.

Once again, guided by her survival instinct, Indira found herself in absolute control of the country, now more than ever, although the manipulation of democratic procedures was bringing her a growing number of enemies, both within India and abroad. But in the early days, the state of emergency was greeted with relief by part of the population, especially the urban middle classes. Even Sonia had the impression that she was in anothercity when she went to take her son to school, and not in the New Delhi of recent times. The atmosphere was of amazing calm. There were no interruptions in the traffic, or demonstrations, or sit-ins, or outbreaks of violence against her mother-in-law. Even the taxi drivers and rickshaw men drove on the right side of the road. Like her, a large part of the population was happy that the strikes and riots were over and they could enjoy a certain measure of peace. In the cities, the people celebrated that they could walk around again without feeling afraid, as the level of criminality had fallen sharply owing to the increased number of policemen and the toughening of the law. Aware of the new atmosphere of seriousness, the civil servants worked full days and with greater efficiency. The trains and planes were punctual, to the relief of those that used them, including Rajiv, who could now enjoy a more stable family life, without the delays of recent timeswhich made him arrive home at impossible hours. Enormous posters with Indira's face on them decorated roundabouts and squares: "The difference between chaos and order," said a slogan next to her photo.

The idea that Indira had restored peace and order in the country also took root abroad. Usha, her private secretary, was the one in charge of bringing and reading out or writing down the articles in the international Press that had to do with the current situation in India. Very often sitting at the table in the dining room she read out the headlines or letters that were published. "The authoritarian government is gaining wide acceptance inIndia", said a headline in the *New York Times*. But there were other openly hostile headlines which provoked worrying looks between Sanjay and his mother. One day Usha was on her own in her office when Sonia came in. The two women greatly appreciated each other.

"Usha, I think it's best if you don't read any of the criticisms that come out in the foreign Press in front of everyone. I'm not saying it for Mummy's sake – as she now called Indira – but because I don't want anyone to give you black looks."

"Thanks for letting me know," Usha told her. She had also noticed that the atmosphere had changed and was wary now of Sanjay's influence over his mother.

They could silence critical voices in India, but not abroad. Dorothy Norman, Indira's best friend for so many years, was overtly hostile towards her. She gathered signatures from American personalities – the writer Noam Chomsky, the tennis player Arthur Ashe, the Nobel Prize winner Linus Pauling, the paediatrician Benjamin Spock, etc. – to publish a text in the Press deploring the harsh measures of the state of emergency and calling for it to be lifted. Among the signatories, humiliating Indira even more, was Allen Ginsberg, the poet she had met in London when she went there to inaugurate the tribute to Nehru and who years later had sung of the sadness of the Bangladeshi refugees. That hurt. The correspondence between the two of them ceased and would not recommence until four years later. Her other friend, Pupul Jayakar, confronted Indira when she came back from a trip: "How can you, the daughter of Jawaharlal Nehru, allow this?" Indira was not expecting it and was dumbstruck. No one dared to defy her openly.

"You don't know the seriousness of what is happening," she

said. "You don't know the plots against me. JP never liked me being Prime Minister. He has not yet discovered his true role... What does he want to be?

A martyr? A saint? Why can't he accept that he's just a politician and that he wants to be Prime Minister?" she answered.

Indira told Pupul that it was her intention to maintain the state of emergency for only two months, and that anyway she was going to take advantage of that time to launch a twenty-point programme to bring the country out of its underdevelopment. Among those measures there were two that were revolutionary: the illegalization of slave labour and the cancellation of poor people's debts with village money-lenders.

Pupul realized it was useless to argue with Indira. The only thing she could do was to listen to her so that her friend could feel free to empty her heart to someone she trusted. Pupul knew her well and knew how alone she felt. Although she deeply disagreed with Indira, she decided to remain close at hand.

19

It was Indira's intention to announce the end of the Emergency on August 15th, 1975, on the same day and in the same place as her father had made his famous independence speech 28 years previously: "A moment comes, which comes but rarely in history, when we step out from the old to the new, when an age ends, and when the soul of a nation, long suppressed, finds utterance…" At that historic moment, those words had left her brimming with emotion. She had declared to the BBC correspondent, "You know, when you go from extreme pain to extreme pleasure, you are left kind of numb. Freedom is something so great that it's hard to assimilate."

Now her car drove along the wide avenues of New Delhi, from where all the beggars and wandering cows had mysteriously disappeared – this was one of the marvellous effects of the order imposed by the state of emergency. She was heading for the Red Fort in order to give back that freedom to the people - the same freedom that she had been forced to hold to ransom – when her chief of protocol gave her some news that upset her deeply. Sheikh Mujibur Rahman, her friend, the hero that she had restored to the presidency of Bangladesh, had been overthrown in a military coup. But that was not the worst: Sheikh, his wife, three sons, two daughters-in-law and two nephews had had their throats cut. The participants in the coup had made certain that a Rahman dynasty would not survive.

Indira was devastated. "I noticed that there was something strange, the moment she began her speech," her friend Pupul would say, standing in the crowd at the Red Fort. "Her tone of voice was forced as though she was trying to hold in powerful emotions, and that voice took away her ability to move people." Pupul was listening carefully to the speech, in which Indira spoke about freedom, about the need to take harsh measures, about the notions of sacrifice and service, about courage, about faith, about democracy

… but not a word about the end of the state of emergency.

Pupul went to see her that night and found her in a state of shock. Indira was convinced that the CIA was implicated in those deaths (which turned out to be true). And she did not want to end up like Allende, as recently she had repeatedly told the British Labour leader, Michael Foot. She thought that what had happened in Bangladesh had been the first in a chain of plots to destabilize southern Asia and to change the ideological colour of its governments. She was convinced that she would be the next victim. The chief of the Intelligence Agency had confirmed that they had discovered several plots to get rid of her. According to Pupul, she was paranoid, suspecting everyone, and convinced that every shadow hid an enemy.

"Who can I trust?" Indira asked her. My grandson is the same age as Sheikh Rahman's son. Tomorrow it could be him. They want to destroy me by whatever means they can, me and my family."

It was the first time that Indira had realized that it was not only she that was in danger because she was Prime Minister. Her whole family, including her grandchildren, were targeted, she thought. She was a prisoner in a vicious circle that she no longer knew how to break. In those circumstances, she thought that it was not the moment to put an end to the state of emergency. On the contrary, it was necessary to take steps to protect herself by intensifying the arrests without trial and the activities of theIntelligence Agency.

Indira felt safe in crowds, but in her house, now heavily guarded, she began to feel she was in danger. The truth is she was sick with fear, tired of wielding power, worn out with so many struggles, and disappointed at the lack of results. She was an intensely patriotic woman and she had absolute faith in the destiny of India. But she realized that her leftist policies had beenunable to pull India out of its poverty. How to make India into a modern, prosperous and strong country? She no longer knew which formula to use, except an iron hand, which went against her own traditions. She had put India, her family and herself in a situation with no way out, and she did not know how to escape.

Instinctively she turned to her sons. The older one, Rajiv, could not be of much help to her. He had expressed his disagreement with the Emergencyseveral times, and he had also done it in public, and whenever he could, in front of his friends. Contact between them was reduced so much that, since he was at work a lot and not much at home, he found out about his mother's tours and decisions from the newspapers. Furthermore, Indira knew that he was not going to feel sorry for her. Even Sonia had expressed regret about anold political rival who had ended up in jail in the first wave of arrests. "It must be terrible for you with your father in jail. I'm really sorry about it," she had told this politician's son at a reception and these words came to the ears of others who wasted no time in spreading Sonia's sentiments in the New Delhi gossip circles. Indira did not harbour a grudge about it; she had always thought that Rajiv was no good for politics and that neither he nor Sonia were able to understand the heartfelt reasons that had led her to take that decision. On the other hand, she knew that Sonia was insisting on going to Italy with the children for a while until the situation returned to normal. Nothing is so contagious as fear...

That left the younger one, Sanjay, her favourite. She saw him as full of energy, strong and loyal. Arrogant, true, able to put his foot in it better than anyone, but a son she could trust, who was at her side and took on her problems. And who, she thought, she could always control. Besides, there was another reason, which had nothing to do with a mother's sentimentality. Sanjay was ferociously anti-Communist and defended liberal policies which encouraged private initiative and the business turn of mind of the people of India. His experience with the Maruti had convinced him even more of the need to free the country of so many bureaucratic obstacles. Indira thought she could use her son to open up the economy and make a turn to the right. And not only out of simple conviction, but out of political need. In effect, radical Communists had infiltrated her party and called for the "elimination of private property as a fundamental right" in the Constitution, among other Stalinist-type measures that they wanted to impose. Indira had stopped them in their tracks stating that any shortcut that did not respect democratic procedures was dangerous. But they represented a threat which could easily cause a split in the Congress Party. Through her *darling boy* Sanjay, she thought she could counteract them.

Indira was so afraid that something might happen to her son that she asked him to move to another room. "I don't want you to stay here, so near the main entrance and the street, it isn't safe," she told him. "It's better if you move to the room at the end of the passage, the one next to mine." A friend asked her the reason for the change and she said, "I don't feel very well. I sleep in my room and Sanjay is in the room next door. If something happens to me during the night, I can call him straight away." The truth was that Indira wrapped herself in Sanjay like one of those Kashmir pashminas that she liked so much and she did so to protect herself from the cold she felt in her soul, not realizing that her son was her biggest problem and, in a sense, her greatest threat.

Sanjay had been left without any money and, convinced now that no Maruti vehicle would ever come out of the factory, he was selling off the structure for scrap iron. He had left the car dealers in the lurch after they had got into debt with the banks to build attractive showrooms and now they were being forced to sell their properties to pay off those loans. As if that was not enough, Sanjay ordered the arrest of the only two dealers who dared to claim back the advance money they had paid.

With the Maruti disaster, cars no longer interested him. Now he took to flying, like his brother. Before the Emergency he had gained a qualification as a private pilot and as he loved speed, he immediately became fond of acrobatic flying. His weakness for machines that went faster and faster and the excess of confidence he had in his own abilities scared most of his acquaintances and friends, who were frightened to fly with him. Maneka ended up being his only passenger.

Sanjay needed a cover in order to be able to operate

parallel to his mother. To justify his extra-constitutional power, Indira decided to place him at the head of a dying organization, the Youth Congress (the youth wing of the Congress Party) and in a ceremony in Chandigarh, the ultramodern capital of the Punjab designed by Le Corbusier, he was named a member of the Executive Committee. But everyone understood the subliminal message: Sanjay was officially Indira's heir. The Prime Minister, who had been merciless to the princes because they put birth before talent, was now succumbing to the same temptation and was setting up her own dynasty.

Rajiv and Sonia watched Sanjay's rise with amazement and displeasure, confused and often embarrassed for him. The Press called him the "Messiah", the "Sun" or "the voice of youth and reason": They saw him always surrounded by flatterers whom they called *chamchas*, which in Hindimeans a spoon, alluding to the curved movement required when handling that item of cutlery. They were tough individuals hiding under a docile appearance, skilled at manipulation, with no real knowledge of the government's problems, and with little education or training, just like Sanjay. A mixture of politicians, henchmen and thugs. The only thing they were interested in was to get what they could out of their closeness to power. They began by revitalizing the coffers of the Youth Congress, organizing themselves into brigades that demanded donations, almost always with intimidation. The shopkeepers of Delhi complained to Rajiv or Sonia that the young men from the Youth Congress were extorting money from them. But Rajiv's protests fell on deaf ears.

"Don't believe all the lies people tell you," his brother invariably told him.

The truth is that no one seemed to take responsibility for the bad things, only for the good.

Because there was also a good side to Sanjay's intentions. As soon as he had been nominated for that position, he added four more points to his mother's programme, which he, personally, ensured were carried out. The four points were: to fight the spread of illegal slums in a campaign to beautify the cities; to eradicate illiteracy and the dowry system and to promote family planning.

In theory, no one disagreed with these measures, especially the fight against overpopulation, caused in part by the success of health programmes which had managed to greatly reduce infant mortality and which had increased life expectancy from 27 to 47 in a couple of decades. In sum, now there were more people living more reproductive years. The advances in agriculture, industry and education could not keep up with the increase in population. There was more wealth, but also more poverty. More education, but also more illiterates. "Nowadays, if we create a million jobs, we already have ten million going for them," Sanjay had said. "Industrial development and the increase in agricultural production are no good if the population continues to grow at the present rate." He was right, that was no way to get rid of poverty. It was not in the idea, which was obvious, but in its putting into practice where Sanjay went wrong, managing to completely discredit the state of emergency, and, in passing, his mother.

In the end it was the poor, those that the state of emergency was supposedly helping, who suffered most. Sanjay's men chose sterilization as the most appropriate method of reducing the population of India. The other methods of family planning had produced poor results. The pill was not available yet and the diaphragm was impossible to use for peasant women who lived without any privacy whatsoever. For a while, hope of controlling the birth rate centred on condoms. Elephants came to the villages with loads of condoms which were supposed to be distributed free among the people, but the children discovered that it was great fun to blow them up and tie them to sticks to play with, and so they intercepted them. The irony of the government's slogan that said that family planning produced happy children did not escape anyone ... Male sterilization turned out to be the cheapest, most efficient and safest method. Furthermore, there was money from the West for carrying out those programmes.

Sanjay began touring the country, encouraging heads of local governments to do better than others were doing. "The head of Haryana has managed 60,000 operations in three weeks. Let's see how many you can get!" he told them. The objectives to be achieved were announced to the heads of district, who were rewarded if they did better, or the opposite - they were transferred or downgraded if they did not. A system like this encouraged the abuse of power. Modest government civil servants had to agree to go under the surgeon's scalpel to get their back pay. Lorry drivers and rickshaw men did not have their driving licences renewed unless they showed a sterilization certificate. The same condition was applicable to the slum dwellers who requested a deed of ownership of their shacks to legalize their situation. An anthropologist named Lee Schlesinger was a witness to how the campaign began, after a lightning visit by Sanjay Gandhi to the village where he was carrying out his research. Local civil servants prepared lists of "candidates", in other words those who already had three or four children, and a few days later police vans arrived to take them to the nearest health centre where, in exchange for 120 rupees, a tin of cooking oil or a transistor, they came out sterilized. Later, when they heard the van was onits way, some men fled into the mountains. However, others had themselves operated twice in order to get more than one reward.

In the cities, people became afraid. Delhi was left without any workmen, which was unheard of in a city where people arrived from the countryside in search of work. Immigrants returned to their villages to avoid the fatal incision to their genitals. In November 1975, the celebration of Nehru's birthday, which included free snacks for hundreds of children, had to be cancelled because the mothers refused to send their little boys in case "Sanjay Gandhi's doctors" castrated them. Soon the official sterilization certificate became an essential requirement for dealing with all people's needs in their day to day lives.

It was inevitable that a campaign like this would soon come up against strong resistance, especially when the false rumour was spread that sterilization led to impotence. To fight that resistance, the government set upa quota system through which the salaries of police officers, teachers, doctors and nurses were paid only after they had motivated a certain number of people to submit to a vasectomy. Naturally, the victims of this pitiless policy were the weakest, the poorest, the most discriminated social groups like the untouchables or certain Moslem and tribal communities which were in principle those who had always supported Indira unconditionally. They did not understand how their goddess, for whom they had always voted, could punish them like that. Was that the reward they were to receive for their loyalty?

Indians were not used to the State dictating the size of their families to them. India was not a dictatorship like China, where decisions taken at the top could be carried out by force. That dictatorial tradition did not exist. Here, children were a very valuable resource, something like their parents' social security, because from the time they were very small, they worked in the fields, in workshops, in textile factories, or begging on the streets. Families were large because the more children there were, the more hands there were and, as a result, the more resources there were. For the poor peasants, labourers and homeless beggars, the possibility of having children represented almost the only act of individual freedom by means of which they could enjoy life. Taking away from the poor the pleasure of making and having children was to take away the only thing they had. But of course Sanjay could not see that as his heart was blinded to the suffering of the poor. Neither did he have any experience in government, in the art of handling civil servants and bureaucrats. By attempting to shake up the stratified administrative hierarchy to make it more efficient, by using methods such as the threat of transfer, dubious incentives to sterilization or the threat of being investigated by the tax authorities, what he achieved was for that tacit brotherhood of bureaucrats, which had been tied together by invisible bonds for centuries, to unite even more in order to defend itself from the attacks. On one hand they flattered him, and on the other they boycotted him. He was too naïve to see it.

As for his mother, she chose not to believe what she was told. Completely distanced from reality by that same court of her son's flatterers who assured her that the reports of abuse were based on unproved rumours, Indira saw the criticism as personal attacks and ignored them with the stroke of a pen.

"People exaggerate a lot," she said to Rajiv when they saw each other at home, echoing Sanjay's words. "You shouldn't believe what people say."

"I've just got back from Bhopal," Rajiv insisted, "and there the Moslems are terrified. They say that the Hindus manipulate the campaign against them... Those people have to be reassured before it becomes a conflict between communities."

"What has to be done is to limit the population by whatever means.

There is no way out for India if we can't do that."

Rajiv also realized that it was impossible to talk to his mother. She did not allow anyone to contradict her. She interpreted everything as a political vendetta, or saw it from a supernatural point of view, which was especially worrying. The influence of her yoga teacher, Dhirendra Brahmachari, was greater than ever. The man took advantage of the Prime Minister's loneliness and he came to have easier access to Indira than her own son, Rajiv. He was able to use that proximity to power in his favour, because during the state of emergency he amassed a small fortune, so much that it allowed him to purchase a light plane. In the city he was known as "the flying saint". Rajiv and Sonia hated him because they realized how much he was taking advantage of Indira. They had been observing him: first he frightened her by talking about supernatural plots against her and Sanjay, and then he convinced her to agree to recite certain mantras and to protect herself with them from those that were seeking her destruction. In this way, he held considerable influence over Indira, which she was unable to shake off. When Sonia and Rajiv tried to put her on her guard, she shut herself up in one of her famous silences. Sonia could not stand the presence of the guru in the house. He was always demanding food and drink whenever he felt like it. He got fatter and fatter, the result of his voracious appetite, and he had no manners.

"He's a real pig!" they said, disgusted at seeing him eat.

"I don't know how my mother puts up with him..." said Rajiv. "She lives in an ivory tower, and if her only contact with the world is Sanjay and the guru, we're in a real mess!"

"Let's go to Italy, really Rajiv, let's give the children a bit of normal life."

When they told her, the expression on Indira's face completely

changed, to such an extent that they immediately regretted having even mentioned it. They understood, even before Indira had said a single word, that it was going to be difficult, not to say impossible.

"I can understand you Sonia. I understand that you're tired of living in this atmosphere," Indira said to her, "that you have to listen to all that unfounded criticism that is showered on me. I understand that you feel like going back to Italy... But can you imagine what they would say if you went away now? They would interpret it as a desertion, as a secret manoeuvre of mine... 'She sends the children off to Europe, then she'll follow, she's preparing her getaway', I can hear them saying it..."

"It's just that we thought it's something we can do now that the children are small," said Sonia. "Later on it will be impossible..."

"Can't you wait a little while?"

Sonia looked at Rajiv and put her head down. He was pensive. Sonia guessed at how torn he must feel inside. Indira went on: "It's just that it's a bad time now..."

"I understand, and the last thing we'd want to do is harm you," her daughter-in-law said as she stood up, even before Rajiv could say a word.

"At difficult times the family has to be seen to be united. It's important for people, for the people, to see that."

Sonia nodded.

"Don't worry, Mummy, we're staying," she told her with an understanding smile.

What was not said in the conversation was equally important. Apart from being afraid of what might happen, Sonia wanted to leave for a while because she was tired of the behaviour of her sister-in-law. Maneka, called her "Italian" insultingly, and acted with the insolence of a queen consort, sheltered by her husband, *deus ex machina* of the state of emergency. For her part, Indira did not mention the aversion she felt at being apart from her grandchildren, whom she adored. She played with them, sometimes she took them into her office and was proud to introduce them to people. They were her great passion. The fact is that Indira had become as possessive and protective a matriarch as her grandfather, Motilal Nehru, the former patriarch of the clan, had been.

20

It was a poor individual who opened Indira's eyes to the reality of the abuses committed in the name of the Emergency. The soles of his sandals were worn out from the five days it had taken him to walk as far as the office in Akbar Road,. He was a young teacher from a school in a distant village. An honest man, idealistic and a fighter, who came to tell Indira how he had been forcibly sterilized, in spite of only having one daughter. The police had overpowered him with blows and had taken him to a dispensary along with other men from the village. He told her about his wife's despair and the despair of his whole family that he would not be able to have any more children now, especially a boy. He talked about whole villages that the police surrounded at night in order to catch the men and sterilize them. For the first time, Indira heard for herself the testimony of a victim of her policy and she was moved by the encounter. "Yes," she admitted, "perhaps Rajiv and so many others are right, after all." She was horrified at what the teacher told her about other teachers who had been beaten for not fulfilling their quota of volunteers for the vasectomy. Suddenly, the truth hit her in all its harshness from the mouth of that brave and bony little man. There was no room for any more excuses. "We have to send an urgent, crystal-clear message to all the regional heads of government," she ordered her secretary, "saying that any individual caught in the act of harassment while carrying out the family planning programme will be punished." Indira was finally reacting.

Sonia thought that then she would adopt some measure to put a stop to Sanjay's activities, but she was wrong. She did nothing. "How can her love for her son blind her to such an extent?" she wondered. "Would I do the same with Rahul?"

"I hope not, I hope you never lose your objectivity," Rajiv said to her, finding it harder and harder to put up with the situation.

Now he practically never even spoke to his brother or Maneka. He hated Sanjay's methods and style and he felt powerless to change things. Powerless before his mother: "The good thing about Sanjay is that he gets results," Rajiv heard her say, referring to the four million Indians who had been sterilized in the first five months of the state of emergency. At that rate, the goal to achieve 23 million in three years was in sight of being achieved, and for that reason, deep down, Indira was satisfied. It was Rajiv, thanks to the relations he had with his colleagues and in the company, who realized first, even before his mother, that disaster was heading their way. He knew that the story-tellers, wandering wise men and fortune-tellers were going to the four corners of this continent country, sometimes distorting and exaggerating the facts to give them epic dimensions, telling of the abuses and suffering that the sterilization campaign had unleashed. The terror those tales evoked and the lack of safety they generated broke the trust that the people had in those who governed them. The state of emergency was beginning to turn against those in power, against Indira. But she could not see it.

"My brother and my mother are betraying the family legacy," Rajiv repeated to Sonia in a desperate tone of voice.

He was trapped in a situation with no way out. He could not leave and yet it disgusted him to stay. He did not like to be identified with everything that was going on. In spite of belonging to one of the most aseptic professions in the world, it was inevitable that his colleagues, and people in general, would tar him with the same brush as his brother. He did not mind confronting Sanjay…

"You're letting down our grandfather!" he told him several times to his face.

"We're modernizing this country!" Sanjay replied.

"You're setting people against you!… The end does not justify the means."

But to say the same thing to his mother was impossible for Rajiv. An Indian son does not stand up to his parents. A certain amount of submission towards the figure of the parents is a characteristic which forms part of the deepest cultural heritage of India. Sonia knew this and therefore tried not to make matters worse. She trusted that the passing of time would end up putting things back into place. Fleeing from the latent tension, they took refuge in their rooms at the back of the house, taking as little part as possible in the lives of the others. They no longer felt that this was their home, as they had before. The writer Kushwant Singh, an assiduous visitor to the house, came to see Maneka one day when Rajiv and Sonia were celebrating the birthday of one of their children. "I realized that the children and each of the women occupied widely separated parts of the house and had little to do with each other." The fights between the dogs reflected the tension of the inhabitants. Sanjay and Maneka had two Irish wolfhounds "as big as donkeys", according to the writer, sitting paralyzed with terror for several minutes in the sitting room when they left him alone with the dogs and a cup of tea in his hand. It was Indira who saved him from that situation by taking them out into the garden. In contrast, Sonia had a sausage dog called Reshma, and Zabul, a quiet Afghan. When the dogs started fighting, Sonia was horrified, and would intervene to separate them, while Maneka watched the scene imperturbably because she knew her dogs were stronger.

In spite of the latent aggression, at home the Gandhis tried to avoid direct confrontation. Communication was reduced to the level of written notes, always polite, to express complaints and disagreements. "Yesterday you left the dog loose in the house, please don't do that again, because it scares the children." Maneka would read the note, but take no notice.

Rajiv and Sonia found support amongst their friends, among whom were Sabine and her husband, as well as an Italian couple who had recently arrived, Ottavio and Maria Quattrochi, a very witty and amusing pair with whom they often went out for dinner. Also part of that group was an Indian Airlines pilot, an Indian couple consisting of a businessman and an interior decorator who was very friendly with Sonia, a journalist and his editor wife and another couple or so. Sonia laughed a lot with Ottavio Quattrochi, her fellow Italian, who was an experienced businessman, the representative of some large Italian companies, and who had a fine sense of humour. Their friends helped them to put up with the unpleasant family situation.

Sonia found out what was happening in Old Delhi from an Indian friend who told her over the phone. She told her that her driver and her cook, both Moslems, had asked her for help, knowing that she had connections with Indira's family. Both of them were terrified because, according to what they told her,

"Sanjay's men are flattening our neighbourhood." They wanted their "mistress" to intercede to save their homes. Sonia knew nothing about it.

"We are always the last to find out. You know what the situation is like at home. I don't know whether we'll be able to do anything."

When she investigated, she found out that Sanjay had ordered the district, a labyrinth of alleys, ruined old buildings and unhealthy slums, to be demolished. A dirty, crowded and polluted district, but containing the soul of the old city. It was part of his programme of "city embellishment". The locals had rebelled, throwing stones, bricks and even Molotov cocktails at the bulldozers. A crowd of women had surrounded the family planning clinic shouting slogans and threatening the workers with castration. The police soon arrived and dispersed the crowd with tear gas. A pitched battle ensued with hundreds injured and a dozen dead, among whom there was a thirteen-year old Moslem boy who had been watching the riot like a film. In the end the police imposed a curfew so the demolition could go on. When Sonia told him all this, Rajiv made a big fuss.

"How is it possible for my mother to allow them to destroy that area? It's one of the districts she herself protected at the time of the Partition riots!"

This time Rajiv dared to tell his mother. "The city embellishment programme is causing great unrest among the population, the poor are being forced to vacate their shacks without the time to collect their things... Hundreds of shacks have been razed to the ground. We're being called even by our friends' servants to do something..."

Indira heard him out, hardly saying a word. Rajiv went on: "Grandfather convinced those people, who are mostly Moslems, to stay and not flee to Pakistan. You know that, Mother. He promised them protection. And now his grandson is kicking them out and beating them!"

Indira had Sanjay called and he immediately refuted his brother's accusations.

"Nonsense!" the young man interjected. "All those evicted are being provided with alternative accommodation."

Indira believed him.

"In this country, there is a lot of resistance to modernization," he murmured.

She always believed Sanjay in matters of politics, or the street. She believed Rajiv when something broke down at home; only then was his word worth its weight in gold.

What Sanjay had said was a half-truth. In Old Delhi, over seventy thousand people, amongst whom were Sonia's friend's cook and driver, had been forced at gunpoint to get into lorries to be taken to their new "residences", a euphemism to describe wretched plots of land surrounded by wire fences on the other side of the River Yamuna, about twenty kilometres from the city. Each family had the right to a pile of bricks to build their new refuge and ration cards to buy materials and food. But meanwhile, they had no roof over their heads.

In the end, the person who made Indira see the truth about the terrible things that were happening was her friend Pupul. She came back from Benares, the holy city on the banks of the Ganges, in a state of shock. The amazing thing, the marvellous thing about Benares is that life has gone on in practically the same way since the 6th century BC. However, Pupul had seen with her own eyes how excavators were destroying ancient buildings to widen Vishwanath Gali, a narrow, winding alley, paved with stones from the river that shone from the patina caused by the feet of the countless generations of pilgrims who walked across the heart of the city. A street where cows had had preference since the dawn of time, and which holy men walked along with their bodies covered in ashes and their hair wild, newly- wed peasants with their brides on their arm, grandmothers with their grandchildren and old men who came from far away to reach the temple of Vishwanath, the Lord of the Universe. Considered the holiest in the world by the Hindu faithful, that temple housed a polished block of granite, the most highly valued relic in Benares, the original *lingam*, a phallic emblem that symbolized the life potency of the god Shiva, the representative of the strength and regenerative power of nature. By prostrating themselves and offering water from the Ganges, the Hindu faithful expressed one of the most ancient forms of Hindu religious fervour. Benares and the temple of Vishwanath in particular, was the centre of that cult. There were *lingams* and *yonis* (the feminine equivalent) everywhere, in the temples, on the small altars set into the facades of buildings, on the steps of the *ghats*, those monumental stairways that sink into the riverbanks like gigantic tree roots, thus sealing the union of Benares with that most sacred of rivers. Every morning, as far back as human memory could remember, thousands of Hindus devoutly anointed the polished surface of the *lingams* with sandalwood paste or oil. They wove garlands of jasmine or Indian carnations that they carefully placed round the erect stone with rose petals and bitter *bilva* leaves, Shiva's favourite tree.

"We want to widen the alley so that cars can go down it," the delegate of the local council who accompanied her told Pupul. Pupul wasthunderstruck.

"What are you going to do with the temples, the gods, all those little altars?"

"We'll move them elsewhere. We are preparing a concrete structure tohouse them all."

"But you can't, they are the guardians of the city, you can't just move them like that…"

Pupul was so indignant that she was lost for words. The man acted stupid. Then he added by way of explanation, "The fact is that Sanjay wants to beautify the city."

"But you can't play around with Benares, it's the holiest of the holy cities… You can't play around with people's faith."

Pupul understood that it was pointless trying to convince the delegate, who was only following instructions. Upset and nervous, she asked him to halt all demolition activity until she got back to Delhi and spoke to the Prime Minister. The man agreed.

When Indira saw Pupul's photos and heard what she had to say, "she hit the roof", according to her friend. "I had never seen her so angry. She picked up the phone and asked her secretary to get the head of governmentin Uttar Pradesh on the line. She exploded when she spoke to him: 'Don't you know what's going on in Benares?' she asked him, before ordering him to come and see her immediately in New Delhi. Then she hung up and covered her face with her hands. 'What's happening in this country?… My God, no one tells me anything.'"

When the head of the Uttar Pradesh government found out what they were trying to with Vishwanath Gali, he was dumbstruck. He too did not know what was going on. Who had given the orders? Everybody knew they came from Sanjay, but his authority was vague and hard to trace. It was impossible to get any explanations out of him. He rarely spoke in public, hardly ever gave interviews and when he did, they were painful. His signature never appeared on official documents. He was the shadow that reigned in the darkness of the state of emergency.

The civil servant subordinates, charged with carrying out his orders, redoubled their efforts in order to ingratiate themselves with him and interpreted the orders in their own way, being even more demanding than what was required. For many, the power went to their heads and they became tyrannical, sharp-tongued people, completely out of control.

21

During the time of the Emergency, Rajiv went from flying the Avro to co-piloting the Boeing 737, a plane which from that time on would make up the majority of the Indian Airlines fleet. After one of his flights to Bombay, as he was going to the hotel in the company's van to spend the night, a long line of police motorcycles and cars, with their sirens blaring and flashing lights piercing the hazy air, forced his vehicle to halt. The deployment was impressive. "VIP!" the driver told him, referring to an important personality going past. When he wanted to drive on, a policeman diverted him to a nearby turnoff. "Who is it?" the driver asked the policeman.

"VVIP!" he answered. "Shri Sanjay Gandhi!"

Sitting in the back, Rajiv raised his eyes heavenwards. That is how his brother was driven around, as if he were the most powerful man in India, even though he had no formal authority either in the Party or in the government. The driver did not miss the chance to tease his passenger: "Little brother goes by, big brother is diverted into the alleys... What do you think of that?"

"That's politics," answered Rajiv humorously, satisfied really at not having to be part of that spectacle.

Untouched by the dismay caused by the opposition's criticisms, Sanjay and Maneka toured the country as though they were royalty, supervising everything, giving orders and instructions and being flattered by obsequious civil servants, ministers and heads of regional governments. The Press reported those tours in every detail. "His picture shines with a light of its own", declared one weekly. "Sanjay is firmly settled in people's hearts", ran another headline. The reality was quite different: at that time Sanjay was perhaps the most hated man in India.

Proof of his immense power was for example that Bansi Lal, the chubby head of the Haryana government and a henchman of his, who had been named as Defence Minister, took his two candidates to Sanjay for him to interview before deciding which one he should promote to admiral. Or when Sanjay visited Rajasthan and had to inspect 501 arches erected in his honour. A similar welcome awaited him in Lucknow, and there an incident occurred, very revealing of the aura emanating from his power. When he lost a sandal on the runway of the airport, it was the chief of the government of Uttar Pradesh himself who bent down, picked it up and reverently handed it to him.

Maneka's family, especially her mother, were suddenly catapulted into stardom. "From being nobody, she became the main lady in waiting to the empress of India, Indira Gandhi," remembers the writer Kushwant Singh. "She became unimaginably arrogant." He met her one Sunday when she went to visit him, accompanied by her daughter. They both wanted to startup a weekly news and entertainment magazine and Sanjay had suggested they should go and see him to ask for advice and to involve him in the project. Kushwant Singh accepted the commission, flattered at finding himself so close to

Indira and her son. "I felt that Maneka was asking too much of Sanjay and that he wanted to involve her in any activity that would reduce the pressure on him," the writer would say. The magazine, practicallywritten, corrected and edited by Singh, was a success, and gave Maneka a power she had not had before as well as social standing that made her happy. Did not the success of *Surya*, as the magazine was called, confirm that she was a worthy wife for the most influential man in the country? At home, that success led to even more arrogant behaviour. Compared to her, who was that Italian woman who only liked cooking and staying at home? Now more than ever, she made her disdain of her brother- and sister-in-law apparent. Not even the children were free of it. A young member of the Congress Party witnessed a scene that revealed the character of the "first lady", as some called her. The phone rang and this young man picked it up, but Mankea immediately snatched it out of his hands. It was a call for her nephew, Rahul. "There's no Rahul living here!" she exclaimed, simply because she did not wish to be interrupted at that moment.

*   *   *

"How can you both live like that?" a close friend asked Rajiv and Sonia. "Why don't you move out?"

"I can't do that to my mother," Rajiv answered.

It was true, at that moment at least they could not. They could see that Indira was changing and about to react. Enough information had filtered through to her for her to finally admit the truth about the abuse committed in the name of her son's campaigns. She began to doubt her advisors and started listening to outsiders. Affected by the growing anger she felt bubbling up amongst the people, she no longer found justification to go on with the repressive measures. She was also affected by the continual requests from different personalities inside and out of India to call off the state of emergency. Her uncle, B.K. Nehru, Ambassador to England, spoke to her frankly and without any beating about the bush about the poor image that India now had, no longer considered a star of civic responsibility shining among the dictatorships of Asia.

Indira had already postponed the elections on two occasions, at Sanjay's request, although the second time she had done it unwillingly. She thought that postponing them was sending the wrong signal to society, as though she were afraid of facing the people. She had proclaimed the state of emergency as a transitory measure, but she did not want to turn India into a dictatorship. The image of her as a "benevolent dictator" that came to her from abroad, concerned her greatly. What would her father say! Sometimes she seemed to hear Nehru's voice coming from the depths of her being, pushing her into making a decision in accordance with her conscience. Furthermore, Indira noticed that she had lost the intimate connection she had with that "vast mass of Indian humanity", and she wanted to get it back. She felt nostalgia for the crowds, she needed to vibrate again to the clamour and love of the people. She missed her earlier electoral successes... How far off now was that tremendous triumph of 1971!

As was to be expected, Sanjay was totally opposed to his mother's plans.

"You're making a huge mistake," he stated. "You might lose the elections, and what will happen then? The report you received from the Intelligence Agency states that the Congress Party will lose..."

"I don't trust those reports," Indira replied. "The Intelligence Agency has been infiltrated by Hindu extremists. They say whatever they feel like..."

"Can't you wait before you end the state of emergency?"

"Wait for what?"

"For some of the political prisoners to come out, and for things to calm down. It isn't that we're against the elections," Sanjay was also speaking for his protectors and henchmen, Bansi Lal and secretary Dhawan, who were now afraid of becoming the victims of possible reprisals. "... But it would be better to release the opposition first and wait a year for the problems to be forgotten and the rumours to come to an end."

Indira stood looking at him, in one of her long silences, a dense silence which spoke of her determination louder than if she had answered him.

This time Indira did not listen to him. The following day, January 18th, 1977, she surprised the entire nation by announcing general elections for two months' time. "It will be an opportunity to clear up all the confusion in public life," she declared. Sanjay was shattered. It was the first time his mother had undermined his authority. She did so again when she ordered the immediate release of all the political leaders and lifted censorship of the Press. The opposition received these measures with suspicion. At this point, they did not trust Indira and were suspicious of her underlying motivation. They were sure it was a trap of some kind. But her old enemy J.P. Narayan, who had been arrested and locked up in a cell during the early days of the Emergency and who then, for health reasons, had been permitted to return home, confessed to a friend of the Nehrus: "Indira has been very brave. This is a great step she has taken." Like him, many had not been expecting it.

The decision to act so quickly, which left Sanjay feeling astonished, was actually the astute manoeuvring of an expert politician. It was a question of taking all of the weak and fragmented opposition by surprise, and not giving them the chance to get themselves organized. It was her best weapon for winning those elections, because not everything was on her side. She wanted to think that the magic that had happened on other occasions would also occur in this contest. She went from doubting that the people still loved her to being convinced of it, in spite of everything.

As always, she launched into the campaign vigorously, touring allover the country, sleeping very little, travelling by any means of transport.As on other occasions, she could count on Sonia, always present, always prepared to help her get herself organized and to make her life easier for her.Sonia felt sorry for her mother-in-law. She could see she was exhausted and yet she was still chasing after a pipe dream: the love and veneration of the people. This time her seduction was not working. Indira came back crestfallen from the rallies. She told Sonia she had heard people shouting against her, voices that called for her defeat, sometimes insults. She had seen people walking away from the meetings, leaving her alone facing a smaller and smaller group of faithful followers. She had to hear many tales about the excesses of the sterilization programme, about the tortures, the arbitrary arrests… She did not know whether or not to believe everything people said, but she ended up realizing that the privileged contact she had enjoyed with the people no longer existed. "I can't bear it," she confessed one day. "They kept me shut up in these four walls." Sonia did not dare to tell her that she had not wanted to listen.

Fighting against the current weakened Indira and she fell ill several times, not managing to get over a kind of flu that gave her a recurring temperature. The blows she began to receive from her own colleagues in the party sank her even further into despair. Suddenly, her Agriculture Minister, a well-known leader in the untouchables community, deserted her ranks to join the opposition. The political life of the country seemed to becomeelectrified. A wave of panic ran through the ranks of the Congress Party. Indira remained impassive in public, but Sonia could guess how hurt shewas. That leader had been a personal friend, a companion on the road, a bastion of the party. His name was Jagjivan Ram and he had called for the immediate lifting of the state of emergency. Later Indira would discover the true reason that Ram had turned his back on her was his opposition to theage limit that Sanjay wanted imposed for standing for election. At the age of 68, Ram – and many others – were left out of the game. When Indira wantedto fix the problem, it was too late. Immediately afterwards, a horde of old comrades took the same path and then there were the defectors to follow. "How strange that you've all kept so quiet all these months…" Indira said tothem, understanding that the rats were beginning to leave the ship… But she knew that politics was made up of betrayals, didn't she? Hadn't Churchill said that there were three kinds of enemies: those who are simply enemies; those who are deadly enemies; and party comrades? What hurt her most was that her own aunt, Viyaja Lakshmi Pandit, Nehru's sister, came out ofpolitical retirement and charged into the ring to denounce that Indira and the state of emergency had "destroyed" India's democratic institutions. After having made these incendiary declarations, she joined a coalition of opposition parties that had been formed under the name of Janata Party. For Indira, more than a betrayal, that was a humiliation. It was then that she got a herpes on her mouth which forced her to give her speeches with her face half-covered by the end of her sari. "What worries me is that I may have scars on my face afterwards," she told Sonia as her daughter-in-law putsome salve on her.

"I'm tired of politics," she said to her suddenly, without any drama or exaggeration, almost without emotion.

Seeing Indira wounded deep in her soul made Sonia realize that high politics and low passions were two faces of the same world. It had never appealed to her, but now, seeing her mother-in-law betrayed and suffering, she felt complete rejection of it. Indira told her friend Pupul, "I'll fight these elections and then I'll resign. I'm fed up. I can't trust anybody."

In view of the opposition gain in strength, Sanjay once again asked hismother to cancel or at least postpone the elections. But she stuck to her guns. So her son decided to stand as candidate MP for Parliament for the electoral constituency of Amethi, next to his mother's constituency, Rae Bareilly, in the state of Uttar Pradesh. It was the territory of the Nehrus and the Gandhis, where victory was guaranteed. If he won a seat, Sanjay would be protected from the revenge of his countless enemies by his parliamentary immunity. Maneka and he were so naïve that in their first speech they praised theresults of the sterilization campaign. They were booed by a group of furious women:

"You have turned us into widows!" they shouted. "Our husbands are no longer men!"

Indira met similar reactions all over the country. One of her speeches was interrupted by a peasant woman who shouted at her: "Everything you tell us about your concern for women's welfare is all very well, but what about the vasectomies? Our men have become weak, and we women have too." In a place near Delhi, another peasant woman who was being asked to vote brought up the subject of sterilization again, and did so in evocative language: "Madam, what good is a river without any fish?" Indira finally realized that in a country with a Hindu majority, where the *lingam* (phallic stone) is venerated as the earliest deity and the source of all life, the campaign of mass sterilizations had been a monumental mistake. And she knew that in politics mistakes are paid for.

After those exhausting tours, Indira would return home with tears in her eyes.

On March 20th, 1977, election day, Pupul went to see her in her house. It was eight o'clock in the evening and the streets of New Delhi were overflowing with previously unheard of joy since the celebrations of independence from the English thirty years before. Groups of people played drums, clowns walking on stilts gave out sweets to the children, the people danced in the streets, it smelt of gunpowder from the firecrackers and fireworks... The sovereign people had voted and were celebrating the fall of the "Empress of India".

And yet the house was enveloped in a disturbing silence. There wasno fuss or lights or cars parked outside as on previous election evenings. There were no children or dogs to be seen. A secretary with a grave expression led Pupul to the sitting room decorated in tones of beige and pale green. Indira was alone, and stood up to greet her. She had aged ten years. "Pupul, I've lost," she said simply. They both sat down and remained in silence, one of those clamorous silences of Indira's which made wordsunnecessary.

Sanjay and Maneka were in Amethi, their constituency. Rajiv and Sonia were in their room, very worried. They knew better than anyone in that house the antagonism the Emergency had aroused in society and they were afraid of reprisals against their mother, against their brother and against them too. They were afraid for their safety, now that Indira had to leave power. Added to this there were many unknown elements arising out of the new situation: where to live? for example, because it was necessary to hand the house back to the government. But, above all, they were very afraid for the children. Sonia was very upset. Now she felt politics striking out at her own flesh and blood. She had seen it coming, but what could she have done to prevent such an outcome? A servant interrupted them, knocking on the door:

"Dinner is served."

The table in the dining room was laid as for any normal day. Sonia could not hold back her tears. Rajiv was serious, gloomy, silent. They only ate a little fruit, while Indira had a good dinner of vegetarian cutlets with greens and salad, as though the defeat had not affected her as much. It seemed more as though she had shaken some weight off her shoulders. Nobody said a word. You could only hear the sound of the cutlery on the china, and Sonia's timid sniffling. There was only an interruption when secretary Dhawan, Sanjay's henchman, came in to announce the latest catastrophic results. Sanjay had lost in Amethi, and Indira in her constituency. A thing never seen before: the defeat was absolute and total, even in their traditional home ground. Indira did not bat an eyelid and servedherself some fruit for dessert.

They went into the sitting room, still without a word, except to exchange banalities with a family friend who came to be with them. They stayed like that for a while, until Pupul announced that she was leaving. Rajiv went to the door with her.

"I shall never forgive Sanjay for having forced my mother into this situation," he told her. "He is the one responsible for everything."

Pupul listened to him in silence. Rajiv went on, "I told Mother the truth about what was going on several times, but she didn't believe me..."

"There were rumours going around that if the Congress Party had won, Sanjay would have been named Home Secretary and people were terrified of that happening," Pupul told him.

"I can believe it. I'm sure he would have tried."

Pupul noticed, in the shadows of the hallway, that Rajiv's eyes were full of tears.

At midnight, Indira left the house to meet for the last time with her ministers and to formally call off the state of emergency after eighteen months, although in practice almost all the measures had already been cancelled. It was a short meeting, in which almost no one said anything. They had all lost their seats. They were facing the biggest disaster that had ever happened in the party. For the first time since independence, the Congress Party was not in power. From there, Indira headed for the palace of the President of the Republic. Shrouded in mist, the old palace of the British Viceroy was fleetingly lit up by the explosions of the fireworks. Once inside, she officially presented her resignation to the president.

On the way home, she saw people celebrating her defeat with joy – children and adults were still on the streets at that time of night – and she suddenly felt afraid. It seemed to her that her house was poorly guarded. When she arrived, she went to Rajiv and Sonia's room. They were still awake.

"It would be wise if you were to take the children to some friends' house," Indira suggested. "... Tonight."

"We aren't going to leave you on your own."

"Just for a few days, until the atmosphere in the city has calmed down. There's a lot of commotion now. I'll feel calmer if you go to another house."

"Let's all go then, you too."

"I can't. I have to stay here. Besides, Sanjay's coming back tonight, so I won't be alone. Off you go, I wouldn't be able to forgive myself if something happened to the children."

At two in the morning, with Rahul and Priyanka half asleep and wrapped in blankets, Rajiv and Sonia left the house as though they were refugees in a country at war. Indira had refrained from telling them that a few days earlier she had refused the offer of the chief of security to bring troops to New Delhi to protect her in case she lost the elections and the opposition decided to organize a march against her home.

"The crowd might get out of control and attack your residence..." the chief of security had told her.

"Don't worry about me," Indira answered. "What I do ask is that you look after my children."

Perhaps Indira never believed she would lose, in spite of the overwhelming indications that she would. Perhaps she felt so protected by the aura of her name, in an almost supernatural way, that she did not realize what was coming her way. Perhaps she was blinded by the idea she had of herself. The journalist and friend, Dom Moraes asked her, "Ma'am, will you be coming back into politics?" and Indira replied, "No. I feel I've taken a weight off my shoulders. I will never return to politics." Perhaps the relief she felt now was because life had put her back in touch with reality. But it was a reality that was hard to take: at the age of 59, she found herself with no job, no financial income and no roof over her head. For the first time in her life she realized that she had nothing. The family home of Anand Bhawan had been donated to the State and was now a museum. Even if she had held onto it she could not have kept it up.

It was four in the morning when Sanjay and Maneka arrived. They did not seem especially depressed or affected by the defeat. They did not seem to be aware of what it meant. Quite the opposite: Maneka told her they had come back from Amethi in a friend's private plane and went on to tell her how Sanjay himself had taken the controls for landing. A perfect manoeuvre, she added. "It was then that I realized the strength and character of the man I had married," she would write later. Neither of them had found out yet that the inhabitants of Turkman Gate in old Delhi had gone home to their neighbourhood full of joy and were threatening to sterilize Sanjay.

Indira gave them one of her meaningful silences and went to bed. It was very late and she was exhausted when she fell into bed. She thought about her grandchildren. The important thing was that they were safe, at least for the moment. Far away, the explosions of the fireworks could still be heard.

22

Indira was really a very perplexing character. The serene, natural manner with which she accepted her defeat left both followers and enemies disconcerted. There were few examples in history of national leaders who had committed political hara-kiri with such integrity. If she felt satisfied in spite of everything, it was because she had given India back its trust in the power of the vote, in a nation that was now more stable and prosperous than before. As for her, she had fulfilled her mission and had a clear conscience. She did not feel responsible for the suffering caused by the measures she had taken. The system was to blame for that, together with bureaucracy and the dirty tricks of the opposition. "With these elections, India has shown that democracy is not a luxury that belongs to the rich," said the New York Times in her defence. Something that all observers, both Indian and foreign, agreed on was that Indira Gandhi's political career was over. They were all wrong, except for an old colleague, a militant in a party on the Left, who went to visit her and said, "You'll soon see. The people will come back to you."

Then Indira turned to her with her eyes full of tears and asked, "When? When I'm dead?"

Usha, her faithful secretary, did not know what to do or say when she went to work the day after the elections. She had never been in favour of the state of emergency and her comments when she read out articles that were critical would almost have cost her her job if Sonia had not warned her not to go on making them. She had not slept all night, but had kept the radio on all the time. When she went into the office, which was next to the dining room, she found Indira sitting at her desk. Smiling, the ex-Prime Minister said to her, "Usha, you have to give back the fat lady."

"Fat lady?"

"Yes, the figurine they lent us from the National Museum."

She was referring to a statue without a head or arms, of no great value, which Indira had borrowed from the museum to decorate her sitting room. Usha immediately found the corresponding receipt and set to work. "I knew that Mrs Gandhi had said that to relax the tension. It was very typical ofher."

It was necessary to move house soon because, in spite of owning a large comfortable house in Dupleix Road, her successor, the Conservative Hindu, Morarji Desai, wanted to make Indira's home his official residence. Throwing her out of the house was a symbol of his victory and of his petty-mindedness at the same time. Indira was hurt. But what could she do? The civil servants who came to check the offices and other rooms were already inthe house with an inventory in their hands. They began to take away objects and appliances that had been prerogatives of the Prime Minister: secret telephones, typewriters, photocopiers, air-conditioning units, office tables and chairs, and all that while Usha and Sonia were classifying documents, putting files away and desperately trying to impose some order on all that chaos.

A few days after she came back with the rest of the family from her friend Sabine's house, where they had taken refuge,

Sonia found civil servants taking away furniture, lamps, cutlery and crockery. All the decoration she had put in over the last nine years, was being moved out by removal men who acted with the arrogance of the victor. The feeling of helplessness became even greater when she noticed the absence of the official servants, the secretaries provided by the government, the guards at the entrance and even the gardeners, who had vanished, some of them without even saying goodbye. Once the boss was gone, the rats were leaving the ship.

Indira owned a plot of land in Mehrauli, in the outskirts of the city, which Firoz had bought in 1959 and where she dreamed of retiring with her family. Rajiv had invested part of his savings in building a country home, but he had run out of money to complete it. But anyway, Indira did not want to be exiled to the countryside. She preferred to stay near her grandchildren, at the heart of things, in New Delhi. She knew the words of one of Napoleon's generals called Desaix, from the battle of Marengo: "It is true that I have just lost a battle, but it is two o'clock in the afternoon and before night falls I can win another one." At this stage, Indira knew that the ideas of success and defeat were both ephemeral in politics.

It was an old family friend who saved her. The diplomat, Mohammed Yunus, generously offered to vacate his house at number 12, Willingdon Crescent, in order to allow the Gandhis to live there. It was where Sanjay and Maneka's wedding had taken place three years before. This new home was quite a lot smaller and Sonia wondered how they were all going to fit in there. The move lasted several days, the time it took to move the possessions accumulated over thirteen years, the belongings of five adults, two children, five dogs, countless boxes of books, files overflowing with papers and documents, pictures, objects, souvenirs from trips, etc. Indira was unwilling to throw anything away: every paper, every gift, every book, was a memory. So they piled up in boxes and trunks in the hallways. In Indira's room there was only space for her bed and her favourite armchair, whose back she used for leaning on and writing. She no longer had a shorthand secretary or even an office of her own. She entertained people on the veranda or in the overcrowded dining room. Sonia organized things so there would always be a vase with some gladioli within sight.

A large part of the work of this huge move fell on Sonia's shoulders, and she had to buy, or borrow from her friends, a fridge, several air conditioning units, radiators, saucepans, frying pans and kitchen utensils. Her sense of family had intensified from living in India. She worked with a perfect sense of organization, which reminded her of her parents during her childhood, when they were poor in Lusiana and had to work all hours to keep their heads above water. Her knowledge of horticulture came back to her and she cleared an area at the back of the garden where she planted lettuces, courgettes, tomatoes and some greens that were unknown and exotic in India, like broccoli. Having known hard times helped her to overcome the difficult patch with more strength than her husband, who could not forgive himself for not having been firmer: "I was unable to put a stop to my brother's activities," he had confessed to a family friend, not hiding his frustration.

As the cook had left and Indira was reluctant to hire another one in case he was a government spy and might poison them, Sonia had to take charge of doing the shopping and preparing the meals. In that family they had never tasted such delicious lasagnas, pasta *a la puttanesca* and risottos as in those fateful days. She had also learned to cook Indian dishes, which she seasoned with milder spices than normal. She was expert at making spinach with cheese and chicken with korma sauce based on ground almonds, coriander and cream. Cooking was also her way of spoiling the family and helping to relax the atmosphere, which was unpleasant. The nun at Sonia's school had said that she had the quality of a peace-maker, hadn't she? That quality kept the family united during that time. Rajiv and Sanjay were still not talking to each other, except for the bare necessities, in spite of the fact that now their rooms were opposite each other down the corridor. Indira insisted on keeping up the custom of eating together at least once a day, but it was almost impossible to have the two brothers sitting at the sametable. Rajiv blamed Sanjay for the family's fall in status, for having gone from being the most highly respected to being like pariahs. It was also true that they lived off Rajiv's salary and the donations of the few faithful friendswho had not abandoned Indira, hoping perhaps that their loyalty would be rewarded at some future time. Sanjay did not bring anything in, rather the opposite: he needed money to pay the horde of lawyers that were defending him from endless accusations that attributed him with the most horrible crimes. He could not bring any money into the family's coffers, but he tried to make up by saying that one of the magnates who was helping them financially was a young friend of his, the owner of a soft drinks factory in New Delhi. Maneka, true to herself, did not help with the household chores, unlike Indira, who did not hesitate to pick up a broom and start sweeping. "Sonia cooked, Maneka ate," said a friend of the family. The result was that the relationship between Indira and Sonia became even closer during that period, which incited young Maneka's jealousy.

Shortly after they settled in, Usha felt that there was no sense in her staying on. She continued going on alternate days, until she decided to leave completely: "I'm going to go to Bombay with my sister," she told Indira, who guessed this was an excuse and that she would not be back. But Usha did not dare to tell her the truth: perhaps she might have stayed if Sanjay and his henchman, secretary Dhawan, had not gone on lording it with that air of arrogance that Usha could not stand. Indira gave a sad smile when they said goodbye. She felt sorry to lose that woman who had been her secretary for the last thirty years. She had trusted her utterly and she knew that Usha knew the innermost secrets of her heart.

Indira was mentally and physically exhausted, as well as worried about the general exodus, the fights at home between her sons and the reprisals that the new government, she was sure, was going to take. She had black bags under her eyes, and it looked as if her whole body had shrunk. As ex-Prime Minister, she was entitled to continuing official protection, but the new head of the government, her bitterest political enemy, Morarji Desai, an orthodox Hindu, wanted to take it away from her just as he had taken away her home.

"What is she afraid of?" he asked one of Indira's ex-ministers. "It isn't a good thing for her to be always surrounded by police officers."

"There's an atmosphere that's hostile to her and her son..."

"No, it isn't that. It's her vanity."

The new Prime Minister immediately launched into a diatribe against women in power, from Cleopatra to Indira, including Catherine of Russia, coming to the conclusion that they had all been full of vanity and were disasters as heads of government.

The campaign of harassment that man unleashed against the Gandhis turned into a real witch hunt. At first, Sonia was surprised to always see the same men following her a certain distance away when she went shopping. The same thing happened with the other members of the family, including Maneka. Indira found out that they were members of the CBI (CentralBureau of Intelligence, the central intelligence agency of the government) who had instructions to follow them and bug their phone conversations.With the arrogance of someone who had never had to face up to a misfortune from which he not recovered, Sanjay sarcastically told the secret service agents who were following him that he would take them in his own car in order to save petrol. One day, they turned up at the half-built house in Mehrauli with metal detectors. "What are you looking for?" Rajiv asked them. They did not answer, but later on he heard them shouting when the detector began to emit a whistling sound. They thought they had found the treasure that Sanjay had buried. The treasure turned out to be an empty canof cooking oil.

It was approximately at that time, in the middle of the heat before the monsoon rains, when Indira appeared late one night at her friend Pupul's house. She often came to visit her, to escape from the tension at home. Once again Rajiv had thrown in her face that: "Sanjay and Dhawan are the ones who have brought you to this." Indira had not answered, and had simply lowered her head. She knew perfectly well that in the final analysis she was the one responsible for everything that had happened and that is why she didnot blame Sanjay. "I've come to sit for a little while and enjoy the peace andquiet," she told her friend. And she sat a while in silence, on the veranda, finding herself again.

Another night of extreme heat she arrived very agitated and with a look of desperation: "I have reliable information that they want to put Sanjay in prison and torture him." Pupul was shocked and did not know what to say. Indira was terribly afraid. "Neither my son nor I are the kind of people who commit suicide, so if we turn up dead, don't believe what they'll be saying…" The fact that in its desire for vengeance the new government was searching feverishly for evidence in order to take revenge on her through Sanjay was an open secret. That they had decided to torture Sanjay was more a product of her paranoid imagination than part of an organized plan. No one knew better than Indira that from a position of power it was relatively easy to manipulate the intelligence agencies. And the former empress of India felt desperately alone. She saw politicians who went to visit her every day, but she could not count on any of them. Those who could help her did not dare to go near the house because they were afraid of the surveillance. On the other hand, the family's financial situation, with so much being spent on lawyers, was becoming untenable. The media, who had so docilely bent to her demands when she had imposed the Emergency – to such an extent that as soon as the state of emergency was lifted, an opposition politician said of the role of the Press: "They asked you to submit and you preferred to be on your knees" – now spent its time earnestly inventing terrible stories, or exaggerating rumours to make it look as though the Gandhis were a band of delinquents. "They accuse me of all kinds of crimes, even of having killed I don't know how many people…" Indira complained. It was true: the Home Secretary had said in Parliament that Indira had "planned to kill all the opposition leaders that she had had thrown into prison during the state of emergency." Five days later, the government ordered the Supreme Court Judge, J.C. Shah to set up of a committee of investigation "to find out if there was subversion of proceedings, abuse of authority, unlawful use of power and excesses during the state of emergency". Another commission was created specifically to investigate everything concerning the Maruti. The government was determined to make Indira and Sanjay swallow the same bitter pill that they had given the country during the state of emergency.

In that atmosphere, the news of the suicide of Maneka's father, Colonel Anand, sounded like the first notes in a wider drama that was beginning to unfold in the middle distance, like the first chords of a funeral march. His body was found face down on an embankment, next to a pistol and a note that said: "Worry about Sanjay unbearable". At first, it was not known whether it had been a suicide or a murder, although Maneka and the closest members of the family were convinced that the colonel had taken his own life. He had already made a similar attempt some time before, by taking an overdose of pills and he had a history of mental instability and depression. He had not been able to bear the sudden fall in reputation and social position. His countless convenience friends had vanished into the thin New Delhi air. The rumour immediately went round that his father-in-law knew too much about Sanjay's shady business deals and that his death was actually a murder disguised as a suicide. But nothing could be proved and as soon as the attention of the Press disappeared, the case fell into oblivion.

Indira was perturbed, and Sonia too. A death like that, at the time when it happened, instilled a vague, deep fear, a mixture of uneasiness and alarm. The fall from power had taken a victim very close by. The blood had reached the river, and where they were least expecting it. Indira became even more paranoid, unconsciously linking the death of Sanjay's father-in-law with the threats to Sanjay. Now more than ever, she felt that she had to protect her son however she could. The news of the suicide arrived abroad and Sonia received distressing calls from her mother. There in Orbassano, the Mainos were following events with growing uneasiness and concern. Gossip from New Delhi reached them, rumours that Sonia and Rajiv were trying to get away and that Sonia had asked for asylum in the Italian Embassy…

"Mother, none of that is true. We are fine, the children too, but I can't talk now, I'll tell you about it later…"

And invariably the conversation was cut short. Sonia refrained from telling her mother that the government had taken away the passports of all her in-laws. Even if they had wanted, now they could not travel to Italy, not even in an emergency.

Indira set herself to working tirelessly with her lawyers to defend herself from the Shah Commission, while publicly she maintained a very discreet lifestyle. An English journalist called James Cameron interviewed her and found her to be "the loneliest and most apprehensive woman in the world", according to the headline he gave to his article. "She is resigned and does not want to talk about anything. She is like a defeated boxer waiting for a miracle. But there will be no miracle for her," he wrote in *The Guardian* on September 21st 1977.

James Cameron was wrong. The miracle that was going to make the phoenix rise out of the ashes occurred in a place called Belchi, a small, inaccessible village in the remote state of Bihar, surrounded by paddy fields, mountains and waterfalls. An idyllic setting which had been the stage for a terrible massacre. The crime had occurred in part because of the atmosphere of impunity encouraged by the new government, whose coalition included extremist Hindu elements. Now high-caste Hindus once again felt they were free to subjugate poor untouchable peasants, as they had done for thousands of years before independence. In Belchi, a group of landowners had attacked a community of landless peasants, exterminating several families and throwing the bodies into a fire. Among the victims there were two babies. The news took several days to get out, before it became front-page news in the national press. The government did not react. Its president, Morarji Desai, who considered the prohibition of killing cows and consuming alcohol to be national priorities, did not think this kind of event merited priority attention. He did not even rush to condemn the crime.

Indira immediately saw the crack in her adversary's armour. She knew what she had to do. She asked Sonia to help her prepare her things to go to Belchi.

"Everyone says that Bihar is a very dangerous place. There are groups of bandits who attack people..." Sonia told her, who, in effect, was well-informed. Bihar was the most backward, anarchical and unsafe state in India. And the poorest too. "You haven't got a security team with you. It's very risky," Sonia insisted.

"I'm not going alone. I'm going with a group of party faithful."

"But in Bihar the party hasn't got a single seat... Will they have the power to protect you?"

"Of course they will. Don't worry," Indira cut her short, "nothing can go wrong."

Sonia did not insist. She knew her sufficiently well to know that nothing would make her change her mind. But she was still worried. In an atmosphere so full of animosity such as in those days in India, anything could happen.

23

When Indira came back five days later, Sonia hardly recognized her. Her sari was dirty and she was all sweaty and covered in dust. She had bags under her eyes and had lost weight. She looked like a beggar. But Sonia, who knew her well by now, spotted a glint in her eyes, like a spark of life. She knew immediately that the trip to Belchi had been a success. Indira told her in great detail all about the epic journey she had just made. Sonia listened to her, entranced.

"It rained so much that all the roads to Belchi were impassable. Of the five hundred sympathizers who had begun the trip with me, following me in a line of cars, I suddenly realized that there were only two left. The others had given up. My idea was to get to Belchi before nightfall, but the roads were so flooded that we had to change the four-wheel drive for a tractor, which in turn ended up stuck in the mud a few kilometres further on. My companions insisted that we turn back, but I told them that I was going ahead on foot. They looked at me as if I were mad. I knew they were not going to leave me on my own, and I was right, and they were forced to go on with me, although they did so unwillingly. After a lot of walking, exhausted and soaking wet, we came to the river, and we realized that it was impossible to cross it on foot. There were no boats out in that weather, or boatmen prepared to take people across to the other side. My companions were ready to go back, but I spoke to some villagers who had come out of their huts when they saw us arrive: 'There must be some way of crossing…Are there any horses around here?'

'No, Madam…' one of them told me.'A mule? A donkey?'

'No Madam. There's only an elephant.''Where?' I asked.

'In the village. It's the temple elephant.' 'Can you bring it here?'

'Yes, Madam, but…' the man seemed bothered and found it hard to find the words.

'But… what?' I said.

'We don't have a *howdah*…' he admitted finally, as thoughembarrassed."

"Do you know what a *howdah* is?" Indira asked Sonia.

"Isn't it a kind of little tower that is put on the elephant's back to carryimportant people?"

"That's right… It's always like that in India, over and above practical considerations there's always concern over status! It's as if that's the only thing that governs people's relationships. So I told them it didn't matter if they didn't have a *howdah*, and then one of them said triumphantly that he would put a blanket on."

Indira was like an excited little girl telling Sonia all about this adventure. Seeing her so alive and sparkling, so direct and close to her, was like a miracle. Indira was transformed.

"You know… I didn't feel tired, and that was in spite of having to stand waiting over an hour in the rain."

"What happened with the elephant?"

"It finally came. It was called *Moti*. The peasants helped me up first and then hoisted up one of my companions, and he sat behind me. When I turned round, I could see his eyes were bulging in terror."

Sonia laughed. Indira went on: "The other one decided to stay behind and organize our return. It was terrifying because the animal swayed a lot and the river water came up to his belly. The man hung on to my sari like a child holding on to his mother's skirts. I thought he was going to start crying…"

They both burst out laughing. It was always funny to hear stories in which the women were in control of the situation. Then Indira's face becameserious.

"It was late when we got to Belchi," she continued, "The survivors of the massacre had been taking refuge in a half-abandoned two-storey building. Suddenly I saw some torches come out, lighting up the faces of the people carrying them: there were old people with their faces all wrinkled, young widows, children with huge shining eyes, dark-skinned men, all of them very fearful and surprised… When they recognized me, they threw themselves at my feet. I think they saw me as a divine apparition. I had nothing to give them except my time, but those people who were so frightened did not stop thanking me for taking an interest in them, for havingcome through so many dangers to go and listen to them. They said my presence was a miracle, do you see? We stayed for several hours, and I heard horrible stories about the massacre. I was crying when I left them… there was so much poverty, and so much pain when the peasants showed me the ashes of the pyre where they had thrown the members of their families while they were still alive, that I was devastated. It was completely dark when we left Belchi. There was thunder, but it was not raining, so a boatmanoffered to take us across to the other side.

Do you know what happened then?"

Sonia shook her head. Indira went on, "As the load was excessive, the boat overturned as we were approaching the other side."

They burst out laughing again. Indira continued: "... We all found ourselves splashing around in the dirty water. I managed to wade to the riverbank. We carried on walking as far as the main road, where some four- wheel drive vehicles were waiting for us. We were soaked to the skin. Then another miracle happened, Sonia. The peasants from the surrounding area who had heard about my visit began to arrive. They brought us fruit, flowersand torches. Suddenly I heard the beating of drums and some women's voices... Do you know what they were singing? 'We voted against you. We betrayed you. Forgive us.' they were saying. They came with sweets and offered me their simple, dry saris to dry myself or change. Some of them even asked for my blessing!"

Sonia realized that Indira had seen the light at the end of the tunnel.She had delved into "the mass of Indian humanity" and had not felt that shewas rejected. On the contrary, she had found her voice again, and an answer.Indira went on to say that the next day she had gone to Patna, the tumbledown capital of the state of Bihar, to visit her old enemy J.P. Narayan, the man whose boycott had pushed her to declare the state of emergency. He was very old, almost on his deathbed. Now that Indira hadbeen defeated and vilified, JP forgave her. They met for fifty minutes, talking about the many memories they shared of the times when Narayan'swife was the best friend of Indira's mother. They also talked about themassacre in Belchi and the fate of the untouchables. Then they posed for the Press. Indira took a crumpled up newspaper out of her cloth bag and showed her daughter-in-law the photo. It was an important photo for Indira, because it sealed her reconciliation with politics. Sonia understood that her mother- in-law was going back into the ring.

"But... weren't you saying less than two weeks ago that you

were retiring from politics?" Sonia asked.

"I haven't gone back yet, and I would like not to go back, but how can I retire?... As long as they want Sanjay's skin, or mine, I'll have to fight to defend us."

Encouraged, Indira decided to leave the next day for her old constituency of Rae Bareilly, where the voters had rejected her overwhelmingly less than four months earlier. It was risky because she could find hostile crowds, since that state had been the main objective of the sterilization campaign, but, to her great surprise, thousands of people turned up to welcome her in the blazing sun. Here too she knew perfectly well what she had to do and say. She came straight to the point and asked forgiveness for the excesses of the state of emergency and then she launched an attack on the Janata coalition which was in power. The people applauded her even more warmly than in Belchi. She decided to make a lightning tour of several towns in the state, repeating the same message. Everywhere she went, the reception was tumultuous. She came home worn out, dirty, exhausted but happy.

The tale of Indira's journey to Belchi spread like wildfire across the sub-continent until it reached the villages set into the foothills of the Himalayas, the mud huts in the desert, the palm leaf shacks of the lowest castes, the plastic and tin shanties of the untouchables in the south... Beyond differences of race, caste or religion, the voice of the poor had found its source of inspiration and consolation again. In spite of feeling that India had begun to forgive her, Indira was still very worried about her situation and the threat of the Shah Commission. Voices in the government were demanding a "kind of Nuremburg trial" for her crimes during the Emergency.

"I'm sure that they will find any pretext to arrest me."

"They won't dare," said Sonia to calm her down rather than out of conviction.

"I've heard that the Janata government has promised not to go after my former ministers in court if they agree to blame Sanjay for all the slipups that occurred during the state of emergency. I know perfectly well that they will betray me. They want to put Sanjay in jail."

Those betrayals hurt her deeply and pushed her towards an abyss of loneliness that made her dizzy. Sonia saw how strong she was and yet how vulnerable. Unlike her mother-in-law, most politicians were in politics out of simple personal ambition and not out of a sense of duty. The mean- spiritedness of that world disgusted her. But she realized that public life, politics seen as service to others, were Indira's *raison d'être* and that she would never change. Although she liked to say that she dreamed of retiring from that world, Sonia no longer believed her. Retiring was a luxury that Indira could not afford.

Given the harassment from the government and the Shah Commission, Indira took the bull by the horns. Faithful to the maxim that the best form of defence is attack, she travelled extensively to strengthen her presence, to get into contact with the greatest number of people possible, to build on what she had achieved in Belchi, the forgiveness of the people. At Agra station, the welcome was so triumphal that there was a stampede that left several injured. Everywhere she began by saying sorry for having harmed so many people, but she also reminded them of the achievements of the state of emergency, especially in the areas of the economy and security, emphasizing that it had been she who called the elections, and that when she was defeated she had accepted the people's verdict with chivalry. In effect, the new government was unable to slow inflation, which was rising out of control again, or to deal with the black market. It was a disparate coalition, that was already showing signs of breaking up.

Her triumphant trips to Belchi and Rae Bareilly annoyed the weak government, which was becoming more and more alarmed at the spectacle of the masses venerating its arch-enemy. It was necessary to do something. On August 15th, 1977, Independence Day, the police arrested her secretary, the carefully coiffed R.K. Dhawan, as well as her former Defence Secretary, chubby Bansi Lal, both Sanjay's henchmen. The net was tightening.

Sonia was afraid. Rajiv was having problems at work, and it seemedas though the management did not want to renew his licence to go on flying 737s. It smelt like a reprisal. His clear position against the state of emergency was not taken into account by the company, in spite of him having a faultless, apolitical reputation among his workmates. On top of the upsets with Indian Airlines came an inspection that the Tax Office set up against Rajiv. The inspection also involved Sonia, who, as a favour to her brother-in-law, had signed documents in 1973 making her the owner of shares in a fictitious company, Maruti Services Ltd. All that, which had already caused a violent argument between the brothers and tension in the marriage, was used as a weapon by the government, determined to prove shady financial dealings which had not actually existed. As Sonia was a foreigner, she did not have the right to own shares or hold any remunerated position in an Indian company without approval from the Central Bank, and this approval never existed anyway. Therefore there had been no infringement of the law. But now Rajiv was forced to prove that his wife had not had a single rupee from Maruti and that she had never had anything to dowith that company. The most they could sentence her to was a fine. The time that Rajiv did not spend flying he spent searching for old papers, or if not, to obtaining them again, to going through a real *via crucis* because of how contorted Indian bureaucracy was. But he kept calm at all times. He had a clear conscience; the business with Sonia was unimportant and he had always paid his taxes religiously. Sonia was perturbed that they might try some dirty tricks with fake documents, for example. Fear was corrosive and deformed her perception of reality. "And what was the reality?" Indira's ideas were clear: "This is a war of nerves, psychological warfare. We have to put up with it, that's all." Sonia did not want to add more paranoia to the atmosphere, but the thought that innocents might have to pay for the sinners alarmed her. When she saw her husband leave the house to declare at the sittings of the Shah Commission, a knot formed in her stomach, and until he came home and she could see him safe and sound, she could not relax. Those hearings were a very unpleasant test because they took place in a disorganized and hostile environment that looked more like the Chinese people's courts than a court of justice. Rajiv always came home agitated. He told how the courtroom was overflowing with people who shouted very aggressively while others ate or even drowsed on the floor. Dressed in black robes with white bibs, the lawyers were seated behind little tables covered in papers tied up with string, under ventilators that made the loose documents go whirling away. A yellowing photo of Gandhi decorated the walls. Every time he or his brother tried to defend themselves, loud booing drowned out their words. The people did not allow them to speak. The face of Judge Shah could barely be seen behind the piles of tomes of the Indian penal code and the bundles of papers that covered his desk. Outside the courtroom, other curious onlookers followed the hearings over loudspeakers. Obviously it was Sanjay who aroused the greatest ill will. Every time he went into the courtroom, he was received with loud whistles and insults. Several times the tension caused real running battles between his detractors and his followers. One of the sessions ended in uproar, with metal chairs being thrown and punches exchanged. Sonia understood how hard it must be for Rajiv to put up with that. He had always hated confrontation and had always tried to lead a quiet life. But, apart from how unfair the situation was, both Rajiv and Sonia were especially alarmed at the repercussions of so much hostility on their children.

However, although they were the centre of the attacks, Sanjay and Maneka took it all much more sportingly, in the real meaning of the word as well as figuratively. On October 3rd, 1977, they were playing badminton on the lawn in the garden at number 12, Willingdon Crescent. At five o'clock in the afternoon, they heard a police car drive up. Two men knocked on the door. One of them was a Sikh, a tall man with a red turban and excellent manners. Indira, who was discussing things with her lawyers, opened the door to him.

"My name is N.K. Singh, from the headquarters of the Secret Service," said the Sikh, squeezing his hands nervously. "We have come to inform you that you are under arrest," he said, looking at the ground.

"Do you mean you are taking me to jail?" "Yes..." muttered the man, visibly intimidated.

"It'll be a good opportunity to have a rest," said Indira.

In fact she had been expecting this moment for some time, just as the whole country had been expecting it.

"Can I know what I am accused of?"

The man read out the charges. They accused her of having coerced two companies into donating 114 four-wheel drive vehicles to the Congress Party's campaign and then of having sold them to the army, which suggested bribery. Also of having granted a contract to a company that had made a more expensive bid than others, which suggested corruption. Indira looked heavenwards: it was all lies. "Were those the horrors of the Emergency?!" she thought to herself.

"Tomorrow you have to go before the court and we will take you there," said the man.

"I want to see the order for my arrest."

The man handed over some papers. Indira went on: "If you don't mind, I'm going to consult with my lawyers. Wait a moment, please."

She went into the house with the documents. She came out an hour later. The Sikh officer was waiting outside, sitting on a step at the entrance.

"The First Information Report is missing here," said Indira. "I do not intend to move until all the papers are in order."

"Madam, it will do no good to make my job harder than it already is." "Don't worry, I'll be here when you come back."

"O.K. I'll send an officer for the missing paper." "You can wait inside if you like."

The man came in, feeling both grateful and uncomfortable. The house was surrounded by police officers and numerous onlookers who were beginning to gather. Sanjay and Maneka had given up their game and had shut themselves in their room. Usha, who found out what had happened straight away, rushed to Willingdon Crescent. "When I arrived, I saw a scene that made me feel sad. Before, the police cordon was there to protect the Prime Minister from possible altercations and demonstrations. Now it was there to prevent people passing through, and to arrest her." Usha managed to get inside. Indira was going in and out of her room and was very busy. She was very happy to see her.

"Usha! How nice that you are here! Could you please help Sonia to prepare my travel bag?"

Sonia was in Indira's room, with her mother-in-law's clothes laid out on the bed. This time she was not very sure what to put in. This was not a journey like the others.

"Where are they going to take her?" Usha enquired. "I don't know. They haven't said," replied Sonia.

"It's best if we put a shawl in, in case they take her somewhere in the mountains."

"I trust you both to do my hair properly for me," said Indira from the hallway. "I want to be as pretty as possible."

"Don't worry about that," Sonia told her, already knowing that her mother-in-law never liked to look untidy, even inside the house. But that desire to look good, that made it seem as if she was going to a wedding instead of to prison, was unheard of. "My God," Sonia said to herself. "And it's an Indian prison!... Why does she want to look so smart?" she wondered.

"Mrs Gandhi is like that," Usha told her.

While they chose a sari for her, Indira took some documents into the kitchen that she considered dangerous if they were to fall into the hands of the police or the Intelligence Agency. The cook made sure they were destroyed in an unusual way, using Sonia's pasta-making machine as a shredder.

Although the phones had been cut off, Sanjay and the lawyers managed to warn members of the party who in turn called the Press. Reporters with television cameras, followers from Sanjay's Youth Congress and a growing crowd of the curious came to crowd up against the police cordon.

The Sikh officer, still waiting for Indira in the hall, was

getting more and more nervous. He did not at all like the spectacle that was being set up around the house. Of all the missions he had been given throughout his career, this was perhaps the one that most disgusted him. Nobody likes to arrest a goddess. He was nervous and undecided about what to do. He tried to be nice to Priyanka and Rahul, but the children responded with hostile looks.

Finally, at eight o'clock, Indira appeared, carefully made up and with her hair beautifully combed, dressed in a pretty white sari with a green border that Usha and Sonia had chosen for her. She looked very distinguished. The Sikh officer was astonished: this would be like arresting an elegant grandmother... Furthermore, when Indira came out of the house, she was received with cheers in the garden and a shower of flower petals. Atthat moment she turned to the Sikh officer: "I want you to handcuff me," shesaid.

N.K. Singh was disconcerted, his mouth left half-open. "Now this little granny was asking to be handcuffed!" he thought in horror.

"Madam, please..."

"I want to leave my home in handcuffs. Haven't I been arrested?...

Well, put the handcuffs on me."

Sonia, following close behind with her husband and brother-in-law, was just as amazed as the Sikh. The policeman, on the verge of a nervous breakdown, went off to consult with his colleagues. He came back after afew moments.

"Madam, we are not going to handcuff you."

"If you don't handcuff me, I'm not moving from here. I'm staying put."

"Please, Madam, don't put me in a difficult situation..." he said, embarrassed. "I am not authorized to handcuff you. Be so kind as to follow me or we'll have to take you by force."

In view of the Sikh's determination, Indira gave way and followed the policemen, while the crowd threw flowers and cheered her. Before he left the house with Sonia, Rajiv asked Usha to remain behind and take care of the children. He did not know how soon they would be back.

Before she got into the car, Indira addressed a group of reporters. "I was to have gone to Gujarat to visit some tribal communities tomorrow. I would ask you to please convey my apologies to the people of Gujarat." Asked about her arrest, she declared: "I have tried to serve our country in the best possible way. The charges against me have no foundation. This is a political arrest."

The car drove off, preceded by a military jeep and followed by a line of vehicles in which her sons and daughters-in-law, as well as followers and reporters, were travelling. The children were left behind, crying, in the care of Usha. History was being repeated again in the Nehru dynasty, as when the police came to arrest Jawaharlal and his daughter tried to prevent their access.

They did not take her to the infamous Tihar prison, where she had ordered the Maharanis of Gwalior and Jaipur and so many others, to be locked up. Her "prison" was actually a spartan but relatively clean room in a police station. With great dignity, she said goodbye to her sons and daughters-in-law at the entrance. She was radiating serenity, because she knew intuitively that by now the news of her arrest, like a common criminal, was already spreading from mouth to mouth among the people to the furthest reaches of their immense country. She knew that if she could give the impression of being a martyr – the reason why she had asked

309

to be handcuffed – she would win that round. Unaware of these manoeuvres, Sonia was looking at her with great sadness and was making superhuman efforts to hold back her tears. The Nehrus were not an effusive family, and less so in situations like this. Neither could she go under now. The police officers on guard snapped to attention for Indira as she went into her "prison". It was hard for them to take in that they had her as their guest that night. The world was back to front. Inside, she was offered food, but she refused it. She was worried about being poisoned. She lay down on the bunk in her "cell" and for a long time she read a novel that Usha and Sonia had put into her bag. She slept deeply and at dawn she was already dressed, freshly showered and ready to face the court.

At nine in the morning, Rajiv was waiting for her in the doorway of the Palace of Justice in Parliament Street, in the centre of New Delhi, accompanied by a lawyer. That morning the usual samosa-vendors and sugar-cane juice sellers were not there, or the scribes who, for a few rupees, would write letters or take down statements for the poor illiterates who were embroiled with the law. The news of Indira's arrest had caused such a stir that at that time the building was completely surrounded by people crowding together. This time, the Janata coalition had sent their own demonstrators too. Sanjay arrived at the head of his people, so when Indira went into the building, she did so to cries of: "Long live Indira Gandhi!" from one side, and "Hang her!" from the other. But she put up with it, stoically, and at no point did she lower her head, not even when a magazine was thrown at her, flying past a few inches from her head.

Inside the spacious hall, Indira refused the chair she was

offered and stood for almost two hours, listening to the arguments about the charges against her. As it got hotter, a poorly-shaven janitor dressed in a dirty white *dhoti* clapped his hands to order the ventilators hanging from the ceiling to be started. The blades began to turn slowly, squeaking as they got moving. The draught made the skirts of her sari flutter, so that Indira felt a little relief. She was almost fainting from the effort of standing in all that heat. But she knew that the gesture of having refused a chair was being whispered from mouth to ear by hundreds, thousands and perhaps later, by millions of fellow Indians… "She remained standing!", "She refused the chair!"… simple phrases that shaped her mythical figure in the people's imagination.

Outside, sympathizers and detractors came to blows. The police intervened and charged them wielding their *lathis*, long bamboo sticks, and later, with tear gas.

In the end, the magistrate declared that Indira was innocent and absolved her. He immediately ordered her unconditional freedom and gave the following sentence: "There is no proof to support the accusation." Sanjay went running out, shouting: "Case dismissed! She's free!" which caused euphoria among some and fury among others, who all came to blows again. The police were forced to fire more cans of tear gas. Indira came out of the courtroom with red eyes and her nose covered, but happy at having won. Rajiv was very excited: "Not even Mother could have dreamed of a better outcome," he declared to a reporter.

In effect, the farce of her arrest got the news on the front page of all the national newspapers and a good many international ones too. The government made Indira seem like the victim of an incompetent administration. They achieved the opposite effect to the one they were seeking:

Javier Moro

they set Indira on the path to her complete political rehabilitation.

Sonia was beginning to understand the reason for her mother-in-law's need to be immaculately dressed. She had managed to project herself as a martyr to justice. She admired her desire to fight and at the same time her mother-in-law's indifference towards the benefits of power; now she was sure that Indira would get back to the top, even if only to clear her name and to be the pride of her people again, especially of her grandchildren, whom she adored. Sonia understood her because they both shared a very deep and intense sense of family. However, she could not see the other side of her mother-in-law's character, because she had never been attracted by power. For Indira, it was a kind of drug. Kissinger himself had said that power was the best aphrodisiac there was, hadn't he? From being a plain, lonely little girl, and then a fragile woman with delicate health, power had made Indira into a formidable fighter, tough and tenacious. She had the bug deep inside and she felt it stirring every time the possibility, however remote it was, arose that she might reach it.

So she did not waste a second; she knew that she had to seize the moment. Once again, Sonia helped her to prepare her travel bag, and this time it would be for a long time because Indira wanted to tour the whole country. In Gujarat, she addressed the people from little platforms erected several kilometres apart. As the day passed, the garlands of jasmine and daisies collected round her neck until they hid part of her face. She would take off the heavy load before she went into the huts of the natives where sheshared their food, on banana leaves, talking to them about their problems: the harvest, education, the lack of health care, etc. One night, as she was driving through a wood, she asked the driver to stop. She had heard a voice. A few minutes later a native emerged, a half-naked man with wild hair and very dark skin. He was carrying a garland of flowers. "Mother, I've been waiting ten years to see you," he said in his dialect as he put the garland round her neck.

The welcome was not always triumphal or loving. The writer Bruce Chatwin, who went with her on part of that tour, was in a car that was mistaken for Indira's. A stone broke the windscreen and injured the driver. Another went through his window and the pieces of glass caused the writer a cut on the shoulder. "That's what often happens to those who walk at my side," Indira told him as she took him to her room to check that the wound was properly bandaged. On another occasion, in the state of Kerala, Chatwin witnessed how a crowd of a quarter of a million, completely soaked by the rain, came to listen to her when it was already dark. Indira went to a balcony on the top floor of a building and sat on a chair that had been put on top of a table. She held a torch between her knees and pointed the beam at her face and torso. And she began to wave her arms and speak, while her followers mixed her up with Lakshmi, the goddess whose many arms moved with a waving motion. The comparison was not trivial: Lakshmi was the goddess of wealth. After some time, she turned to Chatwin, who was sitting below her on the table.

"Mr Chatwin, please pass me a few more cashew nuts," she said, bending down towards him. The writer gave her a handful and was perplexed to hear Indira add, "You have no idea how exhausting it is to be a goddess."

24

Prime Minister Morarji Desai admitted what a mistake it had been to arrest Indira, and he was not prepared to repeat it, in spite of the reports from the Shah Commission, which proclaimed that the decision to impose the state of emergency had been unconstitutional and fraudulent as there was no "evidence of threat to the integrity of the nation", an arguable conclusion. Among the ills caused by the Emergency, Judge Shah emphasized the arrest of thousands of innocent people and a "series of illegal acts that led to human misery and suffering". The unfortunate thing was that the judge's well-known pro-government tendency took away some of the Shah Commission's credibility. It was a very subjective interpretation of the evidence, and furthermore, it was not binding.

So they forgot about Indira and concentrated on her son, who was not legally safe, although it could never be proved that there was diversion of public funds or bribery in the Maruti affair. The most problematic charge against Sanjay was that he had destroyed a satirical film called *The tale of two armchairs,* in reference to the power that he and his mother wielded during the state of emergency. The producer of the film had appealed to the Supreme Court to get the judge to OK the censorship and then obtain the certificate to show the film. But then

Sanjay and his henchman the Minister of Information had ordered the copies and negatives of the film destroyed, in an act that subverted the course of justice. They were found guilty of that.

And so Sonia was once again witness to the arrest of another member of the family, this time her brother-in-law. It was much quicker than in Indira's case. In five minutes he was taken away in handcuffs to the infamous Tihar Jail, where he had sent so many opponents of his mother's. Indira, who was travelling in the south, caught the first plane back to Delhi. She went directly to see him in jail and found the whole family there, as well as a large group of reporters and television teams. The hug she gave Sanjay went round the world, as well as the advice she gave him: "Don't lose heart, be brave, this is going to lead to your political rebirth. And don't worry, remember that I, my father, all of us have been to jail." Indira was worried about the effect that prison might have on Sanjay. "What I'm afraid of," she told Rajiv and Sonia, "is that they might hurt him physically."

In spite of the tension, the family reacted as one in the face of adversity. Sonia promised to make a meal for her brother-in-law every day which Maneka would take to prison for him. The young woman was excited at the new situation. To her it felt as if they were going through an incredible adventure and deep down she was enjoying her new role because she felt her husband needed her more than ever.

In 1979, Sanjay was imprisoned six times, although he did not spend more than five weeks locked up. The same thing happened to him as to his grandfather, Nehru: prison brought out the best in him. He had no qualms about mixing with all

315

kinds of prisoner; he organized sports tournaments, team games and shifts to clean up the prison. When a prisoner fell ill, Sanjay took care of him. If he felt it was necessary, he would spend hours at his side. As soon as he went into any of the jails he became the undisputed leader there.

While Sanjay survived going in and out of jail and the courts, his mother was gathering her strength, convinced as she was that she would be able to regain power, and with it security and dignity for her and her family. She was prepared to fight like a lioness to protect her cubs. It was a lioness who sent the message to Sanjay in jail on his birthday: "Remember, everything that makes you strong, hurts. Some are left crushed or damaged, very few grow. Be strong in body and mind and learn to bear things…"

Indira was trying to re-form her base, the party, which was divided between the unconditional followers, ready to go with her to the ends of the earth, and those who said that Sanjay was responsible for the disaster in 1977 and who did not want him in the organization. In addition to this there were numerous ministers who had betrayed her before the Shah Commission, confessing to lies in exchange for legal immunity. In those circumstances, re-forming the party became almost impossible. So Indira went to the root of the matter. She decided to split the organization and only hold on to the most loyal members. So she became the president of the Congress (I) Party – the I for Indira – and the logo chosen was the open palm of a hand, like a blessing. She also demanded loyalty to her son from her loyal people. "Those who attack Sanjay, are attacking me," she had declared on several occasions. Her desire for power pushed her subconsciously to perpetuate herself in power, which is why the figure of Sanjay fed her dynastic ambitions.

Sonia thought she had already gone through the worst with the arrests, the harassment, the fiscal persecution of her husband, but from the moment that Indira announced the creation of her new political formation, life in Willingdon Crescent became much more irritating and uncomfortable. The house was open day and night. People came at any hour to visit Indira. The members of her party, with expressions that went from euphoria to anguish, came and went as if in their own homes. They would meet unexpectedly in secret, organize themselves, plan new strategies, and decide what tactics to use in each constituency. Added to all this there were the frequent visits from lawyers who continued to guide Indira and Sanjay through the ins and outs of the law. Sonia would suddenly come across members of the secret services in the dining room who had come to question her mother-in-law or her brother-in-law. She no longer knew if the people who swarmed through the rooms were allies or enemies. She found it hard to keep up with preparing cups of tea and snacks for the numerous visitors that Indira received on the lawn, under some improvised awnings in the garden or in theentrance hall of the house, which sometimes seemed like the waiting room ata train station. Indira seemed happy with so much hustle and bustle; the confusion did not bother her. She was in her element, in the atmosphere in which she had been brought up as a little girl. Furthermore, she had Sanjay with her. If he was not in jail or with his lawyers, he worked very closely with her, looking for a way to use the Youth Congress to boycott the work ofthe current Janata Party government.

"It reminds me of those days in Anand Bhawan when we were preparing some protest action or other..." said a delighted Indira to Sonia, who was on the verge of tears.

317

Neither she nor Rajiv could stand the lack of privacy. More than once it happened that they came across party members arguing heatedly in their bedroom because they had not found a better place to do it. The disorganized and unsettled atmosphere, the constant threats and the uncertainty of the future set their nerves on edge. That was not the life they had chosen for themselves and their children. Now their friends could not even come to see them. Where would they entertain them? All this confusion made Sonia fear for the safety of the little ones. "What if someone slips into the house with the intention of kidnapping them or hurting them," she wondered. Besides, she was worried about the effect that the tension within the family would have on them. Sonia and Maneka had stopped speaking to each other because the latter was still not helping out with the household duties. Pupul, who was a privileged witness at that time, wrote: "It's incredible that, in those chaotic circumstances, Sonia could deal with all the housework without it getting her down."

The next step that Indira took was to stand for election in a small constituency in the south. She had heard rumours that the Janata government was preparing a law to sanction politicians who had committed crimes against the people, such as making it impossible for them to vote or be elected. If Indira managed to get into Parliament, she could be certain that these measures would not affect her as she would be protected by her parliamentary immunity. She had chosen the constituency with extreme care. Chikmaglur was a small district among the green hills of Karnataka, a state in the south west of India, where a Moslem saint had arrived from Mecca in the seventeenth century to plant some red seeds that were unknown until that time. It was the start of the cultivation of coffee, which was still being carried out three centuries later. For Indira, it was a perfect area: over half of the electorate consisted of women, of which half belonged to the so-called "lower castes". In all, more than half the population lived below the poverty line. The area was also a bastion of the Congress Party. The MP for the district, who resigned in order to give his place to Indira, was an old, well- respected leader.

The little villages perched in the hills were surrounded by exuberant semi-tropical vegetation. Indira enjoyed the bucolic scenery. She visited the coffee plantations to speak to the harvesters and their families. They were simple people, satisfied with the little that they had, isolated from the political life of the rest of the country. Indira discovered that the news of her defeat in 1977 had still not reached the interior of the district. An old lady picking coffee there had still not heard that Indira was no longer Prime Minister. When they told her that she could end up in jail if they proved the charges against her, the old woman asked, with tears in her eyes, "What charges?", as though the great people of this world could never do anything wrong. Those people were ingenuous and innocent.

Indira did not leave a single village unvisited. Everywhere she went the welcome was very warm. The women came up to her to touch her face because they had never seen such pale skin. Their eyes held a tacit understanding of what it meant to be a woman, to bear the weight of childbirth, children, hunger and death. The older ones thanked her because her government had set aid programmes in motion thanks to which they were able to eat rice for the first time. Before, they survived on the harvest of wild wheat, and many of them had no clothes to wear and went around dressed in banana leaves. That is how remote and backward Chikmaglur was, and that is how grateful the women there were.

While her rivals made speeches about democracy as opposed to dictatorship and reminded voters of the excesses of the state of emergency, Indira talked about the spiral in prices, the shortage of basic foodstuffs and the growing poverty. In that place, the Emergency had not been noticed. As if that were not enough, her adversaries smoothed the way for her by mocking her in a manner that could only occur in India. At a huge rally, they placed an enormous poster of Indira in which she was represented in the form of a menacing cobra. Underneath there were the words: "Look out. In these elections a powerful cobra is going to rise." The effect was totally counter-productive. The authors of the campaign did not know that in Karnataka the cobra was venerated and considered an animal that protected the land. Another poster showed arrows from the Janata Party killing a snake called Indira. But in Chikmaglur, killing a cobra was considered a very bad omen.

It poured with rain on election day. Even so, three quarters of the population turned out to place their vote. Indira returned to New Delhi and two days later, while she was with Sonia and Rajiv in the Russian Embassy, celebrating the USSR's national day, she was informed that she had won by an ample margin of seventy thousand votes. The ambassador raised his glass to toast Indira's victory. In two years, the woman who had been beaten at the polls in such a humiliating way was returning as MP in Parliament for a remote constituency in the south.

Four days later, Indira was flying to London. She had managed to get a diplomatic passport for herself and she had wanted Sonia to go with her. She was the only one who could, since she had an Italian passport. She had invited her so that her daughter-in-law would have a change of air and also to thank her for her dedication to the family. In recent times, the discord at home had almost turned into hysteria. Maneka's erratic and uncontrolled behaviour was a source of constant tension. She reacted to the pressure and uncertainty by bursting into frequent attacks of anger against everybody, including her husband. In one of those fights, Maneka pulled off the ring that Indira had given her for her wedding and thrown it on the floor in fury.

"How can you dare to do that?" Indira burst out. "That ring belonged to my mother!"

Maneka went out, slamming the door and Sonia bent over to pick it up.

"I'll keep it for Priyanka," she said, and in effect, years later, her daughter would wear her great-grandmother's ring.

The marriage between Sanjay and Maneka was explosive, just the opposite to Rajiv and Sonia's. In that unusual home, Sonia behaved like a perfect Indian daughter-in-law, and Maneka like an exuberant Neapolitan. "Chaos reigns supreme at home," Indira confessed to her friend Pupul. "But Maneka is barely twenty-one... Sanjay still has long periods in jail ahead of him. We have to understand her and forgive her hysteria." The witch hunt had made them all pay a high price in nervous tension, even Sanjay himself, on whom the thirty-five criminal charges brought against him by the Janata Party in two years had left a mark. One day, while the family were having breakfast at home with some relatives who were visiting them, Sanjay protested because the eggs were not cooked as he had requested and he threw the plate on the floor. Sonia was the one who had cooked them for him and she left the room angrily. Indira did not say a word in criticism of her son, although it was quite obvious that she was upset.

When Sonia had had enough, she went out with her friends,

one of them a decorator and the other an editor, to have lunch in a small Chinese restaurant in Khan Market, or to the American Embassy Club where she was not recognized. Or she went out into the garden with a hoe in her hand to take care of the kitchen garden. The broccoli she had managed to grow was a sensation among her acquaintances.

The ten-day trip to London was not a holiday, but it did Sonia good to be out of the house. London brought her memories of a very happy time in her life. She had thought she would get away from the unbearable atmosphere of Indian politics, but that was not the case. Politics came after them. Indira had agreed to that trip in order to rehabilitate her battered reputation abroad, and she was greeted with great expectation and a lot of mistrust. She had been warned that she could find hostile audiences at the different acts that she would attend, so for the first meeting with MPs, Sonia feared the worst.

"Mrs Gandhi, what went wrong in your state of emergency?" one MP asked without any beating about the bush.

There was a long silence. Indira stood up, adjusted the skirts of her sari and took the microphone.

"We managed to alienate almost all sectors of the community at the same time," she replied in a simple, direct manner.

Her frankness caused general laughter and caused the tension in the atmosphere to evaporate. Among those present was a woman who, although she was on the opposing side of the ideological spectrum to Indira, she professed great admiration for her. It was Margaret Thatcher, who was about to become Prime Minister. Perhaps because she was a woman, she understood Indira's mixture of fragility and firmness and saw the reason for many of her reactions during the exercise of power. The future "Iron Lady" had no qualms about admitting that she was facing a master. That trip served mainly to allow Indira to recover her democratic credentials.

What with meetings with the Press, with representatives of Indian communities and visits to English politicians – which irritated the Indian Ambassador exceedingly – there was hardly time to go to the theatre or the cinema or to go shopping in Woolworth's and to look for books in Foyle's, the famous bookseller's. Those little trips were like balm for Sonia. In those streets that shone with the rain, nobody recognized her, she felt safe and she did not have to depend on an escort and could go around on foot and notneed to depend on a car... What a luxury! In spite of all the difficulties in recent times, her relationship with her mother-in-law was closer than ever. Sonia did not hesitate to admit that she loved her like a mother. Although Indira did not show it openly, her preference for Sonia was well-known. She inspired the kind of trust that Maneka could never inspire in her. But in spite of that, she always defended her, at least in public. "Maneka has to put up with a lot of pressure," she said by way of excuse for her. The fact is that Maneka worked hard in her mother-in-law's cause. She had managed to uncover a scandal that had affected the Janata Party. Photographers from her *Surya* magazine had obtained pictures of the Prime Minister's son, a married man of 40, in bed with a teenager. In a country with such prim habits, that scandal had the effect of making the persecution of Sanjay by the Janata Party look ridiculous and of making the Prime Minister look ridiculous too. Maneka was very proud of having done her bit in this battle. But deep inside, she felt that she could never take the place that Sonia held in Indira's heart, and that upset her.

While they were walking along Oxford Street, doing some last minute shopping for the children, neither Sonia nor

Indira could imagine that in New Delhi the government was making a last, desperate attempt to shoot her down again. As her political resurrection became more certain, the investigatory commissions multiplied in number to try to link her to all kinds of crimes. The accusations went from the macabre to the absurd, from "conspiring to kill an ex-minister" (who had actually died a natural death) to "diverting public money and illegally getting rich" (which was obviously false). Perhaps the most absurd of the charges was that of having stolen four chickens and two eggs, an accusation which, as soon as she got back from London, forced her to travel to the distant state of Manipur, in the east of India, a journey of three thousand kilometres, to stand before the local judge. The case was dismissed and Indira was able to return to New Delhi.

In Parliament, where she was greeted with shouts and cheering, the Privilege Committee, a group that watched over the abuse of power among political leaders, had presented a motion against Indira, accusing her of having harassed four civil servants who were investigating Maruti Ltd, when she was Prime Minister. The report concluded that she was guilty, but before it could be processed in court, the leaders of the Janata Party decided to punish her, making use of their majority in the House. They passed a Parliamentary decree asking for "Indira to be jailed for one week and then expelled from the House." Now the ones who were committing abuses were those in power themselves. They had condemned her before she had been judged. It was nothing but revenge, easily explained by the fear they felt that she might rise again. One thing was to have Indira travelling round the country, but it was very different to have her speaking out in Parliament. So they used a trick to get her out: first jail her, which was not entirely legal, and then apply the law that automatically expelled from Parliament anyone who had been sentenced to a term in prison. Actually they crossed the line of what was legal. And they did it on precisely the day that the ex-Prime Minister of Pakistan, Zulfikar Ali Bhutto stood before the Pakistani Supreme Court to defend himself from a death sentence passed by a lower court. It had been planned by Zia Ul Haq, a coup general who had organized a sham trial. The shadow of that unfair sentence reached as far as New Delhi, menacing Indira and her son. If those in power passed over the rules of play, everything became possible in that lynch-crowd atmosphere. By acting illegally, Indira's enemies did away with the last vestiges of the moral superiority with which they had taken over power as representatives of a nation traumatized by the experience of the state of emergency. Suddenly, they were the ones who had become tyrants who locked people up without trial, thus subverting the will of the electorate.

Under the dome of Parliament, Indira defended herself with controlled passion and fury: "Never before in the history of any democratic country has one person, the leader of the main opposition party, been the object of such calumny, defamation of character and political vendetta on the part of the party in power." Once again she said how sorry she was for the excesses of the state of emergency: "I have already expressed my regrets in many public arenas, and I do so again now." Her words were frequently interrupted by an uproar of cheering and booing that echoed loudly in the concave dome of the building.

"I am a small person, but I have always been faithful to certain values and objectives. Every insult against me will turn against you. Every punishment you inflict on me will make me stronger. My voice cannot be silenced because it is not an isolated voice. It does not speak of me, a fragile, unimportant woman. It speaks of significant changes for society, changes which are the basis of a real democracy and greater freedom."

Having finished her speech, Indira stood up and, turning her back on the MPs, walked towards the exit. When she reached the door, she turned and gave them a long, hard look. Some were sitting with their legs crossed, dressed in their white cotton *kurtas* and their *pashmina* shawls, others were wearing the characteristic hat that Nehru had used, others the Moslem *fez*, very few were dressed in Western clothes. It looked like a crowded, old Oriental court. She raised her arm, with her hand facing outwards, whichwas the symbol of her party:

"I'll be back!" she said.

Sonia had made some exquisite pasta for dinner. There was also guava cream for dessert and little mango cakes from Allahabad, which Indira liked a lot because they reminded her of her childhood. She arrived an hour late, exhausted. Her features reflected the tension she had just experienced.

"They'll come for me at any moment..." she told Rajiv and Sonia, before telling them what had happened in Parliament.

Sonia was unable to eat a thing. As often happens, the people who are closest suffer more than the victims themselves. Fear overcame her again, mixed with an unpleasant feeling of insecurity, as though they were living on quicksand that was ready to swallow them all up. Indira would be arrested again, and this time she would not sleep in a police station but in jail. Her enemies had won a battle. Rajiv and Sonia were downhearted.

"Why don't you call Priyanka and we can play a game of

Scrabble?" asked Indira at that point. She loved to play with her granddaughter, who was very sharp and won a good number of the times they played... Whatbetter company than that of her darling girl at those moments of uncertainty?

25

The next day, Indira was arrested as she left Parliament, amid a huge demonstration of support and cries of "Long live Indira Gandhi!". This time she did not ask to be handcuffed. The police van where she was put made its way with great difficulty through the crowd. She was taken to Tihar Jail, whose name alone was enough to terrify the most hardened criminals. But unlike the Maharanis of Jaipur and Gwalior, she was not locked in a cell with prostitutes and common delinquents. She was put in the same huts where the leader of the opposition had been held during the state of emergency. She was on her own – quite a privilege. Two female guards took turns to watch her. When they brought her something to eat she refused to even try it.

"I do not intend to eat anything that has not been brought here by my family," she said imperiously, knowing that she could only trust food from Sonia's hands. The guard went out to discuss it with her superiors. As usual in India, there were long conversations that seemed to go on forever.

Meanwhile, Indira spent her time looking round her cell. The noise from the yard and the other women prisoners could be heard. It was spaciousand was generally better than what she had expected. It had a wooden bed with no mattress, and there were bars on the windows, although they lacked glass or blinds. It was very cold. At the end of December, the temperature can come close to zero at night.

Indira was blocking the window hole with a blanket to keep out the cold and try to have a little privacy when the guard came back.

"You have a visit."

Sonia and Rajiv were waiting for her in the visiting room, a large room with peeling walls, some tables and metal chairs and a lot of people, mostly poor, bony, young men who had come to see their wives and mothers who had been locked up. The lower part of the walls was covered in red stains, the vestiges of the countless gobs of spit of all the people who chewed betel leaves. It smelt of urine and rancid incense. As they had already been there to visit Sanjay, they were not horrified. But they seemed upset and it was Indira who had to raise their spirits.

"I'm fine, really. I'm going to take advantage of the time to do some reading. They let me have up to six books ... aren't I lucky?" she said sarcastically. "They've made a kind of special washroom for me and I'll be able to have a shower in the morning with hot water. The cell is quite clean but it's all so horribly ugly, as you can see... How are the children?"

"Priyanka wanted to come and see you, but we thought ..." Indira's face lit up.

"Oh yes!" she said, smiling. "Bring her. It's good for her to see what a jail is like. From a very early age, we Nehrus have visited our relatives in jail... We must not lose the tradition."

They laughed. As usual, Indira was not letting herself be beaten down by adversity. Not once did she allow the slightest sign of self-pity to show. It was enough for her to be convinced that she had moral right on her side.

"I'll come to bring you your food..." Sonia told her. "Don't bring much. I'm not very hungry."

Sonia went twice a day to take her food prepared at home. She had to put it all through a metal detector. Then a female guard inspected the containers. Sweets were forbidden because on one occasion a prisoner had offered his jailer a sweet with some narcotic substance inside it and had managed to escape. Neither were bananas permitted in the women's section: the authorities were so Puritan and suspicious...

One day Indira told Sonia that she had received two anonymous telegrams. One said: "live frugally". And the other advised her to count the bars to help the time go by. "I've counted them. There are twenty-eight," she told her. She also said that she kept to a strict routine which helped to pass the days. She woke up at five o'clock and did her yoga exercises. After that she drank a glass of cold milk – which Sonia had brought the day before – and went back to bed until seven. Then she washed, did a little meditation and read a little. The afternoons seemed never-ending, but she did not complain. She spent the time thinking, withdrawing into herself and, curiously, resting. She experienced the best moment when her granddaughter went to visit her. Everybody in the family said that Priyanka was just like her grandmother. She had personality and was wilful and determined. Indira adored her. Rajiv and Sonia had to get involved in very lengthy discussions to get the prison authorities to allow the little girl in. It was a happy reunion in gloomy surroundings.

Before they left, Indira asked Sonia to do her a favour.

"I'd like you to send a bunch of flowers to Charan Singh from me with a note for his birthday."

"Charan Singh?" asked Sonia in astonishment. "Yes, him. Will you do it please?"

"Of course," Sonia replied, bemused.

Charan Singh was one of the leaders of the Janata Party. He had been Home Secretary and the man responsible for her first arrest. Now he had been relegated to a ministry of less importance. Indira knew what she was doing. The Janata government still had three years to run, but she had received information that the members of the coalition were involved in a fight to the death. Charan Singh was resentful of the Prime Minister, Morarji Desai, the man who had insisted on taking away Indira's home and protection, because he had dismissed him as Home Secretary. Indira thought that she could open up a split between the two leaders, and incite his ambitions so that the government might fall like a piece of rotten fruit. That was the purpose of the bunch of flowers.

As soon as she came out of jail, there was a letter waiting for her from Charan Singh inviting her to his residence to join the celebrations for the birth of his grandson. In that reassuring family setting, Machiavellian negotiations took place, in which both political adversaries worked out a strategy to overthrow the government of Prime Minister Morarji Desai. In exchange for annulling the new Special Tribunals Law under which Indira and Sanjay could be accused without the usual legal protection, Indira offered the support of the Congress Party to defeat Morarji Desai. And once overthrown, she promised to help Charan Singh to become Prime Minister, which would allow him to satisfy his lifelong ambition. It was Sanjay who took charge of the delicate negotiations, ensuring he left no loose ends.

The result was that the coalition split apart and Morarji Desai's government fell, but Charan Singh could not, or would not, revoke the special law, so Indira pulled out her backing, and his government lasted less than a month. In order to get out of the mess, the President of the Republic dissolved

Parliament and called new elections for January 1980. Indira had manoeuvred with experience, coolness and efficiency. Just as she had told MPs after her speech, she was getting ready for a comeback, and she would come in through the front door.

A few months earlier, she had been thinking about giving it all up. She and Sanjay had even talked about retiring to a small town in the Himalayas. The wise man and philosopher Krishnamurti, a personal friend of Pupul's, had recommended that Indira leave politics and she had replied that she did not know how, with 28 charges open against her. She did not want to end up like Zulfikar Ali Bhutto, who had been executed by hanging on April 4th, 1979 in the courtyard of the central prison in Rawalpindi. The Pakistani dictator, fearful that Bhutto might make a political comeback, like Indira was doing in India, had managed to manipulate the courts to finish off his rival. Here it was not so easy to manipulate justice, because India wasstill a democracy. But danger was lurking.

"I have two alternatives," Indira had told Krishnamurti, "either I fight or they shoot me like a duck in a fairground stall."

Now there was no going back. Power was within her reach. True to herself, Indira went out to grasp it. Armed with two suitcases that contained half a dozen raw cotton saris, a thermos flask for hot water and another for cold milk, two cushions, several bags of dried fruit, a box of apples and an umbrella to shade her from the sun, she headed out to the furthest reaches of the sub-continent. She travelled seventy thousand kilometres, spoke at an average of twenty rallies a day, and altogether reached an audience of one hundred million. She was seen or heard by one in four voters. She immediately realized that her second spell in jail had made her immensely popular. A martyr and a heroine. In comparison, the candidates from the coalition that made up the Janata Party seemed like old dinosaurs. They were competing not so much with a tiny lady candidate aged sixty-two as with a living myth, a legend dressed in a sari and dusty sandals who aroused the passion of the people. Her message was simple, miles away from any abstractions or ideologies: "Vote for a government that works for you". Sonia could not imagine that, years later, she herself would use the same slogan.

Just like in the good times, Indira won hands down in the elections. Sonia was expecting it because she had gone with her on some of her tours round the villages and she had seen her moving totally at ease among the crowds of ragged people, saying a kind word to an old man, doing something nice for a handicapped person, smiling at a woman, giving a flower to a little girl. The memory of that fantastic campaign remained engraved on her mind, and years later it would be of enormous use to her.

When the results were made official, the house was flooded with friends, journalists, party members, industrial magnates, neighbourhood shopkeepers and people from right across the spectrum of society. There were flowers everywhere. Her friend Pupul found it hard to make her way through the crush of people. When they saw each other, Indira almost burst into tears. "She was very emotional, and a little vague," her friend would say. "Although she realized that the tide had turned in her favour, the shock of her victory left her feeling knocked out." Taking in that she was Prime Minister again and that with one stroke of the pen all her problems were solved, took its time. But she reacted immediately.

"What does it feel like to be leader of India again?" a Europeancorrespondent asked Indira. She turned to him with a fiery look.

"I've always been the leader of India," she answered drily.

Another journalist, surprised at the massive presence of poor people, said to Indira that she must have done something good for them in the past for so many of them to turn up, to which she replied a little cryptically: "No, the ones we have helped are where they cannot be seen."

Sanjay was at her side, smiling, wrapped in a salmon pink shawl, like a young Caesar. He had won too, in the same constituency that had rejected him three years previously. Now his power would be somewhat legitimate. Life was smiling at him for another reason too. Maneka had become pregnant a few months before, when the situation was very bad for both of them. They had come to wonder what sense there was in bringing a child into the world in the middle of so many threats. Now that veil of uncertainty was lifting and the future looked very promising. Maneka, very excited, chatted to reporters and friends, proudly exhibiting her bare belly, showing between her top and the skirts of her sari. Rajiv, Sonia and the children were all over the house. Once again, they seemed like one big happy family.

Those who had been the victims of the campaigns of nationalization and abolition of privileges did not share that joy. The photo of Indira smiling next to Sanjay, which filled the front pages of the main newspapers on the following days, made more than one in that huge country feel a shiver of fear. Mother and son were returning to the attack. In their now decrepit palaces, the heirs of the maharajas received the news with cynicism... What could she take away from them now that she had not already taken away?

Such was the hatred that Indira inspired in many families of the old aristocracy of the country that once, on a visit to Bhopal, she was invited to have tea in the home of the heirs of the old *begums*, who had governed the sultanate for generations. Indira never knew that the slice of chocolate cake she enjoyed so much was tainted by a gob of spit, a hidden gift from the lady of the house who, *noblesse oblige*, nevertheless treated her with the utmost deference.

On January 14th 1980, Indira was sworn in as Prime Minister before the President of the Republic, surrounded by her family, a few friends and party comrades, in the resplendent Ashoka hall of the former Viceroy's palace, whose paintings on the ceilings and walls told the mythological story of age-old India. It was the fourth time she had done so in this same setting, whose grandiosity evoked the enormous power that she was being granted. This time she did not swear on the Constitution, as on previous occasions, but in the name of God. She had always been a little superstitious, unlike her father, but now mentioning the Almighty was a surprise. Perhaps she admitted deep inside that her return to power was due more to destiny than to her own merits or the failings of her adversaries. Perhaps so many attacks had left a dent in her armour, and she needed comfort. She had always felt respect for the supernatural, a legacy she attributed to her mother, a deeply religious woman. She had always listened to astrologers. That date had been chosen by her yoga teacher, the guru Dhirendra Brahmachari. According to him, it was a favourable day as it corresponded to the winter solstice in the Hindu calendar. For twenty years, this curious character, who also practised astrology, told her the lucky or unlucky days for certain activities. Lately, his influence had diminished considerably. Indira looked at him with suspicion because the Shah Commission had brought his shady dealings into the open and questioned the origin of his fortune. Even so, she continued to ask him about good or bad days before taking a decision. At her age and after what she had been through, Indira did not want to take any risks by tempting fate.

Just after the swearing in, Indira went straight to the President's palace, to her old office in South Block. She could not trust the majority of her former ministers and colleagues because they had betrayed her. Neither did she want to surround herself with figures that people might identify with the state of emergency. She had to choose the members of her cabinet from among a hotchpotch of MPs without much experience, many of them from the ranks of Sanjay's Youth Congress. To the surprise of many and relief of some, she did not give her son any portfolio, in spite of his legitimacy as validated in the polls. She did not want to expose him too much. She preferred him at her side, wanting to train him and see him mature under her protection. She had complete confidence that Sanjay would be able to revitalize the party and ensure that the rural development projects would be properly carried out. And she did not want to repeat the errors of the past.

Meanwhile, Sonia took charge of the move again. Indira's victory meant that they were all returning to number 1, Safdarjung Road. It was becoming urgent to make more space again. First of all, Indira wanted to send a dozen Hindu priests to purify the house where Morarji Desai had resided while he had been harassing her. She had found out that her rival was an assiduous practitioner of urinotherapy, an ancient custom that consists of drinking a glassful of the first urine of the day every morning on an empty stomach. To ensure that there was not a single glass left from the old tenant in the house, Sonia and Indira busied themselves collecting them all, placing them in a box and sending them back to the administration. She also sent a team of bricklayers to knock down the Indian-style bathroom that her rival had had built and replace it with a European-style one, with a toilet and bath tub. When they moved, it was as if they had never been away from that house. "An air of renewed elegance reigned in all the rooms, which were again full of servants and enormous vases of flowers falling in cascades", Pupul would write. Sonia once again took on her role as housewife extraordinaire in that special home, where dinners and receptions had to be organized for a continual parade of personalities: Giscard d'Estaing, Mobutu, Yasser Arafat, Andrei Gromyko, Jimmy Carter, etc. They all came to strengthen ties with one of the most powerful women in the world.

Family life became pleasant again. The new situation and

greater space made the atmosphere more relaxed. The fights stopped, and, even better, the silences. Everyone was attentive to Maneka, who was about to give birth. During the pregnancy, Sonia had tacitly made peace with her sister-in-law. She had chosen to forget the old bickering, the mood swings, the nasty comments, to concentrate on her duty as "elder *bahu*" – elder daughter-in-law – and to help Maneka with her experience. She kept an eye on her all the time. The family comes first. Definitely, Sonia was by now very Indian. Although the two sisters-in-law were like chalk and cheese, they managed to reach a kind of *entente cordiale*. Indira, who was beside herself with joy when she thought about her new grandchild, had already chosen a name for him: Firoz, like her husband. Maneka was not convinced and wanted to call him Varun. Sanjay settled the matter. The little one would be called Firoz Varun.

Rajiv no longer had to spend almost all his free time, outside flying time, in the Tax Office. Once again, he could spend time on his family and his hobbies, such as photography or the radio. He was a wonderful father. He never missed an event at school, or reading a story if he got home before the children had gone to bed. Photography gave him a lot of enjoyment; it was a form of relaxation after the concentration required by his flying, often at impossible times. His hobby had grown over the years. He liked to experiment with filters and new equipment, he never missed an exhibition and he subscribed to specialist magazines. He also encouraged his children to take an interest. He taught them to develop their visual sensitivity by asking them to identify different tones of green in the garden. Later, he advised his son to note down the exposure time and speed at which he took photos so that he could correct them and improve. His camera was always there on special occasions: birthdays, anniversaries, family celebrations, etc. and if he was at home when a photographer came to take a portrait of his mother, he would take his camera and join in the session. He always enjoyed a special sense of camaraderie with photographers. He gave his mother a miniature folding album that she took with her on all her trips. "Rajiv, give me some more recent photos," she asked him repeatedly when she tired of always seeing the same ones. Indira loved the photos of her grandchildren. She chose the ones she liked on contact sheets and asked Rajiv to enlarge and frame them. Her office was full of them.

At night, Rajiv shut himself in his workshop and got in touch with radio hams all over the world. He had bought a radio transmitter in a self- assembly kit and nothing made him happier than to connect up with Pier Luigi, Sonia's childhood friend back there in Orbassano, on clear nights without any interference. Protected by anonymity, talking by radio with people all over the world was another way of travelling and, at the same time, forgetting who he was and relaxing.

On February 16th, 1980, one month after Indira's swearing in, an extraordinary phenomenon occurred in India which had not been seen for almost a century: a total eclipse of the sun. Rajiv set up a telescope in the garden, helped by Rahul and Priyanka, who were very excited about the idea. In addition they had special dark glasses, which Rajiv had obtained from a pilot colleague. Sanjay amused himself adjusting the controls of a radio-controlled plane. His liking for making model aeroplanes had developed after the government took away his pilot's licence without giving any reason. Now he was waiting to get it back in order to return to what had become his favourite hobby: flying. Long forgotten now was his passion for cars, buried by the Maruti fiasco. Pupul, who had been invited by her friend to see the event, was drinking a cup of tea on the veranda. When the time forthe eclipse approached, Indira, influenced by the gloomy predictions of well-known astrologers who had announced earthquakes, floods and disasters of all kinds, sent Maneka to her room. Considered as a direct threat to the unborn child, no pregnant woman should be exposed to its evil influence. Even in matters that had nothing to do with politics, Indira was in touch withher electorate. Most people chose to hide in their huts. Hindus do not go out during eclipses since they are considered harmful because symbolically, the light is hidden. Some fasted, others made offerings or recited mantras toward off the danger. When the moon began to hide the sun, a mysterious light enveloped the house and garden and the shadows disappeared. Indira stood up and went to lock herself in her room until the end of the eclipse. Her guru, Brahmachari, had told her that the eclipse was especially dangerous for her and for Sanjay, and she preferred to believe him. Rajiv, Sonia and the children, all with dark glasses on, watched in ecstasy as the moon passed in front of the sun. Pupul followed Indira to her room. "This was not the strong Indira of the days before the state of emergency," she thought. "It surprised me how influenced she was by ritual and superstition. What was she afraid of? What shadow, what darkness walked beside her?"

The following months were marked by family harmony and happiness at enjoying a normal life again. The attention that Maneka received from her mother-in-law, her sister-in-law and her husband, who went with her to all the checkups because he said that she was terrified of physical suffering, made her feel like a queen. Just like his brother Rajiv, Sanjay joined in the whole process of the birth. Firoz Varun was born on March

13th, 1980 with no complications. He was the icing on the cake in the family's improved fortunes. From that moment on, the spirited Maneka began to enjoy her role as mother and wife, advised by Sonia, on whose shoulders the early care of the baby fell. Indira was so happy that she had him in her room so she could sleep with him. She did not care if she did not sleep a wink.

Once again, because of his closeness to his mother, Sanjay enjoyed irresistible power. He was involved in all aspects of life in India, from the capital's air corridors to the congestion in the hospitals, from plans for rural development to the protection of animals, a favourite cause into which his wife had dragged him. Word went in New Delhi that before a year was out he would be Prime Minister, but his mother was not prepared to allow that. When the members of the legislative assembly of the Congress Party in Uttar Pradesh chose Sanjay as their leader, they asked Indira to name him head of the government of that state, the largest in the country. Maneka could already see herself enjoying the perks that came with that job, including living in a palace full of servants. But Indira refused point blank. She told her son's admirers that he still had a lot to learn before he could take on a responsibility like that. Sanjay protested and argued with his mother, but she did not give way. In the end, he calmed down and did not insist any longer.

Although he was still surrounded by a court of flatterers, Sanjay was not the same man as he was before. Even his detractors began to admit that, in effect, he possessed qualities that the country needed in that difficult situation. They recognized his enormous capacity for work and his proven ability to take tough, unpopular decisions. In fact, what was happening to him was what had happened to his grandfather,

341

Nehru and to Indira. Everyone in the family had taken a long time to mature as adults, and had done so after facing great challenges. At the age of thirty-three, Sanjay was on his way to becoming a responsible man, without the stridency or aberrant behaviour of the past. His mother was convinced that, after a good political apprenticeship, her son would go from being an inexpert and impulsive young man to a visionary and energetic politician. He had all the genes to achieve that, she thought. The incredible thing is that many people in India also thought the same, something that was unthinkable only six months earlier. Either the country had lost its memory or the pull of the Gandhis among the people was still the only chance of salvation for millions of Indians.

Rajiv, Sonia and their children spent those months dreaming about the holidays. They had decided to spend a few days in Italy, and were thinking of doing it in June, when the heat is at its worst in New Delhi. They intended to meet up there with their friend, the Indian actor Kabir Bedi, who in those years was known all over the world for his starring role in the *Sandokan* series, and who had promised to visit them. In addition, this time they were thinking of driving round the north of Italy. They intended to hire a car and visit the region of Asiago and the village of Lusiana, where Sonia had been born. She wanted to show the children the place where she had been brought up, introduce them to the locals and the relatives that were still left there. A journey into the other family roots.

The day they left, before they said goodbye, Maneka showed Sonia a bag, which contained something she had bought, with the idea of using it.

"You aren't going to believe it…" "What is it?" asked Sonia, intrigued.

Maneka took a cookery book out of the bag. They both burst into laughter. It was the last time they would be seen laughing together.

26

If it had not been interrupted, that would have been a perfect holiday: relaxed, fun and interesting. The children perfected their Italian, Sonia got on with her shopping for European clothes and Rajiv did the same with his photographic material. In the end, they did not even have to hire a car: Sonia's sister, Anushka, lent them a convertible that was the delight of the children. In it, they toured the north of Italy, in the opposite direction to that of the patriarch, Stefano, when he had left his home town of Lusiana in search of a better future in the industrial belt of Turin. Thirty-five years later, his daughter and grandchildren were returning to the Asiago mountains, like a normal Italian family on holiday. On the way, they stopped at beautiful Lake Garda, surrounded by olive groves, fields of lemon trees and thick cypress woods; they walked around Verona along the wide streets of red marble, were seduced by the charm of Venice and bathed on the beaches of the Adriatic. They went up the Asiago mountains through a countryside that reflected the splendour of spring. Mauve, white and yellow wild flowers grew at the side of the road that wound among beech woods. The fields where the cows grazed were swathed in an intense green colour and in the background the Alps reminded them of the view of the Himalayas from the plains. In Lusiana, the village the family came from, the air was so crystal clear that it made them feel like drinking it in. The temperature was perfect. And to think that now in Delhi, grandma, uncle and aunt and especially little Firoz would be putting up with temperatures of 45° in the shade while they waited for the rains to come! From the car, Priyanka and Rahul laughed when they read the signs over the shops: "Maino Bakery", "Maino Trattoria", "Café Maino", "Maino Bros. Petrol Station"... How the different branches of the family had prospered since the time after the war! thought Sonia. They were welcomed with great affection and curiosity: everyone wanted to meet the prodigal daughter of the town whose extraordinary destiny they followed in the Press. They were all surprised by the same thing: the family's simplicity. Sonia was dressed with good taste, in tight trousers and sleeveless T-shirts, a luxury that she could not allow herself in India, where a woman could show her belly but it was considered poor taste if she showed her shoulders. They had photos taken outside the stone family home, the last house in Rua Maino. It had stood uninhabited for three decades. They were treated like royalty, to such an extent that they had no time to accept all the invitations and all the visits.

They went back to Orbassano, where Stefano and Paola were waiting eagerly for them. They had been so worried when they followed the turn of events in India during recent years that now they felt a pang in their hearts every time their daughter and their grandchildren went away, even if it was only to the Veneto, or just to spend the afternoon in Turin. Added to that disquiet was the worry they felt for their youngest daughter, Nadia, who had married a Spanish diplomat who had just been stationed in New Delhi. On one hand, they were happy because the two sisters were going to be able to keep each other company; on the other hand, they did not like having themso far away. They joked that they could not escape the karma of India. The eldest daughter, Anushka, who lived in the flat in the lower part of the house on Via Bellini, intended to open an Indian handicrafts shop in a shopping centre near Orbassano. She had called her eldest daughter Aruna.

Rahul and Priyanka were happy to return to their grandparents' house because their cousins, Anushka's children, lived downstairs, so the children had a wonderful time in that large family house, playing in the garden or the street. They played the same as Sonia when she was a girl, when she wrote the days of the week in chalk on the road and spent hours hopping from one box to the next. Stefano felt very happy with those family gatherings. He had built the house to have all his daughters and their families under one roof, hadn't he? They joked that he must have been Indian in another life as all the family liked India so much... Sonia's old acquaintances were surprised that their old friend should still have such a humble attitude and dressed so simply, with only small, discreet jewellery. One local lady said laughingly, "The Cinderella of Orbassano didn't let the marriage she made go to her head". That is how the local press described her since her marriage: "the Cinderella of Orbassano", a name that made Sonia feel embarrassed: "How twee," she said. For Rajiv too the holiday in Italy was the best relaxation he could have wished for. Getting away from New Delhi was a luxury. Jumping on Pier Luigi's orange Vespa and going to the Allegro electronics shop in Corso Rei Umberto to buy parts for his radio that he could not find in India and not being recognized was a pleasure, as was visiting the fabulous Egyptian Museum – where Sonia, as a teenager, used to meet up with her friends to get out of the cold in the streets – without being immediately surrounded by a mass of people asking for an autograph or pointing at them. But the pleasure would not last long. At the end of June, Sandokan's visit to Orbassano caused a real stir. Suddenly the children and young people of the town came to Via Bellini to have a close look at this prince of Borneo who had sworn revenge on the British in the imagination of Emilio Salgari. There was such a fuss that Sonia suggested they leave the house. They ended the evening in a pizzeria in the nearby town of Avigliana, happy and laughing.

And suddenly, at dawn on June 23rd, the phone rang. Sonia felt a knot in her stomach. It was not a normal time, and she immediately thought it could be a call from India. Her mother confirmed it, on tiptoe and in a whisper, in order not to wake the rest of the family. "It's a long-distance call... from New Delhi." Sonia got up, wrapped her dressing gown about her and went into the sitting room to pick up the phone. Amid all the interference, she recognized the nervous voice of one of her mother-in-law's secretaries. Now she was certain that it would be very bad news. "Madam... Sanjay has had an accident... He's dead." Sonia's mind went blank and she did not hear the hurried explanations the secretary gave her. When she hung up she was stunned. She went back to their room. Rajiv was stirring. She waited a few moments to tell him, as though she wanted to give him a few more seconds of happiness that she knew, once he was awake, he would not see again. In the deepest part of her being, Sonia knew that this catastrophe was going to affect her life and that of her family profoundly.

*   *   *

A few hours later, they were flying towards Rome on their

way to catch the Air India flight that went from London to New Delhi. They travelled in first class, together with other friends and acquaintances, among whom were Maneka's mother and sister, whose holiday in the English capital had been interrupted. Also on board the plane there were an ex-minister, an industrialist and a businessman, all of them old family friends and very upset by the circumstances. Each of them had got hold of information about the accident and during the long flight they were able to work out what had happened.

Sanjay had crashed at the controls of his latest toy, the Pitts S-2A, which he had acquired thanks to the mediation of the corrupt guru, Brahmachari. At seven o'clock in the morning, he had turned up at the New Delhi flying club and had invited a pilot friend out for some acrobaticexercises. His friend was unwilling to fly with Sanjay because he knew he lacked experience, but in view of his insistence, he ended up agreeing. They were doing loops in the sky and diving over New Delhi for twelve minutes, then they flew over number 1 Safdarjung Road, where he had been talking tohis mother barely an hour earlier.

"Be very careful," Indira had told him. "They tell me you're very rash…"

"Don't take any notice," Sanjay had answered.

According to a witness, the plane went up into the sky like an arrow and then began a dive as though it was preparing to do a loop, but it could not recover. It crashed in the diplomatic district, on some empty land, less than a kilometre from number 12, Willingdon Crescent.

A month before, the director general of Civil Aviation had informed his superiors that Sanjay persistently violated the security protocol and was therefore putting his life and the lives of others at risk.

"The director of aviation told the Air Force Minister, who agreed to talk to your mother about it, but, for whatever the reason, he did not."

"If no one did anything, it was out of fear of going against Sanjay, I imagine…" said Rajiv.

Later they would find out what had happened exactly. The report from the director of civil aviation had fallen into Sanjay's hands and he had reacted, in his usual way, by forcing the man to take voluntary leave without pay. He had replaced him with his second-in-command, a malleable man who would not give him any problems. The fact is that Sanjay had died because he was rash and arrogant, because his thirst for power was such that it accepted no limits.

Nightfall in flight was very quick, because of the speed of the plane and because of the rotation of the Earth. They must have been over Syria, or perhaps Turkey. Below, turquoise-coloured lakes could be seen and the little lights of the cities as they embraced the night. No one was watching the film. No one in the group of friends and relatives wanted to eat a thing. Amteshwar, Maneka's mother, was visibly upset. "A widow at 23… and with a three-month old baby," the woman kept saying. In under three years she had lost her husband and her son-in-law. She had gone from being at the top to being ostracized, and then back to the top again… And now what would happen?

"You have to do all you can to keep the families united," the three family friends advised Maneka's mother. "Now that Sanjay isn't here, you have to close ranks around Rajiv."

Sonia's hair stood on end when she heard that being said.

She was about to shout "No!" loudly, but she stopped herself. She knew they would try to persuade Rajiv to fill the vacuum his brother had left. Sonia was very clear about it: that meant the end of their happiness. She was prepared to fight tooth and nail to prevent that happening.

The plane landed in Delhi at two in the morning. A wave of intense heat welcomed them. The funeral chapel had been set up in the Safdarjung Road house where a line of people – ministers, friends, strangers – had filed past the remains throughout the day, silently and in good order. Indira, very nervous, had been going from one room to another all night long asking if there was any news of the travellers, because subconsciously she was afraid that another misfortune could occur.

Rajiv, Sonia and the children had already been informed of what they were going to find but even so the shock of arriving home in those circumstances was terrible for them. When they saw Sanjay's body lying in a coffin in the sitting room, among those walls that still seemed to echo with the sound of his nervous, open laugh, Rajiv and Sonia went to pieces. And when Indira saw Rajiv crying disconsolately, she also broke into sobs. Once she recovered her serenity, Sonia observed Indira: her eyes were red and swollen behind her dark glasses, her complexion was ashen, and she walked with a stoop as though she found it hard to stand upright. "Where am I to go after this, daughter?" she asked her in a ragged voice. As she said it she pressed her hands over her stomach, in a gesture that poor peasant women make when they weep for their dead. They embraced again and stayed like that in silence a long time. Less than ten days previously, Indira had set Sanjay up in his first official office, after naming him secretary general of the party. Now, suddenly, there was only a dead body lying there: she had been left without her son, without a companion, without an advisor and without a successor. Then Sonia saw Maneka, whose movements seemed disconnected. She had spent the whole day crying and repeating: "Sanjay no, please… Anyone but not Sanjay…" Rajiv hugged her and said a few affectionate words to her. Sonia too could not hold back the tears when she hugged her. The children, tired and upset, took it all stoically. The distant crying of their cousin, little Firoz, broke the silence.

Sonia immediately set herself to tending those who were sitting with the body. She helped to place mattresses on the floor so that all the friends and close relatives could rest. She also made sure there would be tea, toast and sweets.

After the effusiveness of seeing them again, Indira told them the details of the funeral rites that she had organized for the following day.

"We'll have the cremation in Shantivana, next to grandfather's mausoleum…"

"I don't think that's a good idea, Mother," Rajiv suggested. "Wouldn't it be better to have a private, more restricted funeral?"

"Perhaps, but Sheikh Abdullah, the head of the government of Kashmir and all the heads of state governments have asked me for a memorable funeral."

"Sanjay had no official role in the government. It may cause problems if you hold a state funeral. Imagine the protests!"

"I know. But it's also true that Sanjay had many followers, and I don't want to disappoint them. It would be like disappointing him."

Rajiv did not insist.

The cremation took place the next day, on the banks of the

Yamuna River. It was too close to where the cremation of Nehru, the father of the nation, had taken place, and however much Indira did not want to see it, her son did not deserve the same honours as her father. Many saw in this gestureof Indira's another sign of abuse of power. Again she had not listened to Rajiv's advice that she should choose another place, not that holy place of pilgrimage for millions of Indians. But Indira let herself be led along by the insistence of Sanjay's friends. She had no strength to fight them and she was probably in agreement with them in paying such disproportionate tribute to her son, as if she could compensate a little in that way for her loss.

With her eyes and all the grief they held protected by enormous sunglasses, Indira was sitting next to Maneka in the front row, facing the pyre. Sonia, dressed in an immaculate white sari, sobbed as she remembered the days when she was newly married when her brother-in-law, her husband and she were an inseparable trio. Behind them, you could see people as far as the horizon. Rajiv had to carry out the rituals: he put the torch in the fire and walked several times round his brother's body, to the sound of the mantras intoned by the Hindu priests. His son Rahul watched him rather apprehensively. His father had told him that it would be up to him, as firstborn, to carry out the cremation rituals when, in the natural order of things, one of his parents left this world. Until that day, the boy had never thought that could happen.

In the afternoon, Rajiv took his brother's ashes in a copper urn to be buried under a tree in the garden at Akbar Road. On seeing the urn, Indira was unable to control herself and broke into sobs. For the first time, she wept disconsolately and uninhibitedly in public. Rajiv held her and kept her on her feet because the woman was literally collapsing. Her pain seemed limitless. Sonia had found out that on the morning of the tragedy Indira had left the hospital where the doctors were patching Sanjay's body together to go back to the scene of the accident. She had been back twice. Evil tongues said that she had gone back to look for Sanjay's watch and keyring because one of the keys was probably from a safe full of all the things the prodigal son had stolen. On the cover of the watch, still according to the rumours, the number of a secret account in Switzerland must be engraved. But it was justa tall story. Indira was not interested in his personal objects, which had been picked up already by the police. What she was really doing was looking for her son; subconsciously she was trying to get him back, not his things. By looking carefully among the burned pieces of metal, Indira had realized the enormity of her loss. All her dreams, her great plans for the future, had also been smashed to pieces among the ruins of the plane.

In the shade of the tree in the garden, Indira managed to control her weeping and recover remarkably quickly. Then they went into the sitting room. The place where the body had been placed was now covered in jasmine flowers. They sat down on the floor, with their legs crossed and in silence, listening to the priests singing verses from the *Ramayana*, the great Hindu epic.

Over the following days, Sanjay's followers erected statues in his memory, named streets and squares for him as well as whole districts, schools, hospitals and even hydro-electric power stations. The whole country frenziedly lived through a posthumous cult to the personality of the prodigal son whom the biggest flatterers came to compare with Jesus Christ, Einstein and Karl Marx. That display of so-called affection was more a desperate attempt on the part of his allies and henchmen to hang on to their privileges and stay close to power, near Indira, than a real show of national mourning. Many others, amongst whom were some of the old victims of his birth control policy, greeted his death with relief. For them it had been a providential accident, which had saved the country from the cruel destiny of having Sanjay as Prime Minister, which everyone thought was going to happen sooner or later.

For Indira, the only positive thing in the tragedy was that it served to re-kindle old relationships and to reconcile her with members of the family and friends who had turned their backs on her during the Emergency. She was particularly happy to receive a letter from her old friend Dorothy Norman: "It's been so long since we wrote to each other that on a certain level I don't know who I'm writing to; on another level, I'm writing to the person I used to know. How I'd like us to be able to talk, although silence is perhaps more revealing than any words. (…) I'm sending this letter as a bridge. Friendships are the most valuable thing in this world which is sometimes so harsh." Indira replied, telling her how moved she had been to receive her letter and that she had so much to tell her that she did not know where to begin: "The past is past, let's let it be. But I have to clear up a few things. The falsehoods, the persistent and malicious campaign of calumny must be refuted…" Indira never admitted Sanjay's negative side or hiserrors.

At home, there was Maneka and little Firoz Varun left. The child sleptin Indira's room with the other grandchildren since Sanjay's death. Their grandmother spent a lot of time looking at the baby as if she might recognize her son in his every move. Rajiv and Sonia were also there, their marriage having survived physical separation, cultural differences, family opposition, the stress of the Emergency and the continual infiltration and corrosion of politics in their lives. They had two intelligent, good-looking children, with nice characters. Until Uncle Sanjay's accident, the most serious thing that had happened to the children had been seeing their grandmother in jail and having lost their dog. "Keep the memory of when you played with her, how much fun she had and all of us had when we took her for walks..." Rajivhad written to them in a letter full of fatherly tenderness, ending in some advice: "You have to learn to live knowing that at some point we all have to die."

The perfect family life they enjoyed seemed too nice and too good to last.

ACT III

SOLITUDE AND POWER

Every time you take a step forwards, you are destined to disturb something. You disturb the air as you move, you raise the dust, you change the ground. You crush things as you go. When a whole society moves forwards, that crushing takes place on a much larger scale; and each thing that you upset, the self-interest you may want to repress, all become an obstacle.

MAHATMA GANDHI

27

Twenty years before, after the death of her husband, Indira touched rock bottom and took a long time to get her head above water again. When her father died, she suffered another existential crisis, which lasted for many long months. But now, less than 72 hours after the death of her son, she was back in her office. "People come and go, but the nation remains alive," she declared to the Press, putting the family tragedy into a national context, as though that way she could get over the accident quicker. She had convinced herself that the Herculean task of governing India could not be left unattended. But her attitude and self-control were only superficial. Deep inside, she was hurt irreparably. Sonia could see she was broken inside, with her spirit in pieces. At night she could hear her getting up and searching for Sanjay in her sleep, and when she woke up she would cry and repeatedly call her son's name. Her face aged, her eyes became harder and she began to drag her feet a little when she walked. She was no longer so careful with her dress, and she did not ask Sonia for advice about her hair or the accessories that ought to go with her saris. On the contrary, she wore her hair pulled back carelessly, and she did not seem to care.

Added to her immense sadness was her concern over Maneka, who spent the days without doing anything.

"I'm afraid her mother's ambition may push Maneka into wanting to take Sanjay's place," she confessed to her friend Pupul.

Apart from feeling melancholic, Maneka was uncomfortable because her position in that house had become very delicate. She felt vulnerable without her husband's protection. She could no longer use him as a shield to defend herself from her mother-in-law or her brother-in-law, who actually both still intimidated her. Her only strength was the baby. On the other hand, Indira was so devastated that she lacked the energy to console the others. In other circumstances, she would have done everything in her power for her daughter-in-law, but now her own pain absorbed her completely. Although on seeing the young widow so alone and so lost, Indira offered to help her in an outburst of compassion. Actually she was worried that being bored and isolated, Maneka might end up leaving the house, because then she would no longer have her grandson near her. That eventuality tormented her.

"Do you want to work as my secretary?... I could take you away with me, and I think that would give you something to think about..."

At first, the offer seemed to satisfy Maneka. Later, perhaps under the influence of her mother or simply because things went to her head or she was immature, she saw it as a manoeuvre to take away her natural right to take over her husband's legacy. Her life with Sanjay had given her the illusion of power, and after she had thought about it, her mother-in-law's offer seemed almost insulting to her. She did not even reply to the offer. "Look at her!... Who does she think she is?" she said to one of her husband's closest friends, talking about Indira.

Neither did Sonia think much of this offer. Although she had forgiven Maneka her insulting treatment during the early days, she did not want to imagine her controlling Indira's agenda. She could see the inexperience and arrogance of her sister-in-law as a potential problem for her mother-in-law, and a threat to the delicate balance of the family. The fact that she did not help with the housework could be accepted, but for her to dig in behind the shield of Indira's power and begin to pull the strings to benefit her own family, which Sonia feared so much, was a danger that had to be avoided at all costs. She told Rajiv about it.

"I'll talk to my mother about it," he told her. "Better if I leave her a note," Sonia answered.

When she read it, Indira realized that Sonia was right. Maneka as a secretary, so close by, could in effect be more of a problem than a help. She was afraid that her impulsiveness would make her even more unpredictable. And she also distrusted the Anand family and their dealings. However, what Indira was very well aware of, even enveloped in her cloud of suffering, was the need she had for Rajiv and Sonia. After all, Rajiv was her own flesh and blood; and she loved Sonia like a daughter. So she did not insist, and the offer fell into oblivion.

The young widow, for her part, found a way of passing the time which gave meaning to her life at the same time: she concentrated on the project of making a book of photos about her husband, a kind of tribute that would include family photos as well as political ones. She asked her mother-in-law if she would like to write the foreword. Indira agreed.

But then an unfortunate incident occurred, which had lengthy and undesired repercussions. The writer Kushwant Singh, who had helped Maneka and her mother to launch the *Surya* magazine, published an article in his newspaper column that suggested that Sanjay's mantle should fall naturally on the shoulders of his young wife, "who had been supporting him and had shared his vision of India, since Rajiv had never shown the slightest interest in politics, and his wife loathes it." The idea had some foundation. The article ended with a sentence that, more than any other, unleashed Indira's paranoia: "Maneka is like her deceased husband, brave and determined, the reincarnation of Durga riding on a tiger." That image of Durga, which had been widely attributed to Indira and which represented a symbolism that belonged to her, upset her deeply. How could two Durgas live under the same roof? She thought that Maneka had schemed with the writer to plot the writing of that article, that she was manoeuvring behind her back in order to compete with her, to steal Sanjay's legacy from her. She began to see her as an enemy in her own home.

Inevitably, and to Sonia's discomfort, all eyes began to turn towards the natural heir, Rajiv. Indira had her doubts: "No one can take Sanjay's place," she told her friend Pupul. "He was my son, but he also helped me like an older brother." She saw Rajiv as too soft and sensitive for the world of politics. Furthermore, he was married to a foreigner, which, in terms of national politics, was considered an insurmountable obstacle. And if he resigned from Indian Airlines, what would they live off? Sanjay was very frugal, while Rajiv and Sonia liked to live well, in European style, without excesses but in comfort.

In this scenario of a wounded family at the peak of power, not only did individuals decide, no matter how powerful they were. Just as important as what Indira wanted was the opinion of her followers, her friends, her relatives, her colleagues in the party, her advisors, her flatterers, her gurus, and the whole country. After having intoned the funeral march for the death of Sanjay, that chorus of voices began to chant a familiar melody, the same one that sounded when Indira was called for the first time to preside over theparty or when they courted her to get her to accept a portfolio in the first government after her father's death. The same voice that in its day had told her "you are Nehru's daughter, too valuable not to have in the government", was now calling for a successor, as though instead of a democracy this were an imperial court of old. It was a chorus as ancient as India itself, whose mythology told the story of an uninterrupted saga of hereditary monarchs. It was a call that came from the depths of that continent country, so inclined to mix temporal power up with divine power. As in classical Greek tragedies, the chorus called for a victim in propitiation. It became necessary to respondto that urgent need that the people had for stability, for continuity, and, why not? for perpetuity. That could only be guaranteed by a dynasty.

As for Rajiv, he kept himself as far away as possible. His relationship with his mother was different from Sanjay's. The affection ran very deep,but was almost British in its form, with hardly any intimacy. He did not offerto help her spontaneously, and she never asked him to, at least not directly. But when Indira began to realize the enormity of the vacuum Sanjay had left behind, and of the urgent need she had of support and physical proximity, one day she confessed to her friend Pupul, "Rajiv lacks the dynamism and concerns that Sanjay had, but he could be of great use to me." "He could be of great help to me": no further words were needed to set in motion the wheels that the chorus of voices had already announced.

It was the friends of the family who began to talk to them, to Sonia and Rajiv, about Indira's loneliness, about the need she had to lean on someone in whom she could trust blindly, to count on a person who would keep windows open on the world for her... And that someone could only be her son. Sonia rebelled against that idea.

"We know what politics is about, the supposed glamour, the flattery," she said, upset. "We've seen politicians close up, with their double talk, the constant toadying, the manipulation, the betrayals, the inconstancy of the media and the people... We've seen what power did to Sanjay and Maneka. We know perfectly well what Rajiv's life will be like if he gets into politics."

Her husband said nothing; and silence gives consent. He was in complete agreement with Sonia's arguments. But he could not prevent it: the picture of his mother, alone and devastated, with the burden of a country like India on her shoulders, weighed on his conscience.

*   *   *

After the article that came out in the newspaper, it was impossible for Indira's situation with Maneka to improve. The young woman got upset when she sensed her mother-in-law's hostility and realized that her presence was not wanted. She had lived all her married life in an atmosphere of very high political excitement, and now she was not prepared to sink back into anonymity. She realized, although she could not put it into words, that that was the condition she had to comply with in order to live under the same roof as Indira. That was the price of peace. But she was not Sonia; she hated even the idea of being a housewife, of spending the whole day between those four walls giving orders to the servants or taking orders from her mother-in-law. Taking care of the baby, with the help that wealthy families had at their command in India, left her a lot of free time. During all those years, she had watched how her husband and her mother-in-law worked, how they planned every move well in advance, and she too began to plan her future, urged on by her own chorus of voices, the chorus of her family and of Sanjay's old friends. "Why don't you have the right to take over yourhusband's legacy? Haven't you given him the best years of your life? Didn't you join in with everything he did? Didn't he love you? You know more about politics than his brother…" They wanted her to react before Rajiv was forced to react. And the chorus of voices left their mark on the malleable mind of the young woman.

The book about Sanjay was the battlefield in the relationship between Indira and Maneka, who hardly dared to speak to her mother-in-law. She noticed she was distant and cold, and felt more afraid of her than ever. Whenshe had to speak to her, the words would not come out, just like when she arrived in that house. She only got proper attention from Indira when she talked about the baby. Nothing when she talked about anything else. Oneday she finally dared to suggest an idea that had been going round and roundin her head.

"As I can see you're so busy, I thought that instead of you writing the foreword, it would be better if the journalist Kushwant Singh does it, based on an interview with you. That way you won't have so much to do."

Indira stood looking at her for a long time, in one of her silences that did not augur anything good.

"No way," she said finally. "You should have done that immediately after Sanjay's death. I would have had time then to write something. But youdidn't consult me. Now I'm not going to write anything and that man is not going to interview me."

It was her personal revenge for the article that had so annoyed her. It was also a way of putting her daughter-in-law in her place. The war had started.

Maneka came out of that conversation with her mother-in-law in a terrible state. "If she doesn't write the foreword, I'll never speak to her again," she threatened to anyone who wanted to hear. Then, alone in her room, she started crying. The draft of the book, with photos she had chosen with great care and love, was spread out over her bed. "Why won't she help me? Isn't it about her son?" she asked amid her tears.

When she had calmed down, Maneka attempted a final approach. She took the book to Indira's room and left it on her bed. Perhaps, when she saw it, her mother-in-law would think again.

Over six months had gone by since Sanjay's death, and seeing those photos again after an exhausting day in Parliament moved Indira deeply. Theangel face that Sanjay had when he was little, the photos of his childhood games, of when he stroked his favourite pet – his tiger - , of his toy cars, of his horse-riding with Nehru, of him and Indira hugging each other… all that past that suddenly came rushing back, like a wound reopened, and left her emotionally drained. She did not sleep a wink that night. She told her friend Pupul that the book was well presented, but that she was determined not to write the foreword. "She had erased Maneka from among the people she loved," Pupul would write, having noticed a symbolic and revealing detail: the door that went into Sanjay's room was shut and the one that went into Rajiv's was open. Indira had moved on from one phase of her life and was preparing to start another.

28

"Rajiv, I'm worried to death about you flying..." Indira said to him one day in the sitting room at home.

"Mother, you are an intelligent person and you know perfectly well that statistically there is more chance of being run over crossing the street than flying in a plane."

"I know, but I can't help thinking about..."

Rajiv stood looking at her. Dressed in a white sari for mourning, his mother looked a wreck. And she was not pretending; he could see she was really distressed. Sanjay's death, which projected its long shadow over the present, had made Indira insecure, and the fears that had always held her in their grip were now magnified. It made Rajiv infinitely sad to see her like that. Just the thought that she needed him and that he could not – or would not – help her, was beginning to torment him. Indira went on: "Did you know that a newspaper in Gujarat predicted that Sanjay would die in June?"

"Mother, please... If we had to believe the predictions of all theastrologers there are in India, no one would be able to live."

"I've been receiving lots of letters warning me that danger is lurking near you, and that's why I'm scared when I know you're in the air."

"Do you know the best thing you can do with those letters? Throw them on the fire..."

"Don't be silly, Rajiv," she replied with a distraught look on her face and an expression of dark despair. "What happened to Sanjay is because we didn't do anything to avoid it happening. We didn't take any notice of the predictions that were right when they gave the exact date."

"No, Mother. What happened to Sanjay is because it was his own fault."

Indira looked long at him. She was not used to Rajiv contradicting He went on: "…He did whatever he wanted, and when the Director of Civil Aviation told him off for not keeping to the rules and risking his life, Sanjay had him thrown out instead of listening to him. You have to see reality as it is, Mother. I'm very concerned that you allow yourself to be influenced by astrologers like that…"

Indira put her head down, as though to let him see that she was bowing to her son's reasoning. Rajiv understood that his mother was trying to make sense out of the tragedy that had overcome her, and she found that sense in the occult forces that her enemies had launched against the family. That old paranoia of hers was more alive than ever.

"Mother," Rajiv said, attempting to bring her round. "If there are evil forces, there are certainly positive forces that protect us too… Aren't there?"

"Were they able to protect your brother?" she asked.

Rajiv looked up as though to say "Not again!" Indira went on: "If I had died, it would have been part of a natural process… I'm sixty-two, I've lived a full life, but your brother was so young…"

Rajiv stood there dejected. His mother was inconsolable. They were silent for a while. Suddenly Indira stood up: "I've got three hours of work left. I must get back."

"You're exhausted and you should rest," Rajiv told her.

"If I don't do that work now, I'll have to get up at four in the morning to do it. Goodnight."

Rajiv remained pensive. He saw his mother go off to her room like a hunched over bird, slightly dragging her feet. She looked as if she was adrift, like someone in a ship-wreck... Where was her boundless energy and her eternal optimism? It was distressing to see her like that. And the question that kept coming back to him was the logical consequence of that: "Have I really got the right to refuse to help her?"

When he told Sonia about his feelings regarding his mother, she burst into tears, perhaps because in moments of lucidity she realized that she was fighting a battle that was already lost beforehand. Besides, she felt that her husband was in a dilemma and he was suffering for it.

"Are you going to throw all that we've achieved overboard?... Your career, the time with your children, your hobbies, our happiness?"

For the first time, there was tension in their marriage. So much that one day, in desperation, Sonia told him: "If you're thinking of going into politics, I'll ask for a separation and I'll go back to Italy."

Never, in all the fifteen years of their marriage, had they had a fight. They had never exchanged harsh words. Sonia had never gone so far. "I fought for him like a tigress, for us and for our children, for the life we had built together, for his vocation in flying, for our friends, and above all, for our freedom: that simple human right that we had preserved so carefully and consistently," she would write later.

But the forces against which Sonia was fighting were much

more powerful than her arguments for individual happiness and family harmony. What weight could the bourgeois wellbeing of a family of four have in comparison with the destiny of India? Those forces, which came out of the deepest history of the nation, spoke in the name of a country of over seven hundred million people. They were the same forces that had once pushed Indira into the political arena and which now called for Rajiv's presence. Two months after Sanjay's death, three hundred MPs, all members of the Congress Party, signed a petition asking him to take on his brother's postand stand as candidate in his constituency. The fact that he was married to a foreigner did not seem to be a problem, perhaps because in the mentality of the people, a woman takes on the identity of her husband's family.

It was the beginning of intense, constant, public pressure. From that time on, not a single day went by without the Press predicting his entry into politics. When reporters asked Indira about the subject, she remained impassive: "I cannot speak about it. Rajiv is the one who has to decide." MPs began to besiege the house. They came to "visit him", which meant trying to convince him. Sonia was forced to make tea with cardamom for all those "vultures" who, according to her, had come to tear the happiness of their family apart before her very eyes.

It was not only public pressure that began to be blatant, but personal pressure too. T.N. Kaul, Rajiv's uncle, a diplomat with an unsullied reputation, was not a man whose advice could be taken lightly. Kaul was thelast name of Nehru's wife and T.N. had always been very close to Indira. His loyalty had resisted the blows of fate of recent years. His son was a pleasant, lively character who had studied at Cambridge with Rajiv and was part of the couple's circle of close friends. The Kauls were very closerelatives, and were very much loved.

"The lives of your mother and your brother were closely linked, even more than it seemed," T.N. Kaul told Rajiv at the first meeting they held. "Sanjay was her communication link with the party leaders, and that is why she has been so isolated since his death. She needs someone close to her, someone who is able to act effectively to hold on to the party's loyalty. And you know how she doesn't trust anyone, except the ones who are very close to her."

"I know, but I also know, and everybody knows, that I was not made for politics... Besides, you know what Sonia's attitude to the matter is."

"I understand that Sonia sees it that way, because she has been exposed to the worst side of public life, but not everything is contemptible orbad in politics. It's supposed to be the noblest of duties…"

Rajiv gestured ironically. Kaul went on:

"It's about serving the people, dedicating oneself in body and soul to others… as your grandfather did, as your brother did, as your mother is doing."

"…As they want me to do." "Of course. It's in your blood."

"I'm not sure it's as hereditary as you think. I stand every chance of losing…"

"If you stand a chance of losing, after having imbibed the atmosphere of politics from the very beginning, just imagine other people… On the contrary, you have every chance of winning. One day you could be Prime Minister."

"No thanks. I've seen my mother weeping after her oldest, dearest andmost faithful colleagues left her in the lurch to save themselves. I've seen comrades of hers, people in whom she had the utmost trust, turn their backs on her and become ruthless critics... Thanks, but I prefer to go on living my life in jeans with my wife and my family, who give me everything I need."

"Rajiv, you know as well as I do that there are two kinds of people who go into politics: a few who consider politics as a way of getting society to move forward, and the rest who see it as a means to obtain advantages for themselves and their group. Those of the second type only care about the things connected with power: the glitter, the flattery, people kissing their feet and venerating them like a god, all the things that Sonia loathes."

"And what is the reward for the others?"

"There's only one. The satisfaction of being fulfilled as a human being."

Rajiv shrugged his shoulders. It was too vague and abstract an idea for his taste. Then he asked: "What does my mother say?"

"She has told me word for word that she does not want to influence your decision; that you are to do as you think best."

"Does she know that you've come to talk to me?"

"Yes. I asked her.. and she told me that if I wanted to talk to you, there was no problem as far as she was concerned."

There was a silence. Rajiv showed him some notebooks and books that he had spread out on the table.

"Do you know that I'm about to make one of the dreams of my life come true?"

"Oh yes?"

"Indian Airlines is just renewing its fleet, and there will only be jets. Until now I've flown as second-in-command on the 737. Next month I'm sitting the Commander's exam. My salary will go up and I'll be able to ask for the Delhi-Bombay route, which will allow me to have better working hours."

Kaul glanced at the compass, the calculator, the maps unfolded with notes correcting direction and calculations written in pencil in the margins…Then with a serious look, he turned to Rajiv:

"So am I to understand that your answer is no?" Rajiv nodded, and added:

"For me, going into politics would be like going to jail." As he felt his uncle's eyes on him, he said:

"…Besides, I don't even have a membership card for the Congress Party."

"Think about it Rajiv. Think about all the sacrifices the family has made for the country. When you were little and you went to Teen Murti House, you did that because your grandfather was on his own and needed help. Like your mother does now. She sacrificed her personal life to serve him. She did it because she was a woman. Your duty as a man is to help her and support her in every way you can.

Uncle Kaul's arguments were convincing and appealed to filial duty and a certain sense of predestination, to an imaginary family mission on a national level written in the stars. Rajiv's were rational and practical. They spoke of simple things, such as living day to day, vocation, the love of the family. But the reality was more complex, a mixture of many people's emotions and ambitions, of fears and doubts, of dreams and hidden rhythms, of history and politics. For months the pressure on Rajiv continued, and therefore it continued on Sonia too. "I spent hours and hours trying to convince her to let her husband enter politics, but no argument seemed good enough for her," Nirmala Deshpande, a family friend, would say. "At every attempt, Sonia very politely, but very firmly, said no." One day Sonia went so far as to tell her: "I'd rather have my children begging on the streets than have Rajiv go into politics."

For the couple it was a terrible year in which they both felt helpless to avoid the approach of the abyss. They were overcome by the strange, perverse feeling that suddenly their lives did not belong to them. They had gone from being masters of their own existence to being the victims of a policy of harassment in the name of grand principles and noble causes which, at that moment, they felt were nothing to do with them. As though that gigantic country could not live without them. Rajiv was torn by the conflict between his duty as a son and his own happiness. Sonia was caught between her husband and her mother-in-law, two people whom she adored. "At the same time," she wrote later, "I was furious and resentful of a system that, as I saw it, demanded a sacrificial lamb. A system that would crush him and destroy him – of that I was absolutely sure."

Rajiv lost weight and could hardly sleep. His sense of duty pushed him towards helping his mother. His love for Sonia and the commitment he had taken on with her pulled him in the opposite direction. Everyone had their reasons, all of them were valid and he was in the middle, confused and unhappy. Then he took refuge in his studies to take the exam as commander of the 737, the only thing that allowed him to remove himself from a reality that was becoming unbearable to him. He, who had always fled from conflict and confrontation, was in anguish at being the target of everyone's demands. "Won't this pressure ever stop? Will this hell never end?" he wondered when he saw the months going by and the chorus of voices becoming deafening.

"I was hoping for a miracle," Sonia would say, "a solution that would be acceptable and fair for all of us."

But that miracle did not happen. On the contrary, every day

that went by, the main actors in this drama found themselves worse off: Indira, ever more alone and overwhelmed by the problems piling up, Rajiv and Sonia, more and more tormented every day.

"I hate to see you like this," Sonia said to him one day, hugging him tight, "I don't want to see you so bad..."

"It's as if they'd stolen our lives away from us..."

"Rajiv, forget what I told you when I was so angry. Forget it all. If you think you should help your mother, do it... I don't want to see you so unhappy. It's eating us up."

"I don't intend to make any decisions without you."

"Do it," said Sonia in tears, with her head on her husband's chest. "Go ahead. Life changes, I find it hard to accept... Deep down, I think I'm going to end up losing you, but perhaps that's selfishness on my part, I don't know... What I do know is that we cannot go on like this."

"He was my Rajiv," Sonia would say, "we loved each other, and if he thought he should offer to help his mother, I would bow to those forces that were now too powerful for me to fight off, and I would go with him wherever they took him."

Sonia once again showed that her love for her husband was more important to her than any other consideration. Was loyalty not the very essence of love? Had she not always followed him? Had she not left her family and her country for him? Had she not become an impeccable Indian daughter-in-law for him? If her whole life had revolved around him, if one day she had promised to follow him to the ends of the earth, now she would have to keep that promise. She would follow him wherever he went, into the nightmare hell of politics if it were necessary. Even if they both ended up burning in the flames there.

After four very long and very intense visits from uncle T.N. Kaul, Rajiv finally said: "… If Mother wants me to help her, then I will."

Kaul sighed.

"It's a sensible decision," he said. "We are sure you can win the elections in Amethi, your brother's constituency, which will give you the legitimacy necessary to work alongside your mother."

"But I don't want to form part of the government, that is my condition. I'm only prepared to work within the Party, because I realize that there is a vacuum and I can see that no one else can fill it."

"The important thing is for you to win your seat in Amethi."
"And what if I lose?"

"You leave the field open for Maneka and Sanjay's followers, and that is very dangerous, do you see?"

"Maneka isn't twenty-five yet. That's the legal age for being an MP in Parliament."

"But she will be by the next elections. There cannot be two different heirs of Sanjay Gandhi. That's why there is a rush for you to accept. And it's fundamental for you to win Amethi."

There was a silence. Rajiv's face had aged. In almost a whisper, he added: "There is an air of inevitability about all this, isn't there?"

"When your mother went to help your grandfather," Kaul told him, "she was not part of the government either," he paused, aware of the huge sacrifice this decision was demanding of the family. "What does Sonia say?" "I would not have taken the decision without her. I'll try to fit my career as a pilot in with politics, as long as I can. Then we'll see what happens."

"It's a sensible solution," Kaul concluded.

After so much accumulated anguish, the decision was a kind of liberation, but without joy. As always in the family history of the Nehrus, what had always won was a sense of duty over and above all other considerations. Sonia shut herself up in her room and did not come out for four days. Her children were unable to console her. They said she spent the time weeping.

When she emerged from the depths of suffering, she was skin and bone and haggard. Over the following days she hardly ate a thing and stopped dressing as elegantly and stylishly as she had before.

29

Rajiv's old dream finally came true and he passed the exams to obtain the certificate as pilot of the 737; but for him the pleasure of crossing the skies in jets was not going to last very long. The closing date for him to stand for the constituency of Amethi, which he was going to inherit from his brother, was coming inexorably closer. The law of incompatibilities prevented Rajiv from holding a public position (Indian Airlines was a State- owned company) and at the same time standing as MP. As it was clear that from here on he would not be able to combine his career with politics, he had no alternative but to make politics into his career. So, one hot day in May, 1981, he took the decision. He arrived home after spending the day in the air, took off his uniform tie, jacket and trousers and put on a white kurta, the "politicians' uniform". He went to the airline's head offices to hand in his pilot's pass and to say farewell to his colleagues and bosses. Sonia saw him leave with her heart bleeding. It was the final farewell to the life that he had chosen in England, when he was looking for a way to earn his living so that they could marry because he was crazy about her.

As was predictable, the couple's life changed from that day. They could no longer be seen at night in the Casa Medici, the Italian restaurant in the luxurious Hotel Taj, or in the Orient Express, in the new Hotel Taj Palace. They changed everything, from the times they did things to the way they dressed. Rajiv wore *kurtas* because it had been suggested that it would be a good idea for him to give a more "Indian" image, and not so European. So he said goodbye forever to the jeans he used to wear when he was not in uniform, he said farewell to the Italian shoes that Sonia bought for him when they were away on holiday, and he wore sandals, although he held on to his Ray-Ban sunglasses, oval-shaped and with metal frames, which were fashionable in those days. The reality was that Indian clothing was nicer to wear and was more appropriate for that merciless heat than Western clothes. The *kurtas* made of raw cotton were worn over pyjama-type trousers or *chowridars*, wide at the hips and narrowing in folds down to the ankles. He also wore the hat typical of members of the Congress Party, and Indira thought that with the age he was exactly like his father, Firoz.

Once Rajiv had taken the decision, he did not look back. If destiny was putting him in this situation, it was better to make the most of it and do it well, as best as he could. The old ideals that his grandfather had talked about at table when they were teenagers – the struggle against poverty, in favour of equality and a secular state, etc. - , those principles that his mother had inherited, he made his own too. He was not leaping into the ring in order to accumulate wealth or power, because they had never attracted him. He lacked any kind of personal ambition, but he had ideas for India. If now he could do his bit for the life of the nation, it was better to do so with as much information as possible.

But he found it hard to shake off his world, which was the world of technology, of proven facts, of concrete things that are ruled by known, provable laws. A plane flies because the air bears the weight of its wings. What maintains the success of a politician? There were many possible answers, many variables, but no certainty, except in his case: he had a last name that was a recognizable "trademark". The intellectuals and Indira's adversaries threw it in his face: "the only qualifications Rajiv has are his genes". The wealthy classes were disconcerted by what they considered as another act of nepotism on Indira's part. But the "great mass of Indian humanity" saw it in its own way, through the prism of tradition, according to which sons follow the vocations of their parents. For centuries, in the villages and cities of India, master artisans, musicians, scribes, cooks, grooms, healers, architects and politicians transmitted the secrets of their profession to their offspring. By getting Rajiv into the life of politics, Indira and her party colleagues did nothing more than follow a well-established tradition. During his first campaign, Rajiv had to make a great effort to fight his own shyness. For someone so jealous of his privacy, being the centre of attention constantly and facing questions from the media was difficult to put up with. "Politics has never been my thing," he declared one day to a reporter who had asked him why he was standing. "I'm standing because I have to help my mother somehow..." His openness made him into an object of scorn, and he soon learned to weigh his words, to always give clear answers that could not be misinterpreted or twisted.

Speaking in public without notes was not easy either, because it was necessary to find a way to say not only what he wanted to say, but also to connect with those who had come to listen to him. The rallies took place in town squares and the organizers did not always have the means to put up an awning to shade him from the sun. Most often, Rajiv would find himself facing a crowd of about a thousand people in the blazing sun. Many would be sitting on mats on the ground, most would be standing at the back, and they would all have come to have *darshan* with a man who was already part of the long list of personalities in Indian mythology. There were many poor peasants, because Amethi was a very backward area in the state of Uttar Pradesh. But there were also shopkeepers, labourers, village notables, Sikh businessmen whose turbans stood out among the crowd, many unemployed young men, swarms of children, some with their worn uniforms based on theuniforms of English schools, Moslem women with their faces covered, Hindu peasant women with multicoloured saris... They were all packed together in spite of the temperature of forty degrees. It smelt of sweat, flowers, dust and smoke from *bidis*, those cigarettes made of cut tobacco known as the "cigarettes of the poor". Before speaking, Rajiv took off the garlands of orange carnations that had faded against the whiteness of his *kurta* and placed them on a table or handed them to an assistant. His style was very different from his brother's. He was not grandiloquent and he did not harangue the masses. Quite the opposite, his humility and his curiosity led him to ask many questions. On his constant trips, stuck in the control cabin of the plane, Rajiv had dreamed of a fairer country, more prosperous, more modern and more humane. Now, at ground level, the reality could be seen differently: the backwardness was tremendous, the lack of resources, desperate, and the poverty, extreme. How was it possible? Where was the system failing? During moments of rest, he took out of a black bag a silver invention that aroused admiration:

"It's a revolutionary invention," Rajiv said. "One day it will be as popular as a calculator or a type-writer, you'll see."

"What's it for?" asked a young party member.

"For many things. I want to use it to have a database and to follow up the improvements we are going to set in motion here in Amethi."

It was a laptop computer, one of the first to be seen in India. Rajiv's method consisted of identifying the failings so that he could then know where to intervene in order to rectify them. Some problems were obvious, such as the lack of roads, which forced the little electoral convoy to drive, sometimes for an hour or more, down narrow dirt tracks between fields ploughed by gaunt oxen, in order to gain access to the little villages. Most of the dwellings were adobe huts which the peasants had to rebuild after each rainy season. Those villages had no kind of communication at all with the outside world. "If at least they could be given a phone connected by satellite!" Rajiv told himself. Yet, there was a ray of hope: when the poorest people were asked what they most needed, they never asked for food or money, or even a hut to live in, or that there might be a well with drinking water in the village – all urgent necessities -. The poorest of the poor wanted schools for their children above all. In the first place, education, and, immediately afterwards, medical dispensaries.

As was to be expected, Rajiv won by an ample margin. Sonia was the first to congratulate him. They hugged each other tight. That victory gave her husband some very necessary support, and Sonia could see that in the look on his face, suddenly more relaxed and confident. It was the justification for many months of torment. Sonia felt that Rajiv was beginning to like the experience, although she missed the past. "Before, our world was recognizable and intimate," Sonia would say. "There were days of concentrated activity and then long periods of leisure. Now it was the opposite. Our lives filled with people, hundreds of them every day, politicians, party workers, all putting on the pressure with their demands and their urgent problems. Time stopped being flexible and every hour that Rajivspent with us became more and more valuable."

What Rajiv still could not get used to was the nuisance the media were. He responded with hesitations and interruptions. "You reporters hurl yourselves at politicians like tigers," he once said, overwhelmed. But at the same time he felt that he was beginning to be appreciated by a growing number of people. The contrast with his brother's personality was so refreshing that it helped him win followers. If Sanjay had left behind the memory of an abrasive, pitiless character, vulgar in the ostentation of power, Rajiv was quite the opposite: a gentle man with impeccable manners, a born peace-maker who used common sense to settle conflicts, and above all a man without any strange contacts or suspicious associates. "I want to attract a new type of people into politics," he declared to the *Sunday Times*, "intelligent, young, Westernized and without feudal ideas, who want India toprosper rather than themselves." He always showed his true face, that of an honest man, kind and with a good heart. Soon they would call him *Mr Clean*. And if that were not enough, he had a nice photogenic family,although Sonia was much more reluctant than he was to be photographedand even less to give interviews. Her fear and hatred of the Press and the media had become a constant in her life.

Rajiv was sworn in as an MP three days before his 37th birthday. He declared himself openly in favour of modernization, of freedom of enterprise and of opening the country up to foreign investment. He poured with sweat under the same dome that had returned the echo of his grandfather's and his mother's speeches. Nehru would probably have felt perplexed to see his grandson in that enormous hall as another representative of the people. But happy too to see that, like he, Rajiv believed that the solution to many of the ills of India lay in science and technology when they were properly applied.

Indira began to smile again. She felt that her son, who took on the role of personal advisor with surprising efficiency, was the ideal person to take on an ambitious project that the government had already embarked upon, aware of the need to improve the country's image. It was a question of organizing the Asian Games, which were to take place in Delhi two years later. The project foresaw the construction of hotels, highways, several stadiums and a district to house the athletes. The initiative would be used too to extend the range of the colour television signal, which could only be received in the centre of the big cities. Successfully carrying out the project required a brain with a capacity for organization, an enterprising and imaginative mind. Indira felt that it was a good challenge for her son and, if it worked out well, it would improve his image and would serve to launch him into national politics. Suddenly Rajiv found himself coordinating architects, builders and financiers, and supervising an enormous budget.

Sonia had no ambition at all to make a place for herself in public life —what Maneka so longed for -, whether it was as a volunteer in humanitarian causes or as a hostess for personalities. She was happy with her position in the shadow of her mother-in-law and she worked hard to ensure the Prime Minister's home worked as efficiently as possible. In those days, Sonia came to be closer to Indira than ever before. "Knowing how deep her wounds were, Rajiv and I became even more protective towards her." Her mother-in-law was deeply grateful to have them nearby. She spoke with great affection and gratitude of the way Rajiv "had offered to take over some of her responsibilities relating to the work in the party." When the one-year period of mourning ended, during which time Indira had worn only white, black or cream coloured saris, Sonia chose for her a beautiful gold sari with Kashmir-style embroidery for the inauguration of an important conference of Asian countries.

"Look, this sari tones in with the decoration of the hall where the conference is going to be held... Do you like it?"

"I love it," said Indira, "... it's perfect for the people following the event on colour television."

Seeing her dressed again in coloured saris, her friend Pupul said toher, "I'm glad you're getting over it."

Indira looked serious and did not answer her. But the next day shesent her a letter: "You said something to the effect that I might be getting over my grief. One can get over hatred, envy, greed and so many other negative and self-destructive emotions. But grief is something different. It cannot be forgotten or overcome. One has to learn to live with it, to integrateit into one's very being and make it a part of one's life."

30

The note of discord was struck by Maneka, who saw with displeasure how her husband's legacy was snatched away from her by his brother, although she knew perfectly well that she could not have stood for election as she did not have the required minimum age. She had always felt deep contempt for Rajiv, and now she began to make declarations to the Press, calling him her "indolent brother-in-law, incapable of getting out of bed before ten o' clock". The idea was implicit that she, the heir to the Gandhi name and the mother of Sanjay's only child, was the most suitable person to one day succeed Indira at the peak of power. "How can Rajiv take on his brother's mantle if he has never liked politics and is married to an Italian?" she said in public. Maneka was the first to use Sonia's foreign origins against the family. Rajiv and Indira immediately smelt danger and asked Sonia to finalize the paperwork to acquire Indian nationality, to which she had a right through marriage. She should have done it long before but she had always put it off out of laziness. In her naivete, Sonia had always thought it was enough to feel Indian and to follow the customs and rites of society to be Indian. She had already relegated her skirts, her tight trousers, her jeans, her sleeveless blouses and her low-cut dresses to the darkness of the wardrobes. She only dressed in European clothes when she went to visit her family in Italy. In

India she only wore saris or the Moslem version of Indian national costume, the salwar kamiz, wide cotton or silk trousers covered by a top with lots of buttons. But that was not enough: now she needed the official sanction, nationality, a passport. So one morning she went to the Home Office and spent several hours filling in papers andreplying to questions from courteous civil servants. A few weeks later she received a letter: "The government of India hereby grants Sonia Gandhi, née Maino, a certificate of naturalization and declares that the aforesaid has the right to all the privileges, rights and responsibilities of an Indian citizen..." Next, among the papers that accompanied the passport, was the number and address of the electoral college where she would have to go to vote.

The only thing that Maneka achieved with her senseless declarations was to annoy her mother-in-law even more. When the young woman showedher the first copy of the book she had designed about her deceased husband, Indira caused a fuss, claiming that part of the text and the captions of the photos were pernicious and distorted the truth. It could not be published like that.

"But it's supposed to be presented in three days' time!"

"You should have shown me the final draft earlier, not at the last minute. You'll have to postpone the presentation for when the changes have been made."

"I can't, it's all been organized already."

"I will not allow the book to come out the way it is at the moment."Maneka left the room furious and slammed the door.

"Maneka!!" shouted Indira. "Come here immediately!"

The young woman came back. This time she did not look like afrightened puppy. She had the defiant manner of a rebellious teenager. She held her mother-in-law's gaze.

"Things cannot go on like this, Maneka. I cannot allow your nonsense with the Press to go on or for you to publish whatever you like about the family."

Maneka hesitated between replying or putting up with the telling off.

Indira bluffed, trying to make her daughter-in-law back down:

"If you want to leave this house, it's up to you," she told her firmly.

Maneka hesitated at the temptation of using the only weapon she could to strike Indira a lethal blow: taking her grandson away from her. Indira went on:

"If you carry on like this, our relationship in the future will be as if I had never met you. You choose: that, or go on being friends."

Maneka clenched her fists and bit her tongue: perhaps this was not the moment to do without such a prestigious relationship. She lowered her eyes:

"Alright, I'll delay the launch of the book and I'll change the captions of the photos."

Indira breathed a sigh of relief. She was aware that she had won a battle, but she was sure it would not be the last. For the moment the crisis had been avoided.

Argumentative and persistent, Maneka became expert at tightening the rope. She had become convinced of two things: one, that there was no place for her in the power structure over which Indira presided, and two, that she could come to rival her mother-in-law. So she decided, on one hand, to redouble her defiant and provocative attitude and, on the other, to develop her own power base by mobilizing Sanjay's now dethroned supporters. Maneka had agreed to go and give a speech in the

city of Lucknow, the capital of the state of Uttar Pradesh...
for a group of dissidents of theCongress Party, led by an old
friend of Sanjay's. Indira was furious: "They're defying me with
a mini-revolt," she told Pupul after Maneka had let her know
that she had gained the support of a hundred or so members of
the legislative assembly of the state of Uttar Pradesh loyal to
Sanjay. Indira sent her a message: "If you go to Lucknow, don't
ever come back to my house." Maneka withdrew and
apologized, but it seemed clear that a confrontation was
inevitable. That slippery, stubborn "kid", who was making
Indira's life impossible, was driving her mad, something which
her powerful political adversaries, who were much more
Machiavellian andexperienced, had not been able to do.

In an attempt to put things right, Indira took her on a trip to
Kenya with Rahul and Priyanka. But the trip that Maneka
would really have liked to make was the one that Rajiv and
Sonia made to London for the weddingof the Prince of Wales
and Diana Spencer. Indira had sent them to represent her, in
order to present on the international stage the one who in all
probability would end up succeeding her. That was a glamorous
trip, rubbingelbows with power and the most distinguished
people in world society.Maneka, on the other hand, was going
off with the children "to see animals".She began by complaining
that she was the only one in the family who did not have a
diplomatic passport. She hardly spoke to her nephew and niece
on the whole trip and she barely answered her mother-in-law
when she called her or tried to cheer her up. She kept herself to
herself the whole time, with a long face, because she did not
really want to be there. In the Embassy in Nairobi, when the
time came to greet the representatives of the numerous Indian
colony there, she did so unwillingly and coldly, to such an
extent that it was embarrassing. She was taciturn and they did

not really know whether she felt bored or if she was simply not interested in anything. Or if she was plotting something. Or all three at the same time.

The one who was plotting something was her mother. Something explosive. She was negotiating the sale of *Surya* magazine to a well- known sympathizer of the RSS behind Indira's back. When she found out, she was furious. The RSS (Rashtriya Swayamsevak Sangh) was a Hindu political organization on the extreme right with almost military discipline, which had been involved in the massacres during Partition. Indira had always considered the RSS as "the greatest threat to India" because of its fanatical and exclusive Hindu nature. She was convinced that this party could one day lead the country into ruin. Had one of Mahatma Gandhi's assassins not been a member of the RSS? The sale of *Surya*, which ended up going through,was a real provocation. Although it belonged to Maneka and her mother, Indira was fully aware that the magazine had been born and was able to function thanks to her contacts and her influence. Family tension came to boiling point. For some months Rajiv had avoided meeting his sister-in-law at home. Now it was clear that Maneka could no longer go on living there.

Seeing that the conflict with Maneka was going to deprive her of her grandson, Indira became very depressed. Of all the betrayals she had been through, she felt that this was the most serious, the most harmful and the cruellest, because it came from within the family, sacred territory, and it affected the child of her favourite son. The imminence of another crisis, this time a definitive one, drained all her energy and made her feel exhausted. She made a last attempt for her grandson's sake. She sent her old yoga teacher and guru, Dhirendra Brahmachari, who still visited her from time to time, to negotiate the repurchase of the magazine, at any price, from the new owners. But they refused the offer. Indira was left with no way out. Hundreds of millions of people, the whole country, waited expectantly for the outcome of this live soap opera, a reality show before its time.

Indira was in London, inaugurating the Year of India, a huge effort on the part of her government to promote cultural, industrial and commercial exchanges between India and the West. She had wanted Sonia to go with her. A large number of politicians, scientists, personalities from the world of culture, the aristocracy and the media attended the opening party. Indira was very moved when Zubin Mehta, who was a Parsee like Indira's father, conducted the orchestra in playing the national anthems of India and the United Kingdom and the audience rose to their feet. It had special meaning because it was the first time the Indian national anthem had been played in public in London, the old capital of the Empire. Even Sonia felt shivers of emotion. Exquisitely dressed thanks to her daughter-in-law's ministrations, Indira was radiant at the different receptions and dinners that went with the inauguration. So much so that it would have been impossible to guess how agitated and anxious she was inside. The messages that came from home announced that Maneka was prepared to abandon the family home permanently and that she had decided to defy Indira openly. Sonia remained silent and expectant regarding the inexorable moment of the split.

In effect, Maneka had calculated the date very carefully, taking advantage of the fact that Indira and Sonia were away, and that Rajiv was too busy with his work and did not go near the house in order to avoid coinciding with her. The young woman had ignored Indira and had gone to Lucknow, where, in front of her husband's followers, she made a heated speech, taking great care, however, not to appear to be disloyal to the Prime Minister. "Long live Indira Gandhi!" "Sanjay is immortal!" said the posters the organizers of the meeting had put up everywhere. "I will always honour the discipline and reputation of the great Nehru-Gandhi family to which I belong," Maneka had ended.

But that show of false loyalty did not soften Indira, who came back from London on the morning of March 28th, 1982, determined to be obeyed. When Maneka went to greet her, Indira cut her short: "We'll talk later."

Maneka shut herself in her room and waited for a long time, until a servant knocked on the door.

"Come in," said Maneka.

The man came in bearing a tray with her food on it. "What's that?"

"Mrs Gandhi asks me to tell you that she does not wish you to join therest of the family for lunch."

"Take it away. I don't intend to eat in my room just because she says so."

The man obeyed. An hour later he came back.

"The Prime Minister would like to see you now," he said obsequiously.

Maneka's legs were shaking as she went down the corridor. The moment of truth had come, but there was no one in the sitting room. She hadto wait a few minutes, which seemed to go on forever, and during which she started biting her nails again, like when she was a little girl. Suddenly she heard noises and Indira appeared, furious and walking barefoot, accompanied by the guru, Dhirendra Brahmachari, and secretary Dhawan, with the fancy hairstyle. She wanted them as witnesses.

Under normal circumstances, Indira would have fought this

battle with her usual skill, waiting for the right moment to act. Now, perhaps because the thought of being separated from her grandson clouded her judgement, Indira fell into the trap her daughter-in-law had set for her. Her words could hardly be understood, and yet she could be heard loud and clearwhen she pointed her finger at her and shouted, "Get out of this house immediately!"

"Why?" Maneka replied, looking innocent. "What have I done?""I've heard every word of the speech you gave!"

"You gave the OK."

Maneka said that she had sent it to Indira for approval. And in effect, Rajiv had sent it on to London by telex. His mother had read it, but had not answered. She had decided to wait until she got home to give an answer.

"I told you not to speak in Lucknow, but you did exactly what you wanted and you disobeyed me! There was poison in every single one of yourwords... Do you think I can't see that? Get out of here! Leave this house right now!" she screamed. "Go back to your mother's house!"

"I don't want to go to my mother's house," Maneka replied defiantly. "You will go to her. Since you've got together with the riff-raff of this

country, to whom you've sold the magazine you started thanks to the contacts I got for you, I don't want to see you again, either you or your mother."

Maneka started to cry, but added, "I need time to get my thingsready."

"You've had all the time in the world. You'll leave here when I tell you. Your things will be sent on to you later. You and your mother are trash!" Indira shouted, completely beside herself.

Maneka went off towards her room, shouting, "I won't allow you to insult my mother!"

But Indira was determined to throw her out. She could not control herself. All the wrongs accumulated since Maneka had come into the house exploded like the gates of a dam bursting.

"Get out! Get out this instant! And don't take anything away from thishouse apart from your clothes!"

Maneka shut herself in her room, and from there she called her sister Ambika to tell her what had happened, so that she could tell the Press andget help. The writer Kushwant Singh found out what was going on from a call from Ambika asking him to go to the Prime Minister's house.

Stormy relationships between mother- and daughter-in-law are part of the age-old culture of India, to the extent that many Bollywood productions are based on stories that recreate those domestic conflicts in all their gory details. What occurred in the home of the highest authority in the country exposed the whole family to public scrutiny in a way that even the most hardened film producers could not have imagined.

About nine o'clock that night, a crowd of photographers and reporters, including a large group of international correspondents, gathered at the gate at the entrance of the house. The police, whose reinforcements had deployed in the surrounding area, did not know who to let in and who not to. So Ambika and Maneka's brother got in without any difficulty, after having visited for eight years. They found their sister in her room, in floods of tears,piling everything untidily into suitcases. Suddenly, while they were deciding how to proceed, Indira burst into the room: "Get out now!... I've told younot to take anything with you."

Ambika, whose viperish tongue was well known to Indira, intervened:"She won't go! This is her home!"

"This is not her home," shouted Indira, with her eyes bulging in fury. "This is the home of the Prime Minister of India!" And pointing at Maneka, she added, "You can't bring people in here without my permission."

Ambika was going to say something, but Indira interrupted her. "Anyway, Ambika Anand, I don't wish to talk to you."

"You have no right to talk to my sister like this!" shouted Ambika, with no intention whatsoever of allowing herself to be cowed. "This isSanjay's house and my sister is Sanjay's wife! So this is her home. Nobody can throw her out."

Indira went crazy then. What her bitterest enemies had not managed to do, those two sisters did. Indira's shouts alerted Sonia who ran to tell Rajivin his office in Akbar Road. Rajiv tried to get the situation under control with the help of a cousin who was helping him with his political business. They asked the chief of security, a tall, burly Sikh, to kindly throw the sistersout of the house. The man replied cautiously, "Sir, I can only follow that order if I have it in writing."

Rajiv was ready to sign a written order, but his cousin stopped him. "Don't do it," he said. "Don't sign anything that might later be used

by the Press against you or the family. Whether you like it or not, Maneka has the right to be in this house. Signing a document to throw her out can only bring you problems."

Rajiv looked at the Sikh, who nodded, totally in agreement with whatthe cousin had just said.

"It isn't wise," his cousin added.

"OK," said Rajiv, giving up and looking towards the end of thecorridor where, suddenly, a deafening noise had started up.

Shut in Maneka's room, the two sisters had put a video of a Bollywood film on at full volume so that Indira, who was exhausted in the room next door, could see that they would do whatever they liked. Meanwhile, they planned their strategy and the exact time they would leave. Secretary Dhawan and guru Dhirendra Brahmachari had to act as messengers. Every time Dhawan went in to tell them to leave, they asked forsomething else. First they asked for dinner, which was served them in the room. Then they told him that the dogs also needed to eat, and the secretary ordered them to be fed and was unlucky enough for *Sheba*, Maneka's Irish wolfhound, excited by the atmosphere of hostility there was in the house, to give him a slight bite on the arm.

It went on like that for a couple of hours, until the sisters ordered theirtrunks, suitcases and parcels to be taken out. When they were already outside, Dhawan came back again, this time accompanied by the guru: "I'm sorry, but we have orders to check your things."

"Very well," said Maneka, "if you're going to search me, let it be out here, so that everyone can see." And she began to open the trunks, deliberately pulling out clothes, shoes, books...

Suddenly, the flashes of the photographers at the gates lit up the night like a minor fireworks display. Indira appeared in the doorway, and told her secretary not to insist on the search. She had realized that her daughter-in- law had won the match and she was beginning to give way. Maneka had done nothing more than to apply one of her mother-in-law's lessons: "Let your enemies do what they want to you, but always in the public eye, so they show the worst side of themselves". When the lamentable spectacle of the search came to an end, Maneka and her sister went back to their room, demanding that her things and the dogs should be sent on ahead of them to their new home. The last of the conditions was that they would not leave without little Firoz Varun.

On that disastrous night, Indira's worst mistake was trying to keep hold of her two-year old grandson. Before the quarrel she had given orders for him to be taken to her room. He had spent the day with a slight temperature. When the servants went to fetch him, Indira refused to hand him over.

"My grandson is staying with me," she said in an attack of irrational stubbornness.

Maneka let her know that if she did not hand over the baby, she woulddo a sit-in at the door of the house until she got him. Very skilfully, the young widow was preparing to exploit her role as victim using Mahatma Gandhi's weapon of civil disobedience. Indira's fight was a desperate one.

She sent for P.C. Alexander, her chief official secretary, who, on being woken in the middle of the night, thought that some international conflicthad broken out. "I had never seen her so distressed, so worried, so anxious, so tense as that night," the man would say. "Her face reflected her indescribable anguish."

"Madam," Alexander said to her, "you have had to face so manycrises in your life, so many political battles, the death of your son. Why are you like this now?"

"Alexander, this girl wants to take Firoz Varun away from me. You know my relationship with Sanjay's son. He's my grandson. They want to take him away from me."

Indira was still beside herself. The suffering caused by the loss of her grandson was clouding her judgement. There was no way to make her see sense, to convince her that her daughter-in-law was in the right. However much she was Prime Minister, she could do nothing against the fact that Maneka was the baby's mother. The rule of law reigned supreme in India, didn't it? The lawyers she made come in the middle of the night to see how she could hang on to the baby all agreed that there was nothing to be done.

"Madam," one of the lawyers said finally, "if you keep the baby, your daughter-in-law will put in a complaint and you will be forced to hand him over to the police, who in turn will give him back to his mother. I suggest you save yourself all that trouble."

The battle was lost. Indira went to her room, and stood looking at the baby, who was sleeping in his cot, breathing regularly and audibly. The woman was in floods of tears. Rarely in her life had she been seen to cry so much and to be so distraught. For her, it was like her son's death all over again. When the nanny went to take the baby away, Indira gestured to her, took him out of the cot and hugged him to her for a long time, aware that it was the last time she would see him. Then she handed him over, shattered inside, wiping her tears away with the end of her sari.

It was after eleven o'clock when, carrying the confused, half-asleep Firoz Varun her arms, Maneka finally left the house and got into a car with her sister. An explosion of flashes lit up the whole sequence of their departure. Photos that fitted the image she wanted to give, of a loyal daughter-in-law treated cruelly by her powerful and authoritarian mother-in- law. "Maneka waving to the reporters from the car," said the caption under the photo that came out the next morning in all the newspapers in India and some abroad. The daily *Indian Express* published an article comparing the efforts of the Prime Minister to kick Maneka out to the act of "killing a wasp with blows from an axe". Indira had lost and she knew it.

Sonia was heartbroken to see her so distraught. She too suffered with what happened, although she had been able to see it coming, perhaps more clearly than Indira herself. She suffered because she had cared for the baby a lot since he was born. She had been like a second mother to him. The baby's birth evoked memories of the family's happiness, found again after the upsets of the Emergency. The harmony had not lasted long, only until Sanjay's death, but it had left a deep impression on all the members of the family. Priyanka and Rahul had also become used to their little cousin's presence, so close to them that they considered him to be like a brother. During the following days, Indira said to everyone who came to see her, "Do you know what's happened? Maneka and Firoz Varun have left the house," as though it had been the considered decision of two adults. The whole country knew what had happened down to the last detail.

31

Painting. Concentrating on each brush stroke, without her hand shaking. Mixing and re-mixing the paint on the palette, finding the correct tone, the right colour. Taking off her glasses and putting them on again. Moving slowly forwards, step by tiny step. Scrape with the spatula, smooth down, clean, add a little colour, start again... For Sonia, her courses in restoring old oil paintings in the National Museum were a kind of therapy that allowed her to forget the commotion at home for a few hours. Those stolen moments provided her with intense, personal satisfaction and now she was sure that this would have been her real vocation if life had not led her along other paths. It was an activity that allowed her to develop her potential, her nature as a perfectionist who liked to fix, repair and patch. To restore something she had to become invisible. It was not a question of inventing, but of interpreting the intentions of the original artist. It was not for rebels who might end up imposing their own criteria. It was for characters like hers, malleable, not fond of confrontation and rather docile, who always ended up adapting themselves best and getting the best out of what there was. Now she could spend time on her hobby because her home was an oasis of peace again, as it was before Maneka came to live there. And that peace helped Indira to calm down, little by little, surrounded by the love of the grandchildren she had left and the certainty that Sonia was taking charge of the house, which meant, for example, organizing a dinner for Mitterand and his entourage, or a reception for Moslem leaders at middayand another for party leaders in the evening.

Sonia always tried to adjust her timetable and commitments so thatshe would have free time with Rajiv and her mother-in-law. She felt that, perhaps to counteract the harshness of life in politics and to get over theupset of the battle with Maneka, both of them needed now more than everthe stability, privacy and the direct and open relationships they could find within the family. Between the four walls of their home, neither Rajiv nor Indira had to weigh their words or worry about what they were saying orwho they were saying it to. Sonia kept a sanctuary for them so they could be protected from the hustle and bustle of politics. So they could enjoy the warrior's rest. "I was dedicated to my husband with unconditional love," she would say. She could have said the same about Indira. Rajiv was deeply grateful to her for having agreed to take the step and change her life, and he told her so: "As the Hindu tradition says, a man is only half a person and his wife is the other half. With you, I feel exactly like that", he wrote to her in a note one day before he went off to work.

At that time, Nadia, Sonia's younger sister, went to live in New Delhi with her husband, a Spanish diplomat. She was a young woman with fine features, dark-haired and with undeniable natural distinction. She was introverted and she liked reading, and the influence of her husband made her become fond of Spanish literature. Her ambition was to become a translator from Italian into Spanish. Now she was too busy with her two young daughters, but she was leaving it for the future... For Sonia, it was wonderful to have her so close by, to be able to organize excursions at the weekends with both couples' children or to go for dinner at friends' homes, where cosmopolitan Indians and Europeans resident in the city got together. Nadia and her husband had a much busier social life than Rajiv and Sonia, because they were part of the diplomatic circle in the capital of India. Meals, cocktail parties, receptions, inaugurations of exhibitions, book presentations, concerts, games of polo, etc., they could be seen joining in many acts and nothing gave away the differences that were emerging within the marriage. A few rumours reached Sonia, but as her sister had not said anything to her, she did not think anything of them. She would be mad to trust the local rumour-mongers.

But one day Nadia went to see her at an early hour, while she was still getting ready.

"How does this look on me?" Sonia asked, referring to the sari she was wearing.

"You look really pretty," her sister said in a dull voice.

"Here I only wear saris. They attack us with the fact that I'm Italian, you know? Actually, I feel just as comfortable either way – European or Indian."

"You could pass perfectly well for an Indian girl, if it wasn't that your jewellery is so discreet, not like the ladies here... Me, on the other hand, if I put on a sari, I look like a tourist dressed up as an Indian."

"Once, the wife of a politician came up to me to see the cross I wear round my neck and she asked me why I was wearing such a fine little chain when a more visible, thick chain could be worn... Here they value ostentation, just imagine, in a country with so much poverty..."

Sonia smiled when she remembered the scene, and when

she turned round, after straightening the sari, she found her sister crying.

"What's the matter?"

Nadia did not dare to say anything. She stammered. Sonia had to use all her skill to get out of her what was wrong. Her husband was unfaithful to her. And word of it had spread in the gossip circles of New Delhi, which added humiliation to the pain.

"How can he be so irresponsible?" Sonia wondered, furious.

The diplomat had turned out to be rather frivolous. He did not even bother to hide his affairs. The most recent one, which he had had with a lady diplomat in the Danish Embassy, was the cause of Nadia's going to pieces.

"He's promised me that he's going to break it off, but I don't know whether to believe him or not."

For Sonia, it was a blow to see her like that. She asked her to be patient, to give him another chance, if he had promised her that. She had become used to having them in New Delhi and it made her sad to think they might have to leave. She hoped the situation with her husband would right itself. Not all men were like Rajiv, that was certain. She began to take a dislike to her Spanish brother-in-law.

*   *   *

Like the split between Nadia and her husband, life is made up of little partings. At the beginning of 1982, the family went through the separation from Rahul. Following the custom inherited from the English, he was sent to a boarding school which was in the foothills of the Himalayas. It had been founded by an English teacher who had stayed on as headmaster after independence. Doon School was an institution with an excellent reputation, created in the image of British schools, where the children and grandchildren of the wealthy studied. At first, Sonia had been opposed to the idea. Separating from her son at the age of eleven is not part of the Italian tradition, although Rajiv reminded her that her own parents had sent her to a convent boarding school in Giavenno.

"Yes, but that was only twenty kilometres away from home."

Doon School was seven hours from Delhi, which, on the scale of India, was a short distance. Even so, it was hard to be apart from the boy. It was the same suffering that Great-grandfather Motilal and Grandfather Nehru had gone through. At that time, the wealthy classes sent their offspring to England when they were seven. Rajiv was as convinced as his great-grandfather that parting from his son, however painful it might be, was an experience that would help the boy to grow up, to be stronger and more independent. What worried him, as much as it did Sonia, was that Rahul should be mature enough to deal with the attacks and cruelty of his classmates. They had already had to struggle with that kind of problem when they went to school in Delhi and both Rahul and Priyanka were the victims of the taunts of some children who made fun of the family. Except that then their parents were nearby to offer their support. "If they get at them when they're far away, who will console them?" Sonia wondered uneasily. "Sometimes they'll say all kinds of nonsense about your grandmother, your mother or me," Rajiv wrote to his son to give him confidence, "but you mustn't worry. Perhaps you'll come across some boys at school who use it to get at you, but you'll discover that most of those things are not true... You have to learn to fight against that kind of provocation... to not take any notice of things that might annoy you, and not let it get to you."

What the boy found out from the newspapers was about the numerous tours his parents made. At that time, Indira travelled a lot, and whenever she could she was accompanied by her son and Sonia. They went to New York together, where Indira was delighted to meet up again with her old friend Dorothy Norman, who described her thus: "There she was, the woman who led a highly complex society of over seven hundred million people, most of them poor and facing all kinds of problems; a woman still overcome by the grief of having lost a son, sadder than before…"

"Yes, I am calmer, sadder too." Indira confirmed. "But would it be fair to ask for more? Life has been splendid to me, both in happiness and in grief. How can you appreciate one without the other?"

Dorothy would remember Rajiv and Sonia with great affection because of the way they were with her. She saw that Indira was very proud of her son: "Rajiv has done a magnificent job with the Asian Games," she told her. The games, inaugurated on November 19th, 1982, the day that Indira was 65, had been a feat of organization. Six stadiums, three luxury hotels and a whole district with accommodation for the athletes had been built in record time. The physiognomy of south Delhi changed forever. Rajivhad come out of his first test looking good, with the image of an efficient, modern leader, and a good manager, although the Press denounced the living conditions of the labourers, mainly immigrants from the south. They were skinny men and women with dark skin, who were cruelly exploited by the legions of go-betweens, contractors, works chiefs, builders, manufacturers ofbricks, cement and steel who handled the budget. It was not an easy task to modernize India. Yes, avant-garde buildings were being put up, but it was done by a mediaeval society, where children worked from dawn to dusk for an amount of money that was stolen from them by those who hired them. Rajiv had realized that the challenge lay in changing that social structure that was eroded by corruption. An immense challenge, because Indian society had had those vices for thousands and thousands of years, including the exploitation of some castes by others. If a salary of a hundred rupees a day was set aside in the budget for a labourer, everybody knew that he would end up getting thirty, at best. The rest was kept by the contractor or the middlemen. Then there was something else that revealed the poverty of the country. A large number of the blood tests carried out on Indian athletes indicated the presence of anaemia. How could they expect to compete with Japanese, Koreans, Malaysians? Because of all that, the games were a bittersweet victory for Rajiv.

Although Rajiv could not always accompany his mother, Sonia did every time Indira asked her. She had never travelled so much: she toured several countries in the east, Indonesia, Fiji, Tonga, Australia, the Philippines as well as other places in South America. When the trip was to Europe, she took advantage and hopped over to Orbassano to give her family a hug. Sonia always avoided the cameras and she did not at all like civil servants who treated her with special deference for being the daughter-in-law of the Prime Minister, which usually pleased the Indian delegation and their hosts abroad. In Washington, Sonia was able to see for herself that Indira was still not connecting with American presidents. This time it was Ronald Reagan, whose attention Indira could not manage to hold for more than a few minutes, as though the ravages of the illness that would attack him later in life had already begun. "Do you realize?" she said to her daughter-in-law after the stopover in Moscow where she had had an interview with Brezhnev. "The future of the human race is in the hands of two old men, firm in their positions, and with no flexibility or desire to initiate dialogue." But at that moment Sonia was more worried about Indira's health than the future of the world. She had noticed that when she was tired her mother-in-law had a tick in one eye, and her eyelids started trembling all the time. And she was sleeping very badly. She would suddenly say odd things: "When I close my eyes, I can see a misshapen old woman who wants to hurt me."

Home in New Delhi, Indira told her friend Pupul, "I've received secret reports that someone is performing tantric and black magic rituals to destroy me. Pupul, do you think there are evil forces that can be unleashed through tantric rituals?"

"Even if it were true," her friend told her, "Why are you reacting like this? By doing that, you're only making those forces stronger…"

"Do I have to ignore those reports then? I get them every day… What shall I do?"

Pupul and Sonia were perplexed. Was that behaviour the result of her inner solitude which she had never really left behind since her childhood, since she waited alone at home for her parents to come out of prison or the clinic? She had not seen her grandson Firoz Varun for almost two years, and both Pupul and Sonia guessed that the pain of being apart from him was ravaging Indira's heart. She kept up her stoic composure, but deep inside she was so hurt, that perhaps she was going crazy.

Sonia did not think so. She attributed Indira's crazy ideas to the evil influence of her guru, Dhirendra Brahmachari, who still wandered around the house, always dressed in orange *kurtas*. He was like a blowfly, which always came back, no matter how hard you tried to chase it away. He was fatter, his matted grey hair hung down on his shoulders, and he had let the nail on his little finger grow until it was as long and sharp as a knife and disgusted Sonia so much that she found it hard to hide her feelings. Everyone knew that the guru frightened Indira with those supposed "secret reports", but no one knew what to do to stop it. It was incredible: the Prime Minister of India believed more in those "reports" than in those of thegovernment's Statistics Department. The fact is that in her times of depression, now more and more frequent and intense, the supernatural acquired worrying importance to her.

There was another reason that explained why she used the services of the guru, and it was because another holy man, a thirty-year old Sikh called Brindanwale, had launched the most serious political challenge of her life.

That man was a simple village preacher, a fundamentalist who called on people to purify Sikhism, return it to its former orthodoxy and fight for a Sikh homeland. The conflict with the Sikhs went back to Partition which, with all its horrors and massacres, caused a trauma in the awareness of this community, born in the fifteenth century to fight against the idolatry and dogma of Hinduism and Islam, the two dominant religions of the time. In 1947, Partition tore apart the country of the Sikhs, the Punjab. "The land of the five rivers" was one of the most beautiful and fertile regions of India, a countryside of golden fields of wheat and corn crossed by rivers of silvery waters. The border between Pakistan and India, drawn by the English, cut the region in half. Western Punjab became part of Pakistan; eastern Punjab remained in India, with a population that was half Sikh and half Hindu. As a reaction, a strong separatist feeling left its mark on the Sikh population.

The curious thing about Brindanwale is that Sanjay had discovered him. Concerned about the progress of the moderate nationalist party which took many votes away from the Congress Party in the Punjab, Sanjay thought that by backing and promoting Brindanwale, he would manage to divide and weaken Sikh nationalism. The problem, which no one could haveforeseen, is that Brindanwale got out of control and ended up becoming a monster who now threatened Indira.

He looked like a holy man who had come directly out of the Middle Ages, with a long, silky black beard that fell to his waist. He had penetrating, dark little eyes, an aquiline nose, a severe, gaunt face and he always wore a turban. He dressed in a long blue gown, and proudly carried his metre-long *kirpan* (sable) in his sash. Almost two metres tall, he was an imposing presence. His speeches, full of fanatic passion, inflamed many Sikhs who dreamed of independence from the rest of India. He had left his wife and children in order to lead a legion of followers, as extremist as he was. Sanjay had not counted on the fact that, as his influence grew and more people gathered around him, Brindanwale's ambition would also grow along with his desire for autonomy. Shortly after the 1980 elections, in which he participated actively in the campaign, supporting the Congress Party and even sharing the podium with Indira on one occasion, the holy man decided he no longer wanted to be the puppet of the Gandhis and broke his connections to the party. In time, he and his followers demanded the creation of a sovereign state called Khalistan, "the land of the pure". The land of the Sikhs.

The problem is that they did so using violence as a means of intimidation and pressure. In 1981, Brindanwale was accused of ordering the murder of the owner of a chain of newspapers in the Punjab whose editorial line was very critical of his activities and ideology. But his imprisonment caused a wave of demonstrations so violent and destructive that the central government intervened.

Hesitating and not really knowing which path to take, Indira herself ordered the Home Secretary to release him when only three weeks had gone by. She did so precisely not to turn Brindanwale into a martyr, but it was already too late. He had gone into prison as a fanatical provincial preacher and he came out a national hero. He made a tour of the large cities during which he proved his immense popularity among the Sikhs of the diaspora. But his return to the Punjab coincided with an increase in the violence. Every day, in the alleys of Amritsar or Jallandar, the bodies of Hindus or Moslems appeared with their throats cut. In several temples, faithful Hindus were horrified to find the heads of their sacred animal, the cow, thrown at the feet of the altars. Added to these bloody provocations there were blacklists published by Brindanwale in the newspapers with the names of the adversaries he intended to eliminate. And he carried out his threats. The son of the murdered owner of the newspaper chain was, in turn, shot down, which spread terror among the media and the population in general. The Sikhs who dared to criticize him also became the target of his attacks. He went back to jail, but his followers continued to kill their opponents. When he came out, he and his army dug in at the Golden Temple complex in Amritsar, the holy city of the Sikhs.

Built in the middle of the shining waters of a broad ritual lake crossed by a bridge, the Golden Temple is a white marble building covered in decorations of copper, silver and gold. The dome, completely covered in gold panels, houses the original manuscript of the Holy Book of the Sikhs, the *Granth Sahib*. The faithful always circle clockwise round the lake; they walk barefoot over the shining marble and have their heads covered by brightly coloured turbans and wear long beards and thick moustaches. Brindanwale's army occupied this place of peace. They got into the building adjacent to the temple, from where they sent out orders to the terrorist commandos to murder, pillage, profane and burn in the villages of the Punjab. While Indira still did not know how to fight this grotesque creation of Sanjay's, Brindanwale received TV teams from all over the world who treated him like a real media star. The police, whose morale was at rock bottom owing to the increase in delinquency and violence, did not dare to enter such a holy place.

Other outbreaks of violence in Kashmir and Assam gave the impression that the nation was heading straight for chaos and disintegration.

The murder of a police inspector as he prayed in the Golden Temple on April 23rd, 1983, killed by shots fired by Brindanwale's men hidden behind the bars of the windows, forced Indira to take a decision. But what decision? To attack the temple with the army and risk provoking the fury of the other Sikhs? To lay siege to the temple until the terrorists had no alternative but to surrender? Indira tried to negotiate with leaders of the moderate nationalist party, while the pillaging and murders continued, but any agreement that did not include full independence for Khalistan was systematically vetoed by Brindanwale. He, in turn, emboldened by the indecision of the central government and by the fact that the murder of the police inspector had gone unpunished, dug himself in in the Akal Takht, the second most holy building in the complex. He got hold of sophisticated weapons paid for by Sikhs abroad and turned the temple into a real fortress. Indira, Rajiv and their advisors waited patiently for the leaders more moderate than Brindanwale to gain control or distance themselves from the fanatical preacher. They thought that time would be on their side, but two years went by and the terrorists were still entrenched there.

"Can the army assault the temple without causing too much damage?" Indira asked the head of the army, General Sundarji, who had replaced her old friend Sam Manekshaw.

The general spread out over the table some aerial photos taken the day before showing that all the windows, doors and other openings of the building were protected by sacks of earth or had been walled up. He explained that the terrorists managed to supply themselves with weapons, food and ammunition through a labyrinth of tunnels that linked them to the outside. That way they could go on forever.

"The chances of causing extensive damage are very high," the general stated.

Aware that religious sensitivity in the country with the most religions in the world could make the fragile balance in the nation explode like a powder keg, the fathers of independence had set up a tacit agreement on holy places in accordance with which they were all untouchable. Brindanwale had entrenched himself behind that agreement, certain that the army would never dare to intervene. Opposite him he had a tired, fearful woman, wounded deep in her soul, worn out by power and lacking in the self-assurance and passion of a fighter which had made her victorious in the Bangladesh conflict.

Feeling she was hostage to some terrorists who did not leave even the narrowest margin for negotiation made her despair. With growing unease, Indira realized that the only solution to this defiance was the use of force. The situation reminded her of the Bangladesh crisis, when she also knew she would have to declare war in the end. Only then there was no internal religious problem at all. The enemy was abroad and the consequences could be weighed up better. Now they were unforeseeable.

411

When her friend Pupul, seeing her so depressed, asked her if it was not all too much for her, at first Indira did not reply, but then she said, "I have no way out. It's my responsibility."

32

In 1983, a year after Rahul had joined Doon School, it was Priyanka's turn to go to Welham School, the boarding school that was the girls' equivalent of her brother's school. It was also in the mountains, some two hundred kilometres from Delhi. Suddenly, Sonia found that she had more free time than ever before, but she was still not able to spend it on herself. She had to accompany her husband to Amethi, his electoral constituency. Now that she was the legal age, Maneka had decided to take his seat away from him in the following elections in the constituency that had been her husband's. Real defiance. The fact that she had disappeared from the house did not mean that his sister-in-law had vanished completely. In her tours of the area, she presented herself as the poor widow thrown out of the house with her baby in her arms, and forced to find a way to live by her evil brother-in-law and his foreign wife. It was not true, but it sounded like those simple, domestic tales of family injustice and envy that the people liked so much. She was presented by her people in Amethi as "a triumph of courage". Now that she did not fear a personal confrontation with Indira, her behaviour became even more aggressive. She put into circulation letters from the family that were critical of Rajiv, and in one speech, Maneka compared Indira to the goddess Kali, "the drinker of blood" – she said literally –

elevating the usual bad relations between a mother-in-law and her daughter-in-law into a frenzy. In this way she took revenge for being excluded from all official commemorations. On the second anniversary of Sanjay's death, she was not invited either, and she reacted by calling a rally for widows and organizing the free distribution of clothing. Maneka's defiance was as depressing or more for the Prime Minister than the much more dangerous defiance of crazy Brindanwale. And it hurt more because it affected the intimate fibre of the family.

"Your mother is also coming to Amethi with me," Rajiv wrote to his son. "It's going to be difficult for her, because at first everyone will be looking at her and she will feel uncomfortable until she gets used to it. She's very brave." For the first time, Sonia realized what the life of an Indian politician on campaign was like. Travelling endless kilometres on roads filled with potholes in cars with very poor suspension, putting up with the heat, the dust, the flies in the numerous villages, being forced to accept a cup of tea, and then another, and then another in order not to hurt people's feelings... The good thing is that now she spoke Hindi fluently and could chat to the peasants, who asked after her children, her mother-in-law and anything that had to do with the turbulent history of the family. "Will Indira be able to see her grandson again?" the women asked, or "Is it true that Maneka doesn't even have enough money for food?" What the peasants were not very convinced about was that Maneka was the real heir to the Nehru-Gandhi dynasty, as was shown in the results in the polls. Once again, Rajiv won.

*   *   *

At the beginning of 1984, Rajiv appeared to be a politician on the up and up. His management of the Games, together with the efficiency he showed in his position as General Secretary of the Congress Party, gained him some real respect, independently of his political lineage. His office wasa model of good organization, a little corner created in his image. Compared to the old dinosaurs in the party, mostly corrupt flatterers, Rajiv was a model of virtue, especially regarding efficiency and integrity. He had broken with the shady figures who had swarmed around his brother, and he had surrounded himself with technocrats, young men with briefcases and executive suits, examples of a modern generation that believed intechnology, statistics and computers. Many of them had been classmates of his at Doon School, others at Cambridge, and they were all more at ease speaking English than Hindi. They lived in the present; they were not intellectuals but pragmatists and they were totally indifferent to anythingthat had to do with religion, ideology or superstition. Both they and Rajiv were opposed to Indira's passive attitude to the Punjab affair. The Prime Minister, following the advice of her guru, Dhirendra Brahmachari, had begun making offerings in the hope that a miracle might solve the crisis in the Golden Temple.

"He has to be got away from the house once and for all," Rajiv told Sonia, talking about the guru.

Indira did not need any more doses of esotericism or more fears addedto the dark thoughts that filled her mind. On the contrary, she needed to havea very cool head and clear vision. She was still deeply depressed. Too many challenges, too much tiredness. Sanjay had cultivated a friendship with the guru, not because he believed in his occult powers but because he was useful to him. The "flying saint" had managed to buy light planes, deal in arms, hire killers and launder money, and those were skills that Sanjay admired and used if he thought necessary. Rajiv, direct and honest, was the antithesis of his brother and of the holy man, a shrewd, vague, astute, dishonest and completely non-Westernized individual. Sonia and Rajiv could not stand him any longer.

"What can we do?"

"I'm going to try to get his weekly TV programme cancelled and cut off the grants to his *ashrams*."

As his stature as a politician and his influence had grown, he managed it. In order not to hurt Indira, Sonia and the advisors closest to her husband extolled Rajiv's achievements, and Indira was finally convinced that her son's strategic plans were the only way to solve the evils of India. Little by little, she began to forget the guru's mysticism and stopped making offerings to the gods to ward off the Punjab crisis. To Sonia's great relief, the guru completely disappeared from the family table. Almost imperceptibly, Dhirendra Brahmachari saw his access to the Prime Minister denied. "I'm sorry, Madam does not have the time to see you," the servants said when he tried to come back to see her.

The month of February that year was the only one in her entire life that Indira did not enjoy the spring, her favourite season, between the cold of winter and the tremendous pre-monsoon rains which begin to lash down in March. During that month, the city fills with colour, the green of the leaves on the trees becomes intense, and the beds full of flowers brighten up the gardens. The temperature is wonderful and a gentle breeze blows at night. In the past, in spite of all the difficulties and problems, Indira had always felt euphoric at this time of

year. Not now. She was isolated and sad, and the Sikh holy
man firmly entrenched in the Golden Temple stole her sleep
from her. She listened to everyone and still did not know what
to do. In situations with no solution, all that was to be done was
to gain time, wait and stay confident, Indira repeated to her
close collaborators.

Following Rajiv's advice, Indira made a last attempt to find a
negotiated way out of the crisis in the Punjab, agreeing to many
of the pro- independence campaigners' demands, but she came
up against the intransigence of the members of the moderate
party and Brindanwale himself. Most of the seven million Sikhs
were as disconcerted by the situation caused by the extremists as
the government. Instead of negotiating, the leader of the
moderate party took the final step that sealed the split, astep
that could only lead to catastrophe. He announced that from
June 3rd, the anniversary of the martyrdom of guru Arjun, the
man who had built the Golden Temple, all exports of electric
energy and grain from the Punjab would be halted. The irony
of the threat could not escape Indira. If thePunjab was the
granary of India, it was because the region had benefitted more
than any other from the "green revolution", the ambitious plan
for agricultural development that first Nehru, and then she, had
launched to put an end to the famines. And now it turned out
that a handful of fanatics were not only threatening to break up
the State, but also to starve the poor in the rest of India, if the
central government did not bow to their demands. The
situation had come to the point of no return. Much to her
regret, Indira was facing the inevitable: getting Brindanwale and
his followers out of the temple by force.

First of all, before even consulting the Chief of Staff, she
wanted to talk to Sonia: "Sonia, I think it's best to take the

children out of school…I'm afraid for them. The Intelligence Agency has warned me that they are a terrorist target. Nothing new there. We're all the targets of those fanatics. But as the situation in the Punjab is still deteriorating, it's getting harder and harder to guarantee their safety in school. They've advised me to take them out of the boarding schools and bring them to Delhi."

"But you only have one armed guard here to protect you when you go out in the mornings to talk to people in the garden!"

"That's coming to an end. They're going to reinforce security heretoo, of course."

"OK, I'll bring them home tomorrow. We'll see how we get organizedto educate them here…"

One of Indira's secretaries interrupted them. The Commander-in- Chief of the army was waiting for her in the sitting room. The man had come with his intelligence reports under his arm.

"Madam, they are armed to the teeth. The terrorists entrenched there are still getting hold of very sophisticated weapons. They arrive there hidden in containers of milk and sacks of grain, and they are sent using money from Sikh sympathizers abroad."

Indira sat thinking. Was there any sense in going on waiting for a miracle? Then she turned to her Chief of Staff and asked him, "How should we proceed with the attack?"

The man puffed. He was uncomfortable. He found it hard to believe inthe success of the mission.

"There are many risks, Madam. It is my duty to warn you. My opinionis that it's best to launch a fast, massive attack, with all the necessaryforce…"

"Better than besieging them?" Indira interrupted.

"They are already surrounded, Madam, and the weapons still keep coming in. I trust more in a fast, crushing attack."

"How much time are we talking about?"

"About forty-eight hours. The shorter it is, the fewer casualties there will be."

"It is essential to have Sikh officers and soldiers present in the attack force. This must not be interpreted as an ethnic aggression, of Hindus against Sikhs."

"No doubt about it. The officer in charge is Commander Kuldip Singh, from the Ninth Division of the Army, a Sikh."

"Very precise instructions have to be given to avoid damage to the Golden Temple. The Sikh community would never forgive us."

"We'll instruct the troops. But those terrorists are hard to deal with, Madam. I can't guarantee anything."

"May God help us."

On May 30th, a suffocatingly hot day, troops surrounded the city of Amritsar. The hustle and bustle in the streets vanished like magic. Shrouded in terrifying silence, the holy city became a ghost city.

On June 2nd the media announced that Indira would speak to the nation that night, at eight thirty. Sonia had breakfast with her, and noticed that she was upset, pessimistic and still undecided. She did not like at all the idea of attacking "a house of God". She told her that her speech was not working out well. In fact she was making so many last-minute changes that her appearance on television had to be delayed until nine fifteen. Finally she spoke, in a serious tone, with an anguished expression on her face. "This is not a time for anger," she said. "The unity and integrity of our land are being questioned by a handful of men who have taken refuge in holy places. Once

419

again I call for the moderate parties not to hand over their authority to Brindanwale." She ended by appealing to the common sense of all the inhabitants of the Punjab. "Do not shed blood, shake off your hatred. Let us join together to heal the wounds." On hearing that speech, her friend Pupul realized that the coming days were going to be tragic for Indira and the country. In effect, while the Prime Minister was speaking, army troops were taking up positions around the grounds of the Golden Temple. Operation Blue Star was about to begin.

The next day, foreign correspondents were invited to leave the Punjab. The traffic of buses, trains and planes was cut off, as well as the phone and telex lines. The region was isolated from the rest of the world in preparation for the final assault. From his sanctuary in the Akal Takht, the building next to the Golden Temple, Brindanwale held out, now with a cartridge belt across his chest over his blue gown, a pistol in his left hand and his sable in his right hand. He declared to a handful of local reporters, "If the authorities come into this temple, we are going to give them such a lesson that Indira's throne will fall down. We'll cut them to pieces... let them come!"

At four in the afternoon on June 5th, army officers with megaphones gave orders for all civilians to vacate the area, and for the terrorists to give themselves up. 126 Sikhs came out, mostly men who had gone there to pray and pilgrims, but none of Brindanwale's followers did so. At night, an advance party of special commandos went into the complex, while helicopters flew in circles over the temple. They met with fierce resistance. Over half of the ninety members of the commandos were killed by extremist fire.

The Chief of Staff immediately informed the Prime Minister

of the losses. The assault could not have had a more discouraging start. But it was not possible to go back now. The die was cast. Indira did not sleep all night, aware that a sacrilege was being committed against the most venerated symbols of a religion. Why had destiny placed her in this pass? What price would have to be paid for what the troops were doing? She felt a shiver run down her spine. One thing she was certain of, and that was that neither she nor her government would come out of that situation unharmed. Karma always gets you in the end. But at eight o'clock in the morning of June 6th, perfectly dressed and made up, she was in the garden talking to a reporter from the *Sunday Times*. The temperature was already touching 40 degrees. The reporter found her tense and tired. His last question was: "What do you think will happen in India when you are no longer Prime Minister, Ma'am?"

"India has lived for a long time, a very long time – thousands of years

– and my 66 don't count for much. India has gone through many vicissitudes in its long history and it has always managed to move forwards."

While the interview was taking place, one thousand five hundred kilometres north of New Delhi, the battle for the Golden Temple was raging. In infernally high temperatures and in the blazing sun that made the gilded dome of the main temple gleam, Indian soldiers were being shot down like ducks in a fairground by the bullets of Brindanwale's men. Once again, over a hundred men fell in the attempt to take the building where the terrorists were dug in.

The instructions received for the soldiers to limit the use of force as much as possible, and to inflict the least possible damage on the main temple, now lacked any meaning. The

Commander, who could see no other solution than to carry on with the assault, sent in the artillery in the afternoon, supported by tanks and armour-plated vehicles. In order to neutralize Brindanwale and his men, they had no option but to bombard the Akal Takht. They inflicted enormous damage on the temple, builtparadoxically by the fifth guru, a real apostle of peace, who had insisted on building it on a lower level than the other buildings as a sign of humility.

After a day of heavy fighting, the Akal Takht was almost completely razed to the ground. Late on the night of June 6th, when the generals went to inspect the place, there was not a single column left standing and the marble walls were blackened and pitted with machine gun fire. In the basement they found the body of Brindanwale. His robe was no longer blue, but black with blood. He was lying there with thirty-one of his men. There were no survivors who would be witnesses to the martyrdom of the terrorist preacher. In another room, the soldiers found some surprising documents: the list of all the victims that Brindanwale had ordered killed, and a huge bag with letters of admiration, not just from Indian citizens but from fans all over the world.

The cost of victory was much higher than the Commander-in-Chief of the army had forecast. Much higher than Indira and Rajiv, who were horrified, had imagined. Operation Blue Star was really a disaster. More than half the one thousand soldiers sent for the assault perished. As for civilians, a thousand pilgrims who could not be evacuated died. Apart from the human losses, the library of the main temple, the one that was not to be damaged under any circumstances and which held the original manuscripts of the Sikh gurus, burned to the ground. For the Sikh community in general, that attack was comparable to what the invasion and destruction of the Vatican would be for Catholics. Unforgiveable sacrilege. Exactly what Indira had wanted to avoid.

33

"I'm afraid for them to play in the garden," Indira told Sonia when she saw Rahul from the dining room window rolling about on the lawn with one of the dogs. The children had come back to New Delhi, after the warning from the Intelligence Agency, which had found their names on a blacklist belonging to a Sikh extremist group. Every morning, they went to their respective schools, under heavy guard. Then they spent the rest of the day at home. They rarely went out. A simple invitation to a birthday party meant a complex security operation. "It's as though a shadow had come into our lives," Sonia said to Rajiv. Very aware that the assault had caused a collective injury to the Sikhs of the Punjab, Indira was convinced that they were going to assassinate her. She was top of those lists. Another group had sworn to avenge the sacrilege in the Golden Temple by assassinating Indira and her descendents for a hundred generations. She told Rajiv and Sonia, who went pale. But Indira wanted them to take the draconian security measures that were being imposed on them very seriously. Following the advice of the police, she wore a bullet-proof vest under the bodice of her sari every time she left the house. She wanted Rajiv and Sonia to do the same.

"It's no joke," she told them.

"I know," Rajiv answered. "And don't worry, I'll put one on

too."

There was a silence. Indira took on a gloomy expression and a sombretone of voice.

"When it happens, I want you to scatter my ashes over the Himalayas. I've left written instructions for my funeral. They're in the second drawer in the desk in my room."

"Don't get ahead of events," said Rajiv sarcastically to relax theatmosphere. "We haven't got that far yet."

But Indira was still agitated. Later she wanted to talk on her own to her grandson Rahul, who was now fourteen years old.

"I'm afraid they might want to hurt you. I'm asking you and your sister not to play beyond the gate that leads to the offices in Akbar Road, please," she said, pointing to the place in the garden where she had seen him playing with the dog. "I'm very sorry that you have to suffer these restrictions, but I would never forgive myself if something happened toyou."

"What can happen to us in here, Grandmother?" "They might kill you, it's as simple as that."

Indira's serious tone made the boy look at her incredulously, as if his grandmother was exaggerating.

"Please listen to me and don't wander off," she went on. "There are many fanatics that would be very pleased if they could do you harm. Do us all harm. What they might do to me doesn't matter. I've done everything I had to and was able to in my life, but you... I don't even want to think aboutit."

Now Rahul was downcast and sad. Indira went on. She left off her protective tone and continued to speak gravely, in a manner that was unknown to her grandson and which made an impression on him.

"If something happens to me, I don't want you to cry for me, OK?

When the moment comes you have to be brave. Will you promise me?" The boy looked up at his grandmother and nodded.

During those months in 1984, Indira travelled round the sub-continent a lot, trips that sometimes seemed to be like farewells, because of the way she spoke about herself and how she would like to be remembered. In some interviews she took stock of her life, in others she talked as though she were above national politics. She had always felt she had the soul of a statesman, and now her global vision bloomed and became clear in speeches full of wisdom. "When a country as old as this one is catapulted into a new technological culture… what happens to the rural mind? Will mystery and sacred things be able to survive? Something inside me tells me that India will survive with its values intact." At the beginning of October, after the last monsoon rains had cleared the sky and the trees and plants were green again, Indira spoke in New Delhi before another huge crowd. It was another of the many dialogues she had been holding with the people of India over the last two decades. She spoke about courage as a supreme value for dealing with the greatest threat that was hanging over the country: the pressure from sectarian groups, castes or religious groups to break up the unity of India. It was a speech that her father would have liked. Yes, the unity of India was a supreme value because it guaranteed the rule of law for each individual, independently of their social, ethnic or religious origins.

On October 11th, an event occurred, thousands of kilometres away, which sank her even further into her dark foreboding. Margaret Thatcher, whom she had met in London, was the objective of an IRA bomb attack in the middle of the

Conservative Party Conference. She escaped death by the skin of her teeth. Indira immediately called her. She understood better than anyone her colleague's vulnerability and panic. Although the Iron Lady showed herself to be impassive in public, inside she was just as distraught as anyone who might have gone through a similar ordeal. The difference between these two lady Prime Ministers, who had been friends for eight years, is that for Margaret Thatcher the attack had been a revelation and a surprise. Nothing like it had ever happened in England before, apart from the assassination of Lord Mountbatten, which was also the work of the IRA, but here the objective was a retired man as he was on his boat with his grandson, not a serving head of State. Indira, however, was much more used to violent death. She had seen the deaths of Gandhi, Sheikh Rahman and Sanjay. Not so long before, the murder of Salvador Allende in Chile had traumatized her and still tormented her. She had always thought that her life would be ended the same way. However, when the Defence Secretary tried to convince her to substitute the police for the army in order to increase her protection, she replied, "Don't even consider that option. I'm the leader of a democratic government, not a military one."

A few days later, Ashwini Kumar, the head of the border police, gave the order that all Sikh security guards stationed at Indira's residence should be relieved of their duties and replaced by others of different religions. But Indira was opposed and vetoed the order. The measure went against her most intimate political credo, which was: in a secular state no distinctions are made between religions. Ashwini Kumar was left perplexed and frustrated. "The Prime Minister is very well protected from an outside attack," he said, "but what if the attack comes from inside?" Indira hardly paid any attention and answered him,

"Aren't we secular?"

That autumn was also the autumn of her life. In November she was going to be 67. She was prey to a bad feeling that the attack on Thatcher had made worse. Without telling anybody, in the middle of October she wrote a document which was later found amongst her papers. "If I have to die a violent death as some people fear and many plan, I know that the violence will be in the thoughts and actions of the assassin, not in the fact of my death, because there is no hatred sufficiently dark to overshadow the love I feel for my people and for my country; there is no force capable of deflecting me from my purpose and my efforts to keep this country afloat. A poet once said of love: 'How can I feel humble with your wealth by my side?' I can say the same of India." Were those the words of a depressed mind? Or was it a premonition? In any event, they showed that Indira felt she had made the right choice when she decided to go on with the family legacy of service to India instead of trying to seek personal fulfilment.

Diwali came, the great Hindu festival of lights, which in this country where everything is myth and symbol, means the victory of light over darkness. The skies over the city were dotted with millions of bright flashes, while the noise of the firecrackers could be heard far away. Light bulbs, little lamps and candles twinkled everywhere. The slum districts looked like Christmas crib scenes and the big houses on the wide avenues of New Delhi wore intricate, showy garlands of lights. Rajiv came back from Orissa to spend the holiday with the family, as he always did every year. True to custom, Indira lit a little oil lamp before the figure of Ganesh, the elephant God, the god of happiness, which was on a little altar in the entrance hall. Then the whole family went on with the ritual of lighting up the house with candles and little oil lamps, and the children began to set off firecrackers. Over the noise of the festival, Indira heard Rajiv say that he had to go away early the next morning.

"Where are you going?" Indira asked him. "To Bengal…"

"Bengal? How funny. Do you know that there they believe that the souls of the dead begin their journey this very day, on Diwali? People there light little lamps to show them the way…"

At that moment, Indira's words did not give rise to any response at all. Within the family they were already used to hearing her say things that they attributed to her state of depression. But Sonia was touched by them and was so upset that in the night she had an asthma attack. It was four in the morning when she switched on the light on her bedside table and got up to go to the medicine cabinet, taking care not to disturb Indira, who was sleeping in the next room. But Sonia was surprised to see her mother-in-law appear in her nightdress and with a torch in her hand.

"Let me help you find your medicines," Indira whispered, obviously not having slept a wink.

She found them and went to get a glass of water for Sonia.

"Call me if you feel bad again," Indira told her. "Try to get some rest."

"That's what I say to you, you must rest… Can't you sleep?"

"No… I'm thinking of going to Kashmir for the weekend. I want to see the *chinar* trees in flower. Have you ever seen them?"

Sonia shook her head. Indira went on in a whisper, "It's the most beautiful tree there is, and it's only found in Kashmir. It's like a cross between a plane tree and a large maple, and in autumn the colours are spectacular… red, orange, brown, yellow. It's a sight that reminds me of my childhood. There's one in Srinagar I've been in love with since I was a little girl.

The most beautiful of all the *chinar* trees... I'd like to see it again."

"That tree seemed to hold special significance for her," Sonia would say. "Was it perhaps the need to say goodbye to her origins, her memories and everything that Kashmir stood for in her mind?" Indira was not sure whether to stay more than one night in Srinagar, because she was worried about Sonia's asthma. But her daughter-in-law encouraged her to go, and in the end Indira took her grandchildren. She wanted to show them that land that was as beautiful as paradise, from where they originated. And the tree while they were there.

They spent 36 hours in Srinagar and the surroundings. But, to her great disappointment, the *chinar* of her childhood had died not long before. The news upset her. As superstitious as she was, the recent death of that centenarian *chinar* tree could not be anything other than a sign from destiny. She did not let her discomfort show and she had time to take her grandchildren for a trip on a *shikara*, those little boats in the shape of a gondola, over the shimmering waters of Lake Dal, covered in lotus flowers. She told them about her last holiday with grandfather Firoz in one of the boats set up as a little hotel. She told them of her love for the mountains, which she had inherited from her father, and how Kashmir had always been, for Nehru and for her, a kind of idea of what Eden was like. Then she wanted to show them a forest that was glowing with the fiery colours of the *chinars*, and then she left them in the hotel. Accompanied by only one security guard, she went off to climb a holy mountain to visit a temple where a wise old man lived. They were together for a few hours. "Indira told me that for some time she had felt death was near her. I also felt it," the wise man would say. He did not want to miss the chance to ask her to open a new building next to the *ashram*.

"I'll come back if I'm still alive," was Indira's reply.

"They returned to Delhi on October 28th and Indira spent a quiet evening with us in the sitting room," Sonia would write. "As usual with her, she brought her wicker stool and files out of her study and started working, glancing occasionally at the television or chatting to us." Indira intended to call general elections very soon, perhaps in two months. That night, Sonia helped her prepare the clothes she would wear the next day to travel to Orissa, on the east coast. Indira chose a maroon sari. The actor Peter Ustinov was directing a documentary about India for the BBC and was going to film her on tour in that state, one of the poorest in the country. In Bhubaneswar, the capital of Orissa, the Prime Minister made an emotional speech in which she spoke about the great moments in the history of India, from ancient times to the struggle for independence. Suddenly, towards the end, she changed the tone of her voice and the expression on her face: "I am here today, maybe I won't be here tomorrow," she said. "It doesn't matter whether I live or die... I will continue to serve my people until my last breath, and when I die, every drop of my blood will feed and strengthen my country, a free and united country." After that, she went to the Governor's House where she intended to spend the night. The governor was surprised at her allusion to a violent death.

"I'm only being realistic and honest," Indira told him. "I've seen my grandfather and my mother die slowly and in pain, so I prefer to die on my feet."

The conversation was interrupted by the news that the four-wheel drive vehicle in which her grandchildren went to school had had a small accident that morning. No one had been injured. But Indira went pale and was very nervous. She decided to return to Delhi immediately.

Sonia was awake when her mother-in-law came in at three

o'clock in the morning.

"How are the children?" Indira asked, very upset. "Fine. They're asleep. Nothing happened to them."

Her chief secretary came to see her. He found her very tired. She was still wearing the same maroon sari, now wrinkled and dusty. Indira was convinced that the morning's accident was part of a plot to kidnap her grandchildren or harm them, and nothing her secretary could say would make her change her mind. Then she insisted on discussing some urgent matters about Kashmir and the Punjab.

"Wouldn't you rather leave it until tomorrow?" the man suggested.

"No, let's talk now. Tomorrow I want to rest a little, I have an interview with the former British Prime Minister, James Callaghan, and at night an official dinner here at home in honour of Princess Anne…"

"Everything is ready for the dinner, don't worry," said Sonia. "I only need you to tell me where you want people to sit."

"I'll write you a note about it tomorrow." Sonia waved goodnight and went to bed.

When Indira finished dealing with matters that were still pending with her chief secretary, she called the other one, faithful Dhawan, to whom she gave instructions to cancel all appointments the next day except for the one with Peter Ustinov, who wanted to interview her in the morning, and the ones arranged with the British delegation in the afternoon. She was very tired.

Two hours later, at six o'clock, she got up. She did her yoga exercises, showered and chose a beautiful silk sari in tones of brown and saffron yellow with a black border. She chose those tones because they remindedher of the autumnal colours of Kashmir and also because she had been told they suited her well on television. For the same reason she did not put on her bullet-proof vest which they had been forcing her to wear since there had been more and more threats on her life. She probably did not notice that saffron yellow was the colour of renunciation according to Hindu belief, and particularly to Sikhism. Then she had some toast for breakfast and a cup of tea in her room while she glanced through the newspapers. Her grandchildren Rahul and Priyanka went in to chat to her for a moment, before they went off to school. When Priyanka kissed her goodbye, she was surprised that her grandmother hugged her so tightly to her. She attributed it to the fear she had felt over the little accident the day before. Then Indira called Rahul and told him, "Do you remember what I told you the other day, that if something happens to me, I don't want you to cry for me?" The boy nodded and, surprised, allowed himself to be hugged.

After breakfast she went into her dressing room, where she put herself in the hands of two make-up specialists from Ustinov's team. Sonia came in to inform her about the menu for dinner. Indira always made sure she did notserve the same food to a guest who was visiting again. They did not have much time to talk because secretary Dhawan immediately came to tell her that the television team was waiting for her in her office in Akbar Road.

"We'll finish off the details at lunchtime," she told Sonia as she left.

Indira crossed the dining room and the anteroom and went out of the house. It was a beautiful day, a clear, bright morning, with no mist. The sun gave the luxuriant vegetation of the garden a golden hue. The temperature was perfect and the breeze was balmy. It smelt of flowers and newly-cut grass. She walked along the path that separated her residence from the party office in Akbar Road, among clumps of flowers and evergreen bushes. A policeman walked at her side, carrying a black umbrella to shade her from the sun. Secretary Dhawan followed a few paces behind, and then a bodyguard. They walked past a large maple which was displaying its yellow and red leaves. At the end of the path, now lined with bougainvilleas, Indira recognized Beant Singh, her bodyguard who was opening the little gate for her which led to the garden where the offices were. It was hard not to see him, because Singh was a giant, a Sikh from the Punjab, wearing a turban that matched his khaki uniform. He was accompanied by another bodyguard, also a Sikh, that Indira hardly knew. As she got close to them, she interrupted the conversation she was having with her secretary over her shoulder in order to greet them. She did so in the traditional manner, putting her hands together at chest-height, slightly bowing her head and saying *"Namaste"*. In response, Beant Singh, her faithful bodyguard of the last five years, took out his gun and pointed it at her. There was a silence that lasted the eternity of half a second, interrupted by the singing of a bird in the upper branches of the *neem* trees. "What are you doing?" Indira asked. At that moment, Singh fired four shots at her at point blank range. Indira raised her arm as though to protect herself. The bodyguard turned towards his companion and shouted "Fire!" The other Sikh guard emptied the magazine of his Sten automatic − twenty-five bullets − into Indira's body. The impact made her spin round before she collapsed on the damp earth of the path. Her eyes were still open. They seemed to look up at the tops of the trees, maybe at the sky. It was sixteen minutes past nine. She fell in the exact place where she had seen her grandson Rahul playing with one of the dogs a few days before.

34

Another bodyguard who had been following a little behind Indira and who was not part of the conspiracy, ran towards her. But before he could reach her, another burst of firing hit him in the ankle and he fell face down. The other people with her, paralyzed with fear and terrified that they were going to be gunned down too, crouched down as though to shelter behind Indira's body. They were expecting the worst. Soon they heard the voices of other security guards who came running from Akbar Road. They thought a violent shoot-out would ensue, but at that moment the two Sikh guards threw down their weapons. "I've done what I had to do," said the giant, Beant Singh in Punjabi. "Now you do what you have to do." It was his way of saying that, in the name of the Sikhs, he had avenged the sacrilege in the Golden Temple. The policeman who had been holding the black umbrella hurled himself on top of him and threw him to the ground. Meanwhile, secretary Dhawan, who had miraculously come out unscathed from the last burst of firing, managed to come out of his stupor and drag himself over to Indira and squat down next to her to help her. More soldiers from the border police corps arrived immediately. They had been on duty in a sentry box in the street, and they neutralized the other killer bodyguard. They took them to the sentry box, where there was a tussle. It was said that they tried to escape. The fact is that they, in turn, were shot down. Beant

Singh died instantly. The other one, seriously wounded, was going to be taken to hospital. Later it became known that in his off-duty hours, Beant used to frequent the gurdwaras (Sikh temples) in Delhi and that he used to talk to the most excitable elements there. The other one had just spent a month on holiday in his town in the Punjab, in the very heart of Sikh nationalism.

Indira's personal physician, that one of the servants had called on hearing the shooting, came panting up and busied himself with reanimation exercises. "The ambulance, quick!" he shouted. "Call the ambulance to take Mrs Gandhi to hospital!" An ambulance was always parked outside the residence as a routine part of the care of the Prime Minister. But at that critical moment, it was not available.

"The driver has gone off for a cup of tea!" said a servant. "Get a car then! Bring a car, now!"

They managed to get a white Ambassador, which they manoeuvred and got into the garden. Secretary Dhawan and the policeman grabbedIndira's inert body and carried her to the car. They lay her on the back seat, and they sat in the front. The car was about to drive off when Sonia appeared, in her dressing gown, haggard, with her hair wet and in a mess andher eyes full of terror. The shooting had caught her in the shower. At first she had thought it was firecrackers, like the ones children throw in Diwali. But the scream of one of the servants made her realize that somethingterrible had happened.

And there was the confirmation of her fears: her mother-in-law lay on the back seat, lifeless. The woman she had identified with Joan of Arc since she was a child had in turn been betrayed and sent to her death by the peopleshe trusted. Sonia got into the car. "Oh, Mummy! Oh my God, Mummy!"she said as she knelt on the back seat in order to hold Indira's head in her hands and hug her and talk to her and keep her going until she breathed her last, in the hope that she might reverse the inevitable course of destiny. The car sped off towards the All India Institute of Medical Science, the same hospital where Sanjay had been taken after crashing his plane. Sonia would remember that trip of only five kilometres as the longest of her life. The traffic was very heavy and it seemed as if they would never get there. New Delhi was no longer the same city as when she had arrived there; now there were hardly any carts pulled by oxen or camels, or elephants in the streets. The population had quadrupled and the road traffic was very heavy. Indira was bleeding to death in her hands and Sonia felt helpless. "Oh my God, go faster!" she repeated as she wiped the sleeve of her dressing gown over Indira's face and tried to clean her wounds. Like a crazy pendulum, her state of mind wavered from blackest black to hope. "What if she's only unconscious?" she asked herself suddenly as the car tried to make its way through, hooting the horn. "Quick!" she said to the driver. "Maybe they can save her!" But no matter what efforts the driver made, it was impossible to get through the traffic. Could any of those sleepy drivers have imagined that in that white Ambassador that did not even have a siren available, lay the body of the woman who had ruled their destinies for over twenty years? In Sonia's mind, questions arose one after another, in disorder, like a volcano erupting. "Where is Rajiv? How can I let him know? Where are the children? I have to send for them! Oh my God, Mummy, please don't die!" There was blood everywhere: on Sonia's dressing gown the bloodstains were bright red, on Indira's pretty sari they had taken on a brownish tinge. The velvet covered seats were also soaked with it, making a huge dark stain. But, even so, Sonia still refused to accept that the worst had happened, and that it was all over now for the woman who until that day had been the pillar of her existence. Deep down, she already felt that the assassins' bullets had claimed other victims: her happiness and that of her family.

At nine thirty-two, or sixteen minutes after the attack, they got to the hospital. But no one had phoned ahead from the house to say that the Prime Minister was about to arrive there. When the young doctors on duty in the Emergency Room recognized her, they went into a panic. One of them had the presence of mind to call an expert cardiologist and few minutes later a team of the most veteran doctors in the hospital came down to take care of Indira. They performed a tracheotomy on her to help the oxygen get to her lungs and they inserted several tubes in order to give her a blood transfusion. They decided to take her up to the operating theatre on the eighth floor. There, the electrocardiogram showed signs of a weak heartbeat. They told Sonia, who was alone in the waiting room. A dim light of hope shone in her tearful eyes. They told her that the doctors were giving Indira's heart a vigorous massage, but they refrained from explaining to her that it was obvious from the dilatation of the pupils that her brain was irreparably damaged. The bullets had perforated the Prime Minister's liver, lungs, several bones and her spine. "She's like a sieve," said one doctor. Only her heart was untouched. Even so, for four hours, the doctors tried to perform a miracle.

Sonia could barely control her trembling. The idea that the enemy was inside the house was terrifying. Who could be trusted? What if some servant or employee or a secretary was involved? It was as if all the certainties in her life had suddenly collapsed. Once again that feeling of having quicksand under her feet, where nothing is what it seems and everything might change from one minute to the next! "Oh my God! What about the children?!" She could not help thinking about Sheikh Rahman and all his family. His sonwas the same age as Rahul. Would they have gone to fetch the children from school? If only she could talk to her sister! But Nadia was not in New Delhi at that time.

It was Pupul Jayakar, Indira's best friend, who arrived first and calmed her down. The children were at home safe and sound and they were as calm as could be expected in the circumstances. Pupul told her that the news had not yet got out and that things in the streets were normal. "I found Sonia in a state of shock," she would say later. "She could hardly speak. She began to tremble and I didn't want to ask any more questions." Pupul had brought her some clothes and Sonia changed the bloodstained dressing gown for a sari. In the next hour, other friends began arriving, together with members of the party and the government. Sonia would have liked to throw them all out of the room, all of them except the close friends and colleagues who had shown their unbreakable loyalty to Indira, so few of them that they could be counted on the fingers of one hand. But that was forgetting that Indira was not only her husband's mother: she was the mother of a whole nation. Her assassination was extremely serious. The country was leaderless, without a hand at the helm. No one yet knew whether the attack had been a specific act of revenge on Indira or whether it was part of a wider plot that would end in a coup. That is what the whispered conversations in the hospital corridors between members of the government and the opposition were about, while the Vice-President talked to top government civil servants in a room on the floor below. They discussed the future of the country, because Indira was already the past. She was about to enter history. At two twenty-two in the afternoon, five hours after having been gunned down by men whose job it was to protect her life, the doctors declared that Indira Gandhi had died. Ten minutes later, the BBC broadcast the news all over the world.

Three thousand kilometres away, Rajiv's Ambassador was going as fast as it could along a narrow road full of potholes in the state of Bengal, avoiding elephants, wagons, motorbikes, lorries piled high with goods and people, lots of people. He wanted to get to Calcutta as soon as possible so that he could fly from there to Delhi and perhaps arrive in time to say goodbye to his mother. His pre-campaign electoral tour had been interrupted when his car was intercepted by a police Jeep two hundred kilometres south of Calcutta. A policeman handed him a note: "There has been an accident at the Prime Minister's home. Cancel all visits and return to Delhi immediately." As they drove through a countryside of glittering rice paddies and adobe villages, Rajiv found out from the car radio that his mother had been gunned down by her bodyguards and had been taken to hospital, where the doctors were trying to save her life. He reacted with calm and self- possession, perhaps because he still nursed the hope that she might survive. After a noisy two and a half hour drive, a police helicopter intercepted his car when they were about fifty kilometres from Calcutta. Rajiv got on board and the helicopter left him at the airport, where an Indian Airlines Boeing was waiting for him to take him home. He completed the journey on the flight deck, with the pilots, who were in radio contact with the capital. The absence of news made him feel that he would not see her alive again. It was by means of a communication full of interference that he finally heard that she had died. He remained still, not speaking and not shedding any tears. The Nehrus do not cry in public when they receive a blow; that he had always been taught. It seemed as if the news had not surprised him, perhaps because he was overcome by a certain feeling of fate, similar to

441

what his mother had felt.

At the hospital, after the announcement from the doctors, Sonia asked Pupul to go home with her to get some clothes in order to dress Indira for her final journey. Besides, Sonia was anxious to see her children and get out of that hospital full of people. Outside, the activity in the streets seemed normal. The news had still not got out.

When she got home and her children asked her: "How is Grandmother?", Sonia went to pieces. Her sobbing drowned out her words. But were any words necessary? Rahul hugged his mother tight and Priyanka ran into the house and came back with the inhaler. Sonia did not need it and gradually she calmed down. Then, after explaining everything to them, Pupul and Sonia went into Indira's dressing room. For her final journey, they chose one of her favourite saris, old rose coloured, and a bodice that had been a gift from an old wise man that she greatly admired.

The children did not want to stay in the house. They also wanted to see their grandmother for the last time, and they did not want to leave their mother in that state, so Sonia and Pupul took them with them back to the hospital. The atmosphere in the streets had changed completely. The shops were closing. "We could see men with anxious faces pedalling quickly to get back home," Pupul would say. As they got closer to the hospital, they saw more and more people walking in the same direction. There was such a crowd that the police blocked the main entrance, so they had to use a service entrance.

At the same time, Rajiv was landing at Palam Airport with his stomach in knots. Neither Sonia nor his children were there to meet him, the only people that he would really have liked to see at that moment. On the other hand, his assistants were waiting for him at the foot of the steps, with some friends and, above all, many politicians from the Congress Party. They were already there. Rajiv immediately knew what they had come to ask him. They had come to demand that, whether he liked it or not, he should be the next Prime Minister of India.

Some friends took him to the hospital. They also agreed with the idea that he should succeed his mother. No one seemed to disagree with what was considered as a natural law. Furthermore, it was the best thing that could happen for his safety and that of his family, because he would have all the power of the State at his command to protect him. It was a powerful argument, which left its mark on Rajiv.

"But that has to be decided by the party and the President of the Republic," he objected. "The President is the one designated by law to choose the person who must form a government."

"He has already taken that decision." "But he isn't even in Delhi!"

"He has already made it known. You have to accept, Rajiv, it's the best thing for you all."

On board the plane in which he was returning from an official visit to the Yemen, interrupted by the news of Indira's assassination, the President of the Republic, an old friend of the Nehru family, had already taken the decision to ask Rajiv to be Prime Minister. And in addition, that he should take over immediately, straight away, without letting any more time go by. The moment was of extreme importance. The death of Indira at the hands of Sikh gunmen made him fear an outbreak of violence between communities, the nightmare of any Indian leader. For that reason it was urgent to avoid a power vacuum, in order to keep the country united in the face of such a threat, which could put an end to constitutional order and, definitely, to India as a nation. That is what he informed the senior member of the party, even before leaving the airport: "We must not leave the throne empty, it's very dangerous." Later, when the President of the Republic explained the reasons for his choice, he said that he had to choose a new Prime Minister from the Congress Party, because it was the party with an overwhelming majority in Parliament. And who better than Rajiv, who had an unsullied reputation and was young and intelligent? There was another reason, which had nothing to do with Rajiv's professional merits, and it was that this was what Indira would have liked. "I knew the way she thought and what she wanted," the President admitted, "even though we never discussed it specifically. I just knew what she was like." So Rajiv found himself with no way out. From beyond the grave, his mother's voice echoed in his ears. If he had never abandoned her while she was alive, was he going to do it now that she was dead? Had he not already taken the decision to go into politics? Was what the country was asking of him not the logical consequence of that? He had never wanted to be Prime Minister, at most to have a post in the government, but sometimes life moves quickly and leaves no room for choice.

As he walked along the corridors in the hospital, Rajiv came across a whole series of people who had been part of his mother's life, including a tearful Maneka, the ineffable guru Dhirendra Brahmachari, who kept repeating that Indira should have listened to him to avoid the danger that was hanging over her, ministers and civil servants, assistants and secretaries who wept in small groups. The party barons were all at the hospital and took advantage of his arrival to let him know that they wanted him as leader of the Congress Party and, in consequence, as the nation's new leader. Everyone took it for granted that they were speaking to the future Prime Minister. "You have to accept," they said to him. "If not for yourself, do it for your wife and children, for your safety. And for your mother, for the memory of your grandfather, for the family, for India."

It was quarter past three in the afternoon when Rajiv got to the room next to the operating theatre. He gave Sonia a big hug and she burst into tears. Perhaps she was remembering that first meeting with Indira in London, when she had felt such panic at meeting her. Who would have thought then that she would love her so much, and that she would leave them like that, alone facing the abyss?

Then Rajiv hugged the children, who were very frightened. The wave of terror that the attack had unleashed had spread like an epidemic. After Operation Blue Star, a group of fanatics had sworn to exterminate Indira's descendants for a hundred generations, hadn't they? Who would be next? "Daddy, Mummy, us?" Who knew if behind any nurse, any visitor, any of the many people walking the corridors of the hospital, another murderous terrorist might not be hiding? Where would the avenging fury of the Sikh extremists stop?

He did not have much time to console his family because people kept asking for him all the time. The country required his attention, not even giving him time to weep for his mother's death or calm his family down. "I remember that I felt the need to be alone with him, even if just for a moment," Sonia would say. She took him off to a corner of the operating theatre, a few metres away from where the doctors were sewing up Indira's body. It smelled of formaldehyde and ether. The white neon light brutally illuminated the devastated features of Rajiv's usually soft face.

"They're going to make me Prime Minister," he told her in a whisper.

Sonia shut her eyes. It was the worst thing she could have heard. Itwas like the announcement of a second death on the same day. Rajiv tookher hands, as he continued whispering the reasons that were forcing him to accept the post.

"Sonia, that is the best way for us to protect ourselves, believe me. Wewill have maximum protection available. That's what we need now."

"Let's go and live somewhere else..."

"Do you think we'll be safe in another country? We're all on the blacklist of the extremists, and those fanatics are capable of striking anywhere. No, Sonia, we have no option but to live under constant protection, at least until the threat is removed."

Sonia wept disconsolately. She knew what that meant. It meant havingto live in a claustrophobic environment, that the children would not be able to enjoy a normal life... Was that living? And what about happiness in all this? That happiness to which they had become so comfortably accustomed?

"I'm begging you, Rajiv, don't let them do this to you," Sonia said."I can assure you it's for our own good."

"For our own good? But that system of protection you're talkingabout has shown itself to be totally inefficient. A Prime Minister gunned down in her own home, and not even a basic emergency team on hand...! Doyou see what I mean?"

"They warned her to get rid of her Sikh guards, but she took no notice..."

"What do you mean? That it was her own fault?"

"She should have listened to the police chief and the head of Intelligence. She would still be with us now if she had."

He hugged her again. She went on:

"My God, they'll kill you too."

"I have no choice, they'll kill me anyway, whether I'm in power or not..."

"Please don't accept, tell them no..."

"I can't, my love. Can you imagine going on living as though nothing

had happened, always afraid, here, in Italy or anywhere else?... That's what would happen if I don't accept. That's how you have to look at it. It's my destiny. Our destiny... There are moments when life gives you no choice because there is no choice possible. Help me to accept it."

"Oh no! Oh my God, no!..." Sonia murmured in a flood of tears. "They'll kill you, they'll kill you..." she repeated as Indira's official secretary, P.C. Alexander, came to interrupt them. The wheel of succession could not wait. It was urgent to set it in motion. He took Rajiv by the arm.

"We have to organize the swearing in," he said in a low voice.

"I'm going home to change my clothes," Rajiv answered him. "I'll be at the palace of the President of the Republic by six o'clock."

Then Sonia knew there was nothing to be done, that once again she had to bow to forces that were superior to her and that she would never be able to control. What could she do against a country that had been left motherless and was now calling for the head of the son? When Rajiv kissed her forehead and went slowly away from her, Sonia felt torn apart inside, and prey to an indefinable feeling of melancholy, just like when she was in the Ambassador cradling the head of a dying Indira in her arms.

In the evening that same day the swearing in ceremony of RajivGandhi as sixth Prime Minister of India took place in the

Ashoka hall of the Palace of the President of the Republic, the same place where his grandfather and his mother had been invested for the same post. Of the six Prime Ministers, three had belonged to the same family and the other three had only governed very briefly. In 36 years of independence, the Nehrus hadbeen Prime Ministers for 33 years. Indira had been the third to die in office, but the first to die a violent death. It was not a lively ceremony, as it would have been under normal circumstances. There was a young man, who had not been given time to take in his mother's death and its repercussions on the nation, pushed into accepting the most difficult and demanding job that any citizen of India could aspire to. Without wanting it or desiring it.

Before accepting, Rajiv had made it clear that he would keep on the previous government, without any new members or changes in responsibilities. Next, he held his first cabinet meeting, in which the discussion revolved around Indira's funeral. They decided to set up thefuneral chapel in Teen Murti House, Nehru's old residence, the little palace where Rajiv had spent his childhood. Usha, the faithful secretary, was one ofthe first to arrive and she described her old boss, lying in the coffin, her bodycovered by a shroud but her face uncovered: "Her face was swollen and colourless. It was just as well she could not see herself like that because she would not have been pleased with the way she looked. She always looked sonice and took such great care of her appearance." Sonia must have thought the same. The television caught a short, intense moment, a gesture that was engraved on the memory of millions of Indians and which spoke, louder than any written or verbal declaration, of the link between the two women. Sonia, very composed, wiped a handkerchief over the corner of Indira's mouth to take the sheen off her skin. As though instead of dead she were alive and still needed her to take care of her. Thus loyalty lived on after death.

After eleven o'clock at night, the new Prime Minister appeared on television, in a speech that was broadcast by radio all over the world. Sonia was at the recording studio, her heart broken to see how power had sequestered her husband, unscrupulously using the Nehru-Gandhi name to keep the country united in a time of crisis. Was it not cruel to have asked someone with so little experience in politics as her husband to accept a post that demanded so much experience, at least in these difficult times?

"Indira Gandhi has been assassinated," Rajiv began saying in front of the cameras. "You know that the dream of a prosperous, united and peaceful India was close to her heart. Because of her premature death, her work has been interrupted. It is up to us to finish it."

His speech, and the tone of contained emotion with which he gave it, reminded many of the speech his grandfather Nehru made after the assassination of Gandhi. At that time Nehru was afraid that the Moslems might be blamed for the assassination, and for that reason he was quick to say loud and clear that the guilty party had been a Hindu fanatic. Thirty-six years later, Rajiv Gandhi made no reference to the murderers of his mother, or to their motives. He referred to the religious nature of the assassination when he called for calm and unity, saying that nothing would hurt Indira Gandhi's soul more than an outbreak of violence in any part of the country.

But violence had already broken out. It began first of all in the surroundings of the hospital, when several taxis driven by Sikhs were stoned and a Sikh temple was burned. Any man in a turban suddenly seemed suspicious. The local Sikhs took their children off the streets and locked themselves in their homes. They put down the blinds and turned off the lights, trying to become invisible. The women peered through the cracks, terrified. Some Sikhs ran to find shelter. For others there was no shelter. They knew that the assassination of Indira Gandhi had made them a target for the anger of the people. When night fell, groups of people gathered in the alleyways, mostly Hindus, some with sticks in their hands, others inciting people to hunt down Sikhs. It was a black night, made even darker by the wave of hatred and terror that came over the city, which hardly slept. The intensity of the massacres increased as rumours arose that the Sikhs had poisoned the capital's cisterns of drinking water, or that a train full of Hindus who were coming from the Punjab had been attacked. They were untrue, but the people believed them. Bands of hooligans, who at first destroyed houses and shops that were the property of Sikhs, then dragged men and boys in turbans out of their homes and cut them to pieces with machetes in front of their horrified womenfolk. In the streets, groups of bullies hurled themselves on Sikhs and beat them to death, or poured petrol over them and then set them on fire. Whole families were put to the knife on trains and in buses. The police did not dare to intervene, out of pure idleness and also because they were really in agreement with taking revenge on that turbulent minority. For three days, while thousands of people filed past the body of Indira Gandhi, among them film stars, heads of State, political leaders, friends, members of the family and thousands of citizens who had never met Indira but who were profoundly sad at losing her, the orgy of violence went on spreading. Over two thousand cars, lorries and taxis were burned, as well as a string of factories that were the property of Sikh families, such as the Campa Cola, the Indian answer to Coca Cola, which belonged to an old friend of Sanjay's who had helped them to get through the hard times. Reporters documented a particularly bad episode in a district on the right bank of the River Yamuna, where a well-organized groupsystematically killed all Sikhs and the police did nothing. They did not even give them a chance to save themselves because they set fire to their homes with the inhabitants inside. One of the reporters who witnessed what was happening phoned Pupul: "Please do something. The situation is appalling," she told her in a frightened voice. Pupul was perplexed. Until only a short time ago she would have known what to do. She would have picked up the phone and called her friend Indira, who would have acted immediately. But now she did not know who to turn to. So she called the Home Secretary, who by chance was meeting with Rajiv at number 1, Safdarjung Road. She told him about the massacres, the rapes, the horror of what was going on lessthan ten kilometres from where they were. "Speak to the Prime Minister," hetold her and immediately passed her over to Rajiv. Pupul repeated what she had already said. "It was hard for me to address Rajiv as Prime Minister, it was hard for me to understand that the enormous power and massive authority that Indira held had now fallen to him." Rajiv made her go to his house, where Pupul told him everything she knew in more detail. The Prime Minister seemed disconcerted and indecisive.

"What shall I do, Pupul?" he asked her.

"It isn't up to me to say what the Prime Minister should do," she answered. "I can tell you what your mother would have done. She would have called out the army and kept order at all costs. She would have gone on television and with all the prestige of her position she would have made itvery clear that she would not allow the massacres under any circumstances."

"Help me to write a speech like those my mother would have

451

written,"

Rajiv asked her as he went to the door with her. "Do it now please, it's urgent."

Pupul did so, but when she sat down in front of the television, Rajiv did not appear. Instead it was the Home Secretary. Pupul thought that his presence was not convincing enough to calm things down. She thought the speech lacked the anguish of a son and the authority of a Prime Minister. In fact the army was not called out to intervene that night for fear of inflaming things even more, so the terror and savagery continued. That lack of decisiveness was attributed by many to Rajiv's inexperience. But the factwas that he was overcome by events, still feeling the trauma of having lost his mother and of finding himself holding on to the reins of power, without really knowing how the mechanisms of that power worked.

Among the Sikhs there was such panic that for the first time in their lives many of them took off their turbans and shaved off their beards andhair to save themselves. Some one hundred thousand fled the capital. The writer Kushwant Singh took refuge with his wife in the Swedish Embassy: "What the crowds were after were the goods of the Sikhs, the televisions and fridges, because we are more prosperous than others. Killing and burning people alive was just part of the fun." As night fell, groups of Sikhs scatteredall over the city seeking refuge. Two of them came to Pupul's house and frightened the wife of the *dhobi*, the laundryman, who at that hour must havebeen joining in the disturbances. At the woman's cries of fright, the Sikhs went running off, but Pupul would have given them shelter that night, as many other Hindu families did too. In the same way as very few Sikhs had been followers of Brindanwale, very few Hindus wanted revenge on the Sikhs. But those who did were so cruel that it reminded people of the times of Partition. In three days, some three thousand were massacred.

On the evening of November 2nd, Rajiv finally came out on television demanding an end to the violence. "What has happened in Delhi since the death of Indira Gandhi is an insult to everything she defended," he said clearly. The next day, he finally ordered the army to intervene, imposing a curfew and sending tanks into the most conflictive districts with orders to shoot anyone who was caught in a flagrant act of aggression.

On November 3rd, as peace was being imposed by force, Indira's cremation was carried out very close to where Nehru's and Sanjay's had taken place, on the riverbank. Rajiv walked seven times round his mother's funeral pyre before putting a torch to the sandalwood logs. The flames gradually took hold as the sun dyed the sky orange, red and gold. An impressive list of personalities were present, amongst whom were George Bush Sr., Mother Theresa, members of European royalty, artists and writers, business magnates, scientists and heads of State. For one elegant lady dressed in black, this funeral held very special significance. Margaret Thatcher remembered Indira's warm words when a few weeks earlier she had called her after the IRA attack. "We have to do something about terrorism…," she had told her.

The silhouette of Rajiv between the flames that devoured his mother's body was engraved forever in the eyes of a whole people, like a torch of hope. "Everything was chaos around him," wrote a well-known journalist, "but he reflected an image of confidence and seemed to be in control of the situation." The British Iron Lady commented, "I have seen in Rajiv the same self-control that Mrs Gandhi had…" The one who was absolutely devastated, and did not hide it, was Sonia. "If someone had painted the scene," said Margaret Thatcher, "her pain would have been enough to communicate the general feeling." Paradoxically, there was no huge crowd of humble folk, of the millions who had venerated Indira like a goddess. Fear of the disturbances and the atmosphere of violence that reigned in the city dissuaded many from paying their last tribute to her.

Faithful to the instructions he had received from his mother a short time before, one morning Rajiv took the bronze urn that held the ashes and boarded an Indian Air Force plane. After an hour's flight, he was flying over the Himalayas, a crest of white peaks that stretched as far as the eye could see. They opened a trapdoor in the floor of the plane for him and freezing air poured in. Rajiv, wearing an astrakhan hat and a thick leather coat with warm, lined gloves and an oxygen mask, took the urn, also wrapped in a leather bag so that the contents would not freeze. He opened the bag and let the ashes fall over the mountains, just as the ritual requires, so that death could turn into life, thirteen days after Indira Gandhi had entered history.

35

Rajiv did not have a moment to stop and deal with his own grief. Political life went on and the leaders of the party advised him to bring the general election forward. They wanted to capitalize on the sympathy vote that Indira's assassination was likely to cause. Rajiv understood that those elections were very important for him, because they would serve to gain him legitimacy in the eyes of the people and not seem merely designated by his mother's followers because of who he was. So he set the date for voting on December 26th, 1984. He wanted Sonia to go with him again to campaign in the constituency of Amethi, where Maneka, with her little son in her arms, was standing as rival candidate. Sonia was now the country's first lady, and just thinking about it made her dizzy. Fate could not have chosen anyone less predisposed to take on that role. A role that would have filled most women with pride and satisfaction, but made her sad, because it made her long for her old life. What a luxury it was to live in safety! What a luxury to be able to spend time restoring paintings, going out with friends, being free and leading a normal, anonymous life! They were still so traumatized that before the trip to Amethi, and coinciding with Indira's 68th birthday, Rajiv and she both wrote out instructions: "In case of my death or that of my wife Sonia in an accident, inside or outside of India, our bodies are to be repatriated to Delhi and burned together, according to the Hindu rite, in a place in the open air. Under no circumstances are our bodies to be burned in an electric crematorium. According to our custom, our son Rahul is to light the pyre… It is my wish that our ashes be scattered in the Ganges, in Allahabad, where the ashes of my ancestors were scattered." Did the saying not go that the cobra always bites twice? In other words that misfortune never comes alone.

Dressed always in a white sari, as was expected in mourning for her mother-in-law, Sonia now discovered that she was much more at home among the crowd in Amethi. "I became a frequent visitor to that place," she would write later. "I knew the people and their problems, and I no longer felt like a stranger among them." But Indira's absence was cruelly felt. She had been the centre of the family universe, a strong, reliable personality, always there to guide, advise, encourage and embrace them. The gap she left was terrible. Rajiv had been left an orphan, without the last figure in his family. One day Sonia was looking for him at home, but no one seemed to know where he had got to. She finally found him in Indira's old study, looking at his mother's things and photos, as though he were looking for signs of her. "He looked very lost and very alone," Sonia would write. "He very often felt her absence intensely." It was inevitable. Wherever he went, even in the most remote corners of the sub-continent, he saw posters with his mother's face on them, always smart with her lock of white hair visible and waving with the palm of her hand turned upwards. There was always someone talking about her to him, about the last visit she had made there, about what she had done for that community, about the children she had blessed and even about the civil servant she had reproached. Indira had left her mark all over the country, and sometimes it seemed to Rajiv that she was still alive, and that she was about to appear to comfort him and encourage him. He had no option but to gather his reserves of courage and mental fortitude to face the memory of his mother stoically.

Rajiv's electoral tour all round the country would have been triumphant if it had not been for the serious accident which occurred in the city of Bhopal, in the centre of India, when an escape of poisonous gas from a pesticide factory, the property of the American multinational, Union Carbide, spread over the poorest districts of the city, causing thousands of dead and injured. Considered as the biggest industrial accident in history, the tragedy in Bhopal, just at the beginning of his career, was seen by many as a bad omen for the man who at all costs wanted to develop the country and tighten links with the elite of the business world. Rajiv immediately decided to visit the disaster zone. He preferred Sonia to stay at home, in case the poison from the factory was still floating in the air, but she refused and went with him. As soon as they arrived, they were struck by the effects of the poisoning. The hospitals were crowded with people who had lost their sight, with mothers crying for the deaths of their children, with orphaned children and men made desperate by the total loss of their families. In view of the scale of the tragedy, his diatribes on the industrialization of India and his call to prepare the country for the twenty-first century seemed hollow words. Rajiv realized the problems that development itself could engender. For a start, he did the only thing he could do and freed urgent aid for the victims and promised that the government would give them fair compensation. But that was never obtained.[1]

Rajiv won hands down in the elections in December 1984, with a better result than his grandfather or his mother had ever obtained. Sonia congratulated him warmly, although she felt intuitively that the news brought them a little closer to the edge of the precipice. For the last three years her husband had been an MP in Parliament only responsible for Amethi, and one of the secretaries general of the party. Now he had 544 constituencies in his care and the responsibility for governing an immense, volatile and sometimes ungovernable country seized up by a huge State apparatus. Had not an English politician written that the chain of the Himalayas seemed small in comparison with the load that a Prime Minister of India bears on his shoulders? The dynasty had received the mandate from the people, a mandate on a national scale, but Rajiv had no illusions about the reasons for his success: "Above all it's been because of my mother's death... No one really knew me, what they have done has been to project the expectations they had of her on to me. They have made me into the symbol of their hopes." The one to lose catastrophically was Maneka, in spite of having run a very dynamic campaign. The wave of sympathy for Rajiv, and perhaps the fact that she was the daughter of a family of Sikh origin, wiped her off the map of politics, at least for the moment. Now it was clear who was the real heir to the mantle of the Nehru-Gandhis.

Sonia and the children found it even harder to struggle to get over the trauma of Indira's violent death because, after fifteen years living in the same house, they had to leave it and move to another considered safer and more appropriate as the official residence of the Prime Minister. It was nearby, in Race Course Road. Now that terrorism had become an inescapable reality of political life in India, the family was surrounded twenty-four hours a day by an impressive deployment of security forces. In part it was a question of an unnecessary display, on show to make up for all the errors they had made with Indira. The responsibility for protecting the Prime Minister no longer fell to a paramilitary force, but to a specialized professional group, the Special Protection Group, created precisely because of the recent assassination. "Their presence put an end to what was left of our privacy and freedom," said Sonia. Suddenly, one day, she had a fright when she was in the garden, with her pruning shears in her hand, and she saw a kind of Martian on a tree branch, totally dressed in black, with balaclava, bullet-proof vest and submachine gun in tow. "I'm on duty," the man told her. On another occasion when she had to go out in a hurry to buy something in the American store, another Martian prevented her, in the doorway.

"Madam, you cannot go out now."

"What do you mean, I can't go out? I need to go to the American Embassy, I have guests tonight…"

"Madam, you have to get used to letting us know a little in advance. We cannot react in an improvised way. There are some three hundred agents in charge of the protection of your family at the moment."

"About time!" thought Sonia, with no option but to call her sister Nadia and ask her to do her a favour and buy what she needed and bring it home for her.

Although it was annoying to live like that, there was no choice but to get used to it. The security agents wanted to prevent Rajiv from carrying on with the custom he inherited from his mother and his grandfather of seeing hundreds of visitors very early in the morning. They asked him questions and listened to him, sitting on the lawn. But he insisted on keeping it up, even if only for three days a week. It was important for him to be able to take the pulse of the people. And he also used it to perfect his Hindi, which he spoke with mistakes in syntax and sometimes in pronunciation.

At home they woke up at six o'clock in the morning with the morning tea which was served to them on a tray. At eight thirty, the whole family gathered for breakfast. Rajiv went straight off and Sonia stayed tidying the house and, if she had time, reading and taking cuttings from the press. The children had stopped going to school the day their grandmother was killed. According to the police, it was too dangerous for them to go to a place where an armed man could easily get in. So now some private teachers arrived at about ten o'clock to teach them at home. Sonia took advantage of that time to go out shopping or to an exhibition. She always went out dressed immaculately, because she was aware that she was subject to implacable public scrutiny. "She has more saris than Imelda Marcos has shoes," said one rumour. What she had was Indira's collection of saris and shawls, mostly gifts, which, as Prime Minister, she had accumulated on all her trips all over India. Sonia had inherited them.

In the evenings she stayed with the children and they looked for ways to amuse themselves without going out, such as watching videos. On Sundays she wanted to keep up the custom of inviting her close friends for brunch, although Rajiv was rarely able to attend because he was so busy. But it seemed to her that it was important to keep up an appearance of normality. All the visitors, including her sister Nadia and the Quattrochis, had to be searched and pass through a triple barrier of metal detectors before being admitted. They got together in the garden and chatted gaily in Italian, French, English and

Spanish, while they tasted Indian treats served on *thalis*, typical little tin dishes. Sonia surprised them with some dishes difficult to prepare in India, such as prawns in garlic sauce, which became a Sunday favourite.

Apart from those stolen moments, normality was a pipe dream. Any little delay on Rajiv's part – and he tried hard to have lunch with the family whenever he could - caused big scares. The only moments of normal life came when they went on holiday to Italy in the summer and over Christmas. There too there was surveillance, although not so overwhelming. In New Delhi, they lived like prisoners.

What Rajiv had to give up altogether was his hobbies, especially photography, in which he had reached a good professional standard. He did not have time to listen to his favourite songs or to attend any concerts of classical Indian music with Sonia and their children. But he was determined to go on being a competent pilot, because it was his passion and furthermore, it gave him a certain sense of security after the uncertainty of politics. He asked a colleague to let him know when his flying licence was about to run out so he could renew it by accumulating the hours required. This he could always do by piloting the planes himself in which he travelled all over the country. But there was no time for anything that was not his activity asPrime Minister. "For me there was only time for action. I set myself to restoring confidence, to restoring friendship and fraternity between communities which had lived together for centuries," he declared.

Rajiv had received a poisoned inheritance from his mother: the Sikh problem. It was fundamental to be able to solve it in order to get back to peaceful general co-existence. He thought that first it was necessary to bring down the tension, so he began

461

by using good sense: he declared that he was open to any compromise to solve the problem as long as it did not constitute a threat to the integrity of the nation; he freed the extremists arrested during the last months of his mother's regime, and he promised to initiate an investigation into the massacres of the Sikhs in Delhi. The leader of the Sikh moderate party, as eager to achieve peace as the Prime Minister, finally signed the initial premises of an agreement. Immediately after that, Rajiv announced elections in the Punjab for September 1985, with the aim of transferring the administration of that state to the moderate Sikhs and making them responsible for the struggle against the extremists. But the terrorism continued, with small bombs in Delhi and the outlying area and, above all, with the explosion of an Air India Boeing 747 in mid-flight from Toronto to Delhi. The attack, which cost the lives of the 325 passengers on board, was attributed to two groups of Sikh extremists. That night, Rajiv met with his cabinet, and Sonia waited up for him until four o'clock in the morning. She was very aware of the size of the threat that was hanging over her husband, and both she and the children were living in terror. They saw the members of the Special Protection Group with scepticism. It was true that they were always there, perhaps too much, but in view of the audacity of the Sikh terrorists... would they really be efficient?

While she waited for Rajiv, Sonia spoke on the telephone with her family in Orbassano. Since Indira's death, her parents were very worried about what might happen to them and they were always watching the news. Any trace of pride that Paola, her mother, might feel about the fact that her daughter was the first lady of India was overshadowed by the fear of another attack. Sonia always reassured them, although her mother was able to recognize the fear in her voice, in spite of the distance and the interference. That day her mother was doubly concerned. Her daughter Nadia had told her she was returning to Italy.

"How lucky you are, Mother, you're going to be near the girls..." Sonia said to her. "On the other hand, I'm going to miss Nadia a lot."

"I'm very unhappy about it. Don't you think they might get back together?"

"No, Mother... Sometimes it's better that way..." Sonia replied, guessing at her mother's distress. Her Spanish brother-in-law had gone on being unfaithful to her sister, and she, tired of it by then, had decided to ask for a divorce. There was no sense in remaining in India. Sonia was being left alone, at a delicate moment, in an apocalyptic atmosphere. She had to bebrave; there was no alternative.

Rajiv kept his cool and did not give way to the temptation to respond to violence with more violence, as his mother would perhaps have done. He granted the Punjab exclusive use of Chandigarh, the city designed by Le Corbusier, as its capital, in exchange for a promise of loyalty on the part of the moderate Sikh party, and he announced economic measures, such as the building of a hydro-electric dam to alleviate the problem of the shortage of energy in that state. He wanted to play his cards right and win over the moderates.

But on August 20th, 1985, it all came apart again. The leader of the moderate party who had been going round the villages and cities of the Punjab calling for the support of the people, "selling" the agreement with Rajiv to his people, was shot down. Once again a tragedy, once again an impasse. The fanatics were imposing their tyranny and boycotting any negotiated solution. In Parliament in New Delhi, Rajiv's ability to get a rapid solution to the problem began to be doubted. But he was not daunted and decided to go ahead with the elections in the Punjab. In the same way as his mother's assassination had catapulted him to power, he thought that the murder of the Sikh moderate would create a wave of sympathy for that party. He was right. For the first time in the history of the Punjab, the moderates won hands down in the polls. The result was a clear victory against extremism.

But the Sikh fanatics were not going to disappear without a fight. In another attempt to create tension, they dug themselves in again in the Akal Takht, the temple razed to the ground during Operation Blue Star and which had then been rebuilt. This time they were claiming that the reconstruction had profaned the temple; in fact, any pretext would do to have recourse to violence. Once again, weapons reached them through the passages and tunnels of the complex. Outside the Golden Temple, young extremists redoubled their attacks against Hindus and anyone who was not considered sufficiently devout, such as barbers and hairdressers for example, whose activity clashed completely with the Sikh precept of never cutting the hair, since what God had created should be respected, including the hair. They were classed as enemies of the Sikh people and in consequence were the targets of attacks by the more orthodox.

"The only answer is military action..." on hearing this phrase, Sonia started to shake. She had heard it before, from her mother-in-law. The result was there to be seen... Indira's son was suddenly at the same crossroads.

Was more sacrilege necessary, when the previous sacrilege had not solved the problem? Where would this spiral of violence end? As if that were not enough, events were repeating themselves with macabre similarity. Just like in the earlier occupation, a police officer was gunned down near the temple, putting the government on the ropes and forcing Rajiv to take a hand in the matter.

"What are you going to do?" a distressed Sonia asked him. "Besiege them until they surrender."

From his office in New Delhi, he personally directed Operation Black Thunder. He gave strict orders to the army and the police not to enter the temple under any circumstances and to seal off the area, blocking all the secret passages, as well as the ways of entry and exit for goods. The waiting seemed to go on forever. In the early days, the terrorists fired into the air and let off intimidating bursts of fire. Apart from these skirmishes, there was absolute silence reigning in the Golden Temple. The waters of the sacred lake reflected the surrounding temples like a mirror, and everything was so motionless that it was as if time itself had stood still. The terrorists were expecting an attack, and even tried to provoke one, but the only response they got were the echoes of their own shots. The army and the police were always unsure whether or not they might be able to get supplies through some channel that had escaped their control, and this kept them in a state of extreme tension. Outside, the inhabitants of the Punjab prayed in silence for their holy places not to be profaned again. Sonia followed it all from home, in New Delhi, and every time the phone rang, her heart missed a beat. Finally, after ten days, Rajiv's voice at the other end of the phone gave her the good news:

"They've surrendered, it's over. The strategy's worked. There's been no violence and no need to go into the temple."

Sonia breathed a sigh of relief, although she was not entirely relaxed. Living without tension was a luxury beyond her reach. The terrorists had failed in their attempt to provoke the government. As always, when people want to repeat history, it ends up as a parody of itself. This time they came out of their hideout half dead with hunger and thirst. More than two hundred of them surrendered. Rajiv's victory became even more patent when the Press published photos of the inside of the temple, which showed the great lack of respect the terrorists had shown for that holy place. There were excrements everywhere, piles of clothes, broken objects and splashes of blood, the result of fights between them. They were completely discredited in the eyes of their fellow believers.

36

Rajiv's critics, who accused him of lack of character, had to admit that his qualities as a peace-maker brought results. The great advantage he had lay precisely in the difference in style between him and his mother and the majority of Indian politicians in general. He brought new blood. He believed that his mother's and his grandfather's Socialist policies made the working and development of the economy seize up. He was convinced that the Licence Raj, which his mother had helped to back up, drowned the enterprising spirit of Indians and encouraged corruption. Speeding up permits in exchange for a bribe was current practice among civil servants. As a pilot in a state-owned company for fourteen years, Rajiv had suffered from the notorious incompetence and knew what he was talking about. His efforts to make the administration more efficient and to relax controls gained him reproaches from Leftist intellectuals. According to them, liberalizing trade and relaxing controls would make India a country that depended too much on foreign capital. They identified him more with the growing middle class than with deepest India. They accused him of having been born lucky, of speaking English better than Hindi and even of taking his in-laws on holiday to the Ranthanbore National Park. Taking a holiday was frowned upon in India, especially for a politician. But Rajiv wanted to invite his father-in-law to see tigers in the same national park where he had spent his honeymoon with Sonia.

Finally Stefano Maino had agreed to visit his favourite daughter. This was the first and only holiday of his life, an opportunity that Rajiv was not going to waste, and that is why he did his utmost to spoil him. Also part of that trip was Stefano's old friend, the mechanic, Danilo Quadra. Sonia was happy to be able to entertain her father after so many years. She felt that it would be his only visit to India because Stefano had never liked travelling and because now he suffered with his heart and was somewhat fragile.

"He's always worrying about you, even before your mother-in-law's assassination," Danilo told Sonia.

Stefano had been very afraid since before Sonia had escaped from his control, since the far off day when he had said to his wife, "They'll throw her to the tigers." He was also afraid for Rajiv, that *bravo ragazzo* as he called him. Too *bravo* to be a politician in a place as turbulent and poor as India, thought Stefano. The spectacle of the poverty moved him, perhaps because it reminded him of his childhood, when he was a cowherd and time went by exasperatingly slowly and his belly was empty. It had seemed as if things were never going to get any better and that the scarcity, boredom and limitations would go on forever, as he saw reflected in the eyes of the young people in Indian villages. Sonia was always telling him off because he was very prone to giving generously to the poor: "If you carry on like that, you're going to have all the beggars in India chasing after you," she said to him, reminding him that the majority of beggars worked for the mafias and that it was better to give money directly to the people that cared for the poor. But this man, sparing with his words and seemingly so hard, took no notice because he could not resist the smile of a child putting his hand in through the open car window. At the end of the trip, when they got back to New Delhi, his friend Danilo confirmed it to Sonia, shrugging his shoulders in a sign of impotence: "There's nothing to be done about it, he likes giving money away to everyone." Stefano Maino was faithful to his own memory.

Rajiv was too "Western" to be able to hide it, and even very British in his manners and in his way of holding in his emotions. Once, defending himself from an attack by the opposition, he said that they wanted to make India go back into the Middle Ages, an expression that belongs to European, not Indian, history. It was true too that his degree of identification with the poor was not as intense as his mother's or his grandfather's, but he thought that if the urban middle classes became wealthier, that would end up benefiting the poor in the villages. The old party dinosaurs reminded him that the important thing was to hold on to the loyalty of the voters, of whom the immense majority were miserably poor. What sense was there in having a policy that would not benefit them in the short term? Did Rajiv perhaps want the party to lose in the next elections? The young Prime Minister found himself trapped between giving greater freedom to businessmen to earn money, and keeping the grassroots loyal, the poor. That was his greatest challenge, and he knew that it was not going to be easy to win. In order to fight against being branded as the "Prime Minister of the privileged", which his detractors wanted to impose on him, and which in a democracy of poor people was very detrimental, he did what his mother would have done: he travelled exhaustively round the country. He even joined in a great pilgrimage in order to improve his image among the masses. According to Sonia, who went with him on many of these trips, her husband was untiring. "He walked so quickly that I had to ask him to slow down so that the rest of us could keep up with him. As he had got used to sleeping no more than four or five hours a day, he used to have a nap between the different stops, giving me instructions to wake him if someone was waiting. Sometimes I let him sleep a few more minutes... Then he would protest, but at least he rested." Sonia witnessed the feeling that he aroused in the people. "People responded more to his personal charm than to the post he held. It didn't matter whether he was in a tribal village in the north, a city in Tamil Nadu, in the heart of rural Punjab or in the slums of Bombay. Rajiv did not belong to any caste or ethnic group. He was Indian and everyone considered him as one of them." He drove his own four-wheel drive vehicle in rural areas. Wherever there were people waiting, he would stop to chat. "If we were delayed," Sonia would say, "they carried on waiting patiently to talk to him, and to see him. In remote places, late at night, a peasant would bring an old oil lamp close to his face and I could see a gleam appear in his eyes as he recognized his smile. He would ask us to accompany him to introduce us to his family, to name his newborn children, to wish the newly married couples in the village luck," How far off was life in New Delhi from those remote corners... from the huts where they shared the little food the people had, where they listened carefully to the descriptions of the deprivation there and where they asked questions in order to find out how they could help them. "I see a lot of love in people's eyes," said Rajiv, "and friendship, and trust, but above all, hope." Rajiv firmly believed that technology could eliminate poverty, or at least mitigate it. He remembered his mother, and the efforts she had made to set the green revolution in motion, taking scientists out into the field and organizing meetings with local politicians and peasants.

When they criticized him for setting aside large sums of money from the State budget for scientific research centres, he defended himself by saying that the farmers of the Punjab would never have been successful if they had not had access to tissue cultivation and genetic engineering. "We can have failures if we experiment," he said, "but if we don't do that we will never get anywhere." The contradictions in India were scandalous: "How was it possible to launch satellites into space and not be able to provide the population with drinking water? he asked himself. He began to discover that it was not from lack of technology, but because of an inability to apply that technology to the problems of the poor. From there emerged an idea of his that he called Technological Missions, an ambitious programme of research in six areas which Rajiv, after his tours in rural districts, identified as priority: drinking water, literacy, immunization, milk production, telecommunications and renewable energies.

As usually occurs with someone who shakes up old structures and ideas, he became the object of scorn. In New Delhi they called him ingenuous, they said he wanted to leap from the oxcart to the mobile phone, something that would yet end up happening thanks to his vision and his forcefulness in those early years of his government. Three decades later, the photo of a *mahout* talking on his mobile from the back of his elephant, which was moving tree trunks, would become the publicity image of an Indian phone company. It was under the government of Rajiv Gandhi, and thanks to the intervention of Indians who lived abroad, mainly in the United States, that an inter-urban and international phone system was installed, functioning via satellite and bringing the phone to all parts of the country, making it available to those poor people who lived in the utmost isolation.

In the capital they also laughed at his slogan "A computer in every village school by the 21st century". It sounded like the dream of a rich kid because, in effect, many schools in the villages did not have electricity, or even a blackboard. But the truth is that Rajiv immediately understood the potential of computers, which years later would serve as a boost for the economy of India. He thought that the industrial revolution had allowed Europe to gain its pre-eminent position and he did not want India to miss the bandwagon of another revolution, that of electronics and computers. Less than a month after being named Prime Minister, he reduced the import tariffs on computer components and computers. Then he gradually eliminated many of the controls over the computer industry and he promoted the use of computers in schools, banks and offices, strongly stimulating local industry. Under his mandate the economy began to be deregulated: "We have to free ourselves of the controls without giving up control," he said. The middle classes went through a much desired expansion for a long time. People were able to buy televisions, radios, cameras, watches and domestic appliances that were previously unavailable because of the very high tariffs, so high that most of those objects were acquired as contraband. They were good yearsfor consumers and for business. For the first time since independence, the creation of wealth was not considered a crime or a sin.

The repercussions of these measures on Sonia's life were immediate, making her work as first lady easier. In preparation for official dinners, she no longer had to go off on a pilgrimage round the markets of New Delhi to find cheese, for example or olive oil or a food mixer. Little by little, the outside world was beginning to come into age-old India and India, in turn was beginning to open up to the world.

But in the eighties the country was still a hotbed of conflicts, and the work of a Prime Minister could be compared to that of a fireman putting out fires. After the Punjab, he spent time on pacifying the region of Assam, in upheaval from the influx of Moslem refugees who were still coming in from Bangladesh fifteen years after the war to seek work. He also worked hard to achieve peace with the tribal communities in the northeast, such as theBodos, the Gurkhas, and the Mizos, in a series of agreements which won a reduction in and even a halt to secessionist violence. On those visits, he had no qualms about wearing astonishing hats or wearing very colourful local costumes as a symbol of friendship, exactly as Indira would have done. He laughed at himself seeing himself like that, and he very sportingly put up with having his leg pulled. He never lost his sense of humour, and was disconcerted when someone did not catch on to his jokes. When Rajiv came home, he hurried to show Sonia and the children the objects he had been given on those trips, whether it was an old woman's pipe from the Mizo, a wicker basket or a carved shell, and which he then kept in his office like real treasures. In his heart of hearts, he knew that achieving peace and securityfor the different peoples of India meant also achieving them for his family,or at least that is what he believed until October 2nd, 1986, when the Sikh conflict reared its ugly head for the last time.

That day, while they were attending a ceremony to celebrate the 117th anniversary of the birth of Mahatma Gandhi in the mausoleum dedicated to his memory in New Delhi, they clearly heard an explosion.

"It's the backfiring of a scooter," a member of the Special Protection Group said, very sure of himself.

Rajiv and Sonia sat on the ground while the priests recited

the prayers in memory of the father of the nation. When the ceremony was over and they got up to go, they heard more explosions. The guard closest to Sonia was injured on the forehead. Panic spread. The people in the crowd shrieked as they scattered. Rajiv protected his wife with his own body when other police officers surrounded them and got them away. "... So it was a scooter!" Sonia repeated in indignation. The frustrated assassin was captured immediately. He was a Sikh, who had fired from the top of a tree. No one was injured, but for Sonia the attempt was a reminder that they could not let down their guard for a moment. She came home very upset, with a great need to hug her children to check that they were also fine, because there was always the possibility that the attack might be part of a wider conspiracy. But this time that was not the case and the Sikh had acted alone.

37

Suddenly, it looked as if Rajiv had got fatter. Could Sonia's penne all'arrabbiata that he liked so much be responsible for that prominent belly? his friends asked sarcastically. No, the guilty party for that bulky torso under a cotton shirt was a thick bullet-proof vest that he was forced to wear since the last attempted attack. From now on, he made his journeys in one of two groups of identical cars, so that no one could know which one he was travelling in. And every time he went out, hundreds of policemen patrolled the city in a state of alert. And the children now only saw a small group of the children of their parents' lifelong friends, who, in spite of being known by the security guards had to submit to meticulous searches before coming into "the fortress", as they called the family residence. Sonia stopped her restoration classes in the National Museum which she had taken up again in her scarce free time, and she began to compile the letters between Nehru and Indira with the idea of one day publishing them. It was a job that she could do at home and which could also serve her husband, who was always seeking good phrases and ideas for his speeches. Digging deep into the family memory, she recognized many of the conflicts and problems that her husband was facing because, in another way and in another time, Nehru and Indira had also had to struggle with them: how to control the power of the bureaucracy, how to calm regional tensions, how to lift the country out of poverty... Contempt for personal safety seemed to be a common trait in the family. Neither Nehru nor Indira nor Rajiv had much respect for "security" in general, because it distanced them from the people and reminded them more of a dictatorship than a democracy. They thought that if someone really wanted to kill them, they would always find a way to do it. Sonia was not convinced. She was beginning to realize that if Rajiv had not ended up asPrime Minister, with all the power of the State to protect them, perhaps now they would all be dead. She went into a cold sweat just thinking about it. The circumstances of life had put her family into a spiral that forced them to flee forwards. As there was no chance of stopping or going back, Sonia had no option but to change, accept her role and find a way to adapt and take advantage of what life was offering her. It was not easy, because the atypical situation of the family created unexpected problems for them. For example, Rahul and Priyanka were coming to an age when they ought to go to college. Where should they be sent? Sonia knew for a fact that they were not going to be safer from Sikh revenge abroad than in India, so the problem became a source of great anxiety. It was then that Rajiv suggested sending them to the American College in Moscow. Of all countries, the USSR was one of the safest and besides, there was no Sikh community there. Sonia did not like the idea, so for the moment they set it aside.

As first lady, Sonia accompanied her husband abroad. They travelled on board a Boeing 747, specially fitted to accommodate the entourage of the Prime Minister, made up of assistants, ministers, journalists and naturally, a unit of agents from the Special Protection Group. During long flights, Sonia would bury herself in a book, something she had loved to do since she was a child, while Rajiv reviewed speeches with his assistants, adding last-minute touches or a suggestion inspired by some of Nehru's or his mother's letters. Rajiv liked those journeys on which he slept little and worked a lot. It seemed as if he was more at ease abroad than at home. "It's good to be among friends," he told Margaret Thatcher as soon as they arrived in London. Sonia tried to make herself as invisible as possible. It was not easy to refuse to attend receptions at which her presence was required or to avoid making speeches. "She is a very reserved woman who does not like to be the centre of attention," explained her husband, to excuse her. There was another reason: it was not good as far as internal politics was concerned for Sonia to be talked about, because automatically her foreign origins would bebrought up, a weak point that first Maneka and then the Hindu fundamentalist Right, were using to discredit the Prime Minister.

But Rajiv felt very much at home among international statesmen. Actually, he had been brought up among them and spoke the same language as they did. He did not project the image of an obscure politician from the Third World, but that of a modern, progressive man with ideas of his own, able to take on any world leader. He was backed by his achievements in his first two years in power, which added up to more than any other prime minister in a comparable period of time. When he was criticized because his policy of economic aperture brought him close to the United States, or vice- versa, when they accused him in the West of moving India closer to the Soviet Union, he liked to repeat one of his mother's phrases: "We keep ourselves straight and we don't lean one way or the other." Rajiv got President Reagan to make an exception to his policy of not selling India technology that could be diverted to countries in the East. He wanted an American super-computer that would help to predict the development of the monsoons with a high degree of precision, something that he thought would be invaluable to the peasants. Reagan understood and agreed to his request.

For Rajiv, those trips meant attending interminable round tables, ceremonies, conferences and treaty-signings. Above all, he enjoyed visiting laboratories and front-runner companies that produced the latest advances in technology and he always asked himself how they could be applied to India in order to alleviate poverty. In Japan, Rajiv praised the "first Asian country to have assimilated scientific knowledge" and underlined the achievementsof his own country: "In 1947, we did not even produce lathes; today webuild our own atomic reactors and we launch satellites into space." He was especially satisfied at having come out with flying colours from what he considered as the greatest challenge of his mandate, the 1987 drought, classed as the most severe of the 20th century and which affected 258 million people and 168 million head of cattle. He took the matter firmly in hand, keeping in close contact with the local civil servants responsible for the programmes of development and aid, ensuring that what was left over in the reserve was distributed appropriately and that the cost of the emergency aid was turned into investments for development, for example by digging wells and carrying out irrigation works. His dedication and almost military planning, which reminded many of his mother's ability for organization, meant that the country did not have to import grain and, for the first time in its history, India came out of a drought on a national scale without famines, without epidemics, without deaths and with a positive gross national product. "It was a great satisfaction for him!"

Sonia would say.

On other fronts, the results were not so encouraging. In foreign policy, Rajiv had inherited a problematic situation in Sri Lanka, partly created by his mother. The former island of Ceylon was a country with a population of 17 million, mostly of Sinhalese culture and Buddhist religion, except for a minority in the north: two and a half million Tamils, professing Hinduism, who had strong racial and linguistic links to the 55 million Tamils who inhabited the Indian state of Tamil Nadu. This minority had always felt sidelined by the Sinhalese majority. They felt that they were treated as second-class citizens, especially since the government declared Sinhalese to be the official language of the island in the 50's. Years of resentment led to the emergence of a guerrilla group, the Tamil Tigers, who sought independence for their territory in the north-eastern corner of the island. For years, the Tigers were able to count on discreet backing from India. The head of government of the Indian state of Tamil Nadu, a former Tamil film actor turned populist, provided them with weapons, money and refuge. Indira turned a blind eye for reasons of internal political strategy, since this man was her only ally in the south and she needed his political backing.

In 1983, the Tigers were so strong that they intensified their armed struggle. The government of Sri Lanka reacted with every means at its disposal and in a brutal manner, so the conflict went into a spiral of terrorism and repression which reinforced even further the Tamils' desire for independence. The very high levels of savagery and brutality on both sides provided a bloody contrast with the Paradise-like beauty of the island. The serene expression of the Buddhas carved in stone by the ancient dwellers on the island soon seemed out of place.

When Rajiv came to power, he came face to face with the problem that an avalanche of refugees were crossing into India, fleeing from the offensive of the island's army. Apart from the logistical problem it meant to feed and house thousands of people, there was the risk that the discontent of the Tamils from the island might infect those on the sub-continent, feeding the desire for independence of the Indian state of Tamil Nadu, one of the states with a very marked personality of its own, and creating more secessionist tension in India, as if there were not enough of that already.

"You remind me of your mother, when she had to deal with the first wave of refugees from Bangladesh," Sonia told him. "At first she didn't really know what to do."

"What has to be done is to fix the problem at source, that's what she would have thought. We mustn't give the Tamils in Sri Lanka reasons to come here. The problem has to be dealt with in Colombo. Like my mother, who had to fix it in Bangladesh."

Rajiv sent a series of special envoys to Sri Lanka, whose mission it was to convince the government of the island to grant a certain degree of autonomy to the Tamils, letting it be understood that if the government made peace with the Tamils, India would promise to completely cut off aid to the guerrillas. But the government of Sri Lanka, having embarked on a military solution, took no notice. It continued with its offensive and imposed a blockade on the peninsula of Jaffna, the territory of the Tamils in the north- east of the island. Petrol, foodstuffs and medicines began to run short.

"They aren't taking any notice. They have to understand that India cannot sit back and do nothing. If they don't invite us to help in finding a solution to a problem that threatens us directly, we'll intervene withoutasking for permission."

"Another war?" said Sonia. "Think about it."

Rajiv planned his move well. In the blockade he saw the opportunity for India to assert itself once and for all. He decided to send five cargo planes escorted by fighters to the Jaffna peninsula to help the population by dropping them forty tons of rice, medicines and various other supplies. It was a gesture moved by humanitarian motives and at the same time by India's desire to reaffirm itself as a power in the region.

The pressure worked. The president of Sri Lanka finally signed an agreement with Rajiv, according to which the Sinhalese government granted wide-ranging autonomy to the Tamils. The agreement also stipulated that an Indian peace-keeping force would be transferred to the island. The Sri Lankan army would withdraw its barracks, and the Tamil Tiger militants would be persuaded – or forced – to give up their weapons. "This agreement not only puts an end to the conflict," Rajiv declared, "it also brings peace and justice to the minority communities of the island."

"Your mother would be proud of you," Sonia told him.

But it was not like Indira's victory in Bangladesh. Rajiv had sold his chickens before they were hatched.

The Sinhalese majority, fearful that their interests would be prejudiced by the concessions made to the Tamils, reacted violently to the terms of the agreement. When Rajiv travelled to Colombo at the end of July 1987 toratify it, the agents of the Special Protection Group who accompanied him tried to dissuade him from reviewing the guard of honour as protocol required. "It may be dangerous," they told him. "Uncontrolled elements may have infiltrated and there's a lot of tension on the island..."

"What? Here we are to sign an agreement that guarantees their peace and security... and you're going to tell them that I'm scared to review the guard of honour?"

His bodyguards, who knew how stubborn their boss could be, did not insist. A short time before, one of them had suffered the anger of the Prime Minister personally. He had dared to complain that Rajiv drove too fast in his Range Rover, a gift from King Hussein of Jordan. He liked to drive from home to his office in Parliament in it, and his guards could not follow him down the streets of New Delhi. Rajiv had found the man too insolent andhad asked for him to be transferred. The pressure of his job made traits of stubbornness and determination emerge in Rajiv which were reminiscent of his brother and his mother.

So he went on with his programme and accompanied the president of Sri Lanka in reviewing the guard of honour, with music from a military band, martial salutes and all the paraphernalia. Suddenly, a soldier dressed inthe white uniform of the navy, broke ranks and threw himself at him, withthe intention of hitting him on the head with the butt of his rifle. Rajiv saw the attack coming and ducked just in time to avoid the blow, which would have cracked his skull open, and which he received fully on his shoulder. It all occurred so quickly that most of those present did not realize what had happened. Rajiv wanted to minimize the incident and refused to be treatedby doctors. He stood listening to the national anthem, putting up with the pain, and he continued with his agenda, imperturbably. Only when he got back on board the plane for the return journey did he allow himself to be treated by his doctor. He would have liked to wait and tell Sonia himself, so that she would not have a fright, but television had already sent the pictures all round the world. Sonia and their children had seen them at home in the sitting room and once again they had their hearts in their mouths. Another small incident had arisen to remind them of the constant danger in which they lived. "For a long time," Sonia would say, "he could not move his shoulder or sleep on his left side."

Rajiv had not yet landed in New Delhi when the Sri Lankan government asked for the military aid clause to be put into practice. A peace force of several thousand Indian soldiers was dispatched to the island with the aim of supervising the ceasefire and disarming the guerrillas and, once their objective was fulfilled, returning. But the troops were regarded with suspicion by both sides: by the Sinhalese majority, which accused them of violating their sovereignty, and by the Tigers, who until then had thought that India was on their side. When the soldiers in the peace-keeping force asked them to lay down their weapons, the Tamils suddenly added more conditions that were unacceptable, making a mockery of the agreement. They went back into the jungle, from where they launched bloody attacks on the peace-keeping force. By having to defend themselves, the Indians ended up being even more involved in the conflict, taking on the role that the Sri Lankan army had previously had. Rajiv came to send almost seventy thousand soldiers, which spread panic in Parliament in New Delhi:

"The Prime Minister is turning Sri Lanka into India's Vietnam!" they accused him from the opposition benches.

Rajiv had been very ingenuous to think that the Tamils would stick to the rules. "They broke each of the promises they had made to us," Rajiv would declare. "They deliberately set out to destroy the agreement either because they were unable or unwilling to make the transition from an armed conflict to a democratic process." Rajiv had put all his money on one card, but the Tamils left him in the lurch. Because he had taken away the backing they had always enjoyed in India, they saw him as a traitor to their cause.

*　　*　　*

Frustration, disillusionment and exasperation were also the lot of a prime minister, especially when the results of regional elections seemed to confirm the predictions of the hawks of his party, who had warned him against a policy that would not give immediate results to the poor. In 1987, the Congress Party lost in several states, causing an increase in discontent among the old guard, who began to question Rajiv's leadership of the party. Added to the Sri Lanka problem and the electoral defeat, there was a scandal that caused irreparable damage to his image as *Mr Clean*. On April 16th, 1987, Swedish radio announced that millions of dollars had been paid in commission to Indian civil servants and members of the Congress Party by the Swedish armaments company, Bofors, in connexion with a contract for the sale of 410 mortars to the Indian armed forces. The contract had been the result of Rajiv's decision to improve the equipment of the Indian army, the fourth largest in the world after the United States, the USSR and China.

Rajiv and his government reacted fiercely to the allegations on Swedish radio, several times denying that commissions had been paid. The opposition smelt fear in the ranks of the government and launched an attack on the Prime Minister with all the means at its command. The Press came to accuse him covertly of having taken a commission through Sonia's family, alluding to the proximity between Turin and Geneva, as though to let it be understood that shady Swiss accounts had been used, handled by the family or friends of the family. There were even reporters who phoned Sonia's parents back in Orbassano, and poor Stefano Maino suddenly found himself involved in alleged arms dealing and payment of commissions! The only thing those calls did was to alarm them even more, because the distance made their anxiety greater, and the fear of what might happen to their daughter and grandchildren was already great. After digging deeper into the affair, the Indian press brought to light the name of a businessman who had been involved in several contracts for the sale of helicopters and arms to the Indian state to the Indian state by Italian companies. Ottavio Quattrochi, the exuberant friend who had been part of Rajiv and Sonia's intimate circle of friends for years, must certainly have received a fat commission in the Bofors deal. From that to insinuating that Quattrochi had passed part of the commission on to them abroad, there was only a short step, which the reporters happily took. What a juicy scandal!

Although no publication could provide proof, the damage was done and Rajiv's ingenuousness and lack of experience did no more than make it worse. Instead of ignoring the baseless accusations, he came out in his own defence in Parliament: "I declare categorically in this high assembly of democracy that neither my family nor I have received any commission whatsoever in these Bofors transactions. That is the truth." But the truth no longer mattered. The important thing for Rajiv's adversaries was that he had taken the bait, that instead of ignoring the allegations from the start, he had reacted so strongly that he had opened up the Pandora's box of insinuations and false suspicions. He again denied that commissions had been paid or that any Indian citizen had benefitted from that contract, and by doing so he sank deeper into the mire of the scandal. In a country where even a postman getsa small bribe for handing over the post to a poor man in a hut, where the practice of the middleman exists in all facets of life and is as old as the culture itself, it was hard to believe that in a contract of a thousand million dollars no one had received a cent. In spite of the fact that a joint parliamentary committee concluded that the process of drawing up and evaluating the contract had been objective and correct, that the decision to adjudicate it to Bofors had been based only on merit and that there was no evidence of intermediaries at the time the contract was signed, Rajiv was already subjected to a public verdict, and that verdict accused him of hiding something. "Perhaps it is true that Rajiv is not involved in corruption," the Press admitted. "But then he must be involved in hiding that corruption!" they immediately proclaimed. When a reporter from *India Today* asked why Rajiv was not responding to this last allegation, he replied in annoyance, "Do I have to answer every dog that barks?" Later, Rajiv admitted that neither he nor his cabinet had known how to handle the problem. In fact, he had reacted like a decent man. He had not done so like a hardened politician might have done, looking for a scapegoat and putting the blame on him. He did not count on the fact that he was moving in the dirty world of politics where the truth was not the important thing, but manipulation of the truth in order to spread doubt and damage the image of the adversary. Sonia was sad for him, and furious at being involved in such a piece of nonsense in such a ridiculous but destructive way, through her family and the Quattrochis. She realized that she had become the target of all the criticisms and that not even in their own home was she free of it. That was the end of the Sunday brunches. Neither Maria nor Ottavio Quattrochi nor any of the businessmen or diplomats they knew ever came back to the Prime Minister's residence again. How unfair, thought Sonia. Especially because she had been a firsthand witness to the general terms of the negotiations. They had taken place over a lasagne that she had cooked personally for the occasion. It was in January 1986, and the Swedish Prime Minister, Olof Palme, on a visit to New Delhi, had come for lunch at home. He and Rajiv had become friends during some conferences on disarmament at the headquarters of the UN in New York. Rahul and Priyanka had also been present at that lunch, during which both statesmen openly discussed the terms of the contract and Rajiv insisted on his veto on intermediaries, precisely to make the cost of the transaction cheaper.

How could Sonia forget Olof Palme, so committed to the problems of the Third World and who shared so many points of view with Rajiv, such as opposition to the apartheid regime or support for the non-aligned countries? Less than a month after that meal, Sonia was horrified to find out on television that, on February 18th, 1986, the Swedish leader had been assassinated in the middle of the street, when he was coming out of the cinema with his wife. My God! Was there nowhere safe left in the world? If something like that happens in Sweden, what can happen to us here in India? Suddenly the Bofors affair became a crusade that the opposition used to throw Rajiv out of his post, although the reporters and newspaper editors felt frustrated at their inability to provide definite evidence of misappropriation of funds on the part of the government. No one seemed to know who had received the money from the Swedish company, not even the government, and Rajiv even less. But everyone admitted now that the clause in the contract which vetoed the intermediaries had been violated. Had members of the Congress Party, disassociated from the government, received it and had the money ended up in the coffers of the party? Had Ottavio Quattrochi received it, using his proximity to power? Was that possible without the person ultimately responsible, in other words the Prime Minister, knowing? Rajiv always maintained that it was not, but the doubt weighed like a ton of bricks. The climate of uncertainty smashed his credibility to pieces. During the first two years of his mandate, he had enjoyed favourable press and seemed incapable of doing anything wrong. Even the opposition had found it difficult to criticize his actions, limiting themselves to criticizing his style: "Indian politics no longer smells of the poor, as in the time of Mahatma Gandhi," a famous journalist from a rival party had declared, "now, with Rajiv, it smells of after shave."

"At the beginning nothing I did was wrong," Rajiv would say. "Suddenly, nothing I did was right. Of course, neither was true." From calling him *Mr Clean*, they began to call him pejoratively *the boy*, with the intention of comparing him unfavourably with his mother. "Would *the boy* be up to it?" was the topic of an editorial in a daily newspaper.

Actually, most of Rajiv's problems had to do with his inexperience in politics and his candour as a human being. He found it hard to set the limits between loyalty to friends and the good of the public. The name of the Bachchan brothers, childhood friends in whose home Sonia had lived during her first days in India, became associated with murky financial scandals. A more prudent prime minister would have distanced himself from them. But Rajiv did not: rather the opposite, he felt resentful because his friends were being criticized. His mother had always said that in politics there are no social relationships, but he was too good a friend to be a good politician. At first, he refused to admit that his friends might fail him and he would rather see a conspiracy among his political adversaries than the truth. However, many trusted friends that he had named as advisors ended up disappointing him. One of them, a pilot, the one asked to remind him when his flying licence would run out and to deal with matters in his constituency in Amethi, was accused by the Press of building a swimming pool made of marble imported from Italy at his home. Once again, instead of distancing himself from him, Rajiv came out in his defence and made a comment that did more political harm than if he had really made an error in government. He said casually that many pilots had homes with swimming pools, a declaration which, made in any country in the West by a head of State who had also been a pilot in an airline company, would not have caused any furore at all. In India it got people's backs up. The opposition threw in his face his lack of respect for "Indian sensitivity". He was very criticized for his habit of taking a few days holiday at New Year with his family in exotic places, such as the Lakshadweep Islands, in the Indian Ocean, or the Andaman Islands, in the Bay of Bengal. In the West it would have seemed reasonable for someone who worked so much to deserve a break, that his children who lived shut up all year might enjoy a few days of freedom and safety, but in a country as poor as India, the fact that the head of the government had a good time was frowned upon. Actually, Rajiv and Sonia continued with their habit of gathering as a family at Christmas and the New Year, but in 1988 they stopped doing so in Italy. In October that year, Stefano Maino had been struck down by a heart attack and they thought it was better to invite the family somewhere that would not remind them of their former gatherings around the patriarch.

Sonia went to Orbassano for the funeral, practically

incognito, and hardly allowed herself to be seen. In addition to the security problems there was a logical feeling of profound desolation and a desire to be with the family, with her mother and her sisters, digging deep into their memories and consoling each other. On hearing the sound of the first spadeful of earth that the gravedigger threw on to the coffin, Sonia shuddered. Part of her life was being buried forever. She would no longer hear the advice of that wise man from the Asiago mountains which, now she could see, had marked her more than she had ever thought.

Back in the house, she was chatting to Danilo Quadra, Stefano's old friend, who went over the last moments of the life of the former shepherd. He told her that they had been playing dominos in Nino's bar, in Orbassano square, as they had done every day for years, and that as soon as he got home, to that house that was a symbol for Stefano of his success in life, he dropped down dead. That he had died without any suffering. A few days later, Danilo told her that Stefano had been annoyed since he had found out about the renewed outbreak of attacks on Sonia in the Indian press.

"'They don't want my daughter there because she's from here,' he told me. Is that true?"

"I don't think so," said Sonia. "The ones that don't like me are those who are against my husband."

"He was annoyed that just because you are Italian, the Indian government avoids any contracts with companies from here," Danilo went on to tell her. "A few days before he died, he told me that Fiat had made a very good offer for the sale of tractors, but that in the end the Japanese went off with the contract... because your husband's government was afraid of being accused of favouring Italian companies. Is that right?" Danilo asked her again.

Sonia looked at him with her dark eyes, swollen from tiredness and grief, and nodded. When she was alone, she went to bed in what had been her room before she was married, and she wondered, as if surprised at herself, Am I really from here? Her father would have turned in his grave if he could have heard her say something like that, but she felt an indefinable feeling of strangeness, of not belonging now to that setting which had been the stage of her youth. As though the death of her father had precipitated the feeling of having no roots. Sonia found it hard to recognize herself in the country of her childhood. Her mind was too far away from the day to day concerns of the people of Orbassano for her to identify with them. In fact she had lived more years in India than in Italy, more years in an environment focussed on the problems of governing a sixth of humanity than in an environment aimed at mere individual well-being. It had been some time since her heart had stopped wavering between the two worlds. She was from there, and her father's death had confirmed it for her, in a secret way, as though the disappearance of the person who had most opposed her designs made her see more clearly where the truth lay.

She stayed inside the house for several days, not wanting to do anything. She did not even have the strength to go and see Pier Luigi; she did not want to talk to anyone, or give explanations, or talk about her life... Was it possible to tell her life? How could she expect anyone to understand the life she led? Only the closest family could understand that, and now not even her father. Dark thoughts came over her... "I should have been more loving towards him," she told herself, "I should have insisted that he come to Delhi more often, and been closer to him and taken him to the doctor and perhaps we could have avoided the heart attack..." It was a litany of reproaches caused by the huge grief at having lost the man who, together with Rajiv, had most loved her. When she closed her eyes, she remembered the tickling of her father's moustache on her cheek, his smell of soap, his smile and his frown, his words, always wise, full of very basic common sense. She remembered when he took her to see a completed job and he showed it to her with the pride of a job well done. "Why has he gone so soon?" Sonia asked herself. She remembered Indira, who had lost her husband to a heart attack, which is like a light going out suddenly. Or when a bomb explodes and leaves a crater. They say it is best to die like that, but Sonia would have liked to say goodbye to him, to tell him how much she loved him... even if just that once. It seemed so strange that her father was no longer there that one night she got up and went to the cemetery, to pray at his grave. She found her sister there, having had the same idea. They wanted to be with him, because sometimes the subconscious mind takes a while to accept what is inevitable. A few days later, Sonia went back to New Delhi and no one ever saw her again in Orbassano.

38

History was repeating itself. Rajiv could not be Prime Minister without provoking the same animosity that his grandfather and his mother had aroused before him. In 1989, parties on the Right and the Left allied themselves with members of the old Janata Party, the coalition that had been born to defeat Indira, with the aim of presenting a common front in the general elections and achieving the same goal: getting a Gandhi out of power again. During the campaign, an episode of fierce violence in the state of Bihar between Moslems and Hindus damaged Rajiv's already tarnished image even more. There were over a thousand dead before Rajiv could manage to quiet the disturbances.

Then he went on travelling round the country, just like his mother, piling up rallies and kilometres and selling the achievements of his government. The difference is that his mother had little protection around her, which allowed to shake hands, give out hugs and, certainly, be in physical contact with the people. Every move that Rajiv made, however, meant the mobilization of some three hundred security agents, who did not allow him to get as close, except in absolutely controlled situations. From time to time, he skipped the protocol, even if he had to argue with his bodyguards, but in general, every one of his movements meant so much in terms of logistics that it had to be thought about to see if it was really worth it or not. He knew that so many limitations made him appear as a distant leader to the masses and therefore he struggled to be free of the surveillance. "I have never been afraid for myself," he declared in an interview. As usual, the one who was more aware of the danger was Sonia.

On campaign, Rajiv travelled in an army Boeing, paid for by the party. It took off from New Delhi before dawn and this allowed him to visit three or four states in one day. In order to reach remote places, he used helicopters which had practiced making emergency landings the day before. He finished the day's work after midnight and stayed in the plane to sleep for a few hours, or in government lodgings. Only someone with the resistance and a sportsman's attitude to life that Rajiv had could stand such a rhythm. No doubt Indians did not profess the same adoration for him as they did for his grandfather, or the almost reverential respect with which they surrounded Indira, but they appreciated this decent man who struggled to prove himself worthy of the dynastic legacy he had inherited. On several occasions his son Rahul went with him, an adolescent with glasses who looked very much like him. For the young man, it was an introduction to the crowds. The people wanted to touch him as if by doing so they might be infected by the magic and power of a Gandhi. Priyanka was not going to be less than her brother, and she insisted that she and her mother should go to the Amethi constituency, for which Rajiv was MP, to pull out all the stops. Priyanka very much enjoyed campaigning with her mother. They were both very popular and much loved by the million and a half inhabitants of Amethi, who now enjoyed the prosperity that Rajiv had promised them during his first campaign. Amethi could now boast of having all its roads asphalted; almost all the villages had electricity and drinking water and a little industrial boom had drastically reduced unemployment. Those were the advantages of having their MP as Prime Minister. Mother and daughter were welcomed with great love and effusiveness. Sonia was the main attraction for the peasants, anxious to place a garland of flowers round the neck of this foreign woman who intrigued them because she was always dressed in a sari and spoke Hindi fluently. "I may be a daughter of Italy, but I am the daughter-in-law of Amethi," she told them to explain her origins, and her smile showed her dainty dimples. As Sonia did not like speaking in public, she preferred to go from house to house, or from hut to hut, and encourage people to vote for her husband. Mother and daughter also improvised rallies at the side of the road, where they explained the same as Rajiv and Rahul thousands of kilometres from there to other peasants even poorer than these. They gave out stickers and badges to the young people, and adhesive *bindis* (the dot between the eyes) with the logo of the Congress Party, the open palm of a hand, to the women. "I only want you to realize how the situation of your villages has improved since Rajiv was elected to Parliament eight years ago…" Sonia said to them, before adding, "Brothers and sisters, if you want us to go on working together, vote for my husband."

Her husband was no longer the novice politician of five years before. Adulation no longer had the same effect on him, and he was hardly embarrassed at all by the songs that were dedicated to him or the flowery adjectives used to describe him. He was impatient to get people to understand the progress achieved, the new policies and the original initiatives undertaken. He shouted himself hoarse explaining how he had solved most of the conflicts inherited in 1984 and how he had managed to put the economy on the path to a growth of 6%, four points more than when his mother was in power, but he had the impression that he had lost his powers of persuasion and that his words were empty. It irritated him to have the feeling that he had done things right and at the same time he had to constantly defend himself from attacks and ill-intentioned insinuations. The fact is that his image had gone from being "the brave son who took on his mother's mantle" to "a European rich boy who lived at the expense of the people". It was inevitable that after calming down so many conflicts, new ones should arise, but the important thing was that India was still united and a country respected internationally with a rising economy. However, the opposition hammered him with an avalanche of slander. Sonia was a favourite target of the critics: a manipulating foreigner who diverted resources away from poor Indians to capitalist paradises with the help of her friends and family, in the purest Mafia style, so typical of her country. The problem of her nationality was so thorny that she was advised not to go and welcome the Pope on his stopover in New Delhi. It was not considered politically correct for millions of Indians to see her curtsey and kiss the ring of the Supreme Pontiff of the Catholic Church. In fact, neither the politicians nor the masses nor the media were used to the glamour of a married couple in the highest post in the government. There was no tradition in India of Kennedys or Blairs, because all the previous prime ministers had been widowed, beginning with grandfather Nehru.

By the end of the campaign, Rajiv had had his fingers burned and was disappointed. He began to have doubts whether his work and the sincerity of his intentions would finally overcome, as he had thought at first. "The real world is a jungle," he wrote to his daughter Priyanka, "but not even the law of the jungle works when you are in public life." His looks reflected his disappointment. He no longer had the serene face and relaxed expression of the past. With age, his features had tensed, his step was heavier, his voicehad lost its firmness, although it was still warm, because he was an affable man.

In the opposition, an exultant Maneka Gandhi was also putting into practice, in her own way, everything she had learned from her mother-in- law. She campaigned in a constituency neighbouring Rajiv's, with all the vigour of her youth and her desire to get revenge. Indira would have been scandalized from beyond the grave to discover that her daughter-in-law had become one of the secretaries general of a new version of the Janata coalition, by which she had managed to be beaten and sent to jail. Furthermore, Maneka was working as a journalist and reporter specializing in the environment, and above all in the protection of animals, a subject veryclose the ideology of the Hindu Right, always very concerned about protecting the sacred cow. The influential magazine *India Today* described her campaigning style: "This is the real Maneka: mature, self-confident, an untiring politician who knows exactly how to win hearts in rural areas. She wears saris with the saffron-yellow and green colours of her party and her head is always covered; the perfect image of a demure but determinedwidow." She had no scruples about using her links with the family to back the opposing party. The slogans, written on brick and adobe walls, offered a curious panegyric of the "in-law": "The storm of revolution: Maneka Gandhi" or "Indira's brave daughter-in-law will give her blood for the nation", as though her relationship to the family was enough to make herinto a potential martyr.

The elections took place from November 22nd to 24th, 1989. The greatest voluntary mobilization in the world of men, women and materials with a single aim came to an end with few interruptions and hardly any disturbances. Three and a half million civil servants supervised 589,449 electoral colleges so that five hundred million people could place their votes in the urns. The whole process, which was enjoyed like a big party, was a reason for pride for most of the population who found in democracy a new God that linked them above and beyond their differences in caste, race or religion. Rajiv won again in Amethi, but the Congress Party, for the first time in its history, did not gain an absolute majority in the national Parliament. Analysts agreed that the Bofors affair had played an important role in the results. Those elections marked the end of what was called the "dominant party system" because no party has ever managed to win an absolute majority of seats in Parliament again.

The rumour had gone round that Rajiv had a flight booked to go to Italy in case of defeat, but that was not true. Shortly before the elections, a close friend, also fond of music, had asked him: "Let's suppose you lose the elections..."

"For me that would mean peace," Rajiv answered. "I'll sit down and listen to music with the children. I'll take up my old hobbies again, like the radio and photography."

But he had said so lightly, owing to his tiredness and exhaustion. Both he and his family were disappointed after all the efforts made. Priyanka, who had inherited Indira's fighting spirit, would not accept defeat.

"Dad," she said, "if the Congress Party has won the most seats, you have the right to form a government... Why don't you?"

In effect, Rajiv had the right to form the government, but he decided not to do so. Even if he had had enough support among the minority parties, he thought that this was not the time to go on.

"I think it's best to stay out of it," he told her. "I'm going to resign. Let the new boys worry about it now. I interpret the results to the effect that the people are not as satisfied as they should be. It's logical after so much expectation at the beginning that now there's been a negative reaction…"

Pushed out of power by the pendulum of democracy, Rajiv felt very frustrated. Not because of the verdict of the people, but for not having been able to do all the things he had set himself to do, and because of his inability to cope in the viper's nest of Indian politics. Now that he knew how hard it was to build something, to change concepts and ideas, he felt dizzy to think how easy it would be to destroy his work of recent years. Perhaps his vision of India had been too innocent: in five years, he had wanted his old nation, so fearful of changes and yet at the same time so wanting them, to undertake a journey of several centuries into the future. Was it not too much to ask of that old Indian elephant? For a moment, Sonia thought that he might leave politics, but when she saw him so downhearted, it was she who encouraged him to keep at it. When a journalist asked Rajiv if he had finally accepted politics as his profession, he answered with good humour, "Yes, except that sometimes I feel like taking a break. I think that's a very human thing to do." Sonia knew that it was impossible for them to go back to their old lifestyle. When her husband looked back, he did so with nostalgia, but he accepted that it was all in the past: "I'm the same as I was before," he said in a television interview, "but what has changed is everything else. I had a very comfortable life, a small family, a well-paid job with a lot of free time… but all that came to an end." Rajiv was imbued with a feeling of fate which made him think that a man cannot complain about his destiny. Recent years had made him grow in a direction that had placed him on a different plane in life. Now the challenges were much greater and the expectations were different. Above all, the responsibility of improving the lives of eight hundred million people had become a priority for him. "That responsibility weighs so much that it changes everything I did and do now. What is not going to change is my commitment to the people of India to improve their lives, and for the nation to take its place in the world." The defeat had not altered his faith. He knew that his name was the only, unique resource for his party, shaken by several defeats in different states. His plan was to go on reforming the party to make it into a more democratic organization, as it had been in the time of his grandfather. A non-denominational party able to cover all trends and beliefs. A common home that would be the best antidote for the growing trend towards religious factions that the country was experiencing. In order to do that work, it was better to be in the opposition.

"With this coalition between Communists and the Hindu fundamentalist Right," he told his daughter, who was always very interested in the day to day details of life in politics, "...what happened with Grandma and the Janata Party will happen... It will fall of its own accord. It's just a question of time until the leaders start squabbling for power, you'll soon see."

Rajiv resigned on November 29th, 1989: "Elections are won and lost...the work of a nation is never done. I want to thank the people of India for the love they have so generously given me." These were words that evoked the words in his grandfather's will, in which Nehru had stated that he was moved by the love that all classes of Indians had shown him. They were words that sounded like a farewell. The appointment that Rajiv Gandhi had with destiny was coming inexorably closer.

Just as he had foretold, the two most important leaders of the new coalition became embroiled in a struggle over the designation of the new Prime Minister. It was a bad start which augured a stormy course ahead. But among the new members of the government was a specially euphoric person who had been part of the family dynasty of the Nehrus. On being named as Minister for the Environment and Forests, Maneka Gandhi finally saw her old dream come true. Now she was in power. Now she had her revenge, and she intended to take it very far. It was one more humiliation for Rajiv, although he was over the scares along the intricate paths of politics, and nothing in the world could surprise him now. For the rest of the family, who had seen how Maneka used their name with a total lack of scruples, it was a bitter pill that only the certainty that the government would be a flash in the pan could sweeten.

For Sonia, having lost the elections meant another move, this time the last one. They had to leave the Prime Minister's official residence and they moved to another Colonial style white villa, all on one floor and surrounded by a large garden. It was at number 10, Janpath Avenue, formerly Queen's

Way, one of the main thoroughfares of New Delhi, lined with flame trees and *neem* trees with very spreading, leafy branches, and whose bitter leaves "cure everything", according to popular belief. Perhaps their protective shade was responsible for curing the melancholy they felt at the defeat because, as soon as they moved, the atmosphere at home livened up. Life became a little quieter and lighter, as if they had taken a weight off their shoulders, the weight of power. Rajiv was still very busy with his work in Parliament and in the party, but the rhythm was more bearable. "He was relaxed," Sonia would write, "almost relieved. Once again he enjoyed simple, day to day pleasures such as uninterrupted meals, sitting on at table with us, watching a video from time to time instead of shutting himself in hisoffice to work." The chef of the exquisite Bukhara Indian restaurant, where formerly they used to go as a family for the Saturday buffet, welcomed themwith open arms when he saw them again after such a long time. They went there to celebrate Rahul's birthday, and his imminent departure for the United States. The children were no longer little, but young adults who devoured the newspapers and were very interested in everything that wenton around them. When they could no longer go on studying at home because they had finished the equivalent of 'A' levels, Rajiv and Sonia had decidedto send their son to Harvard University, thus putting an end to the family tradition of educating the children in England, as three generations of Nehrus had done. Priyanka preferred to stay in New Delhi, studying psychology at Jesus and Mary College. Her obsession with politics worried her father so much that he mentioned it to Benazir Bhutto, when they met for the last time in Paris, as guests of President Mitterand to celebrate the bi- centenary of the French Revolution.

"Please," Rajiv told her, "when you see her, try to convince her not to get into all this."

If she was going to listen to anyone, he knew his daughter would listen to Benazir, whose own father had been murdered after a parody of a trial under the orders of the military dictator. It was another example, close by and terrible, of the fate that awaited those who allowed themselves to be seduced by politics. "She doesn't realize how dangerous it is," Rajiv insistedto Benazir.

He thought that as he was out of power, the threat hanging

over him and his children would diminish, but the reports that reached him regarding his security kept him worried all the time. The threats against his life had increased. In 1984, he was top on the lists of three terrorist groups. Fiveyears later, he was number one for a dozen organizations, including the Tamil Tigers. The Punjab problem seemed to have been solved, but there were other conflicts, especially between Hindus and Moslems, potentially equally as dangerous. "You have both lived in very difficult circumstances for a long time: five years in an area limited to the house and the garden," Rajiv had written to his children on one occasion. "That is the time in your lives when you should have lived in freedom, meeting people your own age and discovering the world as it really is. Unfortunately, the circumstances have not permitted us to offer you normal lives." That letter hinted at a feeling of guilt and at the same time of fate. Rajiv was aware that he was not master of his own destiny. What had catapulted him into politics had been anaccident, then a terrorist attack had brought him to the highest position in the government of the nation, and, finally, the Bofors scandal had put him in opposition. He had not been able to change the direction of events and inthat letter he seemed to excuse himself for the suffering it all might have caused to his children.

In fact, the defeat in the elections was a blessing for Sonia. In August, they went to Mussoorie, in the mountains, and Rajiv drove the car himself. Itwas their first escapade together for 19 months and there, with the chain of the Himalayas as a backcloth, they celebrated what would be his last birthday.

Then, at Christmas, when Rahul came back from Harvard, the whole family went to spend a week's holiday at the country house in Mehrauli, the one that Firoz Gandhi had bought with the aim of spending his last years there quietly with Indira. They had never been able to live in that house, the details of whose construction Rajiv had supervised for years and paid for outof his savings. "It was the first time we had stayed in a house that was entirely ours," Sonia would write. Rajiv took care to ensure that everything was just as it should be. The children helped to take out all the garden furniture and clean the aging inside while he prepared something to nibble, because he preferred that to formal meals. They hid the chocolate that he liked so much because they thought that since he had left power he had put on some weight. They remembered the Holi festivals they had spent there in their childhood, throwing coloured powder all over each other and ending up filthy. They played badminton and Scrabble and Sonia began to clear part of the garden of weeds with the idea of planting a small kitchen garden. The countryside had always called to her, since her childhood in Lusiana. How she would have liked to have her father there with them for that holiday! How he would have liked the house! She thought about him a lot. In her weekly phone calls to her mother in Orbassano, she almost let herself becarried away be the reflex of asking after her father.

"We enjoyed every minute of the six days we spent there," Sonia would remember. "It reminded us of our lives as they were back at the beginning, and the flavour of the lives we would have had if we could have chosen them for ourselves." Many friends were surprised that they were still as romantically in love as the first day. "I wasn't surprised because theywere always very much in love," Christian von Stieglitz, the common friend who had introduced them in Cambridge and who went to visit them during those days at the house in Mehrauli, would remember. "...For work reasons, I went to Delhi a lot at that time, and it was pleasure to see them always so lovey-dovey after so many years of marriage. In private, they were always kissing and holding hands." On December 9th, 1990, Sonia's birthday, she received a present from Rajiv with a note: "For Sonia, who does not change with time, who is even more beautiful today than when I saw her for the firsttime sitting in a corner in the Varsity restaurant, that lovely day..."

39

But, as usual, the interval of happiness was brought to a close by political events, which moved forwards more quickly than Rajiv had expected. India was sliding down a dangerous slope, pushed by one of the parties of the coalition in power, the BJP (Bharatiya Janata Party), the old Hindu fundamentalist Right that had so castigated Indira. The party had grown until it had become the most dangerous adversary of the Congress Party and a potential danger to the unity of the country. Backed by the RSS, an extremist militant organization, the BJP called for a "Hindu India" where the minorities would have to live under the thumb of the majority, not as equals. This philosophy was diametrically opposed to that of Nehru and the Congress Party, because it denied the founding principle of modern India, which was a non-denominational state that proclaimed the separation of State and religion, and the equality of all religions before the law. The rise of the BJP coincided with a worsening of religious violence in the north of the country. These were disturbances that did not settle down of their own accord, but lasted until the forces of order put a stop to them. The origin of those disturbances was always the same and they were usually set off by a trivial detail, such as a dispute over the boundaries of a piece of land, or a space on the pavement, or because a pig urinated on the wall of a mosque or a dead cow was found near a Hindu temple. Whatever it was, as soon as the spark flared, the violence spread stunningly fast, fed by rumours, always false, which magnified the original incident, turning a mere confrontation between two individuals into a holy war between religions. The community organizations and politicians who identified with one or other of the factions, fed the fire of discord, so that from words they moved on to blows, then to knives, and so on until they were using Molotov cocktails and bullets.

In India, conflicts of caste and religion began to feed on each other from the eighties, specifically after the entire population of a village of untouchables in Tamil Nadu took the decision to convert to Islam to escape the rigid Hindu system of castes. Those poor people even changed the name of the village, which from Menashkipuram came to be called Rehmatnagar. The Hindu fundamentalists screamed blue murder: "Hinduism is in danger!" and accused the countries of the Gulf of financing the Moslems of India. The reality was that the untouchables were finally reacting to centuries of oppression at the hands of the landowners, who in that area were high caste Hindus.

Then, an apparently inoffensive event inflamed the spirits of the Hindu fundamentalists even more: the broadcasting in 1987 of a series based on the *Ramayana*, the most popular Hindu epic, the closest thing Hindus have to holy writings. The television adaptation, a mixture of soap opera and mythology, consisted of 104 episodes which were screened on Sunday mornings. It was such a smash hit that state television asked another Bollywood producer to film the *Mahabharata* epic. Both series became the soaps with the greatest audience in the whole world. 85% of Indian viewers saw all the episodes, a unique figure in the history of television.

When the series were being shown, activity stopped all over the country. Taxis, bicycles and rickshaws disappeared from the streets. The phones stopped ringing. Prayers and cremation rites were postponed. Civil servants, housewives, shopkeepers, prostitutes, prisoners, water-sellers, sweepers, children, poor people digging amongst the rubbish... everyoneleft what they were doing to get in front of a television in someone's house, in a shop, in the village square, or peeping through the windows of the houses of families that were privileged enough to have that extraordinary appliance. Many spectators believed what they were seeing word for word, as though the gods that came out on the screen lived in the world of men. When the god Rama came out in the series, they lit a little oil lamp and started to pray there and then. In India, the most underprivileged sectors of the population are indifferent to the Western distinction between past history and current affairs, between truth and myth. For them, everything istrue. The most hardened politicians, starting with Indira, always knew how to use that flickering frontier between people and gods in their favour.

These two series unleashed a real tide of Hindu fervour. In fact the fervour had always existed, and had grown with independence, as a reaction to so many centuries of domination by the Moguls and then by the English. Nehru and Gandhi, very aware of the danger of this kind of fundamentalism – similar to that of the Sikhs or the Moslems, or the fundamentalism of Christians in other parts of the world, but more dangerous still in India because it was the majority religion -, tried to preach the virtues of a non-denominational state and to emphasize unity between Hindus and Moslems. Mahatma Gandhi paid for it with his life: he was assassinated by militants of the RSS, an organization that later became affiliated to the BJP. At the beginning of her mandate Indira was very aware of the problem and had to firmly confront hundreds of naked holy men at the doors of Parliament who were demanding the prohibition of killing cows.

Rajiv and other members of the Congress Party were witness

to how, for political purposes, the BJP exploited the religious feeling created by the screening of the series. In 1987, in agreement with two powerful social and paramilitary organizations that were ideologically similar, the BJP started a campaign that they called a "historic apology". The aim was to knock downan old mosque built in the former Hindu capital of Ayodhya by a general of the Mogul emperor Babar in 1528. They claimed that the mosque had been built on the spot where the god Rama had been born.

For the Indian Moslems, the campaign of the BJP and its allies was a direct attack on their rights and their religion. Preventing the Hindu hordes from destroying the mosque became a symbol of their survival. The ingredients for a complicated and violent conflict were all ready and waiting.

In 1989, after the elections which cost Rajiv his job, another Hindu fundamentalist organization associated with the BJP launched a national campaign for every village of more than 2,000 inhabitants to pay for a brick destined for the construction of a temple to Rama less than thirty metres from the site of the mosque. It was a provocation for the Moslems. In Parliament, Rajiv urged the government to take a hand in things. The new Prime Minister sent the forces of order to interrupt the construction of the temple, but he was not able to get the different leaders to sit down at the same table to negotiate a peaceful solution to the conflict. For his part, Rajiv made the gesture of visiting a very venerated Hindu holy man who lived on the banks of the Ganges, a man who firmly believed that India was the common home of many religions, and that it should go on being so.

One year later, the Hindu BJP turned the screws of provocation a little tighter. One of its leaders, a tall, serious and charismatic figure called

L.K. Advani, made a call for thousands of volunteers from all over the country to converge on Ayodhya with the idea of galvanizing the chauvinistic passions of the Hindus. He personally led a pilgrimage which left from a small city in Gujarat, and he did so on board a motorized carriage which displayed large portraits of the gods and with loudspeakers that recited verses from the *Ramayana*. The peasants rubbed their eyes incredulously when they saw the procession go past followed by volunteersdressed exactly the same as the heroes in the series they had seen ontelevision. That march raised the temperature of the tension on both sidesso much that, in principle reluctant to intervene against one of the members of the coalition, the government ordered Advani's procession to be stopped before it reached its destination.

In reprisal, thousands of volunteers from the BJP attacked the Ayodhya mosque, armed with bows and arrows. A shiver of panic ran through the whole country. What would happen if in every district, in every village, in every city in the sub-continent a religious war broke out? Had the violence unleashed during Partition not been enough to inoculate India against confrontations based on religion? The consequences could be so terrible that it did not bear thinking about: atrocities against innocent people, the dismemberment of the country, perhaps a civil war. But the leader of the Hindu party seemed immune to common sense. Everything went in order to win votes, including placing a nation of 850 million peopleon the brink of the precipice.

The police had no option but to act forcefully to protect the mosque from destruction. There were a dozen dead, some militants, some police. The Hindu party attributed the violent outcome to the police, and its leader,Advani, announced that he was withdrawing his support for the government. Long before Rajiv had predicted, the first government tosubstitute him had fallen.

"Are you going to ask for elections to be called?" his daughter asked him.

"No, the party is not ready yet. I don't think we'd get any more votes

now than in the previous elections. I prefer to wait."

Rajiv, the head of the party with the greatest representation in Parliament, found himself again in a key position. A rival leader of the Prime Minister who had just been ousted, asked for his support to form a government. Rajiv agreed to give it, but from outside, without being part of the new cabinet. An astute manoeuvre, which gave him control without having to take responsibility for what the members of the new governing coalition did. The fact was that Rajiv did not trust this leader very much, or his ministers, among whom was Maneka Gandhi, and he did not want to be associated with this administration, which he foresaw would be disastrous. He was convinced that in a question of months the people would be desperately calling for the return of the Congress Party to power. Then would be the time to call elections.

Rajiv's predictions were correct. The cabinet created by the new Prime Minister offered the most depressing collection of rogues even by Third World standards: "An extraordinary collection of the most pitiless and immoral opportunists to have ever entered the political arena of India," according to the description of William Dalrymple, an English writer living in New Delhi.

The split did not take long to come, and it occurred in a ratherstrange way. Sonia was once again very angry about the matter of security because, after losing the elections, the new government had taken away the highly trained bodyguards from the Special Protection Group, as if the fact that Rajiv was not in the government might make the threats disappear. The change had been so drastic that Sonia and Priyanka lived in a perpetual state of fear every time Rajiv went away on a trip. From being protected by hundreds of agents on every journey, he went out of the houseaccompanied by a single bodyguard, a good man, faithful and helpful, called Pradip Gupta: "If anything happens to Rajiv it will be over my dead body," he once told Sonia when he saw she was so uneasy. But it was poor consolation. Rahul shared the same anxiety. He often called from the United States to check that nothing had happened to his father. In March 1991, he was so worried about the details that his mother told him about how shoddy the security measures were that he insisted on spending the Easter holidays at home,. He accompanied his father on a tour of the stateof Bihar and was astonished to see for himself the lack of care and resources and how exposed Rajiv was to any aggression. Sometimes the police were pushing the crowd aside and left him on his own in the car, other times they did not get far enough ahead and Rajiv was once again left exposed. Before he set off again for the United States, Rahul said a few words to his mother which she did not really want to believe, but which turned out to be premonitory: "If you don't do something about it, I'm afraid the next time I'm back will be for Dad's funeral."

The problem was not only the lack of support from the government, but also that Rajiv was obsessed with the idea of keeping close to the people. He had been told that he had lost the elections because he had projected the image of someone distant and almost arrogant. The presence of bodyguards was an impediment when it came to forging an image as an accessible politician, which was what he wanted. "Living under a terrorist threat or death threat has never bothered me," he had declared. "I have never let it interfere in my way of thinking. Yes, it has caused me problemsbecause of all the fuss that security implies... but if I have to die for what I believe, I would not hesitate."

Christian von Stieglitz spent a few days with them in those days, together with Pilar, his Spanish wife. "Pilar did not know New Delhi, so Rajiv took us on a tour. We got into a little Suzuki that he drove himself, and roared off, with his bodyguards following as best they could in a white Ambassador, until he managed to lose them. It can't have been easy to be one of Rajiv Gandhi's bodyguards! I couldn't stop thinking that he was taking too many risks. I remember one afternoon we went to the Qutub Minar, the highest monument in the city. Rajiv was between my wife and me chatting to us as we walked among the ruins. At a given moment, I turned round and saw that about a thousand people were following us a certain distance away, not daring to get too close to us. They were very surprised to see Rajiv strolling around like just another tourist. We carried on walking and suddenly Rajiv bent down and picked up two little white flowers from the ground. He went over to the crowd and gave them to a little girl who was looking open-mouthed at him with her big, dark eyes." When Christian made a comment about the risks he was taking, Rajiv answered: "I can't distrust the man in the street. I have to live my life."

The one who could not live was Sonia. One weekend when they were spending some time at the house in the country at Mehrauli, it was she who noticed two characters who were watching the house and who were not the usual bodyguards. She told Rajiv, and he went out to ask them who had given them orders to watch them, and that is how he discovered that it had been the head of the local government, a man who belonged to the party of the new Prime Minister. Annoyed and disconcerted at what he considered an unacceptable intrusion into his private life, Rajiv called the Prime Minister and demanded that the surveillance be taken away, and he also called for the resignation of the head of government who had given the orders. "It was a matter of trust," said Rajiv. "I had placed my trust in that man, and we backed his government. And now I discover that we are not to be trusted and they set two policemen to watch our house. What does this mean?" The new Prime Minister tried to play down the matter and tried to calm Rajiv's anger, because he had no other way out. As regards his own party, he could not fire civil servants or local heads of government at the request of the leader of the Congress Party. On the other hand, if Rajiv took away his support, he would lose control of Parliament. But Rajiv insisted on getting to the bottom of the matter. As the man did not respond to his demands, Rajiv threatened to boycott Parliament. So, four months after being sworn in, that Prime Minister was forced to present his resignation to the President of the Republic.

Now the time had come to celebrate another general election, which the electoral commission set for May 20th, 23rd and 26th, 1991. India was in the middle of a crisis, which could make it easier for a party in opposition, such as the Congress Party, to return to power. Apart from the rise in Hindu fundamentalism, Kashmir was undergoing an escalation in violence. On the economy front, the management of the recent governments had been disastrous. Inflation, caused by the increase in the price of crude oil because of the Gulf War, was out of control and threatening to cause serious social problems. Rajiv proposed a programme based on stability and economic reform, including more privatizations and fewer controls on industry and commerce. The enemy to be beaten at the polls was the BJP, the Hindu party, which was taking shape as an organization on the rise with a programme that was potentially dangerous for the country's stability. The other parties, including those of the coalition leaving power, could only aspire to a limited number of seats.

Once again, Rajiv set off on campaign, sure of his victory. Politics was like that, like a reflection of life itself, where nothing is permanent and everything changes all the time, sometimes with dizzying speed. He wanted to start the campaign with Sonia at his side, and he piloted the plane himself, landing in Amethi on May 1st, 1991. It was the first of 600 stops that he had to make in twenty days. A crowd was waiting for them when they got off the plane. Among them there were many women who came up to welcome Sonia. One of the reasons for her huge popularity in Amethi is that Sonia had an amazing memory, and remembered the names and faces of women she had perhaps seen for only five minutes on previous trips. She identified fully with those peasant women who touched her with almost child-like curiosity just to check that she was flesh and bone like them. She intended to spend three weeks camping in her husband's constituency, asking for the vote house by house, while he went round the sub-continent. At the end of the day, before going up the steps to the plane, Rajiv turned to his electors and said a very simple phrase, but which later turned out to be prophetic: "I don't think I'll be able to come back again, but Sonia is staying to look after you." Sonia felt a stab in her heart. Not because she was going to be left on her own, because the warmth of the people and the kind attitude of the local members of the Congress Party made her feel at home, but because it was the first time in 23 years of marriage that they were going to spend so much time apart, almost three weeks.

That night, while she was in a tent trying to get to sleep lying on a *charpoi*, a camp bed made of plaited ropes, and struggling with the heat and the mosquitoes, Sonia remembered the last time she had been in Amethi. It was in February, the month when they celebrated their wedding anniversary. She had come there to open a campaign of vaccination against polio. She thought they would not be able to celebrate their anniversary together, because Rajiv had planned to travel to Teheran over those days. He was going with the aim of launching a diplomatic initiative to put an end to the Gulf War. But one night, like that one, although not so hot, a note had come to her from Rajiv asking her to please cancel her commitments in Amethi and return as fast as possible to Delhi to go with him on that trip. "I feel as though ... I want to be with you, only you and me together, the two of us, without hundreds of people flapping around us as usual." said the note. When Sonia arrived in New Delhi, around midnight, she found Rajiv nervous because he thought they would not arrive in time to catch the flight. She discovered that he had already packed their suitcases and everything was ready for the journey. In Teheran, after the official commitments, they went out to have dinner alone in a restaurant. How long had it been since they had been able to allow themselves such a romantic luxury? They could not remember... Rajiv gave her a present that he had brought from Delhi, some beautiful, simple earrings, just the kind of thing she liked. When they got back to the hotel, he picked up his camera, which he always travelled with and they took a photo of themselves with the automatic button, a thing they had never done before.

"Madam, madam!..."

A voice from outside the tent interrupted her daydream in a whisper. Sonia got up, put on her dressing gown and went out. A young man, a party follower, handed her an envelope. It had come from New Delhi and was from Rajiv. Sonia opened it and found a rose, with a hand-written note. She read it, smiled, showing her dimples, and went back to her *charpoi*. "It was a love letter," she would confess later.

Priyanka arrived in Amethi a few days later to keep her company. They visited an average of fifteen villages a day. They listened to people's complaints about a pension that did not come, a blind child who needed money for an operation or an old lady who complained that after the previous elections, the Congress Party people took no notice of them. Sonia took notes and gave instructions to her assistants. "Have faith," she told the supplicants, "I'm going to make sure this is sorted out for you."

In one of the villages, Priyanka witnessed an extraordinary event, bearing in mind her mother's aversion to speaking in public. Without Rajiv having asked her, Sonia got her courage together and made her first speech before a crowd of several thousand people. "My husband has worked a lot for your wellbeing and I work for my husband... Only the Congress Party can represent you in a worthy fashion. Take my husband's hand..." Priyanka laughed to see her exhorting people to vote for the Congress Party, and, furthermore, in an amusing way. The sentences in Hindi with a slight accent came out easily for her, she smiled and seemed to be having fun, perhaps because there were no reporters; they were all humble folk who did not intimidate her. The most surprising thing was that she had done it of her own accord, as an act of selflessness for her husband.

They both returned to New Delhi on May 17th, exhausted, sweaty and covered in dust, but optimistic about the final result of the elections. The following night, when Rajiv came back from his tour and came in through the front door, they were speechless. "He was exhausted. He could hardly speak or walk. He had not slept or eaten decently for weeks. He had been campaigning for about twenty hours a day. His hands and arms were covered in scratches and bruises. His whole body ached. Thousands of admirers had touched him, had shaken his hand, given him brotherly hugs and slaps on the back. It broke my heart to see him in such a state." His fingers were so swollen from the number of handshakes that he had had to take off his wedding ring. But he was happy, his heart full from so many demonstrations of affection, so much enthusiasm. His deficient security service had allowed him to go out and find what his grandfather and mother called "the love of the people", and he came back moved because the people responded. "In Kerala and Tamil Nadu they have the custom of pinching your cheek, and that is why mine is so red and swollen," he told Sonia as she placed a footrest for him so he could stretch out his legs, "...and sometimes, in Moslem areas, they kiss you, you know, one, two three kisses and then that special hug that almost breaks your back... My whole body hurts, but it doesn't matter." They sat quietly chatting for a good while, exchanging impressions of their mutual experiences. Rajiv was satisfied because he had managed to show the people that they mattered to him. But he was not sure he would win: "It's going to be a tough fight," he told her. That night he slept for five hours, quite a luxury, before he left for Bhopal, where he held a rally for a hundred thousand people on May 19th. The city was still traumatized by the catastrophe in 1984. The multinational responsible for the accident had reached an agreement to pay a sum of money in compensation to the victims, but the money had still not reached the hands of those that needed it. It was diverted by corrupt civil servants and intermediaries. Once again it was the system that failed.

After Bhopal, there was only the south left, "friendly country", as the members of the Congress Party called it. First he came home and he was so tired that he fell asleep in the sitting room, relieved to think the campaign was coming to an end. Three more days and they would all meet up there, because Rahul would be coming to spend the summer holidays. He was expected to arrive on May 23rd. Sonia and Priyanka were also happy. They were more certain than Rajiv that he would win the elections by an ample margin. The whole family had made a huge effort to put a Gandhi and the Congress Party back at the head of the country. Indira would have been proud of them all: that was "being a family".

On May 20th, Rajiv and Sonia left the house at 7.30 in the morning to place their votes. At that hour the temperature was still bearable. The crows seemed to greet them from the branches of the trees with their harsh cawing. Rajiv, dressed in a white *kurta* and with a tri-coloured scarf round his neck, drove the car along the wide avenues, which were almost deserted, but at the entrance to the electoral college a small crowd was waiting for them and a television team. Sonia looked splendid in a red *salwar kamiz*. They greeted people left and right putting their hands together at breast height and Rajiv signed some autographs while they waited for the college to open. Behind them, the line was beginning to grow. A young volunteer from the party came up to Rajiv with a tray on which there was incense, sugar and flower petals with the idea of making a *puja* (offering) right there in order to begin the day on an auspicious note in his honour. Whenever she was with her husband in a public place, Sonia closely observed anyone that came close, trying to guess whether they had any hidden intentions, a suspicious-looking lump, an unusual gesture. Her paranoia gave her no peace. Perhaps because of that she was scared when the man with the tray, intimidated by Rajiv, dropped it with a crash which made everyone jump. Sonia tensed up and then began to sweat copiously. Rajiv noticed his wife's distress and asked for a glass of water for her. When it was her turn to vote, she was so upset that she could not find the paper with the symbol of the Congress Party on it. For a moment she thought she would have to leave without voting. When they left, as they went towards the car, she told Rajiv, who laughed. "He held my hand," Sonia would remember, "with that warm, calming touch that always helped to dissipate any feeling of anxiety." It was perhaps the last occasion on which Rajiv was present to calm his wife, because after he left her at home, he went off for the next tour. In the evening he expected to come back to New Delhi to change the helicopter for a plane and leave for a destination in the south, where the elections would take place two days later.

But that evening, Rajiv surprised them by coming home. Sonia and Priyanka were happy to see him, even if only for a short time. Rajiv had a quick shower, then had something to eat and called his son in the United States: "I'm calling to wish you luck in your exams, Rahul, and to tell you how happy I am that you'll be home soon... It's going to be a great summer... I love you ... Bye bye." Then he kissed Priyanka. He had to go again, but the good thing was that that would be the last stage of the electoral tour. He was calm, he was going to the south, safe territory, not like the north, with so much upheaval and danger.

"Can't you stop now?" Sonia asked him. "This trip will not change the results..."

"I know, but it's already been organized... Come on, one last push and we'll come out on top... Just two more days and we'll be together again," he told Sonia with that captivating smile of his.

"We said goodbye tenderly..." Sonia would remember, "and he left. I stood looking through the crack in the curtains and I saw him go off, until I lost sight of him... This time forever."

40

The next day, May 21st, 1991, Rajiv embarked on a helicopter to visit several cities in the state of Orissa, in the east of the country. It was an exhausting trip, and at night he was so tired that he thought he would catch up a little on his missing sleep and cancel the last visit he had planned to a village in the neighbouring state of Tamil Nadu. It was called Sriperumbudur. Besides, a report from the central government's Intelligence Agency had expressly advised him not to attend meetings in Tamil Nadu after nightfall, because the Tamil Tigers had considerable support among the population in that state. He was hungry, and the local party leader, a young professional woman that he had recruited for the Congress Party, invited him for dinner at her home, but he was still thinking about the people who were expecting him in Sriperumbudur, about all the effort that his party comrades had invested in organizing the rally, and in the end he did not want to disappoint them and he declined the invitation for dinner. The party deserved a final effort.

"I'll sleep as much as I like with Rahul, Priyanka and Sonia around me," he told one of his companions.

"So you aren't going to take any notice of the report from the Intelligence Agency then?"

"If I had to listen to all those reports, I'd need to have given up the campaign long ago. Besides," he added, "political violence is rare in southern India, we all know that. Here the elections are more like a village festival than a serious political event."

When he boarded the plane, he was pleasantly surprised to find that the local leader had sent some pizza and pasties for him. He had hardly taken the first bite of his dinner when he was told that the plane could not take off because of a technical problem. "That's better," Rajiv said to himself, only thinking about having a quick nap. "So we'll stay here." He got off the plane and got into an Ambassador that took him to the government lodgings. But on the way, an official car caught up with him.

"Sir," said a policeman through the window, "the problem has already been solved, the plane is ready for take-off."

For a fraction of a second, Rajiv hesitated whether he should go on or return to the airport. In the end, he allowed himself to be carried along by events and told the driver to turn round. Back on board the plane, he sat down, put on his seat-belt and when the plane was beginning to taxi down the runway, he realized he had left his food behind in the car.

He reached Madras at half past eight in the evening, attended a short press conference, had a soft drink and went on by road. He was sitting in the front, next to the driver, with the window open. On the Ambassador's dashboard there was a small fluorescent light that shone on his face so that people could see him in the dark at night. He stopped in a village where he held a twenty-minute rally, and at half past nine he was already in the next village at another rally. On the way, he took advantage of the time to chat to reporters. That day he was accompanied by Barbara Crossette, the correspondent from the *New York Times* and a specialist in Asian matters. At they went through the villages, the car made its way slowly among the crowds, and the people, with expressions of delirious joy on their faces, threw flowers. "We're expecting good results in this area," Rajiv said to the reporters. As soon as he got out of the car, his followers fought to place garlands round his neck, while others gave him scarves and shawls. At a given moment, he stopped to greet a woman who was being squashed by the crowd. He placed a silk scarf round her neck and said a few words to her. The woman covered her face with her hands and held the scarf to her chest. Barbara Crossette was surprised at the lack of protection he had. "More than a hundred times, any one of the hands that reached into the car to touch his arm or shake his hand could have stabbed him or shot him."

They went on. All along the road there were coloured lights and posters welcoming him. From time to time, Rajiv indicated to the driver to go more slowly or to stop the car so he could get out and shake more hands as he asked people to vote for the Congress Party. The curious thing is that he said it in English, because he did not speak Tamil. When he had to explain something longer, an interpreter did it for him. He put the notes and letters that he was given by people into a grey airline bag that he always had with him. Barbara Crossette interviewed him for the last time. She asked him if he took vitamin supplements or had a special diet to put up with that outpouring of energy, bearing in mind the temperature of 40 degrees and the poor condition of the roads... Rajiv burst out laughing.

"These Americans!" he must have thought. "Most of the time I don't eat anything. I keep going with this..." he answered, pointing to a couple of thermos flasks, one of coffee and the other of tea. He indicated that the only concession to comfort was the white sports shoes he wore. Then he talked about his favourite topics: "The people are frustrated because the system is not efficient, and does not feed their aspirations. We have to find a way to improve it drastically. But, above all, I am determined to put an end to all the controversy over religion. We want complete separation between religion and politics. The mixture of them is explosive, not only here, but all over the world."

At ten o'clock that night, the local leaders in Sriperumbudur, a small agricultural village of no interest at all, announced the leader's arrival. The people were watching a display of dances typical of the region, very colourful and noisy, a normal thing at electoral rallies, as the important candidates never arrived on time. The two hours' delay on the expected schedule did not take away people's desire to cheer him and throw firecrackers to celebrate his arrival. Rajiv jumped when he heard the first bangs, but he was told that it was the usual way to greet an important dignitary in Tamil Nadu. Normally, at an act like this, in the north, there would have been a metal detector arch at the entrance to the compound. But there was nothing like that here, except for the efforts of the faithful bodyguard, Pradip Gupta, to keep people back and prevent them from touching the man he protected. Rajiv stopped in front of a statue of his mother and ceremoniously placed a garland of carnations on it. The crowd was made up especially of friendly-looking men, dressed in *longhis*, cloths wound round their waists, and short-sleeved shirts or collarless *kurtas*. After the tribute to Indira, Rajiv walked along a red carpet towards the stand where the local party leaders were waiting for him sitting round a long table. He accepted with his eternal smile the garlands that were being presented to him, stopping to shake someone's hand, responding to the greeting of another, taking off the garlands piling up round his neck and throwing them to the women, arguing with the local police officers who were trying to keep the crowd back, laughing and joking with everyone. He got his incredible energy from contact with the people, thus linking back to the example of his grandfather and his mother.

Among the crowd there were two women of about thirty. One of them was short, with dark skin and glasses. Her name was Dhanu. She was wearing a denim jacket over an orange Punjabi costume, which consisted of a long skirt worn over wide trousers, unlike the rest of women in the south, who usually wear saris. She looked as if she was pregnant. No one suspected that the reason for her corpulence was that under her jacket, stuck to her body, she had a nine-volt battery, a detonator and six grenades with shrapnel wrapped in plastic explosive. The other girl was called Kokila, and she was the daughter of a party worker. Rajiv put his arm affectionately over her shoulders as she recited a poem in his honour. Dhanu, with a garland in her hands, managed to make her way through, and stood behind Kokila. When the girl finished her poem, it was Dhanu's turn, but just when she was going to hand her garland to Rajiv, a woman police officer stopped her with her arm. Rajiv smiled at her. "Let everyone have their turn... Don't worry, it's all right." The policewoman desisted and turned round, not suspecting that in that way she was saving her life. Then Dhanu approached Rajiv to put a garland made out of sandalwood shavings carved into the shape of petals round his neck. Rajiv thanked her with his beautiful smile, and following the tradition, he took off the garland to hand it to a party comrade who was behind him. Meanwhile, Dhanu bent down to touch his feet. Rajiv did the same, to show humility, as though saying that he was not worthy of that greeting. But the woman tricked him: she was not touching his feet in a sign of veneration, but pulling the cord that activated the detonator.

The explosion was apocalyptic. "When I turned round," said Suman Dubey, Rajiv's assistant and an old friend of the family, "I saw people flying through the air as if in slow motion." Barbara Crossette, who had stayed at the back, saw "a very intense explosion...and then people falling all round, in a circle, like the petals of a flower. In the place where Rajiv was supposed to be, there was a hole in the ground." The shrapnel had killed the murderess, Rajiv and seventeen other people. Panic came overthe crowd and the police, who did not know if that was an isolated explosion or if there would be more. The dust and smoke cleared to leave the spectacle of the massacre in full view: dismembered bodies, smoking, black earth, burned objects. Curiously, the dais was still standing, what had been blown to pieces was the people that had been sitting there.

"I was looking for something white," Suman Dubey would say, "because Rajiv always wore white. But all I could see was black, burned things." Other party workers approached and found Pradip Gupta, Rajiv's faithful bodyguard. He was still alive, lying on his back with his eyes wide open, suffering in his own flesh the prediction he had made to Sonia: "If anything happens to Rajiv, it will have to be over my dead body..." He died a few seconds later. Under his body, someone found a white sports shoe. It was Rajiv's. A party colleague tried to turn what was left of the body over, but could not do it because it was falling to pieces. Rajiv had literally been eviscerated by the explosion, his skull was fractured and had lost almost all the brain mass. He had died instantly. Fifteen minutes after the explosion, the phone rang at number 10 Janpath Road.

41

The person who picked up the phone was Rajiv's secretary, who was working in his boss's private office, in a distant wing of the house. The family was asleep. In her bedroom, Sonia heard the phone in her sleep and it sounded like a scream.

"Sir, there has been a bomb attack," said a faltering voice, muffledby interference.

"Who's speaking?"

"I'm from the Intelligence Agency. I'm calling from Sriperumbudur."

The secretary's throat closed up."How is Rajivji?" he asked.

The man did not reply. The secretary could hear how the man speaking coughed to clear his throat before speaking again.

"Sir, the fact is..." he began to say, not finishing the sentence. Nervous, the secretary urged him:

"Why don't you tell me once and for all how Rajiv is?" "Sir, he's dead," the man let out and immediately hung up.

The secretary was left with the receiver in his hand, his eyes unfocussed, trying to take in what he had just heard. The slight hope that it might have been a false alarm evaporated as soon as he hung up, when the phone rang again. A member of the Congress Party in Tamil Nadu confirmed the news. There was no longer any doubt. Immediately, theother lines began to ring, making an unbearable racket. The secretaryhurried out.

"Madam, madam..."

He met Sonia in the corridor, having just come out of her room, tyingup her dressing gown.

She could hardly open her eyes. Her hair was in a mess. She knew that a call in the middle of the night could not mean anything good. Thecall she had received one night in the family home at Orbassano telling her that Sanjay had died was engraved on her memory. Now she was prey to a similar feeling and her stomach went into knots. But what left her icy cold was the scared, almost hysterical look on the secretary's face, a man usually calm and measured.

"Madam, there's been a bomb..." he stuttered.

Sonia gave him a severe look. Her face was puffy with sleep. "Is he alive?"

The secretary was unable to answer. The words would not come out. Neither were they necessary. Sonia had stopped listening to him. Her wholebody contracted as if she had had an electric shock and from the depths of her mortally wounded soul a harsh, guttural cry arose. Seven years after the conversation she had had with Rajiv in the hospital operating theatre where they were sewing Indira's body together, in which she begged him not to accept the post that his mother had left vacant because he would be killed, the prediction had come true.

"Nooooooo...!!"

Her cry woke Priyanka, who appeared in the hallway, also in a dressing gown, looking worn out and astonished. She was dumbstruck, incredulous, deathly pale. She got hold of her mother and took her into the sitting room as best she could. Never in all her nineteen years had she seen her in such a state of despair. No one had ever seen her cry like that. The sobbing was so loud and lasted so long that the first party colleagues to arrive at the house heard it from the street.

Priyanka could not comfort her. Suddenly Sonia began to cough and choke in such a way that the secretary feared she would lose consciousness.

"It's an attack of asthma," said Priyanka. It was so violent that she felt very afraid. "I'll be right back," she called.

She ran to her mother's bathroom and searched feverishly for her inhaler and anti-histamines. When she came back into the sitting room, she saw her sitting on an armchair with her eyes almost turned up, her mouth open and her head thrown back, trying to get air like a fish out of water. She thought she was dying. In fact, part of her had died with her husband.

The medicines took effect and managed to stop the coughing, but not the sobbing. However much her daughter tried to calm her down, Sonia was inconsolable. Her weeping fed on itself, as insistent and regular as the waves pounding on the beach. Priyanka turned to the secretary.

"Where is my father's body?" she asked.

"At the moment they are taking him to Madras."

"Please help me to do what's necessary to get us there," she asked. Priyanka took charge of the situation, showing admirable maturity,

cool-headedness and sense of organization. She spoke to the first friends of her father's and leaders of the Congress Party who arrived looking perplexed and desolate, some of them weeping their hearts out. She even spoke to the President of the Republic on the telephone. She asked him to put a plane at the family's disposal. Deep down, something inside her prevented her believing that her father was dead. It was like a reflex that protected her from pain and allowed her to act. Subconsciously, she found it hard to accept something so catastrophic without checking that it was true, and that is why she needed to see her father as soon as possible.

"Do you think it's wise to go there?" the President of the

Republictold her.

"Please, Mr President, I must insist. My mother and I have the firmintention of going to Madras this very night."

"OK. I'll talk to the army to have an Air Force plane put at yourdisposal. Then I'll come by your residence to give my condolences."

"Thank you. We'll be expecting you."

Now she had to give her brother the news, in Harvard. There it was lunchtime. She managed to get a classmate to give him a message that he should call home urgently. An hour later, his sister and his mother gavehim the worst news of his life.

"I knew it, I knew it!" said the young man crying and biting his lip."I knew it was going to happen."

That feeling of frustration and impotence accentuated the pain of everyone in the family.

"We did what we could...""Do you think so?"

"Of course we did."

They told him to come on the first flight out, as they were beginning to organize the funeral and they were waiting for him.

It was about eleven o'clock and the news had already spread round New Delhi. A crowd was gathering at the gates of the house. From inside, Priyanka and Sonia could hear hysterical cries and laments. Friends of the family, colleagues, ministers, policemen etc. kept arriving. It was a real invasion. The Press took up positions at the gate and in the street. The people still did not know against whom to direct their rage: against the Sikhs, the Moslem or the Hindu fundamentalists, the Tamil Tigers, the Assamese, the Dalits...? There were many grudges in such a densely populated country. Suddenly, they directed it against the national and international television teams. The people gathered there began insulting them. Some friends who were passing through the gate at the wheel of their cars were received in an ugly manner: Ottavio and Maria Quattrochi were booed and had a stone or two thrown at them, and the same occurred with the leaders of the opposition, who had come to give their condolences. The fury of the crowd extended to all of Rajiv's adversaries. A mob tried to attack the nearby home of one of his fiercest critics, one of the leaders of a caste of the untouchables, when he was in government. Such was the atmosphere in the streets that the President of the Republic was unable to get to the house. He found a frantic, desperate crowd of people. They threw themselves on the bonnet of his car, weeping and sobbing.

"Shall we disperse them?" the security officer asked the President. "No. Let's turn round. I don't want things to get even more heated."

Back in his residence in the former Viceroy's palace, the President phoned Sonia. She was a little calmer and was able to thank him for his condolences and the facilities he had ordered for that singular journey.

Dressed in a white *salwar kamiz*, her hair combed back and tied back in a bun, as soon as Sonia hung up she left the house with Priyanka. Outside, a car was waiting for them to take them to the airport. Uncle Kaul was driving, the one who had tried so hard to get Rajiv to follow in his brother's footsteps. The car made its way with difficulty through the crowd that was packed around the house. The streets were more and more turbulent. Groups of people gathered on the street corners and at the roundabouts, in a state of mind that went between rage and grief.

"I hope the government acts soon and doesn't allow the same to happen as after Indira died," commented Uncle Kaul.

The flight lasted three and a half hours, the time a jet takes to cross the sub-continent from north to south. Below, in that dark stretch of land scattered with little dots of light that indicated the cities and villages, India slept. In a few hours it was going to wake up to the tragedy of another political assassination. In a few hours, they thought, the country will be steeped in sorrow. Nobody spoke during the flight. Only Sonia's sobs couldbe heard.

It was still dark when they arrived in Madras at half past four in the morning. The plane taxied to the old terminal, lit up and surrounded by a growing crowd. Rajiv's body was there. At the indication of the President of the Republic, they had taken him there to avoid Sonia and Priyanka having to drive into the city. Sticky, damp air enveloped them as soon as they got off the plane. They were very nervous because the moment was approaching. The moment when they would see him for the last time. What were they going to find? Were they ready for it? Could they stand it? They asked themselves these questions as they walked down the steps of the plane and greeted the dignitaries who had gone there to welcome them. Here too the authorities were afraid that disturbances might break out, the governor told them. The crowd was seeking a scapegoat and feelings in the city were running very high. For that reason they had taken the necessary steps for the flight to take off before dawn. When she recognized Suman Dubey, Rajiv's loyal, old friend who had miraculously come out unscathed from the attack, Sonia threw herself into his arms to cry.

But they did not see Rajiv. They could not. They were told that the body was in such bad shape that it had been impossible to embalm him. The only thing they saw was two coffins. One contained Rajiv's remains and the other the remains of his bodyguard, Pradip Gupta. From then on it all happened very quickly. Holding tight to each other, mother and daughter watched as the coffins were put into the hold of the plane. They went back up the steps into the plane. Once inside, Sonia asked for the coffin to be placed beside her. With one hand she put a garland of flowers on the coffin, while with the other she covered her face with a shawl towipe away her tears. Priyanka, seeing the coffin tied down there, had to admit what her sub-conscious had been refusing to accept, that her father was in that coffin, or rather what was left of him. Then she could not hold itback any longer and she broke down. She suddenly realized that she would never see him again, that never again would her father's love and warmth comfort her. She held on to the coffin and sobbed there for a long time.

The plane was already taxiing along the runway. Suman Dubey and Sonia calmed her down, got her to sit down and did up her seatbelt. At that moment Sonia made a gesture that Rajiv no doubt would have appreciated. As she realized that the coffin of the bodyguard Pradip Gupta had nothing on it, she went and placed a garland of jasmine there too.

It was daylight when the plane took off, on its way back to the capital of India. Rajiv Gandhi's last journey was beginning.

ACT IV

THE HIDDEN HAND OF DESTINY

You do not know the limits of your strength, you do notknow what you are doing. You do not know who you are.

Euripides

42

That's it. It's all over. In spite of Rajiv not holding any official post, sixty-four countries have sent an official representative to the funeral. Rajiv had something special, which made him well loved by those that had dealings with him.

The ashes are already on their way to the ocean, dissolved in the Ganges, mixed with those of his great-grandfather, Motilal, his grandfather Nehru and his brother. The individual grief is only a part of the huge vacuum he has left behind. The serving and security staff are sad and disoriented. Even the dogs at home are downhearted. The rock that everyone could hold tight to during the ups and downs of a chaotic, unsafe world, has disappeared. How can they believe that he is no longer there? Sonia and the children feel his presence all the time, especially at night, in their dreams. The unconscious moves more slowly than reality, finding it hard to catch up, and that is why waking up is especially difficult. At other times they wake up with a start and come face to face with reality, and thenthey realize that this is their worst nightmare.

The important thing is that it all went off peacefully. The bloodbath has been avoided, not like after Indira's assassination. The government called out the army in time and decreed seven days of national mourning. What it has been impossible to avoid are the several suicides and immolations in the interior of the country. Eternal India is still alive in the hearts of the people.

Now, even his political adversaries agree that Rajiv was a decent man. In death, they praise the leader they denigrated in life. The Press too, who first extolled him and then vilified him, examines its conscience. One morning, Priyanka shows her mother an article from the *Hindustan Times*.

"Read it, Mother. They have published a tribute here that seeks to exonerate the attitude the media had to Daddy."

Sonia is proud of her children. They have been equal to things. Thank goodness she had Priyanka near her to organize everything, to keep the house in order, to go and fetch Rahul and choose the place for the cremation. She could not have done it. It is impossible to take decisions when you feel dead in life. She thinks that Indira would also have been proud of them.

Sonia puts on her glasses and starts reading. The text has the merit of its frankness: "We pulled his leg because of his Gucci shoes, his Cartier glasses, his designer jeans, his trips with his wife in Air India jumbos... We laughed at his Hindi, even though ours was worse... The fact is that we were full of resentment and envy... We knew deep down that he had travelled more than the rest of us put together and that he had a better vision of the problems of India than we could ever have, pontificating in our columns. His natural elegance, his good looks and his manners gave him an unfair advantage over everyone else. He had so much to live for, so much to do in spite of our scruples and our criticisms." Sonia is crying when she gives the article back to her daughter. "Why has a good man had to pay such a high price when on top of everything he had done a good job?" she wonders. There are so many questions and so few answers that Sonia despairs. What she does know is that her husband has ended up being the victim of a system that asked the impossible of him. Ah, if only he had not gone into politics, if only they had let Maneka take on the role of heir... Maneka, who appeared at the funeral with Firoz Varun and who murmured a few words of condolence with tears in her eyes.

Now Sonia and her children want to know who assassinated him. The police say it was the Tamil National Liberation Front terrorists... But are they sure? When will they be able to confirm it? And above all... When will justice be able to be done? Justice is poor consolation, but at this point it is the only thing left.

"Madam, you have a call," a servant interrupts. "It's long distance."

Since her sisters have gone back to Italy after spending a few days comforting them in New Delhi, Sonia talks to one or other of them on the phone every day, and they insist that she should go back. They think that in time she will realize that there is no sense in staying on in New Delhi, apart from the fact that it is dangerous. But Sonia is clear on the matter and has already told her mother. India is still her reason for living, even if it has stolen her heart. Here is where her dreams are buried.

"This is my life," she repeats to her sister Nadia on the phone. "I can't leave this country now and set myself up abroad, where I will always be a foreigner. I realized that when Daddy died."

"At least, move house..."

"Why? Do you also think it's jinxed? That's what the Press say here..."

"No, I don't believe in that rubbish, I'm saying it because in that house everything will remind you of Rajiv..."

"That's precisely why I don't want to move. You know, being left a widow is not like getting divorced. Besides, from the security point of view, this house is adequate."

Security! How hollow that word seems from a distance away. Two assassinations, and Sonia still believes in it. How stubborn a sister can be... But fear can only be understood if it is experienced from the inside. The Sikhs' threat to Indira that they would kill her descendants for a hundred generations stayed engraved on Sonia's mind. How to forget a threat like that, which, in addition, was confirmed with her mother-in-law's blood? Now, with Rajiv, she knows that the thirst for revenge knows no limits. Never will she or her children be able to live in complete peace, because they are who they are. Never, not here or in Italy or anywhere else. Better to accept that. At least in India she again has all the apparatus of the State to protect them. "The security of the Gandhi family is in the national interest," the President of the Republic declared pompously a week after the attack. About time too, thinks Sonia... The fact is that the acting Prime Minister, acting under the orders of the President of the Republic, has assigned them maximum protection. Once again they have the Special Protection Group at their disposal, which had already proved its effectiveness when Rajiv was Prime Minister. Sonia has not been able to avoid making a bitter comment:

"The police have let me know that if you had not withdrawn the SPG's protection from Rajiv, to which he had a right, he would have been saved from the attack."

"Soniaji," the Prime Minister replied imperturbably, "you know perfectly well that if Rajiv had insisted, the government would have provided it for him again."

"I'm not so sure."

How can she be? How can she believe the word of a politician? It is true that Rajiv had not requested it, but she had. She had insisted several times, but always in vain. Priyanka had insisted. Rahul too. The fact is that no politician had any special interest in giving Rajiv greater protection: those in his party because it separated him from the masses and therefore reduced his chances of success, those in the opposition because if something happened to Rajiv, the predominance of the Congress Party would come to an end. Everyone came out winning if Rajiv was left defenceless.

*   *   *

After so much coming and going, after seeing so many people, after so many tears spilled, Sonia suffers the reaction. Little by little she begins to assimilate her new situation, and a terrifying question emerges: How to go living without Rajiv? How to find the strength to go on without him? Now it is the hardest part, to invent a life for herself. The consolation of religion is no help to her. She says she believes in all religions because perhaps she does not believe in any of them. She has the consolation that her son Rahul is staying there all summer. The young man is shattered. Added to the sadness of having lost his father, there is a strong feeling of guilt at not having moved heaven and earth, for not having faced up to him and forced him to demand more protection... Sonia and Priyanka also feel a little guilty, but what could they do against Rajiv's will and the will of the apparatus of the State? The fact is that the family home once again becomes the fortress it was before, with fences in the street, metal detector arches, surveillance cameras, watchtowers, sentry boxes and a hundred or so armed policemen lurking all round the area. Security.

*   *   *

The attack has not interrupted the elections, only the last two days have been postponed. The Congress Party has won comfortably in the south, because of the "empathy factor" caused by the assassination, but they have been defeated in the north. Maneka has also been defeated in her constituency and she has lost her seat in Parliament. The great surprise of these elections is the spectacular advances made by the BJP, the Hindu party that Rajiv had identified as the "enemy to be beaten". They have multiplied their seats by a hundred. A spectacular and terrifying rise. How can you not feel afraid when the leader of a Hindu paramilitary group, an ally of this party, has given a tribute to the assassin of Mahatma Gandhi? Is that not something that would not be allowed in most democracies? asks Sonia, as scandalized as most of the visitors she receives. Can one so easily attack the pillars of a nation with total impunity? With the excuse of giving their condolences, many MPs and party members go to sound her out, sometimes even quite late at night. They go to discuss who should be the definitive successor to Rajiv at the head of the Congress Party. They do not dare to say that she should take on that post, that if she did it there would be some hope of fighting against the advance of religious sectarianism. They know she does not want to hear of it. Did she not reject outright the presidency of the party, which they went to offer her on a silver plate while Rajiv's ashes were still warm?

However, Sonia listens to them carefully: that so and so represents the wealthy too much and has a poor image among the poor, that so and so is disloyal and cannot be trusted, etc.

"What do you think?" they ask her.

"I would be inclined to go for Narasimha Rao, I think that is who Rajiv would choose... But why don't you decide who is to be the next leader?"

"Because this party, with personalities as imposing as Nehru, Indira and your husband, has never had the need to develop a succession mechanism and it needs someone to guide it... You, for example," one of them dares to let slip, looking straight at her.

Sonia struggles to stay composed and calm. Don't they understand that I'm not interested? She has told them a hundred times that she does not want to get into politics, that she is not going to participate in any rally or event connected with politics. If she continues to receive them it is out of fidelity to her husband's memory, because she thinks he would like it. Keeping up these relationships is like keeping him alive in a small way. She does not want to cut the umbilical cord that links her to Rajiv's world, to Indira's world, to the family legacy. She does it for herself and for her children. A friend of hers feels obliged to warn those that come: "Don't bother Madam talking about her going into politics. It hurts her a lot. Remember that she's in mourning for a husband who never wanted to go into politics."

Many will remember her dressed in a white sari with a black bodice and no jewels, as tradition requires in the period of mourning, except for her wedding ring, sitting on the edge of the sofa in Rajiv's study, with the family portraits looking down on them from the walls. The office desk is exactly as it was when he left it. She has not wanted to move any of the objects there and no one sits on his chair, now covered with the flag that was wrapped round his coffin. No one will ever sit there, not even her. In spite of her elegant bearing and her effort to remain composed, the tears slip out from time to time, and she hides it by rubbing a handkerchief over her face. From all the crying she has perpetual bags under her eyes and her gaze is watery. She has lost a lot of weight, the marble-like pallor of her complexion is tinged with grey, and she has an expression of infinitesadness in her eyes.

But her opinion carries weight. So much weight that even she is surprised. In the end the MPs listen to her. Once they are convinced that Madam prefers Narasimha Rao, they arrange an internal election for the MPs to vote him in. The party finally puts in this old friend of the Nehru family as Prime Minister of a coalition government, a minority one because the Congress Party needs thirty more seats for a majority. The Press seizes on this power by influence, which it calls *the Sonia factor*. The same thing has happened to her as happened to Indira when Nehru died: she automatically inherited some of the family's power. For some it is a question of "charisma", for others it is the "name". If that day she had mentioned another name, it is likely that Rao would not have come out on top. It is not so easy to get away from politics. Power follows her, power wants her. Power needs her.

The Rao government seems weak. The way things are, no one would bet on its survival, or on the party's survival either. What is the Congress Party without a Gandhi at its head?... An organization sentenced to disappearing, permitting the Hindu party, the BJP, to take over the ground lost. It is serious, because that party defends the dangerous idea of "a Hindu India", which for many is a recipe for disaster. And no one can even imagine the consequences for the country and the rest of the world of a disaster on the scale of India... That is why the pressure on Sonia is redoubled. For those politically responsible for a totally disconcerted Congress Party, and for a large part of the population, she represents the last sentinel of a dynasty that has been struck a death-blow.

"Can I do you any favours, anything you need, can I help you in any way?" This is how the Welfare Minister announces himself in his singsong voice as he comes into the Gandhi home.

In the leadership of the Congress Party they cannot think what else to do to win her over, to get her to think again and agree to come into the fold.

There are so many of them wanting to see her that she decides to establish visiting times, from five to seven in the evening. She spends the mornings answering the thousands of letters of condolence that she and her children receive still from all over the world. She insists on reading them all, and she tries to answer the ones from acquaintances personally. To the others she sends a printed note of thanks signed by hand, in English or in Hindi. In the evenings, after the visits, is when the feeling of loss and solitude becomes harder to bear. For moments she forgets that now Rajiv isnot going to come home that night. So many years accustomed to waiting for him to come back that she still has the reflex of that useless waiting. Fortunately she is surrounded by her family. Her mother, Paola, now lives with them, and is still secretly hoping that Sonia will decide to go back to Italy. But she does not want to insist any more, the last time she did, Sonia got upset. Priyanka and Rahul are very attentive to their mother. From time to time some friend or other turns up for dinner and the atmosphere livens up as they prepare the meal.

The close friends are few and far between, the faithful ones. Among these are the Bachchan brothers (one of them, Amitabh, has become the biggest star of the Indian cinema), a decorator that she met as soon as she arrived and her husband, a couple of journalists and editors, former colleagues from Indian Airlines, old friends of the family like Suman Dubey and his wife... The Quattrochis have gone back to Italy, although even if they were here, she would not be able to see them... Her friends do not talk to the Press, and they do not say anything that might be interpreted by Sonia as a betrayal of her confidence. They know she is a woman who is very jealous of her privacy. She does not want her grief to appear on the pages of the glossy magazines. She is very annoyed with the foreign Press which projects Priyanka as the heir to "the dynasty". The reporters who followed them during the campaign in Amethi did not fail to notice the young woman's magnetism, with that penetrating look of hers, and none of them was able to resist comparing her to her grandmother.

Many foreign dignitaries on their way through the capital also want to see her and she is happy to receive them, because that way she can share memories of the many trips she made with her husband. In the Ministry of Foreign Affairs they cannot understand why Yasser Arafat, Nelson Mandela or King Hussein want to talk to a person who has no official position. "What's happening with the protocol?" they ask. But Prime Minister Rao rejects those objections. If the foreign dignitaries wish it to beso, the government does not need to deal with the question of protocol, he answers them. Those in power treat her, and her children, as members of a ruling family. The Gandhis, dead or alive, are still revered, as though India recognized their divine right to reign there. Now, together with the big pictures of Indira which adorn public buildings, there is also the photo of Rajiv smiling from beyond the grave. The family is still very present in the minds of millions of Indians.

Little by little, her children and her friends help her to find some sense to life without Rajiv. Sonia is aware that she needs to get her lifeback to normal as soon as possible, even if it is only for her children's sake,as they will have to go back to university. "What has happened cannot bean obstacle to their leading a normal life." She is obsessed with that idea. All her life she has wanted nothing else, and she still talks about it as if she could attain it. Then she corrects herself, and says, "... a life as normal as possible." Yes, that is the goal, the only viable goal.

And although she can no longer live *with* Rajiv, she can live *for* him. For his memory. So that his dream does not disappear. Her friends suggest she creates a foundation, somewhat in the style of American presidential foundations, which hold the legacy of each president. It would be a response to the terrorists who murdered him, a way for his ideas and his vision to survive. Sonia chooses the date of June 20th to sign the act of constitution of the Rajiv Gandhi Foundation, because it is also a way of giving some meaning to Rahul's birthday, who is 21 that day. Surrounded by her children and her friends, she puts her signature to the document that establishes the creation of an institution aimed at promoting the application of science and technology to the service of the poor. Sonia has the impression that in that way Rajiv is still alive in death.

On August 20th, the day that Rajiv would have been 47, they go to pay tribute to him at the *samadhi*, the mausoleum in the shape of a lotus flower erected on the site where the cremation took place. It is not far from the respective *samadhi* of Sanjay, Indira and Nehru, all symbols which evoke the considerable price of power. Sonia wears a white sari with ablack border. Her eyes are distant and it seems as if her spirit is far away, in some place that only she knows. Perhaps she is allowing herself to be carried away by her daydreaming and she is making plans for life with Rajiv, like before, and she is managing to scrape a few seconds of happiness together in this way, even if they are imaginary. It smells of the incense the priests burn in makeshift braziers. Standing between Priyanka and Rahul, the three of them seem absorbed and involved in their own thoughts, while the Hindu religious chants follow one another like an endless litany. In the background the noise of the city can be heard. Suddenly Maneka appears, alone, the last person they want to see there at that moment. Sonia tenses up as her sister-in-law approaches the *samadhi* and places a floral offering on the polished marble. Then she follows the tradition of walking round the mausoleum and goes past Sonia and her children, but they do not greet each other. Her presence has broken the serenity of the act. Sonia, annoyed, decides to bring it to an end and goback to the car.

43

Five months after the assassination, the electoral commission announces local elections in Amethi, and again the chorus of voices makes itself heard. The chorus that called for Indira after Nehru's death, and Rajiv after his brother's death, is now calling for Sonia. Former colleagues of her husband's call on the Prime Minister to convince her to stand in Amethi as Rajiv's successor. They know that Sonia has a special link with the people in that constituency. The adulation reaches unexpected lengths when a party member declares unashamedly: "If Sonia wanted to wear shoes made out of my skin, I wouldn't hesitate to give it to her." But the family is losing patience: "What do these militants think?" exclaims Priyanka, beside herself. "That we have to go on sacrificing our lives? That's enough politics!" It seems like an aberration to them that the balance of a whole nation of almost a billion inhabitants rests on an Italian widow, but that is what they believe at the pinnacle of the government and the party.

Given their failure to convince her, they try other methods. Rao's government decides to make a donation to the Rajiv Foundation of ten million rupees, payable over five years, as though that way they could make up for the loss of her husband. Sonia gets even angrier and sends a letter to Rao: "We thank you personally, and your colleagues, for this generous offer, but it would be better for the government to design its own humanitarian projects and programmes and to finance them directly, honouring the memory of my husband in that way." But it is too late, the scandal blows up. As soon as the news of this supposed donation becomes public, the opposition attacks what it calls the *Rome Raj*: "A government that can steal from the poor to give ten million rupees to the family of RajivGandhi is capable of anything."

Tired now of so much manoeuvring and manipulation, of this new, unnecessary scandal that the opposition gets the most out of with great relish, of all the pressure that does not respect her grief, of the Press speculating all the time about her role, Sonia decides to follow the adviceof her children and go off on a trip to Europe and the United States for a while. The trip serves to distract her from the confusion in India and allowsher to rest mentally and set her thoughts in order. She is more determined than ever to keep Rajiv's legacy alive without having to get into the mire ofpolitics herself. But is that possible?

*   *   *

When she gets back, the police inform her that they have identified Rajiv's assassins. The investigation was made possible thanks to the heroic work of a local photographer from Sriperumbudur, a young man called Haribabu. That fateful night, the reporter had waited impatiently for the leader's arrival. As soon as Rajiv got out of the white Ambassador, Haribabu had bombarded him with his flash shots, to such an extent that the bodyguard, Pradip Gupta, waved at him to stop being a nuisance. But, not concerned about saving rolls of film, the photographer went on with his work. Who knows when a personality as important as Rajiv Gandhi would be back to that remote corner? His persistence cost him his life. Haribabu's body was blown apart by the shock wave. His remains were found twenty metres away from the place where he was originally. What the police discovered was his camera among the smoking remains of the conflagration. Miraculously, it was intact. When the roll of film inside it was developed, the last faces that Rajiv had seen in his life appeared, among which was that of Dhanu, the suicide terrorist.

"Take a good look at the photo," the chief of police tells her. "She is your husband's assassin."

Sonia's hands sweat when she takes it to see. It is deeply disturbing to see the face of the person who has done them so much harm like this. From being an abstraction in her mind, the murderess now appears as an apparently normal woman. "How could she do something so awful?" Sonia says to herself, staring at her, as though seeking some external sign of her evil, as though she could get inside her mind, look into her soul and guess why she decided to kill him. The policeman points with his finger to the face of a dark-skinned man, a southerner, in one corner of the photo.

"The police special investigation team has managed to identify him. He's a terrorist known as Shivarasam, a leader of the LTTE (Liberation Tigers of Tamil Eelam). Madam, this confirms what we all knew already: that your husband was the victim of a plot by Tamil extremists."

"His murder was the revenge of the Tamils for the military intervention on the island, isn't that so?"

The policeman nods.

"The extremists turned against him, Madam, just like a tiger, forgive the repetition, who strikes out at the one who has come to bring him his food."

When she thinks about it, Sonia discovers that there is a horrible link in the deaths in the family, as though its members were the architects of their own destruction. Indira died because of a problem that Sanjay originated by creating the Brindanwale monster to control the Sikhs politically; Rajiv has died through a problem originally created by Indira, who for years provided support for the Tigers in order to gain the votes of the Tamils in India and not lose the electoral grassroots. Had she not heard Indira often say that the worst thing about politics was not doing what you really thought you should do from fear of losing support? Both of them ended up paying for the error they made at some moment of weakness, of lack of faith, the error of putting short-term political considerations before the long-term general interest of the country. And errors cost dear in politics. Sonia, Priyanka and Rahul's blood runs cold when they think about it. It is the most expensive lesson of their lives.

*   *   *

Unlike the Congress Party, the Hindu fundamentalists are very satisfied with their electoral results. They realize that the campaign to destroy the mosque in Ayodhya and replace it with a Hindu temple dedicated to the god Rama, has brought important political returns. The disturbances have turned into votes. So why not go on? In October 1991, extremist Hindu organizations affiliated to the BJP arrange to purchase the land all round the mosque. Immediately afterwards they begin works to level the ground. And as the last straw in provocation, they announce that on December 6th they will start the construction of the temple. When the Moslems scream blue murder, the government sends a team to Ayodhya to assess the situation, and they find a large concrete platform put up by the extremists next to the mosque. It is a flagrant violation of the law that had forbidden things to be changed after the last riots. The government team is dismayed to find that the local government has turned a blind eye, but the explanation is very simple: its leader is a member of the BJP.

Concerned about a possible escalation in violence, the Home Secretary in New Delhi sends 20,000 men, who are distributed in different barracks located less than an hour from the mosque. But, on the other hand, a hundred thousand Hindu militants start arriving, dressed up as heroes from mythology, with tridents, bows and arrows, and they camp in the area. Some leaders of the BJP invoke the pacific and symbolic nature of the gathering.

"We have our own public order agency," they argue to the authorities.

The authorities decide not to send the soldiers to the grounds on the morning of December 6th, the date announced for laying the first stone of the temple. "We did not want to provoke them", they would say later, when the seriousness of that error came to light.

In the area around the mosque only the state police are present, a small force, poorly motivated and even worse equipped to hold back the passions of a gigantic crowd. At half past eleven in the morning, while half-naked holy men covered in ash begin to intone psalms and prayers on the concrete platform, some militants approach the mosque with a threatening attitude. When they try to stop them, the only thing the agents of public order and some policemen achieve is to be stoned by the angry crowd.

"We will build our temple right here!" the militants shout enthusiastically.

An intrepid young man manages to jump over the police and climb the walls of the mosque until he gets to one of its three domes. The crowd see this as a signal to attack. Armed with axes, picks and shovels, an avalanche of militants launch themselves at the mosque. The police flee in terror.

Half an hour later, the militants are walking over the roof

waving bright yellow flags and cheering. While some throw hooks tied to ropes to stick into the roofs of the minarets, others attack the base withsledgehammers, hammers and picks. At two in the afternoon, the firstminaret falls, and with it a dozen men who were destroying the roof with axes. But it does not seem to matter, human life does not matter, what is important is to bring down the symbols of their Moslem neighbours. An hour later, the second minaret falls. Then the last one, and finally the central dome. In a single afternoon, a monument that has witnessed countless disturbances in history, which has borne the lashing of 400 monsoons is reduced to rubble by the fury of a few fanatics.

Most Hindus in the country are not in agreement with a minority of extremists forcing the government to bow to their will. If the forces that could have stopped the sacrilege are at hand, why did the order to intervenenot come? In those days of terror, many Indians miss Indira; with her in power in New Delhi, they think this would probably never have happened. They attribute it to an act of cowardice on the part of the government of Narasimha Rao, who does not want to be seen as "anti-Hindu" in a country with a Hindu majority.

The demolition causes six deaths among the militants and some fifty casualties. The leaders of the BJP are arrested by the police and held in protective custody. An influential local priest expresses the wish that Ayodhya may become the "Vatican of the Hindus" and makes a call for violence. The first step, he adds, is to cleanse the city of its minorities. The militants respond heatedly to this war cry and launch themselves into an orgy of violence, burning Moslem homes and then whole districts. Soon the violence extends up and down India. The Moslems come out on to the streets, attack police stations and set fire to government buildings. The worked up crowds use all kinds of weapons, from acid to shotguns, including slingshots and daggers. The Press tells of cases of children being burned alive, of women shot at point blank range by policemen. The spectre of Partition has reappeared.

There are thousands of deaths all over India. The army imposes a curfew. The country is paralyzed with fear. Planes do not take off, trains do not run. The nightmare of Nehru and Gandhi, of hatred between communities, is becoming a reality before the astonished eyes of the people, who see how co-existence between neighbours is replaced by hostility and suspicion. Moslem and Hindu children no longer play together as they have done for over a thousand years now. Their parents no longer trade with each other and relations come to a halt. Moslems are beginning to be required to prove their loyalty to India. At cricket matches against Pakistan, they are forced to display the national flag on the fronts of their homes, and to cheer on the national team. They are forced to be on the defensive, but in Kashmir, where they are the majority, the roles are reversed. There, Moslem extremists launch a jihad against the Hindu Pandit community, where the Nehrus come from. Over a hundred thousand of them are forced into exile. Both processes feed on each other, while the people, who are not accustomed to dealing with politics in terms of faith and religion, ask themselves a multitude of questions: can a government be trusted if it does not honour its commitment to protect an ancient place of worship?, can a community be trusted if it expels so drastically those who profess another faith? "Like the minarets that crown this old mosque," *Time Magazine* reported, "the three pillars of the Indian State – democracy, a non-denominational state and the rule of law – run the risk of being knocked down by the fury of religious nationalism."

*   *   *

For three years, Sonia has been shut in the house, completely involved in the task of organizing the family archives. She has written a moving book about her husband for which she had had to dig deep into some one hundred thousand photos, five hundred speeches and numberless notes. A voracious reader, she went through her period of mourning among books, bundles of papers, photos and documents. She has also edited the second volume of letters between Nehru and Indira, intense, moving correspondence. "You cannot get away from the family tradition," wrote Nehru from prison to his daughter, "because it will pursue you and, whether you want it or not, it will give you a certain public standing that you have done nothing to deserve. It is unfortunate, but you will have to put up with it. Although, after all, it is not a bad thing to have a good family tradition. It helps us to face the future, it reminds us that we have to keep alive a flame and that we cannot lower ourselves or debase ourselves." Sonia cannot get that letter out of her head. Written in another time and in other circumstances, its echo reverberates inside her because it holds an inevitable truth.

What is happening around her now turns her stomach. That thegovernment, led by a Congress Party Prime Minister, has not been able to prevent the catastrophe in Ayodhya, cuts her to the quick. It is an insult to the ideology, to the very essence of the party. Is it possible that the sacrifices of Gandhi, Indira and Rajiv have all been for nothing? she wonders in bewilderment. Has all that pain been for nothing?

In a meeting of the board of the foundation that bears her husband's name, she proposes they issue a strong declaration of condemnation of the government.

"The foundation is a non-political body," one of the patrons tells her, a former member of the Congress Party and an old friend of Rajiv's. "There is no need to make any comment about a political matter."

Sonia shakes her head.

"Rajiv and the other members of the family are identified with laicism, with the desire not to mix politics and religion. I have the impression that if the foundation does not express its condemnation, we arebetraying the legacy of our family."

"But if you do that, you are getting involved in politics. You have to know that if you involve yourself against what the Congress Party does, you are giving fuel to the adversaries, to the Hindu extremists..."

"It is not a question of making politics or not. It is a question of principle. I cannot remain impassive at what is going on."

She does not intend to remain silent, she does not care who is in government. She repeats that hers is moral authority, not political. Has Prime Minister Rao not committed the same mistake in dealing with the crisis in Ayodhya as Sanjay committed in his day with the Sikhs and Indira with the Tamils? Are the lessons of the past no good for anything? It is quite clear that Rao did not send in the army in time to prevent the destruction of the mosque in order not to alienate the Hindu electorate. He sacrificed peace in the country for a short-term electoral benefit. That is notthe politics that Sonia is prepared to support, no matter who may fall, even if it is the Congress Party.

So she goes ahead with her idea and writes a declaration of condemnation in severe terms, in which she attributes a large part of the responsibility to the government of Narasimha Rao. Inevitably, a political storm is unleashed. "She is getting involved in politics and she's against us?" they ask each other in the government in astonishment. As was to be expected, the opposition enjoys the spectacle of this internal struggle within the Congress Party, which is added to other struggles between different leaders. In the party, they are devouring each other, it is a real viper's nest. The Hindu extremists applaud.

But Sonia is very clear about it. Being faithful to her commitment to preserve the memory of her husband and the family has nothing to do with the fate of Rajiv's men in politics, especially when there are no reasons to back them. She thinks that doing nothing is being disloyal. And Rajiv is still very present in her memory. Everything she has done in her life, she did for him. Now too, in that respect death has changed nothing. He lives on in her. He is her *raison d'être*.

And besides, she has another grievance against Rao's government. The trial of the conspirators arrested by the police shows no sign of ever beginning. As a result of the interrogations of those detained, the police have discovered a meticulously drawn up plan to put an end to Rajiv's life. They know it was designed in the depths of the jungles of Sri Lanka by the official leadership of the terrorist organization, which used the pool of activists they have in the south of India because they needed local Tamils who could not be identified by the accent from the island. The police have discovered a whole support network for the terrorist organization, with a structure in which those who lent their safe houses only knew that they were fighting for the cause; those who were closer to the leadership only knew that the mission consisted of assassinating a politician "hostile to the struggle of the Tigers"; and only the leaders knew who the target was. Those leaders feared that if Rajiv had got back into power, he would have sent the Indian army back to the island again, which would have hurt their cause.

Sonia and her children are disappointed and angered that all the good work of the police runs the risk of coming to nothing because of the inaction of the courts.

"Wait a little longer, you have to be patient..." Rajiv's former colleagues tell her again and again.

"If it is slow, justice is not justice... Don't we all know that?" says Sonia, repeating another phrase she has heard a thousand times at home when Indira was alive.

"This is not the moment to attack the Congress Party. It is so weakened that it would be fatal. Especially if it comes from you."

"Neither my children nor I will go on waiting for much longer."

Sonia, involved in the work of the foundation, goes round the country like she has never done before. It is a rediscovery of deepest India, this time alone and seeing it with different eyes. Whether it is to inaugurate the Lifeline Express, a train made into a travelling hospital to operate for blindness, or providing aid material for the areas most affected by the riots, launching literacy programmes or opening a cancer hospital in a remote rural area, her presence attracts a growing number of people who invariably give her a warm welcome. At feeling herself loved, she learns to be more communicative, not with the Press, of which she is still suspicious, but with the women with whom she shares tea and a chat, and with the children whom she hugs and to whom she gives gifts. Her work deeply satisfies her. She takes on the old family commitment with the poor of India with vigour and efficiency, and she does it her way.

But if she is committed to the people and has principles and the power that comes from belonging to the Nehru family, can she be silent at the inefficiency and laziness of the authorities, whatever side of the fence they are on? Is silence not like approving of the government's behaviour, which has brought the country to the brink of the abyss?

On August 24th, 1995, the fourth anniversary of Rajiv's birthday, now tired of waiting, and concerned about the increase in confrontations between communities, Sonia takes the floor, and does so in Amethi. Ten thousand people deliriously cry: "Sonia, save the country!" as she slowly goes up the steps to the stage, with her head covered by the end of her sari. Her hands tremble because of how nervous she is and she seems unsure of herself, in contrast with her daughter Priyanka, who greets the crowd in a relaxed fashion.

"Mother, look how many people there are! Don't you think you ought to wave to them?"

Sonia listens to her daughter and raises her arm. The thunderous response from the people emboldens her. Flanked by Priyanka, she gives free rein to her anger: "For four long years the government has been incapable of arresting my husband's murderers and bringing them to trial," she declares in almost perfect Hindi. "If the proceedings into the assassination of an ex-Prime Minister take so long to make any progress, what will happen to the common citizen with matters pending justice? I am sure that you understand what I am feeling." In the midst of a hurricane of exclamations, she continues: "Today, the ideals of Nehru, of Indira and of Rajiv are under threat. There are divisions everywhere. The time has come to restore their principles and I will be with you in that effort." "Sonia, save the country!" the people reply, feeling love for this brave and worthy widow. They admire her for her self-denial, her faithfulness to the family and her sacrifice. Before she gets into the car, a reporter comes up to her:

"Does your speech mark the return of the Gandhi dynasty to the political scene in India?"

"No," replies Sonia. "I have no political ambitions. I always speak as president of the Rajiv Gandhi Foundation."

But the whole of India has heard her message. The next day,

her photo with her arm raised, accompanied by her children, is on the front page of all the national newspapers. In the eyes of millions of Indians, Sonia is no longer seen as the housewife who lives in the shadow of her husband and her mother-in-law, and she becomes the public figure responsible for the legacy of the family.

What happened to Rajiv and Indira is now happening to Sonia. Contact with the people cheers her, comforts her and takes her out of her existential anguish, making her forget the contradiction there is in taking on the legacy of such a political family when she herself detests politics. The result of the following elections, those in 1996, does not surprise her at all. She is so well informed that she already knows the party is not going to get even two hundred MPs. But it does not even get 140, a historic disaster. Rao dissolves the government, and resigns as Prime Minister and leader of the party.

A few days later, she receives a visit from a group of dissidents from the Congress Party who once again have come to ask for her advice in choosing the next president of the organization. But Sonia refuses to give her opinion. This time, aware of her power, of "the Sonia factor", she does not even mention who would be her favourite to take over. She does not want to be manipulated.

The one who has come out victorious in these elections is Maneka, who has again won a seat in Parliament. Going back and forth from the benches, the sister-in-law has made herself an image of her own as a defender of animals. She is named as Minister of the Environment again, but her joy does not last long. Because of pressure from the enemies of the coalition, the new Prime Minister is forced to dismiss her a few days later. It is ironic that Indira's Indian daughter-in-law, a political and talkative woman, should fight so much

561

for a piece of power while the timid, apolitical foreign daughter-in-law goes on rejecting offers of leadership.

Because the leaders of the Congress Party come back to the attack, aware that the absence of the widow is the most important presence in the party. The situation is catastrophic, they tell her, the party is falling apart, the country is rushing towards the abyss of religious wars. There is not a day when someone does not come to repeat this to her. The internecine fighting within the largest political organization in the world is emptying it of the best militants, who are deserting en masse. The new leader, who is elected at the cost of bitter disputes, is an individual who does not inspire respect. He spends the evenings at home, lying on the floor with his head on a pillow, drinking whisky and smoking non-stop, while talking about politics, gossip and sex. Sonia knows that this man is not the solution, rather the opposite. In spite of the constant pressure, she still does not let them twist her arm. "What about Priyanka?" they ask, as if the daughter would do just as well as the mother. It does not matter who it is, but it must be a Gandhi, it is the only thing that can save the organization. Only a Gandhi can hold together the different tendencies, the different egos. Only a Gandhi can galvanize the battered morale of the sympathizers. In the once all-powerful Congress Party, a party with 112 years of history behind it, there is despair. "Millions of party militants are prepared to give their lives for you. How can you allow the Congress Party to fall apart before your very eyes?" they repeat. It is said so much that Sonia begins to feel a vague guilt complex, her conscience afflicted by a kind of pain. Can I go on being a silent spectator in the face of the disintegration of the party for which Rajiv gave his life? The question perturbs her. Suddenly it is as if the ground has given way beneath her feet. Besides, she is tired of so much pressure and she has been subjected to it constantly since Rajiv died. She is also tired of so much adulation. But above all she is tormented. If the Congress Party falls apart, the family legacy comes to an end. Thinking that Rajiv's sacrifice was in vain makes her lose sleep. Her daughter shares her worries.

"Something has to be done," Priyanka says to her, "otherwise the BJP will end up destroying everything we have achieved, from grandfather down to Daddy."

When an old friend of the family, Amitabh Bachchan, whose house she lived in when she arrived in New Delhi and who has become the most popular film star in India, comes to visit her, she shares her uneasiness with him.

"I wonder if by failing the Congress party, I'm not failing Nehru, Indira and Rajiv," she confesses.

"Don't confuse them with the leaders there are now," Amitabh replies. "These are a bunch of vultures who want to take advantage of your family's power of pull for their own political ends. Don't let yourself be deceived, don't give way."

"Of course, you're right," she tells him.

But Priyanka does not agree with Amitabh.

"So," she tells her mother when they are alone again, "we are going to let the country fall apart and not do anything then?"

Sonia answers her with another question.

"Don't you think the family has already done enough for the country?"

But doubt grips her like a gloomy embrace, as though it can guess that her resistance is about to give way to the inevitable.

*   *   *

Months later, another visit from another old friend of Rajiv's sows more doubt in Sonia's mind. He is one of the most highly valued leaders of the Congress Party, an upright man called Digvijay Singh. His opinion always carried weight in Rajiv's time.

"We're heading straight for disaster," he tells her suddenly. "With this new president, we aren't even going to get a hundred seats in the next elections. Do you know what that means?"

Sonia makes a face in displeasure. The man goes on:

"It means the disintegration of the party, the end of the Congress Party. And perhaps of India as a nation."

There is a long, dense silence.

"I know your position and that of your children as regards taking on your family's mantle, but given the extreme gravity of the situation, I have come in the name of Rajiv's colleagues to ask you to do it. I know what you think of politics, we all know. I know you're going to say no, but I would be remiss in my duty if I did not insist. And I wouldn't do it if I knew there was a better solution."

"I have always thought that you had pull, that you could perfectly well be a good president for the party," Sonia tells him.

"I don't have enough backing. I may have in the future perhaps, but not now. At this time of extreme gravity, the solution is up to you or your children."

"Are you telling me that if I don't go into politics, I'm failing in my responsibilities?"

The man does not dare to reply.

"I want to make you see another side to the problem," he goes on. "Let us suppose that the Congress Party disappears... What will happen to your security? Whether you go into politics or not, there are a lot of people who see you as a threat because of what you represent. Those who are against the founding principles of the Congress Party are also against you. And unfortunately they are legion, every day more. Even if you never go into politics, the fact of having stayed on to live in this house is in itself a political act."

Sonia does not answer. Her head is spinning. Digvijay Singh goes on:

"If they took protection away from Rajiv, they will take it away from you, don't have any doubts about that. If the Congress Party disappears as a political force, who is going to pay for the enormous security deployment that you and your children need?"

Sonia shivers, because she knows he is right. Would they dare to leave them unprotected? Everything is possible in this dirty world of politics. There are enemies out there, and also within the party, the same ones who withdrew protection from Rajiv. Some for one reason, others for another. It is clear that if the party goes under, they will be left defenceless. But if she agrees and goes into politics to save it, is that not tempting the devil? Is it not exposing herself even more to the bullets of any madman? There is no way out in the labyrinth of her life. It all ends up getting mixed up in her head: the sense of responsibility and the fear, the hatred of politicsand the need for security. For the first time, Sonia begins to realize that power not only needs her, the family also needs the protection of power. Otherwise, it is quite clear: the legacy will no longer exist, the sacrifice of Indira and Rajiv will fall into oblivion and perhaps they – Sonia, Priyanka or Rahul – will also no longer exist.

44

While Sonia struggles with all her doubts, Indian politics continues to fall apart. The concept of nation created by the Congress Party during the struggle for independence, and which advocates a pluralistic, non- denominational and diverse nation (the opposite of Pakistan, a nation created around a religion), is still losing ground in an alarming manner. The same adversaries against whom Mahatma Gandhi, Nehru, Indira and Rajiv fought, are those who are now gaining adepts with their idea of a Hindu India, like an involuntary echo of Pakistan. What will happen if they get hold of power? Will there be ethnic cleansing? Then there is the lamentable spectacle of corruption. A hundred or so MPs in New Delhi now have a "criminal past", which means that they have been accused of several crimes, but not formally convicted. If Nehru could only see this! Once they are elected it is practically impossible to convict them, and for that reason politics is becoming an important incentive for delinquents of all kinds.

The corruption is so grotesque that a leader on the rise in the biggest "untouchables" party in India, a middle-aged woman called Mayawati who has become rich overnight and claims that her followers are "very generous", has been caught red-handed giving out licences to her builder friends to put up a huge theme park around the Taj Mahal. The scandal has forced her to abandon the project, but it has not taken any votes away from her. The newspapers publish photos of her receiving her interviewers sitting on a real carved wooden throne covered in gold leaf in her palatial home in Lucknow. She celebrated her birthday in style, using official procedures and public funds. And she is not the only one.

It seems that instead of progressing, the country is moving back to the times of the corrupt maharajahs. It is going back to its old ways, like when it was made up of a myriad kingdoms that fought amongst themselves, weakening each other, making the Mogul and British invasions easier. If the Congress Party ends up smashed to pieces in the coming elections, the only large national party will die. Now all that is left are kingdoms of gangs who fight, not for their ideology, but to win the favour of their electors, more and more grouped together in castes or regional communities. Politics is fragmenting. How far will that fragmentation go? As far as the disintegration of India? The analysts do not discount that. Some say that India was the Nehru family, that without them India is not even a nation.

*   *   *

During one of her nights of insomnia, Sonia feels pressure on her chest again. Sometimes it is the cold that starts off an asthma attack, other times it comes with no apparent explanation and yet others it is due to stress. Her bronchial tubes feel narrower and make the passage of air to her lungs difficult. The feeling she is drowning, that when she inhales no air comes in, is very distressing. Chronic asthma cannot be cured, but youlearn to live with the illness, as Sonia has done. She knows that yoga has helped her a lot. Yoga teaches you to breathe. When she notices the first symptoms that night, she starts looking for her inhaler and her medicines. But she cannot find them in their usual place, they are not in the bathroom cabinet or on her bedside table. "I must have left them in the office," she says to herself. She wraps herself in her dressing gown and goes out of her room.

In effect, the inhaler is on the desk in the office. Sonia sits down, puts it in her mouth, presses just as she breathes in and takes some deep breaths. She feels the effect immediately. That's it, she can breathe. She relaxes. The house is almost silent, except for the sound of the wind in the leaves on the trees in the garden and her deep breaths in and out. The room still smells of cold incense, just as when Rajiv was alive. He liked to have some sticks burning when he was working. He used to say they helped him to concentrate.

Suddenly Sonia looks up and sees the picture of Indira. Then the one of Nehru. And then the one of Rajiv. "Why are you looking at me so insistently? With such enigmatic smiles?" That night, in the shadows, they look as if they are alive. Sonia puts her inhaler away in her pocket and, before putting out the light, she looks at the pictures again. She cannot hold their gaze and she looks down, as though she is ashamed. She turns out the light and goes back to bed in her room. But she cannot get to sleep and she does not want to take a pill in case she gets used to them. She turns over and over in bed, gets tangled up in the sheets, turns on the light, tries to read, feels tired, and puts the light out again. She cannot get the photos in the office out of her head. "I'm failing them," she says to herself. "I'm betraying them. My God, what shall I do?"

She needs to talk to her children. Rahul has just arrived from London, where he has found a job in a finance company after finishing his studies in the United States. Priyanka has a boyfriend, a young man she has known since she was little. The next day, sitting at the breakfast table, Sonia tells them about the feeling the photos in the office gave her.

"Every time I walk past them, I have the impression they are looking at me, as though they expected something of me..."

"They do expect something, Mother," Priyanka says. "The same thing happens to me and I'm ashamed that I'm doing nothing while everything is falling to pieces. What would Grandmother say? I'm sure she wouldn't like it... We have to avoid the party coming apart."

"And how can that be done?" her brother asks.

"By campaigning for the Congress Party in the coming elections," answers Priyanka.

Rahul shrugs his shoulders. "Let's not get into that mess."

"I think we have to think about it," answers Priyanka, who has her feet firmly on the ground. "You know, Mother, I've come to the same conclusion as you, although by another path. We cannot remain as spectators. It's as if... as if it's immoral!"

Little by little, they start weighing up the pros and cons of a decision that apparently changes everything, but which finally shows it is deeply logical.

"There are times when one's preferences have to be left aside, don't you think?" asks Sonia, with a serious look on her face.

Her children do not answer. She goes on:

"I would be prepared to campaign for the Congress Party in order to try to save the organization, but not to take on any government position. Will you help me?"

"Of course," her daughter says.

"Do you remember what your great-grandfather said to Grandmother Indira in that letter?... That she would never be able to get away from the family tradition. How right he was! I think we too cannot get away from it. It's like a second skin to us, whether we like it or not."

Rahul finds it difficult to accept his mother's decision,

because he cannot see that she is happy. He knows she is going to go down a path that really repels her. He knows she is doing it because she has inherited the same sense of duty that Indira and Rajiv had. But in the end, the young manunderstands what is at stake.

"Mother, I'll give up my job and I'll go with you to all the rallies,"he says to encourage her.

*   *   *

Sonia likes to serve the tea herself to people who come to see her. This time it is not a usual visit, it was she who called the leader of the Congress Party and an old friend of the family, Digvijay Singh, the onewho told her a few months before that they were heading straight fordisaster. He is a tall, good-looking man, with natural elegance emphasized by the clothes he is wearing: a white *kurta* and white pyjama-type trousers. He has come without delay, in spite of having had to spend the night on a train. But if Sonia calls, people take notice, because she does not usually ever call. Sonia hands him his cup of tea, which gives off the scent of jasmine. Before she sits down, she glances quickly at the photos on the walls, as though asking for their approval for daring to do what she is proposing.

"What would happen if I campaigned for the Congress Party?" she says all of a sudden.

The man burns his lips and splutters. Can what he is hearing be true? he wonders. He had no idea what he was going to find, and that is why the question has caught him unawares.

There is a silence, a dense silence, which Sonia uses to offer him a linen serviette embroidered with a G.

"Madam," he replies, wiping the corner of his mouth, "that would have a galvanizing effect on our ranks. We would win overwhelmingly in the polls."

Sonia is serious, meditative. The man's eyes light up. "Do you really think so?"

"I am convinced of it."

"For me, it is a very difficult decision to make." "I understand perfectly, Madam."

Sonia goes on:

"I am not a born leader, you know that, it is not something thatcomes naturally to me..."

"I don't think the ability to lead is something innate. Look at the example of Indira. She was timid and at first she didn't speak very well. Or your husband. Everything can be learned. And in politics you learn even faster."

"Do you think that can be learned?"

"I'm sure of it. Just look at the number of people who come to see you at any event. It's as though they are drinking in your words... Besides, we can prepare you. You have the advantage of having at your disposal the large reserve of talent there is in the Congress Party, unless the partydisintegrates so quickly that they all end up leaving before the elections. But we still have the best specialists in the fields of the economy, the administration, or science and technology."

Sonia remains looking at him, but she says nothing. She has the hermetic expression of a person who is resigned to accepting the inevitable.

Shortly after that meeting, Sonia discreetly carries out some paperwork, in her own way. She heads for the headquarters of the party in Akbar Road and she fills in the form that goes with the request to join the organization. She returns home with her membership card in her hand, which links her even more closely with Nehru, Gandhi and all those who fought for the ideals of an independent, free India. She goes into her office and before she puts it away in a drawer, she gazes at the pictures.

She gives a timid smile, as though she were no longer ashamed to look them in the eye.

*   *   *

On December 28th, 1997, Sonia publicly announces her decision to go into politics and stand as a Congress Party candidate in the coming elections. The news goes round the world. No one understands the reason for this *volte-face*, not her mother or her sisters or her friends or the public in general. The leaders of the party make a great show of welcoming her, but some are suspicious because they know that this "neophyte" will end up ruling them. Evil tongues spit their venom: Sonia is getting into politics in order to cover herself from the Bofors scandal, say some. Sonia wants to be Prime Minister, say others. She's finally showing her true colours, a third claims. Maneka Gandhi does not miss the chance to add her bit. "She waves like a windscreen wiper on a car," she says, referring to Sonia's greeting to her enthusiastic followers when she came out of the party headquarters. And she adds in an interview in the weekly *Panchjanya*: "Sonia will not be elected because she is a foreigner... The only thing she wants is to be Prime Minister one day so she can have a comfortable life. That post is like a toy for her, she is not aware of the difficulties involved in it..."

Sonia refuses to make any comment about her ex-sister-in-law. What she tries to do is to protect herself from the criticism and mockery, wherever they come from. She has always known that she would be subjected to even more intense public scrutiny than before. It is part of a politician's life. That is why she wants to be as well prepared as possible.

Aware of her limitations, she surrounds herself with the best specialists: a historian, a sociologist, a jurist expert in constitutional law, an ex-director of the Intelligence Agency, an expert in political science... In general, they consider her a "conscientious student" who, for example, quickly learns the customs and usage in Parliament. But she makes a few mistakes. When they introduce her to an influential leader of a caste from the state of Uttar Pradesh, a brilliant man, with an analytical mind able to explain to her the delicate balance between the castes, Sonia tells him frankly: "In the Congress Party, I want caste considerations to be minimized." The man gets up suddenly and says he will be back when Sonia has a better idea of how important the subject he is talking about is. Occupational hazards.

The moment of her entry into politics coincides with her daughter's wedding. Priyanka marries a jewellery designer, the son of a tin magnate from a city near New Delhi. Sonia is not very happy about the marriage; the groom has not finished university and, even worse, some members of his family have links with extremist Hindu organizations affiliated to the BJP. But that does not seem to bother Priyanka. She is in love with a man, not with his family, and in that she thinks like a European, not like an Indian. She has taken a decision and is going to go ahead with it.

"Priyanka is being faithful to the family tradition," Rahul tells his mother sarcastically. "She's marrying someone with whom she has nothing in common. What's wrong with that?"

"That is precisely the problem."

"Problem? What did Great-grandfather Nehru have in common with Great-grandmother? Nothing. Grandmother Indira and Grandfather? Nothing either. Uncle Sanjay and Maneka? And you and Dad... you said yourself that you were from very different worlds. Sometimes it works, other times it doesn't, you never know."

"If your sister and you are going to gang up on me, I don't

intend to open up another front," Sonia says, smiling again.

The cream of society attend the wedding of Priyanka, daughter, granddaughter and great-granddaughter of three Prime Ministers. Sonia, very elegant in a maroon and gold sari, welcomes the President of the Republic, the Prime Minister and the top leaders of the party. The atmosphere is charged with expectation at this event labelled by the Press as the "wedding of the year". Never as much as today has the "ruling" family been the source of so many comments and so much gossip. Since Sonia announced her entry into politics, some predict her imminent failure, others show their satisfaction at having found a leader able to help the Congress Party rise up again. They say that the mother has agreed to make the sacrifice of going into politics for the sake of her children, the real natural heirs of the dynasty. Among the guests there is also a tall, good- looking boy, that Priyanka has insisted on inviting. He is her cousin, Firoz Varun Gandhi, Maneka's son, who is studying at the London School of Economics. He has come alone, without his mother. Whether it is Priyanka, Rahul or Firoz, the party leaders have absolute faith in them. They consider them to be born leaders, charismatic and able to decide the fate of millions of people. Now their mother has taken the first step, they are convinced that the future of the Congress Party, and of the nation, will be in their hands. It does not escape them that Priyanka, radiant, is wearing the splendid sari made of cotton that her great-grandfather Nehru wove in prison. The same one that Indira wore at her wedding, and then Sonia at hers. A real symbol, that red sari.

*   *   *

A real symbol too, the fact that Sonia begins her campaign

where herhusband ended his, in the city of Sriperumbudur. She has to get over the emotion of being in the place that Rajiv saw for the last time. She has to getover her shyness, her nervousness and her asthma attacks when speaking in public. "I am here before you, surrounded by security measures, in the same place where Rajiv was alone and unprotected and facing his murderers. His voice has been silenced, but his message and the ideas he defended are more alive now than ever." She no longer makes mention of the slowness of justice with the bitterness she had before. Finally, in January 1998, the judge presiding over the case against those accused of murdering her husband has passed sentence: the death penalty. Those convicted have appealed to the Supreme Court, but their chances of having their sentence commuted are minimal. It is no comfort to Sonia, who has always been opposed to capital punishment. She would prefer them to be locked up behind bars.

Making reference to her foreign origins, the weak point that her adversaries are already using against her, she adds: "I became a part ofIndia thirty years ago, when I came into the home of Indira Gandhi as the wife of her elder son. It was through her heart that I learned to understand and love India." These are simple words, said in a natural, pleasant way, punctuated by a slight smile. She repeats them over the period of a month, during which time she travels thirty thousand kilometres, one of thosemarathons that several members of her family have had to undergo. In her speeches, which she reads directly in Hindi, she also speaks about sacrifice,about stability and above all about laicism. She explains that she has launched into the campaign as a reaction against the distress she feels about there being politicians calling for votes in the name of religion. "You have to choose between the forces of harmony and progress or those who seek to exploit our differences in order to gain power." She takes advantage of any occasion to apologise for the mistakes of the past, such as Operation Blue Star in the Punjab, or the demolition of the mosque in Ayodhya. She takes on the failures of others with total humility. She speaks with the feeling of being infused with a mission. The crowds attend her rallies not just from the immense curiosity she arouses, but because Sonia is able to combine emotion with a forceful political speech. Her campaign provides a note of freshness and novelty to the general panorama. The most sceptical leaders are surprised at Sonia's efficiency when it comes to filling rallies with people and galvanizing the electorate. At the end of the campaign, the *Times of India* carries the headline: "From evasive empress to long- suffering wife and powerful politician, the transformation of Sonia Gandhi seems complete."

Sonia does not gain an overwhelming victory, but she gets 146 seats for the Congress Party, and ensures that voter participation increases significantly. That is to say, she avoids a catastrophe. Recognized as the saviour of the party and in order that in the future the organization will not disappear in internal squabbles, the leaders decide to raise her to the presidency. Sonia Gandhi becomes the fifth member of the house of Motilal Nehru to take on the post. Ah, if only Stefano Maino could see her now!... How distant now are the Asiago mountains, those evenings spent by the warmth of the fireplace with her sisters waiting for the *zuppa* for dinner, those never-ending masses in the church in Lusiana, the smell of snow at the end of autumn, her girlish dreams of wanting to live in a city and not in the country, milking cows... And all of it because her eyes met his in a restaurant in Cambridge.

Eleven months after her wedding, Priyanka comes across a piece of news in the newspaper about her father's murderers.

One of the female terrorists convicted is about to be executed by hanging, along with three accomplices. One of them is her husband. The woman, who goes by the name of Nalini Murugan, married him in jail in Vellore, a city in the south, and they had a baby girl. Every afternoon, the little girl goes to visit her mother in prison for half an hour accompanied by her grandmother. Priyanka, deeply saddened by the news, talks to Sonia and her brother about it. Is it really necessary for more people to die? Has there not been enough tragedy already? Does a little girl have to be left an orphan? Sonia and Rahul are just as upset. None of the three of them is in favour of the death penalty. Justice has been done, and to a certain extent that has served for them to be reconciled with the drama they have been through. But for an act of State to leave a child an orphan because of the wrong-doing of her parents is something that seems unfair to them.

"It isn't going to be any consolation to us," says Sonia. "Rather the opposite," adds Rahul. "What can we do?"

"Ask for clemency for the mother," Priyanka suggests, "and get the execution of the others postponed indefinitely."

When the President of the Republic receives Sonia at a special audience in his Rashtrapati Bhawan residence, the former Viceroy's palace, he is astonished at what he hears, after all the protests Sonia has made regarding the slowness of justice. "My children have been left without a father, and that is enough," Sonia tells him. "Our argument is that no other child needs to be left an orphan. We do not want that tragedy to engender even more tragedy. I ask you to do whatever is possible to get a pardon for Nalini Murugan so that she can bring up her daughter."

When they come to take the young terrorist woman out of her cell, she is convinced it is for her last journey. But they take her before the judge of Vellore, who informs her that her sentence of capital punishment has been commuted to life imprisonment. "I hope this serves some purpose, even if only to call attention to the futility of acts of terrorism, which only lead to destruction and death," Rahul declares to the Press. Then, thanks to Sonia's mediation, Nalini obtains a visa for her little daughter and her paternal grandparents so that they are able to travel to Australia, where theyare taken in by exiled members of the Tamil community. The child will be able to be educated in an environment not stigmatized by the situation of her parents.

45

Sonia has brought hope back to the biggest party in the world, although she has not put it back in power. She has not managed to halt the rise of the Hindus of the BJP, whose results allow them to lead a coalition and form a government. Will they go on whipping up rivalry between communities? Will they go on pushing the country towards the brink of the precipice? At least the new Prime Minister, Atal Bihari Vajpayee, is a moderate, cultured man, well-respected in political circles. Will he manage to control the more extremist members? The whole country asks itself these questions, especially in view of the programme, which is enough to make anyone tremble: a Hindu India, reform of the Constitution, construction of the temple to Rama in Ayodhya, etc.

It is logical that many people have their trust in Sonia, who has to take on the role of leader of the opposition since she is president of the Congress Party. Back home in Italy, relations, friends and neighbours gather round the television to follow the amazing story of this daughter of their land. The Cinderella of Orbassano has given way to the supplicationof her courtiers and has launched herself after power in that land... But does it not make her feel dizzy? Is she not afraid of being killed? Is she notafraid for her children? Why does she not leave it all and come here to set up a home interior shop and live quietly? They do not understand what is running through this woman's head... a woman who has fallen in love with a prince and may end up as a queen.

Eight years after Rajiv's assassination, the doors of Parliament are opened to Sonia. As she goes up the steps, she remembers something her mother-in-law said about hers not being a normal family, "because they expect miracles of us." Was it not a miracle to be in that immense, round, singular building in the heart of New Delhi, where the aspirations of a nation that now has a billion inhabitants converge, where Nehru, Indira and Rajiv defended their ideas? Where she now has to defend her ideas. Shehas come from so far away, she dies of embarrassment when people look ather, and yet she has accepted that challenge that is so contrary to her temperament in order to protect the family of the man she has most loved and to save the country from the yoke of the fundamentalists. Will she be able to perform those miracles?

What a lot of travelling, how much joy and excitement, how many disappointments and tears shed!... And above all, what a lot of love for her husband, whose warm presence she feels in this place where he was so often. She concentrates on the memory of him, and asks him for protection on October 29th, 1999, when she has to give her first speech. Her whole body is tense. She has been to the bathroom five times thinking about the step she is about to take. She is aware that there are five hundred pairs of eyes closely watching her every movement, a torture for a woman who is unhealthily shy. But she does it out of the same sense of duty because of which her husband launched himself into politics. She is not doing it out of pleasure, but out of love. From that immeasurable love she gains the energy to swim against the current, to overcome her own wishes, to put up with all the staring from those occupying the Press stand, the visitors' stand and the diplomatic stand, which are full to overflowing. On the government bench is Maneka, recently named as Culture Minister for the coalition led by the BJP. Both sisters-in-law represent the most opposite factions of the ideological spectrum, like a metaphor of the division the country is suffering. If only Indira could see it! On the Congress Party bench, there are at least a dozen colleagues ready to help Sonia, if she should need some information, in case she makes a mistake, in case she puts her foot in it. She is the very picture of elegance, with her shiny black hair falling in soft waves over her shoulders, her silk sari in tones of pastel green, her proud bearing, her direct gaze.

She puts on her glasses. She has come prepared with a text printed in very large print so that it does not look as if she is reading, an old family trick. A text in which she complains that the present regime is claiming reforms that were originally promoted by the Congress Party, specifically, by Rajiv. She takes no notice of the boos and whistling that come at her from the bench of the coalition in power. On the contrary, she goes ahead and denounces the latest manoeuvres of the government to discredit her husband in the Bofors affair. "Suspicion cannot be cast on a man who is innocent and, furthermore, who is not here to defend himself," she exclaims. Her emotional speech causes a very favourable impact on her MPs, who see for themselves that Sonia is able to take the bull by the horns in a matter as delicate as the Bofors affair. Suddenly, it is as if memories of a smiling, jovial Rajiv were reappearing. But everyone is asking themselves the same question: What is going to happen when she has to attack or defend specific economic options? What will happen when her speech does not have an emotional charge to it?

Over several months, she dares to make short speeches in Parliament relative to current affairs, although she avoids commenting on economic matters. In that respect, she fully trusts a man she met when the firstgovernment was formed after Rajiv's murder. He is a Sikh called Manmohan Singh, an ex-Cambridge student and a brilliant economist, the architect of the reforms that managed to lift the country out of the economic crisis in the nineties, known for his irreproachable reputation for honesty. He followed in Rajiv's wake and he is committed to modernizing the economy. His influence on her is so great that the old Socialists and Leftists in the Congress Party look at her with suspicion. "Isn't she going tolead us away from the old Socialist ideas in order to set us on a course towards liberalism?" they ask each other in alarm.

At first, her role as leader of the opposition confuses both her party colleagues and her adversaries. As she is afraid to deal with thorny questions, she shares them out among different MPs who are considered to be specialists, whether in foreign policy, economic policy or legislative matters... But those opposite her furiously attack that fragmented opposition, without a helm, without any weight behind it, and without any force. In the ranks of the Congress Party, the MPs come to fear sessions in Parliament as much as or more than Sonia herself. She defends herself poorly from all kinds of accusations, launched without any basis in order todamage her image. The worst are those from Maneka, who as Minister for Culture suddenly finds herself placed over the charitable and family institutions that Sonia administrates and who, in order to make her power quite clear, orders a series of audits, alleging suspected financial irregularities. She is finally enjoying the taste of revenge. But her fury is such, her rage and personal ill-will towards Sonia are so obvious, that the other parties in the coalition protest at that gratuitous persecution. So, in an abrupt manoeuvre, she is removed from her position and put at the head of the statistics department, where her inquisitorial activity is neutralized.

The deficiencies in Sonia's role as leader of the opposition ("a leader who hides", as those in the government accuse her) are compensated by her efficiency when it comes to leading the party. The old satraps who thought they could manipulate her quickly realize that that she will not allow that to happen. She has been too close to Indira not to have learned the lesson. But, in addition, Sonia undertakes thorny reforms that had always been postponed by previous leaders. For example, she gets the Congress Party to be the first party to keep a quota of 33% for women at all levels of the hierarchy. It is harder to attack corruption, but Sonia does not hesitate. Under the new mantra of integrity and transparency, she gets the party to only accept donations by cheque in order to make accounting easier and she demands that all members with a certain influence pay their dues punctually, proportionate to their position in the hierarchy. The people in the top positions are forced to pay a month's salary to the party. These are profound changes, which many see as personal triumphs. "The Congress Party is getting ready to clean up the system," she says in a threatening tone to some sceptical, and in many cases corrupt, MPs, who are already conspiring to get rid of her.

They take advantage of the fact that her role as leader of the opposition leaves much to be desired. Sonia does not dare to communicate directly with the other leaders in opposition from embarrassment and shyness, which leads to a great lack of coordination. It is quite clear that she does not know what the game of politics is about. It is hard for her to hide her lack of experience and self-confidence, which makes her an easy target for the attacks of the coalition in power, which challenges her and humiliates her every time there is an opportunity. "They don't know what I'm made of!" she says one day to her children, coming out of a session in Parliament during which she has been slated. She has caused great embarrassment because she had nothing to say when the Prime Minister asked what the Congress Party's position was on nuclear deterrence, a matter about which she knew nothing. So she swears to herself that it will not happen again, and she calls for the best experts in nuclear security and defence, including those who are not part of the Congress Party's think tank, in order to understand all the ins and outs of this complicated subject. When she is sure of herself, she goes back to Parliament. She seems like a different woman: "At the last session, the honourable Prime Minister laughed at me because I did not answer his question... But it is a subject too important to be answered amid the laughter of his MPs. Now I ask you: What is your position on this matter?... You only mention three words: minimum credible deterrence. Do you think that those three little words make up a serious policy?"

In May, 1999, the BJP government loses its majority in Parliament and the advisors and old leaders of the Congress Party think that Sonia's time has come. They think they can articulate the formation of a coalition to govern. They need the magic figure of 272 MPs and they are convinced they have that number. They are already dreaming about the share-out of ministries: perhaps so and so will fight for the Home Office, and so and so will go to the Foreign Office... The mood in the party's ranks is exultant. They are so sure they will take power that they push Sonia to announce that she is in a position to quickly form an alternative government. For Sonia, it represents the chance to get even for the constant attacks on her. At last she is going to be able to stop her adversaries in their tracks. When she comes out of the old Viceroy's palace, where the President of the Republic has called all the parties to invite them to form a government, she is surrounded by television cameras. "We have 272," she states. Actually she meant that an alternative government was possible as a majority of MPs was against the BJP. But the Press announces it in its own way: "Sonia Gandhi is going to head a new government." The country seems suddenly inflamed at the prospect of an Italian woman taking power, but the suspense does not last long. Sonia does not get the magic number because many small groups opposed to the BJP, and in particular the Socialists, refuse to back her as Prime Minister because of her foreign origins and the strong anti-Congress feeling there is among many parties. The fiasco is as big as the expectations aroused. She looks bad to her followers, and ridiculous in front of the entire country. Her haste shows the public her lack of experience in the political arena as well as her excessive dependence on her advisors.

"Mother, drop it now," Rahul tells her.

"Now? Do you think I can? I don't intend to go without defending myself."

Little by little, Sonia is learning. "She is a fighter really and that is very good for the organization," says one of her colleagues on the bench. She is forced to fight because the Press and her political adversaries redouble their attacks on her. They laugh at the accent of "the Italian woman", as they call her insultingly. They claim she is arrogant and cold, they say that she does not know the Hindi alphabet and that her speeches are transcribed into the Latin alphabet, which is a lie. "She reads her speeches as if she was reading her shopping list," writes a well-known journalist. But if enemies are good for anything, it is to learn from them, and Sonia learns tenaciously. Gradually, she puts fire and passion into her speeches, she increases the number of trips, meetings and personal contacts. She maintains that she is not arrogant, just shy. But it is a struggle that wears her out, because it is sterile. It is based on prejudice, on a male chauvinist attitude and on an exaggerated form of nationalism that masks her adversaries' desire to keep her out of power at all costs. In the most extremist circles, they even accuse her of being an agent of Rome, asthough she were a Vatican spy who had infiltrated the labyrinth of Hindu politics... Her father had a prophetic vision when he said that they would throw her to the tigers. Well, there his daughter is, in the centre of the arena, avoiding the claws.

Nothing affects her as much as the challenge that comes from her own people, from members of her own party. One day she receives a letter signed by the chief of her party's parliamentary group and two other MPs, in which they cast doubt on her ability to ever be up to taking on the role ofPrime Minister, in view of her poor record as leader of the opposition. In the letter they suggest that the Constitution be amended in order to keep thetop posts in the State - President of the Republic and Prime Minister - only for Indians by birth. After the fiasco of the failed coalition, this is a blow below the belt that Sonia feels bitterly. Not because they want to prevent her from being Head of State one day, which she does not aspire to ordesire anyway. But she is hurt by the lack of confidence, she is hurt that they want her as a fairground attraction, nothing more. As an advertisementfor the elections, as a pawn who lends her name – and her whole life – to a party that really only despises her. It hurts her to realize that she is alone when she had thought she was in friendly territory.

When she gets back home that afternoon, all she has on her mind is being with Priyanka and Rahul. Her daughter immediately realises how hurt her mother is. Rahul is annoyed:

"Drop politics once and for all, Mother!" he says.

"I think Rahul is right," adds Priyanka. "There's no point in going onlike this."

"The moment has come to throw in the towel," Sonia

admits. "Please help me to write a letter to the parliamentary group of the Congress Party," she asks.

Priyanka takes some paper and a pen and together they write a very clear, concise text: "Some colleagues have expressed the idea that because I was born abroad I am a problem for the Congress Party. I am hurt by their lack of confidence in my ability to act in the best interests of the party and of the country. In these circumstances, my sense of loyalty to the party and my duty to the nation oblige me to present my resignation from the position of President of the Congress Party." Further on she adds, "I came to serve the party, not to acquire a position or to hold power, because the party was facing a challenge that questioned its very existence and I could not remain impassive at what was happening. Just as I cannot cross my arms and do nothing now." Sonia gives a long sigh: "Free at last!" she says to herself.

A disaster. Her letter causes a real cataclysm in the party ranks. Her closest collaborators are dismayed by the decision. After the trouble they took to get her to take charge, and now the barons who see their power within the organization threatened throw it all overboard! When the members of the parliamentary group ask her to reconsider her decision, she answers that she is very hurt by the display of xenophobia surrounding the matter of her origins.

"For that to happen in the BJP, an ultra-nationalist party, or among the Socialists, is already sad enough," Sonia adds, "but OK, I was prepared to defend myself as long as the party backed me. What I could never have imagined is that my own colleagues would attack me in this way. So I'm leaving."

The parade begins: the chief ministers of the states governed by the Congress Party come to pay homage to her at her house. They threaten to resign en masse: "We are heads of government thanks to you. Why should we go on if you aren't with us?" they tell her.

The earthquake caused by her resignation is so huge that thousands of followers camp outside the gates of number 10 Janpath Road to ask her to come back. "Sonia, save the Congress! Save India!" they chant. One afternoon when Rahul comes home with a friend, several party leaders intercept him: "You have to convince your mother to withdraw her resignation." Among the crowd blocking the street there are women weeping and begging Sonia not to abandon them. One morning, as she leaves the house, as her Ambassador makes its way through the crowd, Sonia is stopped by an old Moslem man who comes up to her:

"Have you thought about the fate of the minorities in a government led by the BJP? Don't you want to fight for us any longer?"

Sonia does not answer and puts the car window up, as the man's words echo inside her head.

The height of desperation among her followers is symbolized by a young man, one of those camping outside her house. He tries to set fire to himself, which causes considerable uproar. The police and security guards throw themselves on him and manage to put out the flames before he is burned to death. The reporters' cameras record the scene so the whole country can see it on the evening news. So the whole sub-continent can see what passions "the Italian", who everyone thinks belongs to them, arouses. Because Sonia does belong to them, because she carries the magical name of Gandhi. And for that reason she cannot leave.

The tragic incident precipitates events. Once again, Sonia receives the party leaders in her house, in Rajiv's office, a group of middle-aged men, dressed in *kurtas* and wide cotton trousers.

"There is no other leader who can keep us united as you can.

There isno one else who can get the votes that you get. That is why we are asking you to stay on as president. The party is behind you. Listen to the shouting in the street."

In the background, slogans supporting Sonia can be heard which the followers crowding round the gates chant at regular intervals. One of the party leaders goes on:

"Don't ignore the signs of affection the people keep giving you... The people who sent you that letter do not represent even a minority within the party, they only represent themselves and their own ambition."

"There is no room for them in the organization," another adds. "We have expelled them. You have nothing more to fear."

Once again they offer her power on a silver tray, again she hears the same arguments, the same flattery, the same old story...

"I have to talk to my children about it."

She is prepared to maintain her resignation, and she has already got an idea of how nice it would be to go back to her collection of Tanjore miniatures, and take up her hobby of restoring old pictures and furniture again. But Priyanka and Rahul are moved by the sudden outburst of emotion and solidarity. They had not been expecting such a mobilization. The three of them are overcome by that curious feeling that the surname they bear does not belong to them, but to India, to the crowds who call for their leadership, and that they are not masters of their own destiny. Sonia hesitates, although now she knows that if she goes back it will be in style. Her friends finally convince her to stay. She cannot leave because of an attack from three rivals who are after her job. Her resignation, they say, will only strengthen the ones who have written the letter and all the xenophobes in India. Again Sonia thinks about Rajiv, about her children, about the family, about the tragedy of power, about her fear of losing security, about her sense of duty... and again she gives way. She does it reluctantly, but the result is that she takes on the highest post within the party again with more strength and authority than before. She announces her return in a packed stadium. So many people that a member of the party comments to a colleague:

"Can you imagine so many people all together without a Sonia Gandhi?"

"Quite simply there wouldn't be a rally now," the other one replies. "Without Sonia, there's no rally; without Sonia, there's no party."

"Even though I was born abroad," says Sonia as soon as the loud, extremely lengthy ovation allows her to speak, "I have made India my country. I am Indian and I will be until my last breath. I got married here, I had my children here, and I became a widow here. Indira died in my arms. If I have decided to come back today it is because the party has given me renewed confidence and hope. I want a party that is prepared to follow me and be ready to die for the principles I have decided to adopt."

So, little by little, learning from all her troubles, Sonia Gandhi begins to get used to the game of politics. Certain reflexes come to her unconsciously, not by vocation, but by contagion, from having lived so many years in that breeding ground. She has cleared the party of its black sheep. Now she has more influence over the organization than her husband had. She has managed it without the skill to share out power, and only with a remote hope of gaining power one day, which shows how demoralisedthe rank and file were.

46

In time she manages to forge a public image of herself as a reluctant politician, averse to politics, which the Press transmits. But she lives in a state of perpetual terror of the media. Every word she says is closely scrutinised by her adversaries in the hope they will discover some sign that she is not as Indian as she claims to be. She lives shut inside her shell, entrenched at number 10, Janpath Road, a fortress more difficult to enter than all the residences where she has lived previously. She lives without any freedom, dealing from dawn to dusk with committees, party members, and delegates who come from every corner of the country to ask her advice, and to ask for her opinion as number one leader. Only the visits from her children provide her with any affection. Her mother spends the winters in New Delhi, and her sisters and old friends come to visit her periodically. But these are visits she keeps secret, so they cannot accuse her of being a "foreigner".

Just the mention of her name is enough to enliven the most boring of dinners or social acts, with opinions being divided vehemently between those who admire her and those who despise her. Two well-known MPs from her party complain at every cocktail party of having as leader "an uneducated Italian housewife". Nothing much in comparison with the venom of some members of the coalition in power, such as the Hindu fundamentalist, Narendra Modi, who publicly calls her "Italian bitch". Sonia knows that her being a foreigner is her Achilles' heel, and thecoalition in government, fiercely nationalist and Hindu, never misses an opportunity to touch that raw nerve. Her radical refusal to give interviews is attributed to the fact that she does not want to define her position. She thinks that this way she can leave her adversaries without any arguments with which to attack her. She does not want to have to say that she is Catholic, although she is not practising. She does not want to have to talk about the Italy where she was born, or about her memories of her childhoodor of her friends or of her family. On the contrary, it seems essential to her that she should be seen to be comfortable with the traditions of her country of adoption. She tries hard and visits holy men in great Hindu temples, as Indira used to do. When the BJP steps up its attacks in Parliament on her "foreign origins", Sonia takes refuge in the temple of the Ramakrishna Mission in New Delhi and spends whole afternoons with Swami Gokulananda, a very respected holy man who ties a piece of red cord roundher wrist as a sign of brotherhood. Sonia has a lot of faith in that cord, she is becoming a little superstitious, just as her mother-in-law was. Every time there is a family celebration, she calls the family priest, who lives in Benares, to come and officiate the appropriate religious rituals. When her first grandchild, Priyanka's son, is born, the *pandit* makes sophisticated offerings as he recites his prayers. Just as Indira chose the names of her children, Sonia is to choose the name of her grandson. "Rajiv?" she suggests. Priyanka is worried that the name might condemn her son tobeing compared all his life with her father. Sonia suggests a name that begins with R. In the end they decide on Rehan, a Parsee name, to connect up with the tradition of their grandfather, Firoz Gandhi. But Sonia insists on calling him Rajiv. In the end it is Rehan Rajiv. Thank God the horoscope the holy man prepares for him predicts fame and fortune for the child, but not a political role for the sixth generation of Gandhis. Mother and daughter breathe a sigh of relief.

But in view of the constant provocation, Swami Gokulananda is forced to come out in Sonia's defence: "She is just as Indian as anyone else," he declares. "She leads a disciplined life and I see nothing wrong in her foreign origins." In Gujarat, the state in which Narendra Modi, her fierce adversary, is head of government, a wave of attacks ends the life of several Christian missionaries, accused by the Hindus of encouraging conversions. "Don't let them provoke you," her advisors tell Sonia, "they want you to come out in defence of the Christians, but don't fall for it, don't do it." She listens to them and decides to remain silent, but then the criticisms change direction. "Why is she distancing herself from Catholicism?" her adversaries ask treacherously. "Why does she have a complex about her own religion?" Sonia realizes that her religion and her Italian origin are permanent stigma, whatever she does. Obsessed with hiding it as much as possible, tired of the Hindu campaign on her faith, on January 22nd, 2001, she decides to make a symbolic gesture of great religious significance. During the Khumba Mela, the great Hindu religious celebration that takes place every twelve years and gathers together tens of millions of people at the confluence of the Ganges, the Yamuna and the mythical Saraswati in the outskirts of the city of Allahabad, the city of the Nehrus where they went to scatter Rajiv's ashes, Sonia decides to take a ritual bath. She goes into the water fully dressed, standing, and makes an offering of flower petals to the sound of the mantras and the wailing of conch shells blown by the *pandits* on the riverbank. With her are some great Hindu holy men, and also representatives of other religions, such as the Dalai Lama. The sandy esplanade between the rivers is full of people as far as the eye can see. It is a crowd as impressive as is the order and total absence of disturbances or violent incidents. Sonia's security service is so strict that the police do not allow anyone closer than two hundred metres from the bank where she is.

In the following days, the photo of her making the *puja* to the gods is published in newspapers and leaflets, and is seen by millions of peasants in hundreds of thousands of villages.Sonia hopes to neutralize her adversaries' criticisms of her in this way. But anyway, she is convinced that the people attach not the slightest importance to the fact that she was born in Italy. Besides, she asks herself... What does being Indian mean? Between an inhabitant of the Himalayas and another from the south, the differences are huge: they do not even speak the same language or eat the same food, and neither do they worship the same gods. They do not even have the same colour of skin. However, they both share the same pride in being Indian. Tolerance is an essential part of the culture of the sub- continent, otherwise... how could that mixture of peoples, traditions, ethnic groups, races and castes that is called India have survived for so many centuries? In a place that has always been able to assimilate diversity, the notion of foreign has no meaning. Her advisors provide her with arguments to defend herself. They remind her that when India won independence, an Englishman was the first head of state: his name was Lord Mountbatten, and he was the last Viceroy of the Empire. The party leaders remember that in 1983, Sonia drew up a will expressing her desire that her body be cremated according to Hindu rites. At the time, it was not probable that Rajiv Gandhi would end up as Prime Minister, and even less that Sonia would take on a political role one day. She did it because she believed in it. Actually, and Sonia knows this, if a person feels Indian, they are Indian. And she says it all the time: "I'm Indian. When I came into this family I became a daughter of my husband's land, a daughter of India..." She is convinced that the people can see her love of India. When she is asked where she gets her moral principles from when she has to take a decision about the family or politics, she does not want to lie and she responds candidly: "I suppose from the Catholic values that are still there, at the back of my mind," and she adds, "I am an ardent defender of India continuing to be a secular state. By secular state, I am referring to one that has room for all religions. The present government is not working in that direction." The ferocity of the campaign against Sonia finds an unexpected echo in Orbassano. An Indian immigrant, a Sikh engineer who works for Fiat, has been elected as municipal councillor for the small Piedmontese district. "If a Sikh can join in the political life of an Italian city... how is it that an Italian cannot join in the political life of India?" asks a Congress Party MP. The BJP reply is furious: "Would they allow that Sikh to end up as Prime Minister of Italy?" asks a nationalist MP. "Of course not!" To support his case he quotes the Mayor of Orbassano, who declared to the Press: "I wonder if we in Italy would accept a foreigner, and a woman to boot, as leader of a party that has symbolized the struggle for independence against foreign domination and which still enjoys great popular support, although less than before. The fact that a number of Indians trust their destiny to Sonia's hands says a lot about tolerance in India." In this debate which transcends continents, an Italian journalist comes to his own conclusion: "No, her origins do not count because she has been absorbed, Indianized, transformed. In that sense, she is no longer Italian." Perhaps she really became Indian in the middle of an asthma attack when she found herself staring at the pictures of the family in Rajiv's office and at that very moment she agreed to take the leap into politics. It was then that she fully took on the family legacy.

Now the avalanche of criticism about her lack of experience and the hate campaign about her origins are making her mature in no time at all. Her personality begins to change subtly as she gains confidence in herself and strengthens her determination to solve the problems of the party, to which she dedicates herself in body and soul. From 1998 to 2004, while two successive coalitions led by the BJP govern India, surprisingly in a very moderate way thanks to the influence of the Prime Minister Atal Bihari Vajpayee, Sonia busies herself with regenerating the Congress Party, simplifying the decision-making process and seeking consensus. She does it in a very different way from her mother-in-law, who was more imperious in her style and encouraged a palace-style culture. Sonia surrounds herself with her children and the experts there are in the Congress ranks, not allowing herself to be influenced by the process of demonization going on against her. She is too busy choosing the right candidates and ensuring that they win favour with the people, state by state, with no rush, but without stopping. Many of her decisions are based on what she has learned from her mother-in-law and her husband, but taking great care to avoid the errors that cost them so dear. For example, she does not change the heads of state government at her whim, as Indira did. On the contrary, she supports them unconditionally, letting them get on with it, and they show their gratitude in their solid loyalty to her. She only has one problem with the head of the Orissa government who, after the murder of a missionary, aligns himself with the Hindu fundamentalists: "The Christian missionaries have to be disciplined," he declares. Sonia dismisses him immediately, showing that her hand does not shake when it comes to making a decision. But exceptfor the odd specific problem, under her leadership the party becomes aforce that needs to be reckoned with again. In 2002, and thanks to Sonia's patient groundwork, the Congress Party wins power in fourteen states, which adds up to over half of the population. In March of the same year,she wins a sweeping victory in the municipal elections in New Delhi,taking three quarters of the seats. All over, the desertions of members stop and the tendency is reversed: the number begins to grow.

*   *   *

On May 11th, 2000, India celebrates an unusual event. Thegovernment chooses a little girl called Aastha Arora, born in New Delhi, as baby number one billion. The news that the country has reached that magical figure causes an outbreak of popular fervour tinged withnationalism. As everything in India is celebrated, on this occasion too, the people come out on the streets to throw firecrackers and hold parties. Hordes of journalists and reporters rush to the hospital and take over the ward where the baby is, climbing on to the beds and tables in order to get a picture of the chosen child. A journalist from the *Indian Express* is dismayed: "Baby number one billion has been welcomed with so many flashes that the doctors are afraid her skin may be affected."

But in spite of the demographic explosion, finally, on the thresholdof the new century, the hope of getting rid of poverty emerges. The results of the economy, which has continued to be liberalized since Rajiv's time, are buoyant. India optimistically experiences a wave of nationalist fervour encouraged from the government led by the BJP. The Press repeats all the time that this is going to be "India's century". It looks as if the country is heading down the path to becoming the great power that it promises to be. After so many years of controls and limitations, all the contained energyand vitality overflow. The universities and technical colleges founded in Nehru's time produce a million engineers a year. A lot, compared with the one hundred thousand from European and American universities. A new generation of businessmen flourishes because of the revolution in computers and telecommunications. Soon India rejoices in coming close behind China in another record, that of being the second largest economy with the greatest level of economic growth in the world. It seems as though that old Indian elephant is stretching himself. The BJP and the Hindus say all the merit is theirs. From the opposition benches, Sonia complains that the economic progress only benefits a booming middle class that worshipsa new god: consumerism.

"In prosperous New Delhi," she reminds them, relying on figures from a recent study published in the newspapers, "one child in four isobese, but in the countryside, half the children aged under three suffer some kind of chronic malnutrition! What kind of progress is that?"

She repeats that the new wealth does not reach the enormous mass of population living in the villages. Rural India still suffers unemployment, the excesses of the caste system, shortages, lack of opportunities, with the further aggravation that the spread of television allows them to see with their own eyes how the other India lives, the India that enjoys itself, prospers and consumes in the big cities. Sonia reminds the government thatIndia, that country so proud of its state of the art research and development centres, is the home of 40% of the world's poor.

"We must not allow ourselves to be carried away by the euphoria caused by the government's propaganda about the benefits of the reforms. Something is not right when the economy grows to the rhythm of the suicides of poor peasants, who take their own lives because they are in debt to local moneylenders and cannot see a way out of their situation."

But it seems as though most MPs do not want to believe her words. These are awkward words really because they tarnish the dream of prosperity and nationalism in which they live. Sonia is preaching in the wilderness, but she does not care if they call her a wet blanket: Nehru and Indira felt a strong commitment to the poor and she is aware that her party has survived because it aligned itself with those most disadvantaged, those whose voice no one wants to hear. Perhaps because she still has the essential innocence of a foreigner, she is still sensitive to the terrible spectacle of poverty that many Indians who have access to a better lifestyle simply do not see. It is like a sub-conscious reflex that blinds them to the abject poverty all around them. Out of sight, out of mind. Not seeing means not suffering. But Sonia's eyes are wide open.

And her voice is heard loud and clear more and more in Parliament: she invariably rejects the achievements of which the government boasts. If peace has returned to the north-east territories, it is not because of action by the government, but because of Rajiv's efforts to forge a peace deal which has allowed the separatist leaders, who were previously insurgents in the jungles, to be today respectable politicians elected by the people. If the situation has calmed down in the Punjab, it has nothing to do with this government either, it is because of the "Punjab agreements" which were Rajiv's work. If the moderate Sikh nationalists have realized the advantages to be had in belonging to the Union of India and they have come back to the path of democracy, it is thanks to her husband.

But the crowning moment of her interventions occurs in March 2002. Suddenly a leader has emerged who speaks

fearlessly and without any complexes, with the forcefulness
that comes from her profound belief in her opinions. Sonia
directly accuses the government of having encouraged another
outbreak of religious violence which has placed the country on
the edge of the precipice again. It is yet another act in the
tragedy of Ayodhya, initiated by members of the government
currently in power. After the destruction of the mosque, the
Hindu fundamentalists came up against the rejection on the
part of the judicial authorities of any attempt to build a temple
to the god Rama on the same site, precisely in order not to
make matters worse. But the militants did not give up and
several groups belonging to organizations linked to the
government continued to travel periodically to Ayodhya to
insist on their demands. "Wasn't it included in the programme
of the BJP government?" they asked. On the way back from one
of those journeys, a tussle broke out between one of those
groups of Hindu demonstrators and some Moslem street
vendors in the station at Godhra, in the state of Gujarat. The
vendors refused to sing songs to glorify the god Rama, as the
Hindu militants insisted, so the Hindus began to insult them
and pull their beards. Word spread immediately and some
young Moslems who were working near the station ran to
defend their fellow Moslems who were under attack. The
Hindu militants got on the train, which moved off under a hail
of stones. Some kilometres further on, the train stopped. A
column of black smoke rose into the sky. A fire had
broken out on board with the result that 58 people were burned
to death, most of them Hindu militants.

Although later investigations determined that the fire was
caused by the accidental explosion of a gas stove, the Hindu
extremists did not hesitate to accuse the Moslems of having
been the cause. The news that some Hindus were burned alive
unleashed the population's desire for revenge. The head of

government in Gujarat, the Hindu fundamentalist Narendra Modi, an ally of the government and Sonia's arch-enemy, declared February 28th to be a day of mourning so that the funerals of the passengers could be held in the city streets. It was a clear invitation to violence. The Moslem districts turned into death-traps. Thousands of infuriated Hindus took it out on Moslem businesses and offices and torched mosques. Instead of acting forcefully to deal with the violence, Narendra Modi declared: "Every action has a corresponding counter-reaction." Those words, interpreted by the Hindu extremists as support from their leader to justify the revenge, marked the beginning of an orgy of violence comparable to that of the tragic events that took place during Partition. But this time, thanks to television, the whole country witnessed the dreadful pictures of women beaten and raped by infuriated militants, and then forced to drink kerosene in front of their husbands and children, who then had to watch them being set on fire, before they, in turn, were murdered. It all occurred in the face of the utter impassiveness of the people, who seemed to celebrate that vengeance symbolized by the fire on the train from Godhra. The journalists who covered the massacres are convinced that they were not spontaneous, as the local government claimed, but were planned. They saw Hindu extremists, with electoral rolls under their arms, pointing out the houses and huts inhabited by Moslems in the mixed districts. They saw them pointing out businesses that were the property of Moslems who had taken the precaution of taking on a Hindu name. The efficiency in the persecution and murders make it probable that there was a certain degree of planning. In total, more than two thousand Moslems were murdered and over two hundred thousand were left homeless.

Sonia is the voice that most heatedly denounces those events. In Parliament, she even accuses the government of encouraging genocide. "Madam, do not use such strong words," the Prime Minister tells her. But Sonia will not be silent. She denounces the dubious performance of the police. "In certain cases, it is known that they even helped the militants to find the addresses they were seeking." To support her she quotes reports from the investigations of groups of defence of human rights which show that the police had received orders not to interfere. "What this massacre has brought to light, Mr Prime Minister," Sonia tells him, "is the horrific, sectarian face of your party, the BJP, which you have been so at pains to hide during your years in office, but which now becomes quite obvious... Besides, how is it possible that you did not bother to visit the places devastated by the violence immediately? Why have you waited a month to do so? We know that Mr Narendra Modi is behind these killings, and we are very much afraid that the central government is too!" For the first time Sonia shows herself to be a great politician, denouncing the government with real, heartfelt passion, shaking the Prime Minister with her invective, not sparing a single one of them. The atrocities she has seen on television have scandalised her: "That is not India. That does not represent my country," she declares. Her interventions mean that the values inherent to the Congress Party stand out more than ever. The claim of the oldest party in India that it represents Indians of all classes and religions is not seen only as something attractive, but essential too. The decency of the Congress Party's principles get mixed up in people's minds with the image and voice of this accidental politician who speaks with her heart on her sleeve.

*   *   *

But the Prime Minster cannot get his party colleague, Narendra Modi, to resign, a measure that was designed to pacify the country. The others will not let him. Better to wait and let the people decide, they tell him. The big surprise is that in the Gujarat state elections, which take place two months after the bloody disturbances, the fearsome Narendra Modi wipes the board again. The reason is that the state is mostly Hindu. His campaign, which was based on a single principle, hatred of Moslems, seems to confirm the old belief of the BJP: if they are well-orchestrated, disturbances based on religious hatred turn into votes. Modi has shown himself to be a conjuror or magician in this art. He takes advantage of the fact that Gujarat borders on Pakistan, which favours the policy of fear of the Islamic enemy.

After the hopes aroused by Sonia, there comes a moment of massive disappointment. At the headquarters of the Congress Party, frowning and with her glasses on, Sonia reads the report on the elections in Gujarat from the secretary general of her party. The atmosphere is gloomy. "The Congress Party has not won a single seat within a radius of 100 kilometres around Godhra, where a train carriage was set on fire, killing some fifty people. The Congress Party has lost all seats in the areas close to the state of Madhya Pradesh and Rajasthan..." The conclusion is that, now, just as at the time of the destruction of the temple in Ayodhya, the policy of community confrontations is paying dividends. The Hindus, the largest majority, are bowing to fear and racism. How to avoid that model taking hold in other parts of India? No one has the answer.

Now that everything seemed to be smiling for Sonia, the result of the elections in Gujarat is a jug of cold water which sets a question mark over her future. On the other hand, encouraged by its victory in Gujarat, the government decides to bring forward the first general elections of the 21st century to May, 2004 in order to take advantage of the prevailing wind and ratify its mandate for another five years. Sonia's critics within the party claim that if the forces aligned with the BJP continue gaining ground at this rate, she will not be able to do anything to neutralise them. She is not seen as being sufficiently solid. The fact that under her leadership fourteen states have changed their political colour is begun to be seen as something insignificant. Sonia is vulnerable again. They reproach her for not having managed to project herself as a politician along the same lines as Indira or Rajiv. Even those most optimistic in the Congress Party have doubts about her ability to lead the party to victory. "Did we make the right decision when we asked her to lead the party?" the same ones who pushed her to accept now wonder. Some of her followers, loyal until now, comment to their party comrades that Sonia is good, but not good enough. They all admit that she has improved a lot, but say that she is not up to it and never will be. And in the Congress Party they are in a hurry to get back into power. The party that has governed India longest has been seven years out of power. It is the longest period of time in its whole history, and it coincides with Sonia Gandhi's presidency. Little by little another conspiracy is forged. The closeness of the general elections encourages personal ambitions. If Sonia comes out unscathed from the plot this time it is because the ringleader dies in a road accident. But discontent reigns in many sectors of the party.

While the debate about her abilities as a leader and her lack of experience continues, Sonia dares to present a motion of censure against the government, accusing it of a series of charges that go from anarchy to corruption. She attacks head on, mixing aggression with witty comments, speaking fluently and amusingly. Since they are a minority in Parliament, the motion is rejected, but Sonia manages to present the image of a leader who could be an alternative to the current government. Far behind now is that novice MP who had to search for words, who remained silent when asked a question, or who turned bright red when she was attacked. The elections are only round the corner, and there is no other leader capable of galvanising the grassroots. The die is cast. There is no going back, not for Sonia and not for the Congress Party.

47

New Delhi, May 10th, 2004. At the age of 57, Sonia is still a very pretty woman, just as she was when she was young. But it is a beauty that bears the marks of the tragedies that have struck her, and that is why her face has an expression that may seem harsh. As a young woman she laughed so much, but now she always seems grave, with a smile that does not quite convince because it emerges from the depths of her sadness. Not only has her face changed; her body language is different now too. Her vigorous step, the way she moves her shoulders under the cloth of her saris, everything about her is reminiscent of Indira. Sonia has become Indian even in her gestures.

When she is tired, a tenseness appears in her demeanour. And today, this Monday morning, as Sonia Gandhi puts her eye make-up on with fine brushstrokes of kohl using the mirror on her dressing table at home in New Delhi, she feels exhausted. She has spent several weeks on intense electoral campaigning, and she has travelled thousands of kilometres all over the Indian sub-continent, almost the same distance as a trip round the world, and putting up with the extreme heat at that time of year. Most of the travelling has been done by car, by helicopter and on foot, but she has also had to go ten kilometres by camel in order to get to a small community in Rajasthan. And she did it just to reach a village of barely two hundred inhabitants, where they were waiting for her with open arms because no candidate had ever deigned to go there before. During those days she has thought a lot about her mother-in-law, about her desire to get to the people's hearts, to reach the remotest village, like the time when she had to cross a river at night on the back of an elephant in order to get to Belchi, a village of untouchables who were traumatised because they had been the victims of a massacre. Like her mother-in-law, Sonia has spared no effort to get her message through to the most remote places. And even if she does not win these elections, she will never be able to reproach herself for not trying her best. As usual, meeting the poor of India has been very gratifying for her. At moments of uncertainty, the words of Mahatma Gandhi that she read one day on the wall in a rural dispensary come into her head: "When you doubt or question yourself, try the following test: remember the face of the poorest and weakest man you have ever seen and ask yourself if the step you are about to take is going to be of any use to him. Will he gain anything from it? Will it give him some control over his life and his destiny?... Then you will see that your doubts will vanish."

An electoral campaign on a national level is tough for someone who has never hidden their aversion for power. Living with that contradiction intensifies her feeling of brutal exhaustion, which prevents her even from changing her sari this morning to go and vote. She decides to leave what she has on. After all, it is white, the colour of widows in India, and today, election day, wearing that sari will be a way of keeping Rajiv's memory alive. Which is like helping herself to stay alive. Because everything she does, she still does to keep his memory, since physically she cannot touch him. And for her children, Rahul and Priyanka, who have supported her so much in the campaign, in life. There is nothing like the pain at the loss of loved ones for bringing people together.

She detests attracting attention and being the protagonist; she hasonly given two interviews in her whole life, and yet she has suddenly found herself galvanizing crowds of up to a hundred thousand people about six times a day in different places. She has spoken fluently in Hindi, with a slight accent, and she has given speeches in the style of Indira, trying hard to convince six hundred million voters to vote for the Congress Party. Sometimes she finds it hard to believe that she is at the head of the largest democratic political organization in the world. If a fortune-teller had predicted that for her in her youth, when she still lived in Italy, she would have called him a charlatan.

What did she say to those millions of voters who listened to her, entranced? She spoke to them about her in-laws, a family that has governed India for more than four decades, but which has been out of power forseven years. She spoke to them about the values the Nehru-Gandhis have always represented: freedom, tolerance, laicism and unity. She insisted that these are no ordinary elections, but a historic confrontation between different values, between diametrically opposed ideologies. A struggle between light and obscurantism; between an India where there is room for everyone and for all religions, and another mediaeval, exclusive India. What is at stake, she repeated, is co-existence between the countless cultures, ethnic groups, castes and religions that make up India. In short,the very existence of the country as a nation.

The cities are plastered with electoral posters. The BJP is very satisfied with its slogan: "India shines", which refers to the good state ofthe economy. With a country that is growing at a rate of 9%, two seasons ofabundant monsoon rains and, finally, a relaxed relationship with the old enemy, Pakistan, they are confident and not at all worried. They think that their rival, the Congress Party, is finished, unable to rise again from its ashes, crushed under the weight of its own bureaucracy. They are convinced that Sonia is a leader not skilled or experienced enough to bring it back to life, and even less to win enough seats in these legislative elections. First of all because she is a foreigner and, secondly, because they think she has neither the charisma of her mother-in-law nor the charm of her husband. They say she has never expressed an original opinion about international events or the direction in which India is heading in the field of the economy. Thirdly, because they believe they have managed to have her considered by public opinion as a mere *gungi gudiya*, a mute doll, manipulated unscrupulously by the old dinosaurs of the Congress Party. And did they not say the same about Indira Gandhi when she stood for election for the first time?

But if her adversaries had followed close behind her over these weeks of campaigning, perhaps they would not be so arrogant. They would have witnessed the tremendous welcome that hordes of women and men gave Sonia and her children, covering them with roses and carnations, chanting their names in a kind of frenzy. "This is not political, it's emotional," a European journalist commented one day to Rahul, now aged 33, who is standing for the first time as a candidate for the constituency of Amethi, that was once his father's. If Sonia loses, her son is already at the starting line. No one can escape the destiny of their surname.

"Who does India shine for?" Sonia asked in her speeches. "For the peasants who commit suicide by drinking rat poison because they cannot pay off their debts?" The crowd received her words with roars of approval.

The slogan "India shines", aimed especially at an urban middle class made up of some 300 million voters, has been contrasted by Sonia with another less glossy one that is aimed at those 700 millions that still havenot tasted the fruits of the economic prosperity: "Choose a government that works for you," she repeats. It is one of Indira's slogans, which she used in several campaigns. The modern method of campaigning of the party in power, which has sent a voice message from the Prime Minister to 110 million fixed and mobile phones all over the country (reaching 355 million voters under the age of 25, a real technological achievement), has been contrasted by Sonia with the traditional style of travelling round India shaking hands, hugging people, connecting with them, immersing herself inthe sentimental adoration of the masses.

Very often, the Tata Safari in which they were travelling had to stop as many as ten times in an hour when it was completely surrounded by peasants whose gaunt faces and skinny bodies were stuck up against the windows. Sonia had to push hard to open the front door of the car and standup without getting out of the car, while the crowd crushed even closer, giving cries of jubilation and waving their arms in the hope of touching her.

On this campaign it has been noticed that her children arouse the same passions, especially Priyanka, who is now 32. It was a revelation to see to what an extent she can captivate the crowds, who have come *en masse* to hear her speak. And that is in spite of her not standing for anyseat. She has just had a baby daughter, Miraya, who, together with the older child, Rehan, keeps her very busy. That is why she has only helped her mother and her brother sporadically. But it was enough for her to wave her arm for hundreds of hands to immediately return the greeting with cries of joy. Rahul has also aroused the passion of the masses: as soon as he opens the window, they fill the inside of the car with rose petals. One day, the engine stalled and the driver could not get it started again. The man got out and opened the bonnet, while Sonia repeated "What chaos, what chaos!" trying to look through the windscreen that was filthy with sweat and squashed petals to see if the driver was able to find the problem. "Mother, stay here in the car," her son said, patting her on the shoulder, frightened that it might occur to his mother to get out at that moment, ignoring the security protocols. In the end the driver came back and managed to get the engine to rev up again.

"What was wrong?" asked Sonia.

"The flowers, Madam," the man replied. "The daisies had blockedthe ventilator belt!"

That does not seem like the image of a political dynasty that is heading straight for failure, as their adversaries predict, and even certain colleagues in the party. It is rather the image of a woman and a family who can tune in to the people, even though few people may want to admit that. The fact is that Sonia has won the respect and affection of her adopted country because she agreed to live the same life that killed her brother-in- law, her husband and her mother-in-law. The people, lulled for thousands of years by the great epics of the *Ramayana* and the *Mahabharata* where the deeds of men rival those of the gods, seem to be grateful to her for that sacrifice, and show it every time there is an occasion. And she does not miss an opportunity to return the signs of affection. During the campaign, after four long, hot days, she could be seen relaxed only on one occasion, in the middle of a dusty plain, when she ordered the electoral convoy to stop and walked off alone to where she had seen a group of nomad women under a shelter of sticks and black plastic bags. Those women had not the slightest idea of who she was. Sonia did not understand their dialect. The photographers had been left behind and no one was going to capture the scene on film. But there, far from the crowds, from the Press and from the party meetings, Sonia Gandhi enjoyed hugging the poorest of the poor of India.

She does not think she is going to win; hardly anyone thinks so in the party, and even less outside the party. The polls all agree: the Congress Party is not among the favourites. "She has no chance" says the Press. But they cannot stop people asking her if she will become the first Indian of foreign extraction to be Prime Minister. In theory, she can, if the Congress Party and its allies win the necessary majority of seats and then they designate her as Prime Minister. Legally too, because the Constitution does not stipulate that only persons born in India can aspire to the top jobs in the government. Aware that the world of India is wider than the nation of India itself, those who wrote the Constitution two years after Partition left the possibility open to everyone; and they did so because the tragedy of Partition had caused such a flow of refugees from Pakistan and Bangladesh that they preferred not to set any limits and not add anything that might incite even more division.

For the moment, with these elections, Sonia only wants to take the Hindu nationalists down a peg or two and help the Congress Party up, pulling it out of the stagnation into which it has fallen. She would feel satisfied with that. She would have done her duty to her family and to the ideals that the members of the family always defended, and which are today under so much threat. She would shake off a little of the weight of that immense legacy that she carries on her shoulders. And perhaps she could rest a little.

Also, even if she does not admit it, some good results would bring a nice touch of revenge on those who vilify her, who have humiliated her unceasingly since she decided to accept the presidency of the Party in 1998. As voting day has come closer, the attacks have got worse. Her detractors have struck her below the belt: they have brought to light that Sonia chose to take Indian nationality in 1983, that is to say one year before her husband became Prime Minister. "Why didn't she do it before, if she had been married since 1968 and she says she feels so Indian?... She did it to help her husband win the elections," they point out treacherously. "Her so- called 'Indianness' is nothing but thirst for power," they add. It is a deceptive argument that seeks to tarnish her image by showing her asambitious. In fact she did it to counteract the attacks from Maneka, who was the first to conjure up the spectre of her "Italianness". Besides, perhaps in 1983 Sonia did not feel completely Indian, perhaps her process of Indianization has been slow and has grown in the shadow of the years and the family tragedies... but who cares about the truth? Her origins have become a hobbyhorse in the electoral battle.

The attacks are so low that at the beginning of April the Supreme Court intervened with a bill to prohibit "slander" at election time. But it was already too late; feelings were running too high. Peace at the polls is still an unreachable dream. Two days ago, Sonia tried to settle the criticism over her origins once and for all. At an end of campaign mass meeting, she addressed her thousands of supporters in Sriperumbudur, the city where Rajiv was assassinated: "I am here, on this soil mixed with my husband's blood. I can assure you that there is no greater honour for me than to share his fate for the good of India." The people do not seem to doubt the sincerity of her words, knowing that in Sonia Gandhi politics and personal life are intricately interwoven. In the end, the restraint in her reactions and the immense dignity she has shown in the face of the dirtiest attacks make her seem even more Indian and more worthy of their trust.

*   *   *

Today she has no voice, and that is why she replies to the butler with a gesture and a smile when he lets her know they are ready to take her to vote. Smart and with her handbag dangling from her arm, Sonia remains transfixed in front of the television. The newsreel is giving out the world news: ten years ago today Mandela, the man she most admires and whom she knows personally, was taking power in South Africa, and in another electoral campaign, in the United States, President Bush is gaining ground over the Democrat candidate, John Kerry, in spite of popular support forthe war in Iraq being at an all time low... Not only in India is politics full of contradictions and surprises.

But what she is anxiously awaiting is the electoral forecast from the well-known astrologer Ajay Bahambi, who became famous when Hillary Clinton asked him to read her hand. He finally appears on screen, and with the firm, decisive tone of someone who is completely convinced by whathe is saying, the bearded oracle states that the party currently in power will confirm its mandate with over 320 seats. That means a humiliating defeat for the Congress Party. The precision of the information and the man's tone of self-satisfaction leave Sonia depressed. She is not afraid of defeat, but she is afraid of being wiped off the board and left looking ridiculous. She presses the button on the remote control viciously and switches off the television. She gets up, but before she goes out, she goes into the kitchen to give instructions. Her children and little grandchildren will be coming for lunch today. She would have preferred to meet up with them at La Piazza, the exquisite Italian restaurant in the Hyatt Hotel, as they usually do on Sundays or when there is something to celebrate. But as she does not want to stir up the controversy over her "Italianness", she prefers to stay at home. This is not the moment to come out in a photo eating pasta.

She waits until it is nine o'clock before she goes out. From living in India, local beliefs have rubbed off on her, and according to an MP in the party who called her this morning from Kerala, in the south, the Rahu Kalam falls between seven thirty and nine in the morning today. This is a time of the day considered inauspicious for undertaking any kind of activity. The astrologers calculate it meticulously and publish it in Hindu calendars. It is not that Sonia believes entirely in those superstitions, but you never know, the ways things are, it is best to have as much as possible on her side...

As soon as she goes through the door that gives on to the garden, she feels the heat like a slap in the face. It is only a month until the monsoon rains come, and until then the temperature will continue to climb inexorably. She puts on her usual, large sunglasses and glances around her: the lawn is going yellow, the flowerbeds that brightened it up in February have already withered. But the shade of the big trees protects the rest of the vegetation. Today the thermometer has gone up to 43 degrees, which does not prevent a group of sympathizers from standing for hours on the other side of the wall of her house waiting on the pavement to have her *darshan*. But they will not be able to see her. With so many security measures, Sonia cannot do what Indira used to do, staying to chat for a while with the people who came to see her at the doors of her residence. Those were other times. Now the Intelligence Agency has let it be known there is a "permanent threat" against her and her family on the part of fringe groups and Hindu xenophobes. Sonia is used to living with that fear around her and she has had no option but to accept it after so many years and so many scares. But the hardest thing, what she will never get used to, is thinking that something could happen to her children, and now to her grandchildren too.

The soldiers on duty in the sentry box at her residence hardly have time to salute her as her cream coloured, bullet-proof Ambassador roars outwith a squeal of tyres, followed by her bodyguards in another car with a spinning light on the roof. Sonia has put the dark glass window down and makes a quick gesture with her hand from inside the vehicle, but they are going so fast she is not sure if her admirers have seen her. It is a short trip from her house to Nirman Bhawan, a complex of government buildings where the office is located where she has to place her vote. It does not take more than ten minutes, especially today, a holiday as it is election day. Andit is pleasant because the wide avenues are lined with large trees that are always green, and many of them are in blossom. The city has changed a lot; it has gone from the three million inhabitants it had when Sonia arrived to over fifteen now. There are colourful petrol stations with shops, just like in Europe, large department stores, shopping centres, cafeterias, restaurants of all kinds, a range of luxury hotels, supermarkets where you can find everything you need, from Scottish smoked salmon to Rioja wine. But the central nucleus is still the same, especially when there is no traffic. It is all full of memories for Sonia. Every corner, every street, every shop: in that patisserie Rajiv used to buy his favourite dessert; in this square her friend Sunita used to live; down that street, leading to Akbar Road, she used to take the children to school; on that piece of land her brother-in-law crashed his plane... And along these avenues drove an Ambassador similar to this one on the day that changed their lives. She thought that car would never arrive. Indira's blood soaked the velvet-covered seats, forming a hugeblack stain.

That is why she feels that her heart belongs to these streets, to this city, to this country. In order to defend herself from all the slander, she has ordered posters put up in her husband's constituency, which show different photos of her life in India, beginning with her arrival when she was Rajiv's fiancée. "What Indian tradition have I broken?" the text goes. "As a daughter-in-law, a wife, a widow or a member of the Congress Party, what tradition have I failed to observe?" Sonia is still traumatized by the virulence of the attacks against her.

The access to Nirman Bhawan is heavily guarded by police officers and soldiers because of her arrival. The officers at the gate greet her by putting their hands together at chest-height and murmuring the traditional *namaste*. They are all smiles. Hers is the only vehicle authorized to enter the premises. Outside her electoral office, number 84, familiar faces are waiting for her and a crowd of journalists, photographers and followers. "How does it feel to be an Italian voting in India?" a malicious old reporter asks her, not bothering to hide his political tendencies. "I feel Indian. I do not feel Italian, not even a tiny bit," Sonia snaps in a hoarse voice.

The officer in charge of her electoral table greets her with a wide smile and places a garland of carnations round her neck.

"Some of our Congress Party colleagues told us you would comehere at seven o' clock in the morning," he says.

"I'm sorry I'm late. I apologize."

"No need for that, please..." the man replies, blushing. "You are the sixteenth voter at this table... It's a good number, Madam. It will bring you luck," he adds as he shows Sonia how the brand new electronic voting machine works. It is the pride of Indian technology. Over a million of these battery-operated plastic boxes, the size of a small suitcase, have been distributed for the first time all over the nation – in the remotest places, on the backs of elephants – in the hope of accelerating the counting and combating fraud.

There will no longer be people killed or injured in the fighting between rival political factions who accused each other of trafficking with the contents of the urns. Now a mere beep after pressing the key next to the name and symbol of the candidate chosen indicates that the vote has been registered in a control unit. In this novel way, Sonia places her vote, like just another person among the millions of Indians who will hear the same sound today during this last day of the general election. Suddenly the members of the Press turn towards an old lady who has come to vote, sitting in a chair that her relatives carry up high. She is 108 years old and is a Burmese refugee. She replies to the reporters in a trembling voice: "I have always voted for the Congress Party because they helped us emigrate to India when China declared war on Burma." She presses the button and ... Beep!

On leaving Nirman Bhawan, on the way back home, there are so many people cheering her on that the car can barely make its way through. So she asks the driver to stop. Sonia gets out of the car and her bodyguards immediately surround her and indicate that she should get back in, but she refuses and gestures firmly at them to stand aside. She does not intend to leave without greeting the enthusiastic crowd of people who chant her name and endlessly repeat the slogans that glorify her. It is the least she can do for all those who are waiting in the blazing sun. Impervious to the nervousness of her bodyguards, she turns towards the crowd, nodding her head, putting her hands together in greeting, thanking them, smiling... everyone wants to touch her and she would like to hug them one by one, if she could. She recognizes the same current of sympathy that has always existed between successive generations of Indians and the members of her family, an almost electric current between her and the people, which is made palpable in an exchange of glances, sometimes a handshake, a communication that crosses all barriers.

When she gets back in the car, she suddenly wonders if this morning's astrologer might not have exaggerated his negative prediction. But it is a fleeting thought. She knows better than anyone that elections can be lost, even though a million people have been cheering for you the daybefore.

48

For these, the first elections of the 21st century, 670 million electors are called to vote, an electorate twice the size of its nearest rival, which would be for the elections for the European Parliament. In order to carry out this organizational achievement and to guarantee the safety of the voters, the elections have been divided into four days over three weeks, with the last day being today, May 10th, 2004. Four million civil servants have been mobilized for seven hundred thousand electoral tables in order to get results that will affect the fate of a sixth of the world's population over the next five years. Technology has been the great innovation in these elections. In the 1999 elections there were only three television channels; today there are over a dozen that broadcast 24 hours a day, not counting the satellite channels. Five years ago there were 1·3 million mobile phones; today there are 30 million. The television has broadcast the smiles, the clothes, the expressions of exhaustion or joy or stupor of the candidates, their expectant looks and also a gesture or two that have cost a politician his popularity. But no one really knows which party will most benefit from television.

The counting will begin on May 13th and the first results will be given out on 14th, at the end of the week, precisely thanks to the speed of the new electronic urns. But for the candidates it will be a long week. Sonia would love to go off for a few days to enjoy the cool of the mountains, but it cannot appear that she wants nothing to do with the great contest. Her colleagues in the Congress Party would not understand it if she did not stay in her place, in the capital, on the front line, defending herself from a last- minute attack, galvanizing her comrades in the party, correcting an unruly MP or so...

*   *   *

Thursday, May 13th, 2004. This morning the first results are expected. In the villages, the peasants take advantage of the heat to make a halt in their labours and gather round a transistor or a television. In a country where everyone joins in other people's celebrations, the great spectacle of democracy is experienced like another festivity, perhaps because celebrating the supreme value of the individual acquires even more value in such a densely populated place. In the numerous villages out of reach of the signal, they will have to wait for the arrival of some traveller with news; there the results may take up to two weeks to be known. In New Delhi there is great expectation in the general headquarters of the two large parties, both in the centre, where the strategies have been decided and the guidelines worked out. They are large halls with whispering air- conditioning, full of television monitors, computers, video cameras, printers and all the paraphernalia of technology. Young men in Western clothes hurry between the offices with their mobiles stuck to their ears and, as a concession to tradition, a cup of milky tea in their hands. In the Congress Party's general headquarters, there are more journalists than party members; these are hiding in their homes, overwhelmed by the defeatist speculation on radio and television. Some of them, the more optimistic ones, wearing the famous hat that Nehru popularized, talk and gesticulate to the reporters who are awaiting the first reactions.

Not far from there, in Sonia's residence, the atmosphere is charged with tension. A dense silence envelops the house, decorated with objects brought from all over India, many of them tribal, exquisitely beautiful pieces of cloth and some antique paintings on glass which Sonia is very fond of. Nothing there evokes ostentation or the fact that this is the home of a special family, except the study, which is still just as Rajiv left it. The photos, in silver frames on the tables, show moments the Nehrus shared with Kennedy, Gorbachev, De Gaulle and other illustrious personages of the 20ᵗʰ century. And there are the famous pictures of Nehru, Indira and Rajiv, hanging in their wooden frames on the white walls. Today they also seem to have a life of their own, as though they were participating in the suspense of the moment from beyond the grave.

Sitting on the sofas and squatting on the floor, Sonia's collaborators happily accept a cup of tea perfumed with cardamom which their hostess offers them. They are all in an uncomfortable silence and the fact is that Sonia prefers to have the television off. She is afraid of the results and she wants to save herself the agony of getting to know the figures bit by bit. She prefers to know it all at once, when it has to be. So close to the end, she is afraid of disappointing "the family". She knows that if she wins, it will be Sonia Gandhi's victory and she has projected herself to the electorate as what she is, a vulnerable, sincere and bold woman; if she loses, it will be the defeat of "Rajiv's widow" or "Indira's daughter-in-law, the "Italian" who was not up to the circumstances and who lacked both ambition and political talent. "Is it really worth winning?"

she seems to ask herself at this moment when all kinds of incongruous and even contradictory thoughts come over her.

A mobile rings to the tune of the Congress Party. It belongs to her friend Ambika, Secretary General of the party and the colleague who has spent the most hours with her recently. The woman puts her cup of teadown on a side table and puts the phone to her ear. She immediately gives a smile and hangs up. "Sonia, our allies in Tamil Nadu have won." The good news relaxes the atmosphere a little. "We won't be left looking ridiculous there," thinks Sonia. Tamil Nadu is a large state, certainly important in the final result, but they are all impatient to know the figures for key states like Uttar Pradesh, Maharasthra or Karnataka. Sonia is bursting to know and at the same time she does not want to know.

A few seconds later another mobile rings. "Sonia, we've won in Maharasthra!" another member of her team announces. The sound of thefax is added to that of the mobile phones: the machine spits out photocopiesof newspapers with messages that come from several party delegations... And all with good news. In an instant the study is invaded by a cacophony of noises, sounds and fragments of conversation. Sonia is disconcerted untilshe receives a call on the private telephone of the house.

"Congratulations Soniaji! We're not only winning, we're wiping them out. In my own name and in the name of all the members of the Congress Party, allow me give you our most sincere congratulations."

"Let's not celebrate yet, we have to be prudent..." she says. "Yes, you're right, but we already know the trend..."

Sonia glances at the members of her team, with a smile that bringsher famous dimples back to life, those dimples that always used to appear when she felt happy.

"I'm going to turn on the television..." she says, getting up.

What the screen shows is a very familiar place: Akbar Road, where the party offices are, less than five minutes from her home. Sympathizers full of fervour carry posters in support and shout slogans "Long live Sonia Gandhi!" "Long live the Congress Party!" while others light firecrackers, and dance and drink in the streets. "They called her a foreigner, but the people have given a clear response to that!" says one follower carrying a flag with the national colours, yellow, green and white. "This is a gift from the gods!" declares a well-known member of the party with tears in his eyes. That first reaction of jubilation leaves everyone amazed, but what Sonia is not prepared for is to hear a cry that emerges from among the crowd: "Long live Prime Minister Sonia Gandhi!". She is thunderstruck, as though the reality of her new situation hit her from the television screen. Stunned by the enormity of what is coming her way, she sits down on the edge of the sofa. She wants to hide her anxiety, but she is so overcome that it is impossible for her.

"Are you all right?" Ambika asks her.

Sonia takes a deep breath and points to her chest, as if she was starting an attack.

"Shall I go and fetch your inhaler?"

"That isn't necessary ... it's passing now."

Actually she is praying she does not have an attack of asthma now. What she is feeling is anxiety, which the cries of the enthusiastic followers in Akbar Road only make worse: "Sonia Gandhi Prime Minister!"

The presenter returns to the results. As the results are given out state by state, it is as if the voice of the different peoples of India penetrated into the study, like an echo coming from very far away, from the villages scattered over the Tibetan slopes of the Himalayas, from the mud huts of the Bishnois in the Thar Desert, from the tribes that live in the mangroves in the south, from the fishermen on their immense beaches in Kerala, from the Moslems in Gujarat who survived the recent massacres of the Hindu fundamentalists, from the millions of slum-dwellers in Bombay and Calcutta... And the voice of the people is repeated, astonishing Sonia, her collaborators, her adversaries, India, and the whole world too. A voice that defies the predictions of the experts in politics, of the television magnates and the opinion institutions. A voice that rebels against the attempted domination of the masses by the media. Not a single expert has been able to guess the spectacular defeat of the party in power. In one foul swoop, the results also wipe out the credibility of so many astrologers, palm-readers and supposed magicians who have spread deceit and lies all over the country. The famous astrologer Ajay Bahambi has made a fine mess of things!...

The initial surprise soon becomes euphoria, when the television announces that the Congress Party is about to get 145 seats, which will allow it, together with its allies, to reach the magic figure of 272 in coalition. That is, the capacity to govern. The 272 that Sonia announced prematurely in 1999, she now has. Added to her anxiety there is a deep feeling of satisfaction. And to cap this day of triumph, the news comes that Rahul has been elected as MP for the constituency of Amethi, a worthy heir of his father. A double victory which brings back into power the family most admired and vilified in India. Immediately, the cries of the crowd that has gradually approached the house and is calling for Sonia drown out the sound of the television. At the headquarters in Akbar Road, the person responsible for security calls the New Delhi police to send reinforcements to number 10 Janpath Road in view of the probable gathering of people.

The BJP loses in 24 of the 28 states in India. It loses even in the bastions it thought were unassailable, such as the holy city of Benares or Ayodhya itself. This time, its conviction that community riots make votes has turned out to be monumental mistake.

"The people have reacted," says Priyanka when she arrives to congratulate her mother.

Every minute that goes by, the slogan of the Hindus, "India shines", seems even more ridiculous, as if the voters had uncovered the falseness of that over-confident propaganda, which left aside most of the people, those that are not to be seen in the cities, but who now take their revenge from the burning plains and the remote villages. The expression in Sonia's eyes conveys the feeling of the members of her party: triumph, pleasure, laughter and, at a given moment, tears. She had entered the electoral race with only the hope of not being completely crushed, and she has reached the goal as absolute winner.

49

"Incredible shock", runs the headline of the special edition of the Hindustan Times, the most widely read newspaper in English in New Delhi, the next day, Friday, May 14th. At Sonia's residence, the huge quantity of messages of congratulations and support have jammed the fax. Letters, telegrams, SMS... from everywhere and via all possible methods, messages of congratulations pour in for the future "Prime Minister". Carlo Marroni, the mayor of Orbassano, sends her a telegram in the name of the 25,000 inhabitants of his city: "We are proud of you and we hope you continue along the path of development and solidarity in the largest democracy in the world. We share with you, with your India, those values that link us all." Paola, Sonia's mother, has heard about her daughter's victory at her home in Via Bellini from a local journalist. Then she received an avalanche of calls. "Yes, of course I'm pleased," she repeats hiding her uneasiness, "but I feel besieged and I have nothing to say." How can she say that she is afraid the same may happen to her daughter as happened to her son-in-law? So Paola prefers to remain silent, and she decides not to answer the phone any more.

Now Sonia's task is to secure a coalition capable of governing. She does not hesitate for an instant to call on her old friend, the brilliant Sikh economist Manmohan Singh, her guru in matters of the economy. With him, she writes an agreement of the minimum conditions in order to get the firm adhesion of the other members of the coalition, which consists of over twenty parties. How far off are Indira's or Rajiv's times, when the Congress Party governed with an absolute majority! Politics now is like a gigantic pot where the dreams, aspirations and interests, more and more diverse, even at loggerheads, of a sixth of humanity simmer. And Sonia suddenly finds herself in the position of chief cook. She has to season the stew well, keeping the Communists from the Left and also the Liberals happy, as well as the regional parties and the representatives of the castes... But the task does not take her unawares: she has spent months making alliances, talking with one group and another, preparing the way. Her invisible groundwork now brings results. As the nuns in the boarding school in Giaveno where she studied said, she has a talent for getting consensus: in that she is not like her mother-in-law, who leaned more towards authoritarianism. What really interests Sonia are great matters of State such as reducing poverty and ensuring economic growth; or how to get peace with Pakistan and solve the dispute over Kashmir. The same is not true of her partners. Most of them are real satraps, petty leaders of regional parties with egos greater than their organizations. Each of them looks after number one and demands ministerial portfolios and specific policies to support the members of their caste or their voters. In exchange for his backing, the well-known leader of one of the poorest states demands the Ministry of Railways, a very important ministry because it employs over ten million people. And they all think that Sonia will be the Prime Minister. Some of them even demand it, because they do not want to be left without her valuable leadership which is going to allow them to enjoy their little bit of power; they think that without her the coalition will have a very short life.

After the announcement that the party is going to name her as leader of their parliamentary group, the whole country takes it as given that Sonia will take on the position. In case there was any doubt, when a journalist asks her if it is true that the leader of the parliamentary group will be the next Prime Minister, Sonia replies: "Normally that is so." Four words which are like four slaps in the face for her adversaries. Sweet revenge, which immediately finds a reply when a leader of the defeated party declares on television that he finds it shameful that a foreign woman should govern India. Another leader of the same party adds that he will boycott the act of investiture of the coalition if Sonia Gandhi is Prime Minister. A shudder of nationalism sweeps the country and even affects members of Sonia's own party. A head of government from the state of Madhya Pradesh, a middle-aged woman named Uma Bharti, a Hindu extremist affiliated with the BJP, announces her resignation claiming that "putting" a foreigner in the highest position is an insult to the country and puts national security in danger. Another woman, called Sushma Swaraj, a respected leader of the defeated party, asks for an interview with the President of the Republic, the Moslem scientist Abdul Kalam, to express the "grief and anguish" the matter causes her. "If Sonia ends up as Prime Minister, I will shave my head, dress in white clothes, sleep on the ground and go on an indefinite hunger strike. I will mobilize the nation against her," she threatens to the media as she comes out of her interview.

But no doubt the event that causes the most impact is the suicide in a village near Bangalore of a card-holding member of the defeated party, the 30-year old family man, Mahesh Prabhu. Before swallowing a can of rat poison, he left a note explaining that he "cannot bear the idea that in a country of eleven hundred million people it has not been possible to find a single

Indian leader to lead the nation." The man leaves a widow and a child of eighteen months, and the whole country disconcerted.

Too much confusion, too much division, too much hysteria... The consequences of her victory are beginning to scare her. It has touched the nerve of nationalism, an irrational feeling that can quickly turn into madness. In spite of the results of the elections having shown that her origins mean little to the people, the matter is still explosive. She has learned her lesson and is so cautious that she speaks to an interviewer from Italian television in English and not in her mother tongue, leaving the journalist absolutely perplexed. How can you make someone who is interviewing you for five minutes understand that you cannot speak to him in his own language even if you wanted to? How to explain what it means to be a foreigner in India and to be so close to power that you can feel its blazing heat? How to tell about the violence that has decimated your family and that lurks like an animal in wait? How to explain all the grief, the pain, the anguish, the fear? How to tell all that, without which it is impossible for anyone to understand her reactions? She would have to start from scratch every time she speaks to a reporter, and there is never time for that.

To make the general anxiety even worse, the Bombay share index, the Sensex, collapses in the biggest fall in the financial history of India, made worse by fear of a government in which the weight of the Left may put an end to the reforms that have already been achieved. Sonia urges the man she trusts, Manmohan Singh, to make some declarations to calm the markets, waiting for things to get back to normal as soon as possible.

She needs to think. The following morning, accompanied by

her children, the three of them discreetly leave the house, but the police are nervous and their bodyguards are even more nervous. It was foreseeable that after her electoral victory security measures would limit her almost non-existent freedom of movement even more. Now she must let them know her movements even more in advance, so that the Delhi police force can be alerted, apart from her personal guard.

A light mist envelops the streets, empty at this early hour. It is the best time of day to avoid the heat and drive quickly. Sonia's car goes along the wide avenues in the new part until it gets to the gardens where the family mausoleums are. The singing of the birds can be heard over the dull murmur from the new motorway that crosses Delhi from north to south. The three of them take a moment to get a grip on themselves and then each of them makes a floral offering, throwing rose petals over the mausoleum. What would Rajiv say about this unexpected victory of his wife's, which again puts the whole family in the limelight? She who fled from the attention of the media like the plague, now remembers the time when her husband was Prime Minister and she left him high and dry with a French television team that was insisting on having some shots of the whole family together... "Not even I can make her change her mind," Rajiv had told the reporter. Now her husband must be laughing up in heaven. He must be surprised, like everyone in India; and proud too, probably; but especially alarmed, for her, for their children and for the grandchildren he has never known. Be careful with victory, it can turn against you and destroy everything in its way. Be careful with the hidden face of triumph, you never know what is hiding behind it. "What about you, Rajiv? What would you do in my place?"

*   *   *

In the successive interviews she carries out that day with different members of her coalition, she avoids mentioning the matter of leadership. She blurts, "I have no particular post in mind," to a BBC journalist.

The next day, May 15th, the most highly respected leaders of the party, alarmed at the idea of being left without a leader, ask her to delay her decision, whatever it is, by a few hours. They want to gain time to allow the messages of support to arrive from their allies in the furthest corners of India. Normally the candidate for Prime Minister goes to the President of the Republic with that endorsement in order to receive official permission to form a government. It is a step that she will soon have to take, carrying in her briefcase those messages that praise her and make it clear that she is the essential leader without whom the coalition lacks any sense. Partners and allies hope that Sonia will finally give way: the party needs to prove to its grassroots that it has found its guide. Added to this is the emotional pressure from her friends, with whom she has shared so many troubles and difficult moments. She has the impression that she will be leaving them in the lurch if she does not accept the job. It is not easy to say to them now: I'm not playing any more. Will they be able to understand? To reassure her they say: "We will accept your decision as final." Sonia still has three days to think about it.

In the afternoon of 15th, after having been formally elected unanimously as leader of the Congress Party Parliamentary group, Sonia Gandhi addresses her MPs. "Here I stand in the place occupied by my great masters, Nehru, Indira and Rajiv. Their lives have guided my path. Their courage and entire devotion to India have given me the strength to continue along their path years after their martyrdom. I wish to remember them today, I wish to pay tribute to them today. The people have reaffirmed that the soul of our nation is all-embracing, non-denominational and united. They have rejected the policies of personal attacks and negative campaigns. They have rejected the ideology of the fundamentalist parties. Soon we will have here, in the central government, a coalition led by the Congress Party. We have triumphed in the face of all the forecasts. We have overcome in spite of the ill-omened predictions. In the name of all of you, I want to express with all my heart my gratitude to the people of India. Thank you."

The hall bursts into a lengthy ovation and then the MPs prepare to congratulate her personally. They all want to get close to the architect of so much joy and expectation, the person who holds the key to power. In that hall that has been witness to so many national dramas, so many bitter arguments, a festive atmosphere now reigns. Sonia is radiant. There is so much commotion that the MPs have to stand in line to shake her hand or, even better, to exchange a comment or so that is sufficiently witty for her to remember it... everything may come in useful in the future. Among the last waiting his turn is a young man, dressed in a white *kurta* and wide trousers, her son Rahul, who has been revealed in these elections to be a promising leader of the youth of the party. Sonia smiles at him affectionately as he stretches out his hand to her, just like the others.

However, the veterans and those closest to Sonia are worried because in all her speech there was not a single word about her role in the new coalition. When they suggest that she should go to the President of the Republic the next day to formally request permission to form a government, Sonia wriggles out of it by saying that the block on the Left has still not confirmed its support, which is really just an excuse. The fact is that she wants to use all the time available to think about it.

*   *   *

After spending a whole day at home with her children weighing up the situation, on Monday, May 17th, she gets her closest allies together. She has something important to say to them. They can see it coming and they are not wrong: "I think I should not accept the post of Prime Minister." She does not say it categorically, as though her decision were firm, she says it as if she wanted to judge the reaction. "I do not want to be the cause of division within the country," she adds, leaving them all uncomfortable and disconcerted. And she goes on to suggest a Solomon-like solution, which causes some annoyance: her idea is that she should go on as president of the party... and that Manmohan Singh should be Prime Minister. It is a revolutionary idea because it means a two-pronged leadership, an experiment in the art of government.

A deep silence greets her words. Sonia goes on, "He is honourable, he has an excellent reputation as an economist and he has experience in administration... I am convinced he will be a great Prime Minister." But the suggestion leaves them cold. It is well-known that Manmohan Singh has no charisma. He is a serious man, a technocrat, not a politician. "It's like saying this victory has served for nothing. The coalition will not hold together without a Gandhi, without the only leader capable of keeping such different groups together," says one of her people. Neither does the idea dazzle the more veteran leaders, some of whom have been members of the party for fifty years. Manmohan Singh has barely been a member for fourteen years: he is a newcomer. Furthermore, he is a Sikh, a representative of a minority which hardly comprises 6% of the population of India. It would be the first time that a non-Hindu took on that post since Independence. How will the Hindu majority take it?

"The people have voted for a non-denominational, secular India, where religion must not influence politics," Sonia reminds them.

But above all it is the fact of not having a Gandhi in the key position what worries her people – a lot. At this point, the mystique of the name counts for more than everything else. "It will be the shortest government in history," some predict. Others will not give up and ask her to think again. Even the two party members who complained in private of having "an uneducated Italian housewife" as leader beg her to agree to be Prime Minister. In one week, she has gone from being a plain "housewife" to being "a friend, a guide, the nation's saviour."

In the afternoon, Manmohan Singh arrives at number 10 Janpath Road, wearing his eternal blue turban, with his white beard, his little black eyes full of intelligence and his resemblance to a fragile bird. It is hard for him to make his way through the crowd of MPs and followers who have come to the call of those meeting with Sonia, and who block the entrance. There are so many people that they do not fit inside the house. They wait in the garden or in the street, in the blazing sun with a temperature of forty- three degrees in the shade, for their leader to make a decision. For Sonia the situation is familiar; she has the impression of having lived through this already, when they were pressurizing her to accept the presidency of the party. But if before it was difficult to say no, now that it is power that is at stake, it is practically impossible. However much she tries to argue, they do not accept her decision. They do not understand how she can refuse the position with the most power, which is the dream of all politicians. It is unacceptable to them, in spite of knowing that for Sonia power has never been a goal in itself. They know that she is in politics out of personal commitment, because fate wanted it to be that way. "It would be a disaster for the party, for the coalition, for the country...", they say again and again. "Sonia, don't abandon us."

Facing a real rebellion in her ranks, Sonia asks them to give her all the time available to her. But the situation becomes so inflamed, the opposition so strong – one of them threatens to set himself on fire bonzo- style if she turns down the job – that Sonia becomes alarmed and capitulates. Two hours after having suggested that perhaps she would not accept the role of Prime Minister, Manmohan Singh comes out into the garden and announces in his bird-like voice: "Mrs Gandhi has agreed to meet with the President of the Republic tomorrow morning." Phew!... A murmur of approval sweeps through the crowd. The announcement relaxes things. Those who begin to leave do so convinced that the pressure has worked, that their criteria have overcome. In the end the leader has agreed to take on her responsibility. The Congress Party will be in power again, at the hand of a Gandhi. History is repeating itself. The crowd goes home peacefully.

For Sonia, the problem is how to get those who venerate her and all those who expect everything of her to swallow that bitter pill. How to get them to see reason? How can they think that she can govern this country on her own? The opposition will give her no quarter: every day they will throw the matter of her origins in her face. Some madman will end up killing her, she is convinced of it. Besides, she does not have much experience either and would soon be burned out.

What she needs is to be alone. In her room, she opens the windows before she goes to bed. She breathes the hot air in deeply. Touch wood she does not have an asthma attack. All her childhood she slept with the windows wide open, in spite of the cold. Today she again feels that old distress. It is a feeling of drowning that comes back every time she has to take an important decision. Every time that she feels unbearable pressureon her.

She turns off the air conditioning and leaves the window open. The breeze makes the net curtains billow, and they move like cotton ghosts. But it is a warm breeze, which brings no relief. A reddish mist lights up the polluted sky over the city. The dogs bark. In the avenue, some three-wheeled van with a broken exhaust pipe backfires.

Finally it all goes quiet, just as she was longing. These last few days her home has been like a madhouse. All that noise that has prevented herfrom hearing her inner voice. She needs silence to get in touch with herself,to listen to herself. To know what to do tomorrow. Or rather, how to do it.

50

Tuesday, May 18th is a day that the members of the Congress Party will not easily forget. Some two hundred MPs from the party are waiting in the chamber in Parliament, the same room that has witnessed the election of twelve Prime Ministers of India, for Sonia Gandhi to announce her decision.

When she makes her appearance, followed by her children Rahul and Priyanka, both with serious, hermetic expressions on their faces, some already fear that the news will not be good. Sonia has come without her portfolio which should hold the letters and messages of support that hundreds of leaders in the Congress Party have sent her to encourage her to take on the job. It is a tradition that the previous Prime Ministers have always followed. Perhaps she is deliberately breaking it, some dare to think, resisting the loss of the last shreds of hope. They are the optimists, the ones who think she will not be able to reject the job after so much pressure.

A deathly quiet comes over the room as Sonia, impeccable in a sienna-coloured sari, with her hair carefully combed back and falling over her shoulders, greets several colleagues, joining her hands at face-height as she makes her way to the microphone. She puts on her glasses to see her notes and tells them: "Since I reluctantly entered politics six years ago, I have always seen clearly – and I have stated it on several occasions – that the post of Prime Minister was not my aim. I have always been certain that if some day I found myself in the position in which I find myself today, I would obey my inner voice." She pauses and the silence becomes more tense, if that is possible. Sonia looks up and gazes at her children and then at the rest of those present. "Today that voice tells me that I must humbly refuse that post."

A violent earthquake could not have caused more of a commotion. A deafening roar fills the room. Sonia speaks louder as she requests silence with her hand in order to make herself heard. "I have been subjected to much pressure to get me to reconsider my position, but I have decided to obey my inner voice. Power has never been a temptation to me..." A chorus of laments and loud protests interrupt her. "You cannot abandon us now!" some shout. "You cannot betray the people of India..." exclaims Mani Shankar Aiyar, an old friend of Rajiv's and an influential politician. "The inner voice of the people says you have to be the next Prime Minister of India!"

"I would ask you to please respect my decision...," says Sonia firmly, but they interrupt her again.

"Without you in that post, Madam, there is no inspiration for us."

A dozen MPs take turns to give their speeches, in which they invoke the example of public service of her husband and her mother-in-law. "You do the same!" they repeat. "You are up to it!"

For over two hours the heated confrontation continues between the irresistible desperation of the MPs and the immoveable determination of Sonia. The speeches go from reproaches that label her egoistic to a certain admiration for the unheard of gesture of refusing power. Some accuse her of turning her back on the mandate that millions of Indians have offered her. Sonia listens impassively to this horde of bereft people, with her jaw tight. In the end, the MPs present a joint resolution for her to reconsider her decision, but she, elegantly and with an ever enigmatic air, tells them that she does not think that is possible. "You have all expressed your points of view, your pain and your distress at the decision I have taken. But if you have confidence in me, allow me to maintain it."

It is a matter of insisting, some of them think. Many remember the crisis in 1999, when she announced her resignation as president of the party. She ended up giving way after the leaders asked her to come back. The problem now is that time is running out. By law, a government has to be formed before the week is out. An MP from Uttar Pradesh reminds them that Sonia's decision does have a precedent in the history of India: "Madam, you have set an example, just as Mahatma Gandhi did," he said, referring to when the father of the nation refused to form part of the first government after Independence. "But that day Mahatma Gandhi had Jawaharlal Nehru. Who is the Nehru today?"

Sonia does not speak about Manmohan Singh, the ace card she has up her sleeve, although those closest to her know this is what she is going to play. When she goes out, leaving her MPs distressed and disillusioned, the Press crowd round her children: "As a recently elected Member of Parliament," Rahul declares, "I would like my mother to be Prime Minister, but as her son, I respect her decision." Priyanka is less diplomatic. When she is asked if it is true that she and her brother have influenced their mother with the argument that "we have lost a father, we don't want to lose a mother," "It is a family matter," she replies with the honest truth: "We have never been masters of our own family. We have always shared it with the nation."

The members of the Congress Party do not throw in the towel so easily. When she gets back home, Sonia finds a crowd calling for the same thing, that she should change her mind. They shout for it, some with tearsin their eyes, others throwing themselves at her feet. All this adulation annoys her. It is like the other face of the hatred her detractors show forher. The one is as unhealthy as the other. As she goes into the house, she come face to face with another challenge, a mountain of letters from the members of the Work Committee of the Congress Party and other affiliates who announce their resignation if she does not accept the top job. Outside, in the street, a follower who is threatening to slit his veins right there is overpowered by the police. It seems as if madness has taken over in New Delhi.

But in this contest Sonia does not give way. Out of common sense, out of a deep personal conviction, because she is sure that her decision is the wisest one for the country, for the family and for her. Right until the last moment they try everything to bend her to their will: they beg her, they implore her, they make veiled threats, but Sonia has become stronger than them all and she does not succumb. Quite the opposite, she ensures she has the backing of other members of the coalition and that they will accept a Prime Minister who is not a Gandhi. She sets the rhythm and all of them, even the most sceptical of them, end up following. That strength is the reward for her triumph.

In addition she has the unexpected support of the Press, which seems to rediscover her and do their utmost to praise her: "Sonia rejects power and lights up hearts," is the headline in the *Asian Times*. "She rejects power, and achieves glory," says the *Times of India*. By saying no, Sonia's popularity has rocketed. By "abdicating" she has introduced the notion of sacrifice into the vocabulary of Indian politics. And she goes from being leader of the Congress Party to being the leader of the nation. A real miracle.

*   *   *

Rashtrapati Bhawan, the former Viceroy's palace, is the scene of a short ceremony which is, however, full of meaning, and which finally puts an end of the power crisis at the end of that turbulent week. On Saturday, May 22nd, after three days of stubborn resistance against the leaders of her own party, Sonia Gandhi witnesses the swearing-in of Manmohan Singh as Prime Minister, in the presence of the President of the Republic. It is a historic moment because it is the first time a Sikh has been named as head of government. The man has not slept a wink all night because a crowd of fellow Sikhs have been celebrating the event outside his residence. How things have changed since the Sikhs were persecuted like animals in the days following Indira's assassination!

After swearing the oath, in a gesture that alludes to the agreement they have come to, Manmohan Singh approaches Sonia and bows slightly. As if he wanted to make it clear that he governs, but she reigns.

It is a historic moment for another reason, charged with symbolism that clearly shows the diversity of India, its capacity for co-existence and its growing social mobility. Sonia Gandhi, brought up a Catholic, hands power over to a Sikh Prime Minister, a man known for his irreproachable honesty, born in 1932 into a very humble family in the western Punjab, an area that now belongs to Pakistan. And she does this is the presence of a Moslem President of the Republic called Abdul Kalam, an expert in nuclear physics, born into an extremely poor family. Less than a century ago, no one would have imagined that this could happen in the country where until recently a person's birth and not his merits determined the course of his existence. And only a month ago, who would have predicted a ceremony like this between three representatives of minority religions?

In a few days, Sonia has caused a silent revolution, whose impact will be felt for years to come. With her refusal, she has demonstrated that that politics is not always the equivalent of greed. She has also shown that a person does not become Indian just by an accident of birth. Being Indian is gained by loving the country, being committed to it and being strong enough to place the interests of the nation before one's own interests. With her historic gesture, Sonia Gandhi has reminded Hindus that the real strength of their nation lies in its tolerance, in its traditional openness towards others, in its belief that all religions form part of a search common to all of humanity to find the meaning of life. It is one of life's curiosities that it has had to be a Christian woman who has brought dignity and trust back to the vast majority of Hindus, those who have never felt they were represented under the previous government.

That night, Sonia returns home with the satisfaction of having done her duty. She has preferred to remain behind the throne, galvanizing the people but leaving power to her Grand Vizier with his turban and white beard.

She is finally going to be able to rest after this crazy week. But, before retiring to her room, she goes into the study to feel the presence of the man she still loves like she did the first day, or perhaps more, if love could be measured. With all the heat, the flowers in the garland round Rajiv's photo have withered a little.

"I'll change them tomorrow," she tells herself.

She stays for a while looking at her husband's picture. She shuts her eyes and concentrates intensely, until she can picture him in her mind. He seems so close to her that it is almost as if she hear his well-modulated velvet voice, with his impeccable English accent, murmuring loving things in her ear... She can almost smell his skin, with than smell of cleanness that is mixed with his own perfume of jasmine. And it carries her back into the past, to lost times, to her best memories, the ones that Sonia keeps in her heart because they are a treasure that they gathered together.

The reverie, pleasurable and painful at the same time, only lasts a short time, but it is very intense because the dead live on in the hearts of the living. When she reopens her eyes, she glances at the other photos. She has seen them millions of times, but today she wants to see them again, and again and again, perhaps because they remind her of the meaning of her life. Rajiv and his smile continue to cause a wrench in her heart, and that will always happen; Indira too, with her ability to laugh at herself, never forgetting a birthday or the illness of one of the children amid all her worries over affairs of State. Now more than ever, Sonia realizes that from Indira she has inherited the "mystique of the dynasty" and that she is applying everything she has learned from her: patience and tenacity, daring, courage and a sense of opportunity... Her gaze comes to a halt on a small photo on the table in which Mahatma Gandhi can be seen with Nehru. In those sad days after her mother-in-law's death during which she took refuge in her correspondence, as if in that way she could communicate with her, she also learned, without realizing it, something about the essence of political leadership. She found a letter from Mahatma Gandhi to Nehru, which was among Indira's papers: "Do not be afraid, put your faith in the truth; listen to the needs of the people, but at the same time make sure you gain sufficient moral authority to make people listen to you; be democratic, but value the only aristocracy that really matters: nobility of spirit."

It has not been an easy journey from the placid existence of a housewife content with her domestic life to the frantic centre of political activity. As she herself defines it, it has been a story of light and shadows, of mystery and the hidden hand of destiny. A story of inner struggle and torment, of how the experience of loss can bring deeper meaning to one's existence. But, in spite of all the sadness, the humiliations, the difficulties and the bad times, tonight she feels more fulfilled than she has ever felt before. As though suddenly she understood something that she felt deep inside, but yet which escaped her, and has to do with her deepest *raison d'être*. "The family I first became committed to when I got married was restricted to the limits of a home," Sonia would later write. "Today my loyalty is to a wider family, India, my country, whose people have welcomed me so warmly that they have made me one of them." Sonia is honest when she says that she is no longer Italian. She is not Italian because she has gone from being part of the Nehru-Gandhi family to becoming the heir of the dynasty. And the Nehru-Gandhi dynasty is India.

EPILOGUE

Paradoxically, by renouncing power, Sonia Gandhi has become even more powerful. The people, who admire the ideals of altruism and renunciation which are so much part of the Hindu religion and philosophy, have moved from considering her as a political leader to venerating her likea goddess. And that makes her the most influential person in India. In the rest of the world, her stature continues to grow all the time. *Forbes* magazine classed her among the three most powerful women on Earth. Not bad for someone who has always despised power.

She is loved by the people not only because she performed the miracle of bringing back the non-denominational character of a countrythat was dangerously adrift, not only because she set at the head of such a corrupt and chaotic democratic system a man of great intelligence, irreproachable integrity and deep experience, but because she has managed to connect with the man and woman in the street. The women value her sacrifice as a mother and wife. The men, the meaning of her struggle. They all admire her dedication to the ideals of the family. They understand the suffering she went through when she lost Indira and then when she was left a widow, in such a tragic manner, and lost such a fine, young husband who should never have found himself in the line of fire. They identify with her.

The grief at the loss of those most loved arouses compassion in those who suffer a life of deprivation every day, anonymously and in silence. But the Gandhis are not loved so much because they belong to an exceptional family, but because of what they have in common with normal people. For example, the family upsets: the contempt Nehru felt for Indira's husband; or the tension between Indira and Sanjay's wife; or the hostility between the two sisters-in-law... none of that has anything to do with greatness of spirit, but quite the opposite, with the day to day lives of ordinary people. If most families go through these domestic dramas in the intimacy of their own homes, the Nehru-Gandhis have always gone through them in the public eye, and in addition they have steered the destiny of the biggest democracy ever known. How not to feel fascinated by such normal characters who, nevertheless, live through such extraordinary circumstances? How not to feel interest in that family that is now divided and at opposite ends of the political spectrum, Sonia and her children devoted to the Congress Party, Maneka and Firoz Varun to the BJP? That is the very essence of what the great sagas of mythology are made up of, filling the imagination of the people since the dawn of time. For many of the inhabitants of the villages and countryside of India, the saga of the Nehru-Gandhis, which has gone on since the 19th century and looks as if it will go on well into the 21st century, is the bridge that links their feudal past and their democratic present and, hopefully, a future that will be even more prosperous. If before dynasties served to preserve social order, now they serve to reinforce the link between the inhabitants of the same nation. They help to unify the country, to cement it in the popular imagination. They have somewhat the role taken on by the ruling families in constitutional monarchies, such as the United Kingdom, the Scandinavian countries or Spain. Such is the case of the Bhuttos in Pakistan, the Bandaranaikes in Sri Lanka, or the Rehmans in Bangladesh. It is a tradition deeply rooted in the countries of Asia, although it is not exclusive to that part of the world. In the United States, political dynasties have regularly produced senators, governors and presidents, as was the case with the Roosevelts, the Kennedys, the Bush family or the Clintons. In other countries, the family does not govern but the mantle has passed from father to daughter, as in the case of Aun San Suu Kyi in Burma. It is no doubt in Asia where political dynasties find the most fertile soil on which to reproduce.

In India, there are many who criticize the dynastic politics of "the family", established by Indira, classing it as undemocratic, but that would be to forget that, although a large part of the electorate is illiterate, it does not mean they are ignorant. In modern dynasties in democratic countries, whether Kennedy, Bush or Gandhi, the position is not inherited automatically, it has to be won, as Indira did, and now Sonia. If, in the past, dynasties imposed themselves on their subjects, today it is the citizens who decide to continue to be governed by clans or families. What is the reason? For some it has to do with a certain feeling of nostalgia which urges the Indian people to recreate the governing class of the past with its hordes of Nabobs, Rajahs, Ranas and all the panoply of king-emperors and satraps.

Others explain it with arguments in the terms of marketing: the surname is a trademark as recognizable as makes of toothpaste or detergent and that helps orientation in the morass of local politics. Others think that perhaps it is a reflex of protection from abuse of power, in the hope that those who are already at the top will be compassionate and magnanimous and will not spend their efforts on pillage and theft, a type of behaviour more given to newcomers.

*   *   *

A logical effect of Sonia's renunciation of power is that the prestige of the Nehru-Gandhi dynasty has been reinforced. In 2006, at a Congress Party conference in Hyderabad, Sonia's staunchest supporters called for a greater role for her son within the organization. The chorus of voices, now so familiar, was calling for Rahul's presence. Sonia replied that she did not intend to influence her son, that he was free to choose his own path. And Rahul asked for time. But, in September, 2008, the torch began to change hands, when he was named as one of the secretaries general of the Congress Party, in a manoeuvre designed to mix youth and experience in the party leadership with a view to the coming general elections. Now Rahul is part of the managing committee, the organism that takes decisions in the Congress Party. For the first time in many years there is a number two in the organization who has the complete support of the number one. For months, Rahul has been going round the country galvanizing his followers and, just like his father, he is beginning to be careless about his personal safety. Several times the agents charged with protecting him have complained that Rahul gives them the slip or ignores their instructions. He realizes, just like his father, that it is impossible to make politics without mixing with the crowds. Many of the conflicts which emerged in the time of Indira and Rajiv have been solved or are on the way to being solved, but a public figure, especially if he belongs to "the dynasty", is always in danger of being attacked by some fanatic or other. To look no further than February 2007, the police arrested a man armed with a pistol at a rally where Sonia was speaking in the city of Almora. It turned out that the man, an employee of the local Post Office, was not part of any conspiracy, he was simply suffering from mental problems.

Recently, the assassination of an old friend of the family in neighbouring Pakistan, has reminded them of the fragility and insubstantiality of their existence. Benazir Bhutto died in a similar way to Rajiv. Both were out of power but were on the verge of regaining it. Both were careless of their safety in the interests of greater contact with the people. The Gandhis know that the attack on Benazir Bhutto is a reflection of what could happen to them at any moment, if they make the mistake of lowering their guard. Can Rahul have learned not to let himself be pulled along by a sense of destiny? His uncle Sanjay would still be alive today if he had been more cautious. His political manoeuvring to control the Sikhs created a monster that devoured his mother; neither did Indira take any notice when she was told to get rid of her Sikh bodyguards. Rahul himself foresaw what was going to happen to Rajiv... Will the members of this new generation have learned the lesson from their predecessors? For the moment Sonia is still there to remind them of it day after day, so that they never forget.

*   *   *

Priyanka is removed from politics and leads a quiet life in New Delhi, taking care of her husband and children. In February 2008, she madea trip to the south of India which put her in the limelight. She wanted to do it incognito, but she was immediately located by the Press. She had been thinking for a long time about visiting Nalini Murugan, the woman serving a life sentence for having participated in the plot to assassinate Rajiv. Almost twenty years have gone by since the attack in Sriperumbudur, but the suffering for the loss of a father does not stop with time. These are wounds which never entirely heal. Priyanka wanted to meet alone with the woman she helped to save from capital punishment when she got her mother to intervene to have the sentence commuted. Why did she go to see to her? "It is a purely private matter," she declared to the Press, "a personal visit that is all my own initiative." Both women broke down and sobbed when they came face to face in the shabby visiting room of the prison. After the visit it became known that they talked about their experiences in giving birth to their respective children, since both had to have Caesarean sections. They spoke about life more than death, which suggests that Priyanka has forgiven her. Are justice and forgiving not essential stages in reconciling oneself with a tragedy? At the end of the meeting, Nalini confessed to her brother that she felt "as if all my sins had been washed away by Priyanka's visit." Hinduism teaches that forgiveness is not a sign of weakness, but of strength. It is a manner of liberation, of finding peace. "My meeting with Nalini was my way of making peace with violence and the loss I have experienced." That was Priyanka's declaration, as concise and simple as it is heroic, and she finished as follows: "I do not believe in rage, or in hatred or violence. I refuse to allow those feelings to dominate my life." The Gandhis have always known how to grow in adversity. May God protect them.

*　　*　　*

Sonia lives an isolated life in her fortress at number 10 Janpath Road, although Paola, her mother, spends the winters with her. Every Sunday she can be seen at ten o'clock Mass in the Nunciature church. Apart from her children, Sonia has only a few close friends around her, the same ones she had when Rajiv was alive. It is not easy to see her, except at official engagements. She does not mix with the jet set of New Delhi and neither does she frequent diplomatic circles. She meets with Congress Party ministers and other coalition leaders as often as they require. On average, as president of the party and leader of the coalition in power, she can come to see some thirty people a day and may examine dozens of reports. Her small office at the Congress Party Committee headquarters is always full of poor people who have come to ask for help. Her secretary has instructions to attend them all.

Faithful to the custom that she inherited from her mother-in-law, she tries to fast one day a week and she does yoga exercises every morning. The woman who one day confessed that she felt uncomfortable dressed in Indian style has today become an elegant lady who only wears saris. She is still fascinated with cloth and traditional handicrafts as well as antiques. She would like to have more time in which to read. She takes advantage of her holidays, which she takes in June every year, to rest at the house of an old friend of the family, the journalist Suman Dubey, in Kosani, in the foothills of the Himalayas, and that is when she catches up on her backlog of reading. She likes those mountains which remind her of the Alps of her childhood and she dreams of building a house of her own, somewhere she can flee to escape the pre-monsoon heat with her children and grandchildren. The trips she makes abroad are usually official ones or to give a lecture. Now she is clearly less tense. She has declared that she is "comfortable" in politics, in spite of the fact that the words of Benazir Bhutto could be hers: "I have not chosen this life. It has chosen me." Perhaps she does not control her own life, but she has the life of the country firmly in hand. Even her opponents admit that she does not put a foot wrong. Both her detractors and her followers agree in recognizing her skill in managing the rules of a government in coalition, something which neither Indira nor Rajiv found necessary to learn at all. Sonia has been able to develop a harmonious relationship with some close political collaborators, a relationship based on mutual loyalty.

Indira could never have had a relationship like the one that links Sonia with Manmohan Singh.

One of Sonia's great successes was the fight against corruption. Was it not Rajiv who calculated that 85% of all the money spent on development in India ended up in the pockets of the bureaucrats? In order to avoid this, Sonia and the Prime Minister, Manmohan Singh, got Parliament to vote in a law that permits any citizen to examine the offers for contracts in public bidding and thus avoid bribery and perversion of the course of justice. People in a position of power are now obliged to be much more careful when they are on the fiddle, because there is the real possibility that they may fall into the hands of the law. Both Sonia and the Prime Minister know that it is in the ability to reform the State, to modernize it and clean up the corruption, that the key to development in India lies, which, in spite of everything, over the last fifteen years, has been the country with the fastest growth after China. If those reforms are achieved it is foreseen that in a couple of decades the Indian economy will be the third largest economy in the world. The country will have left behind its archaic past and will have conquered a future led by science and technology. Nehru's old dream will have come true then.

At the present time, the poor only have the consolation of the official projections that predict an income per head 35 times greater by then. The poor are Sonia's greatest concern. Perhaps it is the result of her Catholic upbringing, or because she bears very much in mind that she was born into a humble family in the Asiago Mountains, but she is still hurt by the contrasts in India. Was it not Indira who said that everything that could be said about India, and its opposite, was true? Bombay has the biggest slum district in Asia and the largest concentration of child prostitutes in the world, but it has just become the fourth city on the planet in its number of billionaires – one of them gave his wife an Airbus for her 44th birthday. How can one get used to these differences? How is it possible that the State is incapable of building latrines in the slum districts, or of supplying chalk to the schools or syringes to the rural dispensaries and yet the space programme is considered as good as that of any Western power, or perhaps even better? The day she gets used to that will be the day she has to leave politics.

What Sonia has done is to surround herself with experts in development like the activist Aruna Roy or the Belgian economist Jean Dreze, who lives in a slum district of Delhi with his Indian wife. Together they have drawn up an aid plan for the rural areas which signifies the greatest attempt ever made by the Indian State to improve the situation of the populations in the countryside. But the obstacles to putting these development programmes into practice are enormous. India, with its tumbledown airports, its crumbling roads, its enormous slum districts and its impoverished villages, needs all its resources to build infrastructure of all kinds, and in that race towards development the fate of the poorest people is still not a priority in the minds of the technocrats who rule the country. The idea that prevails in government, that development will end up including more and more people and that in that way poverty will be eliminated, was the idea defended by Rajiv. "But when?" Sonia asks, not forgetting the commitment she acquired with the poor who voted for her. She resists the excessively technical arguments of her own allies, the men that she has put in power, including the powerful Finance Minister. For him, those programmes are too distant from orthodox economics; for her, they are essential in order to give meaning to the power that the people have entrusted to her. Did not Victor Hugo say that "all power is duty"? Sonia has that very much in mind, and does not flinch in her struggle. In the districts where she has managed to have the programme to guarantee a hundred days of employment put into practice, the peasants have noticed the difference. It is the difference between poverty and abject poverty. The programme does not stop them being poor, but it avoids them falling into the abyss of abject poverty, which is when despair is added to a lack of material things. It is the difference between life and death. The other programme is harder to implement. It is a question of giving the peasants bank credits at very reduced rates of interest in order to free them from the tyranny of the debt they have contracted with local loan sharks and which often pushes them into suicide. It is a problem that comes from far back, and Indira wanted to deal with it at the time of the Emergency. It is difficult to solve because most of them are illiterate and do not know what it means to go into a bank. The important thing is to give them a way out, a light of hope, and that they should know that no one has to take his own life just because he cannot repay a handful of rupees. Thanks to Sonia, the "poorest of the poor", as she calls them according to the expression popularized by Mother Teresa, another European woman who left her mark on India, have a faithful ally. An ally who keeps them in mind all the time, every day and at every moment, whether she is in power at the top, or out of power.

BIBLIOGRAPHY

I feel especially indebted to five books which have been particularlyuseful to me:

Adams, Jan and Whitehead, Philip, The Dynasty – The Nehru GandhiStory, Penguin Books, 1997.

Frank, Katherine, Indira: The Life of Indira Nehru Gandhi, Harper Collins,2002.

Gandhi, Sonia, Rajiv, Viking-Penguin, India, 1992.

Jayakar, Pupul, Indira Gandhi: a biography, Penguin, New Delhi, 1995.Kidwai, Rasheed, Sonia, Penguin, 2003.

Additionally:

Alexander, P.C., My years with Indira Gandhi, Vision Books, 2001.

-     , Through the Corridors of Power An inside Story, Harper Collins.

Ali, Tariq, The Nehrus and the Gandhis, Pan Books, 1985.

Ansari, Yusuf, Triumph of Will, Tara-India Research Press, 2006.

Asaf, Ali Aruna, Indira Gandhi: Statesmen, Scholars and Friends, NewDelhi, 1985.

Bhagat, Usha, Indiraji through my eyes, Penguin, India, 2006.

Bhanot, Arun et al., Sonia Gandhi, a biography, Diamond

Books, 2005. Carras, Mary, Indira Gandhi in the crucible of leadership, Beacon Press,1979.

Chatterjee, Rupa, The Sonia Mystique, Virgo Publications, New Delhi,2000.

Chatwin, Bruce, ¿Qué hago yo aquí? (What am I doing here?), El Aleph,2002.

Dhar P.N., Gandhi, The Emergency and Indian Democracy, Oxford Uni.Press, New Delhi, 2000.

Frankel, Francine R., India's Political Economy, Oxford India Paperbacks,2005.

Gandhi, Indira, Letters to an American Friend, HBJ, New York, 1985.

What I Am, in Conversation with Pupul Jayakar, Indira Gandhi Memorial Trust.

My Trust, Vision Books.

Gandhi, Maneka, Sanjay Gandhi, Vakis, Feffer & Simons, New Delhi,1980.

Gandhi, Sonia, Two alone, two together, Penguin, 2004.

Living Politics, Nexus Institute, 2008.

Rajiv's World, Viking Penguin, India.

Gill, S.S., The Dynasty – A Political Biography of Premier Ruling Family of Modern India, Harper Collins Publishers, India.

Guha, Ramachandra, India after Gandhi, Harper&Collins, New York,2007.

Khilkani, Sunil, The idea of India, Penguin, 1997.

Lapierre, Dominique and Collins, Larry, Esta noche la libertad (Freedomtonight), Plaza y Janés, 1975.

Luce, Edwards, In Spite of the Gods, Doubleday, 2007.

Malhotra, Inder, Dynasties of India and Beyond Pakistan – Sri Lanka –Bangladesh, Harper Collins.

Masani, Zareer, Indira Gandhi, Hamish Hamilton, London, 1975.

Mehta, Ved, Portrait of India, Farrar, Strauss & Girould, New York, 1970.

Rajiv Gandhi and Rama's Kingdom, Yale Univ. Press, 1983.

Mehta, Vinod, The Sanjay Story, Jaico Pub. Co., Bombay, 1978.Moraes, Dom, Mrs Gandhi, Jonathon Cape, 1980.

Nanda, B.R., The Nehrus, The John Day Co., 1963.

Nath Mishra, Dina, Sonia the unknown, India First Foundation, 2004. Nehru, Jawaharlal, An Autobiography, Oxford University Press, 2002.

The discovery of India, Penguin, New Delhi, 2004.

Nugent, Nicholas, Rajiv Gandhi – Son A Dynasty, BBC Books.

Paul, Swaraj, Beyond Boundaries, Viking, 1998.

Prakash, Surya A., Issue of Foreign Origin – Sonia under Scrutiny, IndianFirst Foundation.

Singavarapu, sir Dr. Ravi, Sonia Gandhi through a different lens, FultusPublishing, 2004.

Singh, B.P. Varma and Pavan K., The Millennium Book on New Delhi,Oxford.

Singh, Darshan, Sonia Gandhi: Tryst with Destiny, United Children'sMovement, 2004.

Singh, Kushwant, Truth, Love & A Little Malice, Penguin, New Delhi,2002.

Thapar, Raj, All These Years, Seminar Publications.

Torri, Michelguglielmo, Storia dell'India, Laterza, Rome, 2000.

Tully, Mark, No Full Stops in India, Penguin, 1991.

Vasudev, Uma, Indira Gandhi: Revolution in Restraint, Vikas, New Delhi,1973.

Von Tunzelmann, Alex, Indian Summer, Henry Holt, New York, 2007. Yunus, Mohammed, People, Passions, Politics, Vikas, 1980.

ACKNOWLEDGEMENTS

I apologize for not being able to mention here all those who have helped me during this lengthy investigation, in Italy and in India, because they prefer to remain anonymous. With all my heart, thank you for the information you provided, without which I would not have been able to write this book.

I want especially to express my deepest gratitude to my wife, Sita, for her support, her company and her good humour during the research trips and the long months of writing.

Without the efficient and valuable support of my editor, Elena Ramirez, throughout the whole process of the book, and without her enthusiasm, this adventure would have been much harder. To you, Elena, my heartfelt thanks, and to all the team at Seix Barral and the Planeta Group who took part in the preparation of the book.

Thanks to Dominique Lapierre, who always believed in this story and encouraged me to write it, and for telling me in passing his anecdotes about Indira Gandhi, who used to see him on his journeys to India.

All my thanks to Michelguglielmo Torri, Professor of Modern and Contemporary Asian History at the University of Turin, an eminent specialist and lover of India, for his advice, his help and his generosity in investing his precious time in clearing up my doubts and in correcting the text.

Thanks too to Alvaro Enterria for his meticulous, perceptive corrections; to Bernadette Lapierre, to Christian and Patricia Boyer.

In India, my special thoughts for Kamal Pareek, who left us in September 2007. I will always miss his explanations, his availability, his way of telling me about Indian things that are difficult for a Westerner to understand, and above all, the pleasure of his friendship.

My thanks to Ashwini Kumar for telling me his anecdotes about the period when Indira Gandhi governed and for providing me with valuable contacts, as well as Major Dalbir Singh, the national secretary of the *All India Congress Committee*. I am not forgetting Mani Shankar Aiyar, a colleague of Rajiv Gandhi's and a minister in the present government, orhis niece, Pallavi Aiyar and her husband, Julio Arias.

Thanks too to our old friends Francis Wacziarg and Aman Nath for always being there.

And to Christian von Stieglitz for having so generously shared with me his memories of Rajiv and Sonia, as well as Josto Maffeo for telling me in detail about life in Orbassano.

Thanks too to Farah Khan, Josefina Young and Nello del Gatto for their help, their company and their hospitality. To Suman Dubey too for acting as messenger. And to Andres Trapiello and Laura Garrido.

Finally, I would like to thank Susana Garces and the KLM airline fortheir continual support and collaboration.

NOTES

CHAPTER 6

1. "Seeing them with their abject poverty, overflowing with gratitude, I felt a mixture of shame and pain," he wrote, "shame at my easy, comfortable way of life and all the politics in the cities that ignores this vast multitude of half-naked sons and daughters of India, and pain on seeing so much degradation and unbearable poverty"
An Autobiography, by Jawaharlal Nehru (Oxford University Press, 2002).

2. "At first, weaving is very boring but as soon as you get into it, you discover there is something fascinating [...]"
Taken from *Two alone, two together*, edited by Sonia Gandhi (Penguin, New Delhi, 2004)..

CHAPTER 8

3. Firoz was the son of a Parsee named Jehangir Ghandy, whose official biography attributes him with being a naval engineer, but other sources state that he was a dealer in alcohol, although there was no connection at all to Gandhi. At the end of the thirties he changed the spelling of his name

to that of Gandhi, the name of a caste of perfume-makers, a common name among the Bania castes of the Hindus of Gujarat, where Mahatma came from.

Ali, *Private Face of a Public Person*, p. 35, note 11, quoted from *Indian Summer*, by Alex Von Tunzelmann (Henry Holt, New York, 2007),

4. Nehru had once described his country as "an ancient palimpsest in which layers and layers of thought and daydreams have been engraved, without any of them having been able to erase or hide what had previously been written". Nehru, *The discovery of India* (Penguin, New Delhi, 2004).

CHAPTER 12

5. "No, Sam. Go ahead. I have the utmost confidence in you." Scene between Sam Manekshaw and Indira Gandhi, taken from *Indira Gandhi: a biography*, by Pupul Jayakar, *op. cit.*

CHAPTER 13

6. "We have been too soft on that damned woman," he told Kissinger. "Look how she's done that to the Pakistanis when we'd warned that old bitch not to get involved." These were his exact words.
Quoted from *India after Gandhi*, by Ramachandra Guha (Harper&Collins, New York, 2007), p. 460 (from documents in Louis Smith, *Foreign Relations of the United States, South Asia Crisis: 1971*, Washington, D.C., Department of State, 2005).

CHAPTER 14

7. "You will see very quickly a child goes through millennia of human history, and unconsciously, and in part consciously too, will live within himself the history of his race."
Quoted from *Two alone, Two together*, correspondence of Indira Gandhi and Jawaharlal Nehru, edited by Sonia Gandhi (Penguin, New Delhi, 2003),

CHAPTER 15

8. "Rajiv has a job, but Sanjay does not and he's involved in an expensive venture. He is very like me when I was the same age –with the rough edges too – to such an extent that it makes me feel sad to see the suffering he has to go through."
Correspondence of Indira Gandhi. Papers of P.N. Haksar (quoted from *India after Gandhi*, by Ramachandra Guha).
9. It was then, in that fleeting yet intense moment of happiness, that Indira decided that once her father had died she would give Firoz all her attention.
According to Uma Vasudev, *Indira Gandhi: Revolution in Restraint* (Vikas, New Delhi, 1973).

CHAPTER 19

10. "It must be terrible for you with your father in jail. I'm eally sorry about it."

Quoted from *Sonia*, by Rasheed Kidwai (Penguin, 2003).

11. **An anthropologist named Lee Schlesinger**
"The Emergency in an Indian village", *Asian Survey*, vol. 17, nº 7, July, 1977, quoted from *India after Gandhi*, by Ramachandra Guha.

CHAPTER 21

12. **"VVIP!" he answered. "Shri Sanjay Gandhi!"**
The word Shri here means something like "Excellency"

13. **When he lost a sandal on the runway of the airport, it was the chief of the government of Uttar Pradesh himself who bent down, picked it up and reverently handed it to him.**
Quoted from *India after Gandhi*, by Ramachandra Guha, p.508.

14. **"I felt that Maneka was asking too much of Sanjay and that he wanted to involve her in any activity that would reduce the pressure on him,"**
Quoted from *Truth, Love & A Little Malice*, by KushwantSingh (Penguin, New Delhi, 2002).

15. **"Indira has been very brave. This is a great step she has taken."**
Quoted from *Indira Gandhi: a biography*, by Pupul Jayakar (Penguin, New Delhi, 1995).

16. **"Madam, what good is a river without any fish?"**
Jayakar, Pupul, *op. cit.*

CHAPTER 22

17. "When? When I'm dead?"
Quoted from *Indira Gandhi: Statesmen, Scholars and Friends,*
by Ali Aruna Asaf (Delhi, 1985).
18. "I was unable to put a stop to my brother's activities."
Indiraji through my eyes, by Usha Bhagat, op. cit.
19. Once again Rajiv had thrown in her face that:"Sanjay
andDhawan are the ones who have brought you to this."
Quoted from *Indira Gandhi, the Emergency and Indian
Democracy,*by P.N. Dhar (Oxford University Press, New Delhi,
2000).

CHAPTER 23

20. While they chose a sari for her, Indira took some
documents into the kitchen that she considered dangerous if
they were to fall into the hands of the police or the
Intelligence Agency. The cook made sure they were
destroyed in an unusual way, using Sonia's pasta-making
machine as a shredder."
Quoted from *¿Qué hago yo aquí? (What am I doing here?)* by
Bruce Chatwin (El Aleph, 2002), according to the interview
between Chatwin and the cook.
21. The welcome was not always triumphal or loving. The
writer Bruce Chatwin, who went with her on part of that
tour, was in a car that was mistaken for Indira's.
Chatwin, *op. cit.*

CHAPTER 24

22. "Remember everything that makes you strong, hurts.
Some are left crushed or damaged, very few grow. Be strong

in body and mind and learn to bear things..."
Sanjay Gandhi, by Maneka Gandhi, *op. cit.*
23. "It is incredible that, in those chaotic circumstances, Sonia could deal with all the housework without it getting her down."
Indira Gandhi, by Pupul Jayakar, *op. cit.*
24. As if that were not enough, her adversaries smoothed the way for her by mocking her in a manner that could only occur in India.
India Today, 16-30 November, 1978.
25. In one of those fights, Maneka pulled off the ring that Indira had given her for her wedding and thrown it on the floor in fury.

People, Passions, Politics, by Mohammed Yunus (Vikas, 1980).
26. "Chaos reigns supreme at home," ... Sanjay still has long periods in jail ahead of him. We have to understand her and forgive her hysteria."
Indira Gandhi, A Biography, by Pupul Jayakar, *op. cit.*

CHAPTER 25

27. "I have two alternatives," Indira had told Krishnamurti, "either I fight or they shoot me like a duck in a fairground stall."
Indira Gandhi: A Biography, by Pupul Jayakar, *op. cit.*
28. "This was not the strong Indira of the days before the state of emergency...What shadow, what darkness walked beside her?"
Indira Gandhi: A Biography, by Pupul Jayakar, *op. cit.*

CHAPTER 26

29. By looking carefully among the burned pieces of metal, Indira had realized the enormity of her loss.
Indira, by Katherine Frank, *op. cit.*
30. "The past is past, let's let it be. But I have to clear up a few things. The falsehoods, the persistent and malicious campaign of calumny must be refuted..."
Letters to An American Friend, by Indira Gandhi (HBJ, New York, 1985).

CHAPTER 27

31. Look at her!... Who does she think she is?" she said to one of her husband's closest friends, talking about Indira.
Quoted from *The Sonia Mystique*, by Rupa Chatterjee (Virgo Publications, New Delhi, 2000).
32. "No one can take Sanjay's place," she told her friend Pupul. "He was my son, but he also helped me like an older brother."
Indira Gandhi: A Biography, by Pupul Jayakar, *op. cit.*

CHAPTER 28

34. "I fought for him like a tigress, for us and for our children, for the life we had built together, for his vocation in flying, for our friends, and above all, for our freedom: that simple human right that we had preserved so carefully and

consistently."
Rajiv, by Sonia Gandhi, *op. cit.*
35. "He was my Rajiv," Sonia would say, "we loved each other, andif he thought he should offer to help his mother, I would bow to those forces that were now too powerful for me to fight off, and I would go with him wherever they took him."
Rajiv, by Sonia Gandhi, *op. cit.*
36. "...There is an air of inevitability about all this, isn't there?"
Rajiv, by Nicholas Nugent (BBC Books, 1990).

CHAPTER 29

37. "Before, our world was recognizable and intimate... Time stopped being flexible and every hour that Rajiv spent with us became more and more valuable."
Rajiv, by Sonia Gandhi, *op. cit.*
38. "You said something...One has to learn to live with it, to it into one's very being and make it a part of one's life."
Indira Gandhi: A Biography, by Pupul Jayakar, *op. cit.*

CHAPTER 31

39. "Sometimes they'll say all kinds of nonsense about your grandmother... You have to learn to fight against that kind of provocation... to not take any notice of things that might annoy you, and not let it get to you."
Rajiv, by Sonia Gandhi, *op. cit.*
40. "Do I have to ignore those reports then? I get them every day... What shall I do?"

Indira Gandhi: A Biography, by Pupul Jayakar, *op. cit.*

CHAPTER 32

41. "If the authorities come into this temple, we are going to give them such a lesson that Indira's throne will fall down. We'll cut them to pieces ... let them come!"

Part of this sequence is based on *Amritsar: Mrs Gandhi's last battle*, by Mark Tully and Satish Jacob (Cape, London, 1985) and on *Truth, Love & A Little Malice*, by Kushwant Singh (Penguin, 2002).

CHAPTER 33

42. "Don't even consider that option. I'm the leader of a democratic government, not a military one."
Indira Gandhi, a Personal and Political Biography, by Inder Malhotra (Hodder & Stoughton, London, 1989).
43. "They returned to Delhi on October 28th and Indira... As usual with her, she brought her wicker stool and files out of her study and started working, glancing occasionally at the television or chatting to us."
Rajiv, by Sonia Gandhi, *op. cit.*

CHAPTER 34

44. "I've done what I had to do... Now you do what you have to do."
Amritsar, by Mark Tully and Satish Jacob, op. cit., quoted from

Indira, by Katherine Frank, op. cit.

45. The bullets had perforated the Prime Minister's liver, lungs, several bones and her spine. "She's like a sieve," said one doctor.

Indira, by Katherine Frank, *op. cit.*

46. "There has been an accident at the Prime Minister's home. Cancel all visits and return to Delhi immediately."

Rajiv Gandhi: the End of a Dream, by Minhaz Merchant (Penguin India, Delhi, 1991).

47. "Please do something. The situation is appalling," she told her in a frightened voice. Pupul was perplexed.

Pupul Jayakar tells this episode in *Indira Gandhi: A Biography, op. cit.*

48. "What the crowds were after were the goods of the Sikhs, the televisions and fridges, because we are more prosperous than others. Killing and burning people alive was just part of thefun."

The Dynasty, by Jad Adams and Philip Whitehead, *op. cit.*

CHAPTER 35

49. "He looked very lost and alone," Sonia would write. "He very often felt her absence intensely."

Rajiv, by Sonia Gandhi, *op. cit.*

50. "Above all it's been because of my mother's death... No one really knew me, what they have done has been to project the expectations they had of her on to me. They have made me into the symbol of their hopes."

The Dynasty, by Jad Adams and Philip Whitehead, *op. cit.*

CHAPTER 36

51. "Sometimes, I let him sleep a few more minutes... Then he would protest, but at least he rested."
Rajiv, by Sonia Gandhi, *op. cit.*
52. "I see a lot of love in people's eyes," said Rajiv, "and friendship, and trust, but above all, hope."
Op. cit.

CHAPTER 37

53. "What? Here we are to sign an agreement that guarantees their peace and security... and you're going to tell them that I'm scared to review the guard of honour?"
The Dynasty, by Jad Adams and Philip Whitehead, *op. cit.* (from an interview with the journalist Vir Sanghvi and Brooks Associates).

CHAPTER 38

54. "He was relaxed," Sonia would write, "almost relieved. Once again he enjoyed simple, day to day pleasures such as uninterrupted meals, sitting on at table with us, watching a video from time to time instead of shutting himself in his office to work."
Rajiv, by Sonia Gandhi, *op. cit.*
55. "She doesn't realize how dangerous this is."
The Nehrus and the Gandhis, an Indian Dynasty, by Tariq Ali (Picador, 1985).

CHAPTER 39

56. "An extraordinary collection of the most pitiless and immoral opportunists to have ever entered the political arena of India,"
Quoted from *The Nehrus and the Gandhis*, by Tariq Ali, *op. cit.*
57. When they got back to the hotel, he picked up his camera, which he always travelled with and they took a photo of themselves with the automatic button, a thing they had never done before.
Rajiv, by Sonia Gandhi, *op. cit.*
58. "We said goodbye tenderly..." Sonia would remember, "and he left. I stood looking through the crack in the curtains and I saw him go off, until I lost sight of him... This time forever."
Rajiv, *op. cit.*

CHAPTER 42

59. "We pulled his leg because of his Gucci shoes...He had so much to live for, so much to do in spite of our scruples and our criticisms."
"For we shall never be young again", by Sanjoy Hazarika, in *The Sunday Hindustan Times*, June 2nd, 1991, quoted from *The SoniaMystique*, by Rupa Chatterjee, *op. cit.*
60. "Don't bother Madam talking about her going into politics. It hurts her a lot. Remember that she's in mourning for a husband who never wanted to go into politics."
Quoted from *The Sonia Mystique*, by Rupa Chatterjee, *op. cit.*

CHAPTER 43

61. "What do these militants think?" exclaims Priyanka, beside herself. "That we have to go on sacrificing our lives? That'senough politics!"
Quoted from *Sonia*, by Racheed Kidwai, *op. cit.*

62. "We thank you personally, and your colleagues, for this generousoffer, but it would be better for the government to design its own humanitarian projects and programmes and to finance them directly, honouring the memory of my husband in that way."
The Sonia Mystique, by Rupa Chatterjee, *op. cit.*

63. In a single afternoon, a monument that has witnessed countless disturbances in history, which has borne the lashing of 400 monsoons is reduced to rubble by the fury of a few fanatics.
Quoted from *India after Gandhi*, by Ramachandra Guha, *op. cit.*

64. For three years, Sonia has been shut in the house, completely involved in the task of organizing the family archives. She has written a moving book about her husband.
Rajiv, by Sonia Gandhi, *op. cit.*

CHAPTER 44

65. "Sonia will not be elected because she is a foreigner... The only thing she wants is to be Prime Minister one day so she can have acomfortable life. That post is like a toy for her, she is not awareof the difficulties involved in it..."
Quoted from *The Indian Express*, May 14th, 1999.

CHAPTER 45

66. "At the last session, the honourable Prime Minister laughed atme because I did not answer his question... But it is a subject too important to be answered amid the laughter of his MPs. Now I ask you: What is your position on this matter?... You only mention three words: minimum credible deterrence. Do you think that those three little words make up a serious policy?"
Quoted from *Sonia*, by Rasheed Kidwai, *op. cit.*

67. Have you thought about the fate of the minorities in a government led by the BJP? Don't you want to fight for us any longer?"
Sonia, by Racheed Kidwai, *op. cit.*

68. "Quite simply there wouldn't be a rally now," the other one replies. "Without Sonia, there's no rally; without Sonia, there's no party."
Sonia, *op. cit.*

CHAPTER 46

69. "I wonder if we in Italy would accept a foreigner, and a womanto boot, as leader of a party that has symbolized the struggle for independence against foreign domination and which still enjoys great popular support, although less than before. The fact that a number of Indians trust their destiny to Sonia's hands says a lot about tolerance in India."
Quoted from *"In Maino Country"*, article by Vaiju Naravane, in *Frontline*, May 8th, 1998.

70. A journalist from the *Indian Express*.
Nirmala Ganapathy, *"Billion baby put through hell"*, May 12th, 2000, quoted from *India after Gandhi*, by R. Guha, *op. cit.*

CHAPTER 50

71. It has not been an easy journey from the placid existence of a housewife content with her domestic life to the frantic centre of political activity. As she herself defines it.
What India Has Taught Me, by Sonia Gandhi (Nexus Institute, Tillburg, 2007),

72. "The family I first became committed to when I got married was restricted to the limits of a home," Sonia would later write. "Today my loyalty is to a wider family, India, my country, whose people have welcomed me so warmly that they have made me one of them."
What India..., op. cit.

The Red Sari

Translation copyright © 2014 by Peter J. Hearn

Edited: www.triunfacontulibro.com

Made in the USA
Middletown, DE
30 August 2024

60071459R00404